Mexican Democracy: A Critical View

Para Dr. E. Figueroa
con el afecto más
sincero del autor

J.F. Johnson

St. Louis, Mo.
8 de Febrero de
1980

Mexican Democracy: A Critical View

Revised Edition

Kenneth F. Johnson

PRAEGER PUBLISHERS
Praeger Special Studies

New York • London • Sydney • Toronto

Library of Congress Cataloging in Publication Data

Johnson, Kenneth F
    Mexican democracy.

    Includes bibliographical references and index.
1. Mexico—Politics and government—1946-
I. Title.
JL1231.J63   1978   320.9′72′082   77-83473
ISBN 0-03-027711-6
ISBN 0-03-028151-2 pbk.

PRAEGER SPECIAL STUDIES
383 Madison Avenue, New York, N.Y. 10017, U.S.A.

Published in the United States of America in 1978
by Praeger Publishers,
A Division of Holt, Rinehart and Winston, CBS, Inc.

89   038   987654321

© 1978 by Praeger Publishers

Printed in the United States of America

Preface

It happened in El Quizá—revenge for the deaths of one's four brothers. Their lives were claimed by an "old hatred" that was later metamorphosed into a "new hatred" also called revenge. And the "new hatred" then took the form of a graceful horseman who rode through the village of El Quizá bearing the assassin's skull atop the pommel of his saddle. Thereby all the villagers could relive the same adventure, along with the graceful horseman, and take sustenance in sips of alcohol at any *cantina,* for in Mexico that is the road to manliness and probity. This happened in El Quizá.[1]

Sadness, hatred, fatalism, revenge—these are psychological constants in Mexican political life. We should quickly note that Mexicans may not be so different from the peoples of other cultures in this respect; perhaps it is that Mexican writers speak of these themes more openly and frequently, or that this impression stems from the likelihood that, in the public life of Mexico, ostensible human probity has often been castigated with violence. There seems always to be an act of wickedness, or a killing, to be revenged. Witness: two investigative reporters in the state of Sinaloa exposed and fought narcotics traffickers; one of the journalists was shot "accidentally" by a military patrol, and his partner was murdered as he sat in his car. "All this did not occur in some distant, obscure country, but next door in Mexico."[2] More hatred and revenge arises from these acts; sadness, fatalism, and violence run in causative circles perpetuating a shadowy eternal cult whose harvest is usually despair.

Knowing Mexicans intimately has often revealed them as taking pleasure in the deliberate expression of fatalistic attitudes, in an ostensibly cheerful way. Some argue that the Mexican is wont to look for messianic protectors. Many years ago an American writer named Wallace Thompson analyzed some of the Mexican's psychic impediments to political development, attributing these to a heritage of "Indian communism." He did not mean Marxism, but he did mean that the Mexicans, because of their Indian heritage, needed white men to look out for them, and he said so bluntly throughout a weird and curious book called *The Mexican Mind.*[3] Mexicans also enjoy flirting with death, perhaps so as to steel themselves against a threatening environment or, as Thompson would have had it, because of their innate psychic need for a messiah, a deliverer-slayer like the Aztec sacrificial priest or *Tlatoani.* Once I purchased a painting from a young Mexico City artist who went into great detail to explain to me that the work I had bought depicted a "hopeful scene." The painting features a number of "living skeletons" in the fires of hell, most of them drinking themselves into a stupor. One, however, has cast his gaze along a ray of light, symbolic of hope, that enters the inferno from outside and above;[4] deliverance reaches even into hell. The painting is called *Day of the*

Dead, inspired by a theme out of a famous work of philosophy by Octavio Paz.[5] The sad happiness of fatalism, the politics of hatred and revenge, all of this is central to Mexican political life.

Wry smiles from a Mexican politician betray what he knows and recognizes: surfaces deceive, ostensible happiness and outward professions of a commitment to change and progress are in fact masks to hide the war of all against all raging in Mexican society. The public interest is not a priority in the average hierarchy of values. Politics is like the life of an ant hill; people cease to exist, are eliminated, and others appear daily to take their places. There is always a struggle for scarce resources, but the fight is not constructive competition. It is a zero-sum game, with each Mexican's welfare inversely correlated with that of his neighbor; i.e., it is rare that one betters himself without the other's losing. Community values are championed only by the most unusual social reformer. In practical terms, the interior of one's home will be spotless, while raw sewage runs through the streets. Faithful churchgoers profess that poverty and injustice are wrong, yet the slums acquire an ever greater percent of the total population while the government does little or nothing. There is much to be sad, fatalistic, and violent about in today's Mexico.

For 80 percent of the population (some 65 million at the close of the 1970s), it is tough being a Mexican. This makes surreptitious crossing of the northern border all the more appealing. There is a folklore tradition about the Mexican who shows his courage, *machismo, hombría,* by going north the hard way, *a la brava,* returning rich. The wealth of North America is a magnet, and few can blame the poor Mexican for trying to get a share of the largesse from what was once his country's own land. Add to this the fact that in many U.S. businesses and industries Mexican labor is genuinely needed. From these circumstances grows a range of conflicts that can be lumped for now under the vague rubric of "border problems." When American and Mexican politicians meet at the border to discuss these issues, the former may genuinely believe that the facade of hope is really true. The Mexican, however, is somewhat more honest, at least with himself; he recognizes deception for what it is. The American politician will convince himself that border improvement programs (BIP) and twin-plant industries (*maquiladoras*) will have a measurably positive effect. His Mexican counterpart is likely to recognize it as an opportunity for self-enrichment, while of course not saying so in public. This leads us to a real-life scenario.

Two American congressmen and one Mexican mayor of a border community, their faces molded as contours of "instant happiness," smile from the front page of a border daily. They are captioned with a bold promise of more twin-plants for Nogales, Sonora, part of a US-Mexico border industrialization program initiated during the 1960s that enables American industries to cut costs by utilizing cheap Mexican labor. The Mexicans supposedly benefit too, but the promise of jobs has lured entirely too many Mexicans to the border. Thousands cannot be absorbed by the maquiladoras. The labor market is glutted and wages are depressed. Many of the unemployed and desperate turn to vice and to illegal border crossing. Announcing more twin-plants will draw an increased population to Nogales. The city's municipal services are hopelessly inadequate to handle the human pressure; corrupt local officials seem unconcerned. My friend in Nogales, a distinguished civic leader, writes

> we are drowning in our own feces . . . today the Abelardo R. Rodríguez school sent 28 children home sick from exposure to the raw sewage that is running everywhere . . . our mayor, who appears in the photo with the American congressmen, has kept news of our health conditions from them . . . but it is doubtful that they really care.[6]

In a word, Nogales, Sonora, has become unlivable. The policy of the Mexican government has been to encourage foreign investment (like the maquiladoras), hoping that "import-substitution" will follow therefrom; i.e., that Mexico will employ its population and begin to make its own goods that can be sold locally or exported, with as a result less dependency upon imports. It seems, however, that the policy of rapid industrialization, which also encourages rural to urban migration, has concentrated the poor in enormous unlivable slums like Nogales, or worse, those containing an estimated 5 million wretched souls that form a ring about Mexico City (whose total 1978 population is estimated at 10 million, including the contiguous environs).

A few social scientists are now becoming concerned with this state of affairs, which is not unique to Mexico. In Latin America generally, the top 30 percent of the total income goes to only 5 percent of the population. The lower half of the population receives only 13.4 percent of overall regional wealth.[7] Efforts in Mexico to reverse the concentration of poor in the capital city or on the northern border have led to regional construction of hopefully labor-intensive industries, like the Siderúrgica Lázaro Cárdenas Las Truchas, S.A. (SICARTSA) steel works in Michoacán. As noted in the pages to follow, however, the SICARTSA experiment has been frustrated during its early years by poor planning and political corruption. Mexico's society and economy must function under the towering shadow of a political monolith that is also a dominant class, the Institutional Revolutionary Party (PRI). The tribute due this political monopoly makes it hard to design and implement a genuine strategy of livability as a matter of public policy. Ostensible political stability, one hallmark of the bureaucratic-authoritarian state, has its costs; skewed wealth distribution and unlivable conditions for perhaps 80 percent of all Mexicans testify sadly to this statement.[8] Nogales and Mexico City are examples in point.

We may question which is worse, a dictatorial government providing social justice and economic opportunity for its citizens or a feeble democratic regime allowing mass starvation. When the regime is a hard-fisted dictatorship disguised as a populist single party "democracy," which still allows the majority of its citizenry to suffer abuse and hardship, it is easier to reach a judgment. Such a regime must inevitably become the focus of popular scorn, hatred, and attack. That, I believe, is what has happened in Mexico during the past three decades. It was, to be sure, a process with more distant historical roots. This study is devoted to a few of those roots and to many of the recent underlying causes and expressions of the Mexican political crisis, looking beyond the tourist guides to Aztec splendors and behind the border headlines proclaiming American gifts of more twin-plant industries. I will let a number of Mexicans tell in their own words how it feels to be the victim of "official truth." One such "truth" is that there is opportunity at the border; more accurately, it is the opportunity to make a surreptitious entry into the United States. Therein lies the escape valve that allows Mexico's policy of neglect to continue.

Mexico's socioeconomic fortunes are intertwined with those of the United States. The two countries are linked by tourism, food production, investment, migration, and geography. Border cities have interdependent economies. When the Mexican peso was dramatically devalued in 1976 (for the first time in some 20 years), both Nogales, Sonora, and Nogales, Arizona, suffered. Mexican pesos bought less on the U.S. side and often could not be accepted. But in such crisis situations the Mexican government is not effective in caring for its people. Much of this is due to political corruption, and herein lie more reasons for Mexican migration to the north. There is a tendency for money and people to get together, and estimates are that in the late 1970s as much as 10 percent of Mexico's total population lived illegally north of the border.

There are many ways to enter the United States illegally. Behind a cluster of bilingual shops on the main drag of Nogales, Arizona, a paved road called East Street slopes upward, passing the dour fronts of border homes and huts; where the pavement ends the street becomes a rocky footpath leading to and from Mexico. This unceremonious international doorway is marked by two metal posts in the chain link fence, giving the impression of a gate that is impossible to close; in many respects that is true. Seen through the aqueous bluish haze of early morning on the desert, that hole in the fence becomes a human funnel for Mexicans escaping north. U.S. Border Patrol officers say it is better to leave this gateway open so the illegal aliens can more easily be controlled, but they also admit that three out of five illegal entrants escape apprehension. Other parts of the fence boast tough metal barriers, spare plates from World War II that were once used to set up emergency air landing strips in the South Pacific. The *alambristas* or fence cutters (jumpers) cannot penetrate this metal, so they tend to be funneled through the gate at the end of East Street.

When the strips of metal that form the barrier were produced, World War II was in process and Mexican laborers were welcome to help solve the manpower shortage in the United States. Now they are unwelcome. An old Mexican tells me that he once worked in a factory in northern Indiana that produced the metal strips now dividing Mexico from the United States. He had contributed to the war effort. Now his sons must cross the metal he helped to produce and do it clandestinely; they lack the worker's dignity that once was his to proclaim. The old man is bitter and he is poor. Now he called a *mirador,* the one who watches for the Border Patrol and collects a few pesos for telling the waiting Mexicans when it is safe to cross through the fence. Despite his obvious personal tragedy, this old man has a composure and dignity.

He reminds me of the story I had read about Macario Vázquez, a once-proud captain who fought in Pancho Villa's forces during the great Mexican Revolution of 1910–17.[9] Macario Vázquez overcame a life of hardship; for a time he retired successfully to a stable life but was ultimately overcome by the complexities of social intrigue and deceit in which he lived. The once-proud captain died ignominiously beneath the falling snow in Chihuahua. He had been a successful revolutionary who could never master the guiding norms of a society he had helped to create.

Like the mirador I spoke with in Sonora, Macario Vázquez was the victim of a political marshland of words, legal articles used to extort the poor, and codes and regulations that trapped life and made it rot from within the human soul.[10] Like Macario Vázquez, the old mirador guarding the escape hole between Sonora and Arizona finally came to harvest the despair of his nation: "what harvest is there when all we have done is sown hatred, shed blood, implanted terror, destroyed our lives . . . this is a harvest of misery, of hunger, of shame."[11] It is the same harvest of desperation reaped today by those who scramble furtively through the border fence. Their lives and those of their progeny clearly depend on luck, for there is not enough to go around and Mexico's dominant political class has already grabbed up the bulk of the largesse. That is a dominant theme of this book.

So acute and obvious had the national scandal of official looting and bureaucratic infighting become that the pages of critical journals are filled with the theme of corruption. The review *Proceso* dedicated a feature story to shakeups within the PRI over public declarations by certain high officials that political parties should justify their existence through service to the nation and not by treating the national patrimony as booty.[12] An opposition journal of Marxist leaning, *Punto Critico,* decried the use of official terrorism against students and workers in Oaxaca and called for the destitution of that state's governor, blaming him for the use of imported American weapons to kill some 30 protesters.[13] That same issue also carried a story of the planned firing of workers who had joined extraofficial unions at the government's steel works at Ciudad Sahagún, a satellite of Mexico City. The magazine *Impacto* predicted that, so long as the PRI exists to serve the interests of corrupt labor leaders like Fidel Velázquez, there will be no democracy in Mexico.[14] Figures on public nutrition showed that in 1976, as the presidency changed hands, seven out of every ten children in Mexico suffered undernourishment.[15]

A reservoir of bitterness has built up in Mexico. President José López Portillo's motto, undoubtedly well-intentioned, has a hollow ring: "Our best assurance of authentic justice is to distribute the wealth, not the misery."[16] Yet, as the decade of the 1970s ends, it seems that misery is indeed the most frequently distributed commodity. The Jesuit publication *Christus* lamented poverty and governmental corruption and attributed to the regime the assassination of priests and labor leaders, citing among others the case of Father Rodolfo Aguilar, killed by official terrorists in Chihuahua while providing a "voice for those who cannot speak for themselves."[17] The Jesuits declare that violence is now institutionalized in Mexico.[18]

The matter goes much deeper than a listing of isolated cases, however. The Mexican political system rewards scoundrels and castigates honest reformers. Among the worst of such instances, one with both national and international ramifications, is that of Carlos Armando Biebrich, once governor of Sonora, deposed for corruption on orders from Mexico City in 1975. Biebrich fled Sonora to Arizona and was subsequently indicted on a range of corruption charges. One of his henchmen, Francisco Arellano Noblecía, was wanted in Sonora for murder and dodged a warrant in Arizona in connection with a narcotics case. President López Portillo arranged to have the charges against Biebrich dropped and gave Arellano Noblecía a job in the presidential team (in fact, Arellano Noblecía was photographed standing behind the president as part of López Portillo's own entourage).[19] The journal *Impacto* carried an article following dismissal of the Sonoran charges against Biebrich, saying that granting him freedom confirmed the sorry rule of thumb that the Mexican "Law of Responsibilities" is a dead letter—only the corrupt get rich in Mexico, despite regular promises of reform each electoral period.[20]

It is unrealistic to ignore political corruption if one's goal is to make a candid assessment of Mexico's own system capabilities vis à vis the staggering problems of poverty, health, and illiteracy. There is an ample literature by Mexican authors alone to dramatize the problem, works like Mario Menéndez Rodríguez's *Yucatán o el genocidio.* This detailed account, with extensive numerical calculations, shows how the Indian henequen farmers of Yucatán were systematically swindled by the state rope-making monopoly *Cordeleros de México* (CORDEMEX). Much of the binder twine used on midwestern farms in the United States has been extracted from the sacrifice of the rural *Lumpenproletariat* in southern Mexico. Keeping double sets of books allowed CORDEMEX officials to get rich. Menéndez's study even implicates the Church in some of the shame of Yucatán.[21] But the clergy in Mexico, as indeed in other Latin American countries, has shed many of its archaic ways since the publication of Menéndez's book, and at least some groups within the Church are now publicly on record for radical reforms and lasting change. It is a bitter irony that some clerics, like the previously mentioned Father Aguilar have been sacrificed by agents of the Mexican regime. Mario Menéndez, whose name reappears later in this book, is now exiled to Cuba. His brothers Roger and Hernán were incarcerated in 1974 without formal charges. At latest word,[22] they had been tortured and were still held captive; their crime was exposing official corruption in Mexico.

For my own "seditious" collaboration with the Menéndez brothers I too was incarcerated and castigated by Mexican "justice." One of my more flagrant "lies" was that high Mexican officials collaborated with the CIA.[23] That episode delayed the appearance of this book by approximately three years. In so far as Mario Menéndez's revelations about genocide in Yucatán are concerned, little has changed. The April 2, 1977, edition of *Proceso* carried an extensive story about the thousands of starving *henequeneros* in Yucatán, who remain under debt peonage to a variety of government lending institutions and elite management cadres who siphon off most of the profits from the harvest. In this recent account, the henequen workers in the village of Motul tried to subsist on less than $1.00 per week. For them a trek north toward the myth of American riches might be worth it, even though their health would permit few, if any, to arrive.

The reader will have been forewarned by now as to potential biases inherent in this book. Hopefully, it will be remembered that the great majority of my sources herein are Mexican and that much of what they write is negative. To a great degree my task has been to organize Mexican testimony around key themes, like system atrophy, political alienation, psychic behavioral determinants, and emigration as an historic response to imperialism, and to combine these insights along with those of selected non-Mexican scholars into a coherent whole. It should be noted that, whereas this edition is new by some 75 percent, it continues and refines the critical outlook that characterized the first edition. Thus scholars of Mexico might profitably read this book along with any of the more neutral treatises that are cited variously throughout. On the basis of my documentation and extensive interviewing of real Mexicans on both sides of the border, I sincerely believe this to be an accurate, albeit grim, portrayal. A good number of Mexican writers whom I have cited concur.

One does not need to travel to Mexico City to view the socioeconomic problems that the Mexican political system is unable to solve; a view across any urban stretch of the border fence will be adequate. A frank talk with illegal Mexican aliens, the *mojados* or "wets" who now enter in droves by night, will reveal the pitiful ambient that they are forced to escape. Many of Mexico's proudest and most dignified workers come north annually to pick food that otherwise might not reach American tables. In a real sense the United States has been subsidized by Mexican poverty. A random scrutiny of the Jesuit publication *Christus* will bolster one's sense of the urgency for reform in Mexico (the May 1977 edition alone contains articles decrying the problems of urban slums, credit shortages and injustices, violence against the Church, and unemployment). Today it is not necessary to search out the obscure anarchist review or the clandestine communist handbill to find out what is wrong in Mexico. Traditionally respectable publishers print criticism of Mexican politics, providing that they do not cross certain thresholds of tolerance, and from within the official regime itself sound voices of protest. The cause of reform in Mexico may be frustrated, but it is by no means dead.

Who will reform Mexico? This is the real question to be raised as a counterpoise to the traditional query "who rules Mexico?" The principal opposition National Action Party (PAN) cannot be expected to do it in the near future. That party also seems to be in atrophy. After some 39 years of struggle as an opposition to the official PRI monolith, what is the PAN's total number of wins? In the time span cited, the PAN won a total of 129 federal deputies (the PRI won 2,327) and 40 mayorships (the PRI won approximately 27,000).[24] Apart from these positions, the PAN won virtually nothing. Between electoral fraud, official violence, public apathy, and the PRI's own loyal support groups, it would be unrealistic to expect anyone to win at the ballot box.

Placed in an historical perspective, this may suggest that the Cuban model of what has been called "charismatic hardship communism"[25] may be next to appear in Mexico's future. The possibility of unification with the United States is also entertained in the pages to follow. And the PRI might even reform itself —improbable, but by no means impossible. However, the raw statistics of opposition politics previously quoted, considered in the light of Mexico's staggering social ills, make it extremely unlikely that political democracy is the answer. Although democracy seems to function in the impoverished milieu of India, that nation's political legacy and hemispheric circumstances are so different from those of Mexico as to make comparison unrealistic. If Mexico is to have democracy (and I am not at all sure that it ever should or will), then in the words of one political theorist it will have to win that for itself.[26]

What could North Americans and their government do to bring about drastic change in Mexico if the only goal of such intervention were improved human rights? Ending the drug traffic could partially dislocate the economies of Sinaloa, Jalisco, Nayarit, Michoacán, and perhaps other states. Stopping the flow of illegal aliens would probably create social anarchy and a financial collapse along the border, this because of a range of factors to be discussed in this book. Cutting off the north-to-south tourism would undoubtedly wreck much of the remainder of the Mexican oligarchy. There is no immediate assurance, though, that such acts would improve the status of Mexican human rights or the quality of life in the short run. In the long run, following a Castro-style revolution, one might expect to see the human condition, the overall quality of life, improve somewhat in Mexico, but the economic costs to the United States might be too great, not to mention the dilemmas of international politics. Instead, perhaps, the United States should lower its immigration barriers and absorb Mexico's excess population while concurrently instilling the ethic of family planning (a component of the lifeboat population ethic). At the same time, using the skills and weapons of international finance, those sectors of Mexican government and industry that are at present not seriously indebted to United States interests could be lured into such indebtedness. When the debts become hopelessly delinquent, foreclosure might complete the absorption process.

In what is to follow these ideas will be explored along with some psychological delving into forces that might render any Mexican reform dubious. Perhaps it is Mexico's destiny to remain an angry reservoir of complacent, fatalistic, manipulated human beings; bitter people, yet festive, whose joyful demeanor often explodes violently; a society whose psychic ebullience has been traced in the minds of some philosophers to an ancient Aztec death wish that lingers on to plague Mexican life. Mexicans may remain a people divided by an intellectual abyss separating their authors' and painters' brilliance from the cruel stupor their hurting masses must endure. From the conquest onward, the styles and norms of Mexican politics seem to have been violent and wanton; as the creator of Macario Vázquez put it, an insatiable vortex of lives crashed to their end without the jubilant sensing of fulfillment. All this occurred in a state whose motto should be *"ladrón que roba a ladrón merece cien años de indulgencia y quinientos de perdón,"*[27] or the ethic of enduring abuse forever. Hopefully, in the mosaic of Mexican political life, a practicable and humane way out of this morass can be found. The apparent Mexican pathology may not be so much a "breakdown in the system," as just the inevitable consequence of the way society is organized politically and economically, and how it is guided morally. Let us see!

NOTES

1. Oscar Monroy Rivera, *Sucedió en El Quizá* (Mexico: Costa-Amic, 1974), p. 14.

2. From an editorial in the *Los Angeles Times* as reprinted in the *St. Louis Post-Dispatch,* February 25, 1978.

3. Wallace Thompson, *The Mexican Mind* (Boston: Little-Brown, 1922), *passim.*

4. *Día de Muertos,* painting by Jorge Espinosa Carrizales, 1970.

5. Ibid. See also Octavio Paz, *El arco y la lira* (Mexico: Fondo de Cultura Económica, 1972), pp. 287–94, for a distinction between religious and political artistic expressions.

6. From a note to the author by Oscar Monroy Rivera, attached to a copy of *Diario de Nogales,* February 14, 1978 (front page story).

7. Robert L. Ayres, "Development Policy and the Possibility of a 'Livable' Future for Latin America," *The American Political Science Review* 69, no. 2, 1975, p. 510.

8. The concept of the bureaucratic-authoritarian state is developed by Guillermo O' Donnell in "Reflections on the Patterns of Change in the Bureaucratic-Authoritarian State," *Latin American Research Review* 13, no. 1, 1978, pp. 3–38.

9. Carlos Chavira B., *Macario Vázquez* (Mexico: Editorial Jus, 1968), *passim.*

10. Ibid, p. 230.

11. *Proceso,* no. 70, March 6, 1978, pp. 6–8.

12. *Punto Crítico,* Año VI, no. 71, March 15, 1977, *passim.*

13. *Impacto,* no. 1407, February 16, 1977, p. 18.

14. *Proceso,* no. 70, March 6, 1978, p. 28.

15. Ibid., p. 47.

16. Ibid.

17. *Christus,* April, 1977, *passim.*

18. Ibid., p. 11.

19. On the front page (photograph and text) of *El Sonorense,* January 22, 1978.

20. *Impacto,* no. 1406, February 9, 1977, p. 61. See also a related article in the semiofficial newspaper *El Día,* October 20, 1977, p. 5.

21. Mario Menéndez Rodríguez, *Yucatán o el genocidio* (Mexico: Fondo de Cultura Popular, 1964), p. 170.

22. See Juan Miguel de Mora, *Por la gracia del señor presidente: México, la gran mentira* (Mexico: Editores Asociados, 1975), pp. 241–44.

23. Ibid., p. 247. Former CIA agent Philip Agee identifies former presidents Díaz Ordaz, Echeverría, and other high Mexican officials as collaborators during his spy residence in Mexico in *Inside the Company* (Penguin, London, 1975), passim.

24. *Proceso,* no. 70, March 6, 1978, p. 9.

25. Edward González develops this concept in *Cuba Under Castro: The Limits of Charisma* (Boston: Houghton-Mifflin, 1976), *passim.*

26. Leslie Lipson, *The Democratic Civilization* (New York: Oxford, 1964), p. 589.

27. Carlos Chavira B., op. cit., p. 244.

Acknowledgments

Let me enter here the traditional caveat about my exclusive liability for the errors of fact, or judgment, or both, in what is to follow; then let me proceed to honor those who helped to get the best of it onto these pages.

To the late Ben G. Burnett I remain eternally grateful for his inspiring example of excellence as a scholar, teacher, and magnificent human being. American academia has been enriched because Ben was here. Most recently I have enjoyed the counsel and professional friendship of Edward J. Williams, John D. Martz, and Miles W. Williams along with that of Richard Millett and Robert Loring Allen, the latter two colleagues having given me important historical and economic insights respectively. The Praeger Special Studies team was simply great, especially Bruce Warshavsky and Victoria White who are bright sensitive persons as well as skilled professionals. My home institutional colleagues Ruth Jones, Lance LeLoup, Harry Mellman, and Lyman Sargent bolstered my resolve immensely through challenges whose psychological nuances defy my ability to explain. I am profoundly grateful that I survived. Thanks are also due the Franciscans of San Xavier del Bac, Tucson, Arizona.

The first edition of *Mexican Democracy,* substantially different from the present volume, was dedicated to María Mercedes Fuentes de Johnson who has since joined me in several research ventures and who contributed significantly to the Mexican border interviews reflected herein. Also since the first edition we have been joined by our daughters Estela Marie and Andrea Louise, something of a set of joint publications in and of themselves; the love and endurance of all three gave this effort a special meaning.

Officers of the United States Immigration and Naturalization Service and Border Patrol who contributed their wisdom are acknowledged in chapter eight. In particular, I am indebted to Michael J. Nolan who embodies that which is creative and humane in the best of professional public administrators. I am also grateful to Nina M. Ogle who assisted me with the report *Mexico's Silent Invasion* and whose research effort was vital to bringing this book to fruition.

Throughout this book one finds the nearly towering presence of a Mexican poet-philosopher whose sacrifices for the cause of probity in political life and whose efforts to help the poor inspired me to give *Mexican Democracy* a new microfocus. Oscar Monroy Rivera, an ebullient civic activist and a brilliant thinker, is not the typical Mexican described by Samuel Ramos or Octavio Paz. Through Monroy's eyes the reader can peer deeply into the Mexican psyche and plot the course of the eventual apocalypse. This book is dedicated to the courage of Oscar Monroy and to his dream of a compassionate Mexico. If, in his role as giant-killer, he is ever able to dethrone only one of the major satraps who dominate Mexican politics his country will have moved a step closer to the good life. In his own words, which I translate freely:

> ... todo escritor y todo poeta que en las horas amargas en que, unos cuantos hombres se deciden a probar fortuna envenenando a través de drogas a otra generación de hombres posibles en la juventud presente; para suprimir a esa generación del patrimonio del amor y la vida; habrá—el poeta y el escritor —de luchar con su presencia peligrosa contra todo envenenador del hombre. Y entonces será la hora del exilio. La hora de partir en busca de hombres más enhiestos. A cualquier patria donde haya una garantía para la vida. Para luchar con las armas de la prosa, con el filo acerado de la poesía, en la defensa de la humanidad.

> ... each writer and poet must come to grips with the bitter reality that some men will decide to try their hand for riches via drugs, poisoning the generation to emerge from today's youth, so as to eliminate that generation from our national stock of love and life; the poet and writer will have to struggle fiercely against the corruptors of man. Then it will be time for exile, the hour to begin the search for men of probity. In whatever country where life is defended, the fight must be carried on with poetry's steel-edged blade, in defense of all humanity.

Oscar Monroy Rivera
León de Galán, Mexico, Editorial Libros de
Mexico, 1977, p. 32.

Contents

Abbreviations

ACNR	Acción Cívica Nacional Revolucionaria (National Civic Revolutionary Action Movement)
CCI	Central Campesina Independiente (Independent Peasant Confederation)
CEN	Comité Ejecutivo Nacional (National Executive Committee)
CIA	Central Intelligence Agency (U.S.)
CNC	Confederación Nacional Campesina (National Confederation of Farmers)
CNOP	Confederación Nacional de Organizaciones Populares (National Confederation of Popular Organizations)
CONASUPO	Companía Nacional de Subsistencias Populares (staple-goods distribution system)
CROM	Confederación Regional de Obreros Mexicanos (Regional Confederation of Mexican Workers)
CTM	Confederación de Trabajadores Mexicanos (Mexican Confederation of Workers)
FSTSE	(Federation of Syndicates of Workers in the Service of the State)
FUZ	Frente Urbano Zapatista (Urban Zapata Front)
INFONAVIT	Instituto del Fondo Nacional de la Vivienda Para los Trabajadores (worker housing program)
INS	Immigration and Naturalization Service (U.S.)
IPN	Instituto Politecnico Nacional (National Polytechnic Institute)
MAR	Movimiento Armado Revolucionario (Revolutionary Armed Movement)
PAN	Partido Acción Nacional (National Action Party)
PARM	Partido Auténtico de la Revolución Mexicana (Authentic Party of the Mexican Revolution)
PCM	Partido Comunista Mexicano (Mexican Communist Party)
PDLP	Partido de los Pobres (Party of the Poor)
PDM	Partido Demócrata Mexicano (Mexican Democratic Party)
PEMEX	Petroheos Mexicanos (national petroleum monopoly)
PIPSA	Productora e Importadora de Papeh S.A. (national newsprint monopoly)
PMT	Partido Mexicano de los Trabajadores (Mexican Workers Party)
PPS	Partido Popular Socialista (Popular Socialist Party)

PRI	Partido Revolucionario Institucional (Party of Revolutionary Institutions)
PRM	Parti Revolucionario Mexicano (Mexican Revolutionary Party)
SICARTSA	Siderúrgica Lázaro Cárdenas Las Truchas, S.A. (steel-production center)
UGOCM	Unión General de Obreros y Campesinos Mexicanos (General Union of Mexican Workers and Peasants)
UNAM	Universidad Nacional Autónoma de México (National University of Mexico)
UNS	Unión Nacional Sinarquista (National Union of Sinarquistas)

Glossary

alambristas	fence jumpers (cutters)
aviadores	phantom bureaucrats or PRI functionaries
aviaduras	the position itself (phantom bureaucrats)
braceros	Mexican contract workers legally in the United States
cacique	boss (political)
camarilla	political power circle or clique
charro	labor boss
coyotaje	corruption; extortion
dedazo	personal designation of an official or candidate
delegación	urban administrative division in Mexico City
ejidatarios	collective farmers
ejido	collective farms
enanismo	dwarfishness
enano	dwarf
gachupines	European-born Spaniards who held political power in Mexico
gobernación	roughly equivalent to U.S. departments of interior and justice with the Central Intelligence Agency mixed in.
latifundio	large landholding
latifundista	owners of large landholdings
maquiladoras	twin-plant border industries
mestizo	person who is a mixture of Indian and Spanish blood
mojados	wetbacks
mordidas	bribes
panistas	members of the PAN
paracaidismo	land occupation without legal writ
paracaidistas	squatters
priista	members of the PRI
procurador	attorney general
regente	mayor of the Federal District
sexenio	six-year term (presidential)
tapado	test candidate for Mexican presidency
Tlatoani	Aztec high priest
vendepatria	he who sells his country to foreigners

Mexican
Democracy:
A Critical View

One

Mysticism and Violence: Psychic Roots of the Mexican Political Consciousness

THE SALIENCY OF ALIENATION: CRISIS AT TLATELOLCO

Resorting to violence as a way of resolving conflict may be a greater constant in Mexican political life than in that of most other Latin American nations. If so, where do we look for clues as to the general principles or laws explaining this aspect of Mexican political behavior? I suggest in this work that at least one fruitful starting place would be the Mexican psyche. To do this thoroughly would require an immense collaboration among social scientists and psychiatric medicine, plus a profound steeping in the humanistic literature which has made Mexico internationally famous in intellectual circles. All of this I cannot pretend to do. For the purpose of the present undertaking, I am equipped only to unite key aspects of the social science dimension with selections from the literary one. Mine is, admittedly, a humanistic social science which stresses cultural anchoring over methodological rigor. This book will attempt to validate that approach by conveying a greater nearness to the political realities of Mexico today. Let me begin with a sample of social science dimensions.

The Mexican sociologist Carlos A. Echánove Trujillo noted pronounced tendencies among many Mexicans to be deliberately quarrelsome, to seek fights, to avoid compromise and seek out confrontation, to use self-deprecating language, to practice empty courtesies as a way of cloaking hostility, to feel uncomfortable upon meeting new people, to indulge in a variety of hypocrisies and expect others to do likewise, and to employ verbal rituals as a way of masking their hostile emotions.[1] These characteristics, in my experience, are more typical of Mexicans than of most other Latin Americans. Such characteristics are also apparent in Mexican political life, in the unwillingness of governments to negotiate with protesting students lest negotiation be seen as weakness. It is better—that is, stronger—to use rifles first and words thereafter. Confrontation is *machismo,* negotiation betrays weakness.

1

Consider now a literary dimension of political insight. It has been suggested by the Mexican writer Carlos Fuentes that the profound and melancholy irony of modern Mexico may be that it devours its own offspring out of inability to assimilate its past. Citing his contemporary Octavio Paz, he queries: "But do not revolutions, like Saturn, hunger for their own children?"[2] Mexico is an endless caldron of slippery political variables, of endless intellectual excitement. It is possible to become so totally absorbed in the quest for new psychic nuances of meaning that one misses the forest because of preoccupation with the trees. My task in this study is to simplify a highly complex constellation of values, styles, skills, and arenas which go into the makeup of Mexico's political system and which reflect in part on the political culture of Hispanic America. In my effort to make the story of Mexico understandable to the general intellectual public, I will no doubt transgress certain venerated concepts that have been elaborated by experts in history, philosophy, and political science. For this I apologize at the onset. It is an unavoidable pitfall.

What we see today in looking across the Mexican political horizon is a series of value layers, each containing precise influences which seek to break through the upper crust (I am still drawing loosely on Carlos Fuentes). Octavio Paz's book *Posdata,* translated as *The Other Mexico,* along with his earlier classic *The Labyrinth of Solitude* are devoted to elucidating that in the Mexican psyche which impels him on toward breaking out of the final restraining crust, emerging into a new world of self-realization and awareness in which fear of unknown demons out of a mystic past can be sublimated, controlled, and channeled constructively. It has been argued that the Mexican's greatest fear lies in knowing his true self and that frustration and aggression erupt out of this syndrome.

The Mexican being resulted from a miscegenation among the Spanish and Indian cultures (the Aztecs and assorted others who were conquered by Cortés in the early sixteenth century). Many Mexicans are not sure of their heritage. They are not sure what it means to be Spanish, or to be Indian. They are *mestizos* or Mexicans and that they often think they more readily understand. Much of the uniqueness of the Mexican culture, and its politics specifically, is disclosed by attitudes toward death. The month of November is especially revealing. During the first two days of that month, All Saints and All Souls days in the Catholic faith, spiritual devotion is given to the cult of the dead. These are the Days of the Dead when people organize fiestas which begin with happiness, later to degenerate into quarrels that still later, reinforced with alcohol, may end in death. Cakes and cookies are eaten in the form of skulls, skeletons, and coffins. Mariachi bands sometimes play their music at grave sites to inspire dead souls to communicate with the living.

These contemporary ceremonies are mild compared with the ancient Aztec rituals in which the high sacrificial priest or *Tlatoani* sliced open the chest of a living person, removed the palpitating heart, smeared blood across the stone faces of various gods, and then eviscerated the sacrificed person, parts of whom were eaten by the faithful or fed to reptiles. It is believed that hundreds of such sacrifices were made yearly by the Aztecs. Today, many unschooled Mexicans repeat a modified version of the ancient ritual on the Day of the Dead by sprinkling red sugar or syrup over skeletons near altars in honor of their time-bound obligations. Few of them know why they do it. It is believed to be a form of communion with the ancient gods, a process, some believe, over which the participants have no control. It is said that, for the ancient Aztecs, to die was a happy occasion (not necessarily for the person sacrificed) because it meant pleasing the Sun God or some other deity who would guarantee a life after death. To die, then, was to be reborn. Perhaps today's Mexicans somehow know instinctively that risking death is no risk at all for one will return, reincarnate, and hopefully in better socioeconomic circumstances.

This is what one gets from some of the literature. No Mexican ever confided such to me in exactly those terms, although I have discussed the subject at length with Mexicans whose friendship I consider intimate; yet at times they were close to such an admission. Many will confess their preoccupation with violence, confrontation, and death. This is especially true of those involved in political life who have learned to accept violence as a basic political skill, who view negotiation as somehow unmanly. Along with this, Mexican political life is typically authoritarian with commands (that are not to be questioned) emanating from above and beyond. To disobey is to invite predestined castigation. No Mexican political actor is likely to admit that he believes in spiritual forces out of the past which compel him to engage in violent political conflict, nor that his psyche is somehow tied up in an ancient death wish. But some of Mexico's most penetrating minds have sensed that it is so. Thus the specter of supernaturalism is raised at the onset. All of this is most likely beyond the province of the scientific method qua science. But it may also be very real. What is believed and acted upon can be more relevant than demonstrating other truths.

What is suggested, not proved, is that the tradition of Aztec pyramid and sacrificial Tlatoani has evolved into today's Mexican governing system. This refers to the official single party, Partido Revolucionario Institucional, PRI, that is superimposed over the government bureaucracy and is one and the same with it. The president of Mexico is a modern day Tlatoani and sits at the apex of the pyramid. All demands made upon the system must be channeled up through the pyramid to the president. Orders for castigation of deviants are supposed to come directly from the president. As we shall see, there have been cases in which power contenders in modern Mexico sought to test the power of the Tlatoani and internal conflict resulted in bloody purges.

The PRI has sectoral organizations (to be discussed later) which lend themselves graphically to the pyramid form. These are the power base of the system representing labor, peasants, and a conglomeration called the popular sector. People outside or within that power base who seek to challenge it, to deny its bona fides, may be punished or even sacrificed. As we shall see, Mexico's political system has a great capacity for human sacrifice. Perhaps this is not a question of conscious manipulation of the present by ancient deities, but merely an inheritance of behavioral norms which compels today's Mexicans to act as they do, to enter into endless conflict and violence. All of this is tied up in the symbolic and rejuvenative capabilities of today's single-party democracy in Mexico.

Here we must regress into Mexico's recent past and then later try to establish at least a symbolic connection between the present and the distant past, or more accurately with that point in history which saw the birth of a unique Mexican national consciousness. I will try to relate at least symbolically one of Mexico's most profound and recent human sacrifice rituals to the downfall of the Aztec empire and suggest a continuity of events having their denouement at the same geographical spot. A coincidence? Perhaps, but a suspicious one. This is what happened.

On the night of October 2, 1968, a political catharsis shook Mexican society. The event has come to be known simply as Tlatelolco. It was the occasion when government troops massacred some 500 student protesters at a place variously known as the Plaza of the Three Cultures (Plaza de las Tres Culturas) or Tlatelolco, located not far from the heart of Mexico City. Tlatelolco is also the spot on which the Aztecs made their last stand of major resistance against the Spaniards under Cortés in 1521 and is the site of ancient Aztec human sacrifice rituals. The events in 1968 became symbolic of the unity of the people against an oppressive regime, that is, a breach opened between the apex of the pyramid and its base. The Tlatelolco massacre has been likened to the reinactment of an ancient death-wish ritual. Since Tlatelolco the revolutionary symbols of the state, including its Tlatoani or authoritarian presidency, have been desecrated publicly and in derogation of established custom. Violent guerrilla insurgency has erupted about the country and in the cities. Many today feel that Tlatelolco meant the beginning of a new renaissance in Mexico, just as the Spanish triumph at the same spot during the sixteenth century signaled the birth of a new nation.

What produced the crisis at Tlatelolco has been analyzed elsewhere by this writer and others.[3] Looking back it appears that on October 1, 1968, an impasse between the government and protesting students crossed the point of no return. The students protested, among other things, police brutality, the holding of political prisoners, and the spending of millions of pesos to host the 1968 Olympic Games. They demanded a public dialogue, an open debate, with their government. They had been repeatedly turned down on this request since early August. The government of Mexico would not negotiate with a mob. A well-circulated rumor called for a mass demonstration at the Plaza of the

Three Cultures on the evening of October 2. There had been many such rallies before, but perhaps none so large as this one; an estimated 4,000 persons gathered to hear speakers demand that the government listen to their grievances. At approximately 7:00 p.m. white-gloved riot police moved into the crowd, swinging clubs and chains against the protesters and spectators indiscriminately. This action was a trigger mechanism which sparked mob behavior. Police units, furiously attacked by the unarmed citizens, opened fire.

The response to this was rifle fire from snipers whom the student National Strike Committee had placed at strategic locations in nearby high apartment buildings. The police retired and the army brought armored vehicles onto the scene. A firefight then ensued with ferocity and chaos until nearly 4:00 a.m. Thousands of Mexicans were caught in the murderous crossfire. Persons running in terror from a nearby movie theater were slugged by the soldiers without provocation. Nearly anyone who moved was fired upon. Automatic weapons swept building ledges where youngsters had climbed to safety. Many innocent people were injured and bodies were strewn about grotesquely. The Italian journalist Oriana Fallaci, herself a veteran of Vietnam reporting, was seriously injured.[4]

When the holocaust was over the army was in control, some 500 students and spectators are believed to have perished, and the estimates of those wounded (many died later rather than report their wounds) go into the thousands. The event brought condemnations against the government from some normally docile press organs. Thirty priests of the diocese of Cuernavaca signed a document sympathetic to the student cause. Yet the students were not without blame. Many of them who attacked the police, with and without arms, did so after first inebriating themselves into a hideous pitch of revelry by consuming a mixture of tequila, rum, and a drug known as cyclopal whose effect is to make one impervious in the face of certain death. Many students reinacted the ancient Aztec death ritual by liberating themselves for a new life, a reincarnation, in this tragic fashion. Soldiers and police as agents of the government played the role of sub-Tlatoanis. Ironically, President Díaz Ordaz's own interior minister Luis Echeverría was the man who gave the orders for the massacre at Tlatelolco. And Echeverría became Mexico's next president in 1970. The succession of Tlatoanis was complete.

The student protest movement shattered certain political traditions like reverence for the president while he is in office. President Gustavo Díaz Ordaz was severely attacked and discredited in the public view as was Luis Echeverría Alvarez. This sullied the subsequent presidential succession as well, but did not halt it. The issues that provoked the violence were many and diverse but central to them all was the naked illegitimacy of Mexico's single-party democracy and its belligerent refusal to allow a politically relevant sector (organized youth) to question publicly the status quo. The students screamed discontent over their society's enormous social injustices, over official corruption and inefficient government. They decried the general lack of socioeconomic mobility opportunities for youth. Consequently, Tlatelolco became a symbol of youth unity, christened with the blood of hundreds of their fellows who were dead. It enabled groups like the National Strike Committee of the National University (UNAM) and the National Polytechnic Institute (IPN) to weld into being a broad group consciousness. Veteran observers and political practitioners in Mexico told me that Tlatelolco became a symbol of group attachment for a newly conscious segment of the nation, pitting not only youth but *el pueblo* (the people) against the government.

Octavio Paz saw the student rebellion of 1968, the *enajenación juvenil,* as a predetermined extension of an Aztec death ritual that has been operative throughout Mexican history since the conquest.[5] His analysis exhibits nuances of an Hegelian dialectic, a march of uncontrollable spiritual forces across the earth. When President Díaz Ordaz and Secretary of Interior Luis Echeverría took the decision to risk the massacre of hundreds of citizens at Tlatelolco, and to injure thousands of others, the government was, in Paz's view, regressing to the behavior of premodern, that is, Aztec, times. Aggression is a synonym for regression. The massacre of Tlatelolco revealed the prevalence of a violent potential for destruction that had been latent in the Mexican people since the death rituals of the Aztecs. In ancient times such death rituals had indeed been conducted at Tlatelolco, a coincidence we noted earlier.

It is significant that Octavio Paz, in order to write *Posdata* both in protest against and in analysis of the meaning of Tlatelolco, had to resign his prestigious position as Mexico's ambassador to India. And it is perhaps equally significant that President Díaz Ordaz felt compelled to speak out on national television against both Paz's act and his book. Octavio Paz was too worldrenowned as an intellectual to be sacrificed like the students. Carlos Fuentes sums up the message of Paz's challenge in a way that is unmistakably clear:

> The official repression, too, was inevitable. Unaccustomed to dissent, the regime panicked; it had no political answers to political challenges. . . . The ritual bloodletting once more took place, ordered from the top of the pyramid by the *Tlatoani* in power, President Gustavo Díaz Ordaz, in the name of a perversion of nationalist and revolutionary theology. The hidden subconscious mechanisms of power probed by Paz were once more in operation.[6]

Paz saw the universities and the new bourgeois middle class as fertile sources of rebellion against Mexico's official party, PRI, which he viewed as an unnatural political monopoly whose path toward dictatorship was then being strewn with insurrection and anarchy. PRI was created as a recourse against military intervention in the political arena, a phenomenon intimately involved in the political alienation that one finds in many other Latin American nations. One of the ways in which the Mexican military was disestablished politically was through the enshrinement of the presidency along with it. The revolutionary Emiliano Zapata, before his death in 1919, had viewed the presidential chair with horror, urging that all such thrones of power should be burned, that power should be dispersed among the people. Zapata was murdered for his heresy. Exactly 50 years later another would-be reformer, ex-PRI president Carlos A. Madrazo, also sought to redistribute power to the localities and died under what many consider to be mysterious circumstances.[7] Paz says that Zapata was right: All thrones should be burned. For when they become institutionalized and bureaucratized their undoing is difficult and painful.

Looking backward still, Paz argues "for the Spaniards the conquest was an exploit [hazaña] but for the Indians it was a ritual [rito] . . . between the two extremes of exploit and ritual the Mexican sensibility and imagination has always oscillated."[8] Tlatelolco was a conquest or exploit for the regime; for the students it was a sacrificial ritual (this is my interpretation of Paz). The Aztec cult required a sacrifice in human blood to reify its omnipotence and to deify the onward phenomenal thrust of the universe that the Aztec rulers pretended to embody. The imperative was for Aztec domination of all other cults and groups, domination by force if necessary.

Modern-day Mexicans institutionalized Aztec domination in a unique way that few people have noticed: the Aztec capital's prehispanic name Mexico-Tenochtitlán, shortened to Mexico, was given to the entire country. This symbolizes, yet personifies, the domination of all Mexico by the capital.[9] The capital, in turn, centered about the ancient Aztec Zocalo that dominates all of Mexico today through the government and the PRI, the official party, which itself is a pyramid of power with the National Palace and Zocalo at its apex.

Mexico's enshrined presidency is the modern-day high priest of the Aztecs, the Tlatoani, who represents the extended and perpetual domination of the Aztec mystique and ritual over a submissive Mexican populace. Every six years another high priest is elected. He is invested with a mission; it is not personal power but a continuity with that of the Aztec past. And along the way he may have to perform sacrificial rituals, like that of Tlatelolco, if the Aztec mystique is to be spared from those who would threaten its perpetuation. The Plaza de las Tres Culturas, today's official name for the ancient square of Tlatelolco, is a counterpoise to the Zocalo which symbolized the perpetuation of Aztec power via the PRI. The massacre of Tlatelolco on October 2, 1968, was a sort of denouement, through blood and carnage, that revealed the historic petrification of the PRI.[10] If a line is drawn on a map of contemporary Mexico City from the Zocalo (power center of the PRI) to Tlatelolco (sacrificial center where the system is purged of its impurities), then in order to form an Aztec pyramid a final point is needed.

This is provided by the national Museum of Anthropology which has been transformed into a functioning temple for worship and adoration of the ancient grandeur of Mexico-Tenochtitlán. It is filled with symbols of death. The museum completes the pyramid. Paz asks why the Mexicans should hold up such a mirror of reverence to their past. His reply is that the true inheritors of the legacy of those who massacred the prehispanic (Aztec) world are not the Spaniards of today but the mestizo Mexicans and the remaining Indians. There is a causal bridge connecting past and present. The Museum of Anthropology and the plaza still known as Tlatelolco form the base of the power pyramid. This is an image, but, says Paz, all images suffer the fatal tendency of petrification, and only with the acid of verbal criticism can such images as Mexico's living-power triangle be dissolved. Progressive thought can break the power pyramid and then Mexicans will be free.

There are a number of ironies in the fact of the Tlatelolco massacre. The Plaza of the Three Cultures is supposed to symbolize the unity of Spaniards, Indians, and mestizo descendents of the conquest. Tlatelolco should be symbolic of Mexico's unity with its past. Today the Ministry of Foreign Relations conducts peoples diplomacy from a towering building at Tlatelolco. It is also the site of a major housing project, reflecting the alleged progressive urban policies of the single-party-dominant political system. Tlatelolco seems always to have been a mystical place, just as in the ancient days of religious human sacrifice.

Inescapably, one encounters in Mexico's writers a fascination with the political and spiritual symbolism of Tlatelolco. Witness the contemporary political novelist Luis Spota (author's translation):

Behind the church of Santiago Tlatelolco
Thirty years of peace and still
Another thirty years of peace,
Plus all the sidewalks and cement playing host
To the fiestas of this phantasmagoric country
And then all the speeches uttered
From the mouths of machineguns.[11]
An entire nation was wounded at Tlatelolco.[12]
A student leader is hooded, tortured by the police, the colonel in charge says "now we will learn, you bastard, who is your second in the National Strike Committee."

"But I have no second, no one in the Committee."

"We will beat it out of you, little son-of-a-bitch . . . and you will also tell me what you and your gang of sick comrades are about . . . tell me now."

"We want only one thing: respect for the laws of the land, for the Constitution."

"The Constitution is ours, managed by the Government . . . if you don't like that, screw you! Now tell me, where did you get your weapons?"[13]

When troops turned their guns on the student demonstrators at Tlatelolco it enraged many persons who previously had little to do with the protest movement. Infuriated beyond control at the horrors of military repression, they grabbed hidden weapons and opened fire against the army.[14] An anomic rebellion erupted at the mystical site. There were more illusory phantasms; Tlatelolco was an urban jacquerie (peasant's revolt) chock full of human variables which scientific rigor will be hard put to explain. Such is the political life of Mexico: it generates new martyrs; its revolutionary mystique is claimed to be endless. In Mexico, "time hungers for incarnation," says Carlos Fuentes.[15] It may be the central truth of today's Mexican political psyche that the nation has fallen schizophrenic, maddened from the quest to know its very self.

To many, therefore, it will seem that Mexican political life is too full of mysterious unknowns to be amenable to social science analysis. Rather than try to gloss over the mysteries, or tuck them neatly away in the verbal architecture of some conceptual scheme, I will simply admit the panoply of unknowns or inconsistencies and try to present them in an orderly fashion. Besides, what is inconsistent to North Americans may seem perfectly normal to Mexicans. That, indeed, was the counsel of one of Mexico's greatest social science scholars, the late Daniel Cosío Villegas. He gently chided North Americans for trying to see and impose order in Mexican political life where it did not exist. And he called them to task further for not understanding that Mexicans have learned to live with their own set of political contradictions.[16] That, to be sure, was part of the trauma of the year 1968. The contradictions in Mexican politics were emerging too rapidly and violently for anyone to find normalcy therein as the events unfolded. Now, with the benefit of a decade of hindsight, a more dispassionate view may be possible. And to illuminate the picture further we must cast yet another glance even deeper into Mexico's past before an attempt at theorizing is made.

COHESION AND ALLEGIANCE: ORIGINS OF THE SYMBOLIC CAPABILITY

If one visits the Plaza of the Three Cultures where the massacre of October 2, 1968, took place, it is quite possible to miss the engraving on a memorial which I translate as follows: "On August 15, 1521, heroically defended by Cuauhtémoc, Tlatelolco fell to the power of Hernán Cortés. This was neither triumph nor defeat, but the painful birth of the mestizo people who form today's Mexico."[17] The names in this cryptic scenario are important to an understanding of the creation of a Mexican national consciousness, hence, the spiritual and ideological foundations of today's Mexican political life.

Looking backward with certain historians into the labyrinthine depths of Aztec legend an important theme emerges. Early Mexican intellectuals and their conquerors in the sixteenth century felt it necessary to create for themselves a past that would lend the appearance of continuity with the future they were determined to erect. It is argued that Mexico is a case in point of colonialism interfering with the creation of an authentic national self-image among the colonized people. Both the colonized Aztecs and the creoles, Spaniards born in the new world, needed a common historical bond. This was even more important for their successors, the mestizos who resulted from the miscegenation of Aztec Indians and Spaniards and who were, in the spirit of the engraving cited above, the first Mexicans.

The Mexicans needed to separate themselves from the loyalist Spaniards, the *peninsulares* or *gachupines* as they were variously called. All Spaniards who intended to remain in New Spain (as Mexico was originally known), their creole progeny, the Indians, and the resultant mestizos, needed to explain why the conquest had succeeded. Cortés had relatively few men against the entire Aztec nation; he also had the help of some warring tribes who opposed Moctezuma's central authority. Cortés's victory in such circumstances required a credible explanation couched in terms that would generate a feeling of national consciousness which future Mexican generations could inherit. Accomplishing this seems to have been done by practicing (acquiescing in) a convenient historical sleight-of-hand, that is, the deliberate fabrication of a myth. (The use of such myths has become a constant in Mexican political life.) Recent scholarship has revealed that "spurious elements in a spurious history [were] predetermined by inherited assumptions and expectations . . . and that . . . the script writers [were] themselves unaware participants in a drama they [did] not fully control."[18]

Or to put this another way, it is alleged that Hernán Cortés sat down with his emperor, Charles V, and explained his famous encounter with Moctezuma during 1519 which resulted in the latter's surrender of the Aztec nation. It seems Aztec legend held that a plumed serpent-god, a phoenix named Quetzalcóatl, would return from the East in precisely that very year. Moctezuma feigned belief that Cortés was the serpent-god returned. Cortés apparently encouraged Moctezuma in that belief, or so he is supposed to have told his emperor. And Moctezuma is said to have reciprocated by pretending to invest Cortés with a messianic role. (The professing of messianic roles has become a standard political skill in Mexico.)

This historical entrepreneurship generated a cultural illusion of continuity. The Judeo-Christian messianic presence, embodied by Cortés, was made compatible with the pagan Aztec phoenix newly returned as a symbol of immortality. This act of creating (fabricating?) a doctrine of historical continuity was not only useful in long-term nation-building, but in the short run it allowed Moctezuma to save face while he surrendered to a Spanish force of inferior numbers, notwithstanding the subsequent decision of Cuauhtémoc to fight to the death to save the Aztec empire. This also enabled the Spaniards to pretend that their coming was the natural denouement of an Aztec prophecy, a psychological advantage in legitimizing their later control over the colonial population and in trying to win allegiance from the subject people by telling them that they were all acting out the Creator's grand design. Thus, it is argued, Quetzalcóatl-Cortés became one symbolic person, the forerunner of a great society to be built, a vital connecting link between the ruptured past and a yet uncomprehended present.[19]

However, the maze of fantasy and fact continues. Through additional machinations of the intellect one is asked to believe that the identification of the Aztec plumed serpent-god with Cortés was tantamount to including Saint Thomas in the equation. Saint Thomas is spuriously alleged to have conducted missionary work throughout Central America and perhaps parts of Mexico. Moreover, there was a professed and certified apparition in 1531 (ten years after the fall of Cuauhtémoc at Tlatelolco and the birth of the mestizo nation) which turned out to be the Virgin Mary come to the Aztec capital and nicely ready to be metamorphosed into a Mexican saint, the Virgin of Guadalupe. She became for the Indians and mestizos the protectress saint against floods, earthquakes, and other natural disasters. (Today the figure of Guadalupe protects Mexican taxi drivers and politicians alike from each other.)

Later, Guadalupe was adopted by the creole population in the seventeenth century as the official patroness saint of New Spain. Here was a spiritual metamorphosis, a tie with the past, yet one which was unique to the new world. Guadalupe became the principal giver of succor and protection for all Mexicans, and since she prefigured the early Church in New Spain she gave seventeenth-century Mexico its own separate spiritual identity, not of European derivation, which was distinct from the Quetzalcóatl-Cortés-Saint Thomas confabulation. This, then, gave to creoles, Indians, and mestizos a special sense of belonging to a common past and the ability to experience mutually the thrust of an ongoing history. They had roots. It ended the Christian-pagan dichotomy of the conquest era at least in theory if not entirely in practice. Surely, most of New Spain's inhabitants were not aware of this identity-forming process in any sophisticated sort of way. But they did welcome the protection afforded by the newly metamorphosed saints and protectors. Had they been left alone spiritually in the new world these transplanted Spaniards and their progeny could have gone mad. Some believe that today's Mexicans are suffering spiritual atrophy, frustration, and aggression, because their political system denies them the protection they once felt they had enjoyed via Guadalupe and others. That might partially explain the urban jacquerie at Tlatelolco.

Out of this miscegenation of races and mystiques emerged a new and powerful dichotomy which would rend Mexico, that is, the dichotomy between

Mexican and Spaniard. This would lay the basis for the independence movement in the early nineteenth century: and out of that would emerge a certain "comingtogetherness" as "creole, mestizo, and Indian were brought closer together (at least in theory) as common heirs to a mystical past."[20] The tying of pagan gods to those of the Judeo-Christian tradition laid a spiritual basis for declaring a new Mexican nation to exist and this, at least intellectually, was essential to achieving independence in the 1820s.

As we have already stressed, Cortés beseiged and conquered Tenochtitlán (Mexico) and defeated Cuauhtémoc in the battle of Tlatelolco of 1521. This was where the Mexican nation was really born. That is what today's Mexican officialdom asks us to believe. The last sacrificial priest (Tlatoani) to lead the Aztec resistance was Cuauhtémoc. He is of great symbolic importance for he sought to undo the selling out of Tenochtitlán to the foreigners. He tried to atone for the treason of Moctezuma and La Malinche. Cuauhtémoc symbolically is anathema to the concepts of *vendepatria* and *malinchismo,* the selling out and betrayal of one's nation. Cuauhtémoc becomes Mexico's first martyr, but by no means its last. As will be noted, Mexico needs its martyrs. Cuauhtémoc, now a name often adopted by patriotic contemporary Mexicans, is venerated along with Guadalupe as symbolic of resistance vis-a-vis a hostile external environment. But emotionally it is really Guadalupe who bridges the gap between the Spaniards, the creoles, the Indians, and the mestizos. Her brown color is no accident. She accomplished what Cuauhtémoc could not do. Guadalupe belongs to everyone.[21]

Part of the illusoriness of Mexico's authoritarian political system lies in its symbolic capability to deceive. A mystical presence such as the Virgin of Guadalupe lends itself to a facade of stability. The Virgin was the protective symbol of those who fought with Hidalgo and Morelos following 1810 in the beginning of the independence movement. Guadalupe is celebrated as a national cult of worship on December 12, a major spiritual ritual for many Mexicans. She adorns the interiors of most public transportation vehicles which pass through Mexico. Guadalupe is the answer to the dilemma of fixing one's origins. And it has been argued that she has a critical dual role, that of the violated woman who is victimized by a wicked outside world, and at once the source of morality and tenderness with which to cement family life. Whether she appears as the mother-victim or as the protectress saint, it is Guadalupe who will steer the believing Mexican to heaven, if not before that to the temporal good life as well. Guadalupe is ubiquitous; so is her duality. Guadalupe is an important part of Mexico's symbolic capability, a spiritual basis for cohesion and allegiance to the nation and she is at once a source of refuge from a threatening political system.

It is very much like the account given by an *Excelsior* reporter concerning today's Otomí Indians. He met a woman who could have been the incarnation of Guadalupe in her dual role of victim and giver of succor. Along with a young girl this woman bore a heavy load of cactus to be sold. The little girl held an axe that her mother used as a basic tool:

> poorly dressed they all looked at us with terror, as if we were going to strike them. The woman maintained a certain beauty but all that she could tell me I knew in advance. Her breasts rose under the ancient worn shirt that she got from a religious charity agency. She was mother earth, the giver of life and at once a beast of burden. Her primitive force and the natural beauty that she gave to her children was sullied by her tatters and rags, her bare feet to which decomposed sandals still clung.[22]

This is the sad duality of Guadalupe in Mexico's phenomenal world of today. The decline of the Otomí woman to tatters and rags may symbolize the social and political atrophy of Mexico as well. And to the extent that the Guadalupes of the real world are also mestizos the implication may be critical.

For the Mexican nation to emerge, the mestizo, who formed the great power base of the independence drive, had to be elevated out of his ambiguous role of an expendable pariah. Octavio Paz writes that the mestizo was not always able to avail himself of the creole's religious and historical syncretism as a way of capturing identity, and

> socially the mestizo is a marginal being, rejected by Indians, Spaniards, and creoles; historically he is the incarnation of the creole dream. His situation vis-a-vis the Indians reflects the same ambivalence; he is their hangman and their avenger. In New Spain he is a bandit and a policeman, in the twentieth century a banker and trade union leader. In Mexican history his ascent signifies the sway of violence; his silhouette embodies endemic civil war.[23]

Tired of exploitation by foreign-dominated elites, the mestizo erupted in civil war early in the nineteenth century and later between 1910 and 1917. Today's revolutionary Mexico was born. The mestizo is the new Mexican man of the 1970s and beyond; his stamp is patent in the political life of Mexico. Thus the mestizo is in a very real sense the embodiment of contemporary Mexico's diverse heritage of two cultures, the Spanish and the Aztec. The mestizo provides the third culture, and thus Tlatelolco, the ancient site of human sacrifice rituals where the Mexican nation was born in 1521, comes to be renamed the Plaza of the Three Cultures, today's site of more tragic rituals which seem to be a self-fulfilling prophecy thrusting onward into the twentieth century.

Octavio Paz also writes that under the Spanish crown New Spain knew a great deal of abundance and stability; not that all the viceroys were good, but the system had a built-in balance of powers with state authority limited by the Church and the viceroy's power balanced by the *audiencias* of the crown. This division of powers made it necessary for the government to seek some level of public consensus from even the masses. "In this sense, the system of New Spain was more flexible than the present presidential regime [of the 1970s]. Under the mask of democracy, our presidents are constitutional dictators in the Roman style. The only difference is that the Roman dictatorship lasted six months, while ours lasts six years."[24]

TOWARD A PARTIAL THEORY OF MEXICAN POLITICAL LIFE

It is the function of the PRI to provide Mexicans with paternalism, to give the masses feeling that they have expression and belonging while at once manipulating them for the advantage of the ruling class. The PRI must attend to Mexico's development in an industrialized world. It is here that the masses, and especially the workers and peasants, may be manipulated in favor of bourgeois interests. To accomplish this the PRI offers Mexicans a father image in the presidential palace to accompany the mother image in the nearby shrine of Guadalupe. Thus paternalism and maternalism are complementary. Carlos Fuentes writes that most Mexicans would rather suffer a paternalistic regime (and complain about it) than have real political freedom. Any weakening of the protective figures of authority makes the Mexican feel abandoned, just as the original Mexican bastard, the son of La Malinche, felt abandoned by the conquering father Cortés.[25] For most Mexicans life is a continued war of all against all. Protective symbols are a way of steeling oneself amidst a hostile environment.

The problem is that although being sacrificed to the gods may have been a happy event to the ancient Aztecs, today's Mexican university student with some glimmer of hope for socioeconomic mobility is not overjoyed when he is bayoneted at Tlatelolco. He does not see the contemporary president as one who will lift up the people to a better life, nor does he recognize any gods who merit his blood. The president has already demonstrated his vanity by wasting public resources on showy international events (Olympic Games) while the masses starve. There is not even a means for the student to communicate his disapproval to the regime (which insists publicly that it is a democracy). When the students confront the regime en masse they are massacred. And about 70 percent of Mexico's total population, while not all students, are still under age 25. When their government massacres them it is a critical juncture for the entire society.

Later in this book I will try to refine the ideas I am about to offer into a partial theory of Mexican politics. Succinctly put, the general proposition can be advanced that the essence of Mexican politics is paternalism and mass manipulation via the symbolic capabilities of the system. The masses can be made to believe (or at least act as if they believe) that the PRI is a benevolently authoritarian regime as long as its dispensation of largesse and public acquiescence in a certain level of poverty continue without interruption. If the regime can invoke attachment symbols from more recent history (to be discussed in Chapter 2) and combine them with an occasional appeal to the ancient greatness of Mexico newly born (Quetzalcóatl-Cortés, Cuauhtémoc, and Guadalupe) then all is well. As long as the material largesse keeps flowing in sufficient abundance, such symbolic manipulations may suffice; however, when the populace becomes aware that the regime is not paternalistic, but voracious and malevolent, then the regime's legitimacy is undermined along with that of the symbols it monopolizes. As Machiavelli counseled his prince, be feared but not hated. The latter brings revolt.

A key point is that today's pyramid and Tlatoani, the PRI and its authoritarian president, are not seen as deities by the majority of the population as apparently was the case with the Aztecs, or even as recently as the era of President Cárdenas in the 1930s. Every time the PRI celebrates a ritual of human sacrifice today it loses popular support, and at Tlatelolco it may have gone just about to the brink of collapse. That Mexicans have numerous psychic hangups will be denied by few who have known them. But it is doubtful that very many of them really believe in reincarnation either. Few want to die for the PRI.

In short, at Tlatelolco the PRI may have profaned many of the symbols which once generated allegiant political attitudes among the Mexican people. In subsequent chapters we will consider evidence of the atrophy of symbolic and other capabilities of Mexico. Not the least of such evidence will be the enormous rush of illegal migrants now flooding north into the United States —and that is not because Quetzalcóatl has been sighted anew on the north side of the border, nor that the Virgin of Guadalupe has just been revealed as a gringa. It is because there is food to the north and starvation to the south. It is hard to manipulate symbols of allegiance, with or without bayonets, when the populace is wretched.

I noted earlier certain Mexican personality tendencies toward belligerent confrontation, verbal abuse, self-deprecation, and others including the preoccupation with death. This may be, as stressed herein, a spiritual holdover from the Aztecs, a part of the death-wish legacy. Or it may simply be that popular faith in traditional symbols is crumbling. Mexico has developed an enormous capacity for cynicism and corruption; indeed these are major political constants today. To pretend to be what one is not is another constant. Charlatanism is rewarded in Mexican politics; and at such a point the treasured symbols of national consciousness seem to be forgotten. Writing during the Cárdenas years, an epoch which many considered truly progressive, the playwright Rodolfo Usigli captured, pejoratively, the spirit of what may have been germinating within the pyramid for years and is causing its atrophy today:

> Everyone here lives by appearances, by gestures . . . look at those who wear
> the general's eagle having never fought a battle; at those who call themselves

friends of the people but who rob them just the same; at the demagogues who
stir up the workers and who call them comrades having never worked with
their hands; at the professors who do not know how to teach and the students
who do not study.[26]

Usigli also wrote that Mexico needs its heroes in order to live and he who
spilled his blood for his country was surely a hero. But he did not say that he
who massacred his countrymen could continue to call himself Tlatoani or any
other patriotic epithet.

It is not surprising, then, to find Mexicans displaying a certain dwarfishness (*enanismo*) as a reflection of both the nation's rulers and of many of its
citizens. The small dwarfs, the Juan Pueblos, are helpless pariahs before the
threatening governmental pyramid. But there are big dwarfs atop the pyramid.
The president has ceased to be a Tlatoani but he is now a ruling dictator-dwarf
(*enano*). This is the philosophy of Oscar Monroy Rivera, creator of *Enanonia*
(Land of the Dwarfs). It is the dwarf mentality that causes Mexico to atrophy.
In characterizing Luis Echeverría as president of dwarfland during his recent
administration (1970–76), Monroy wrote of the crimes the president is compelled to commit against the people and then hide:

> He picks his victims without the application of any judicial or moral norm,
> not even to create the appearance of legitimacy. Soldiers and policemen in
> Enanonia are those who are charged with the primary responsibility of
> palliating, cloaking, muzzling, doing anything necessary that will cover up
> the crime. Better said, it is they who make sure that the jobs are "clean."[27]

Regardless if we are talking of Mexico, Enanonia, or Tenochtitlán, the
essential question is whether the regime has been able to accompany its symbolic manipulations with a distributive capability that will create a substantive
foundation on which allegiance is to be based. But here is the nub of the
dilemma. Mexico's political system is that of one party, superimposed over the
government, where thousands of phantom bureaucrats (*aviadores*) drain away
the public resources. The one-party system allows token opposition only to
create the facade of democracy, but only the facade. Thus there is no effective
loyal opposition that has a vested interest in correcting abuses. The handful
of opposition congressmen who are allowed into the congress for showcase
purposes are easily rendered helpless. The single-party PRI claims to be the
exclusive inheritor of political legitimacy in Mexico. All the symbols, beginning with Guadalupe, Cuauhtémoc, and the rest are the exclusive province of
the PRI. No other group can effectively challenge this hegemony within a legal
context, although key individuals can be co-opted. Even groups can be co-
opted. But a real challenge, via an honest public election, is something the
regime fears greatly. So opposition groups are left only with the option of
extralegal challenges. From there comes the violent guerrilla activity. Many

insurgent terrorist groups formed after Tlatelolco. The events leading to that tragedy had begun within a legal context. The government's intransigence forced them into extralegality. As one North American scholar put it quite appropriately, the Mexican regime treats bona fide groups as if they were enemy nations.[28]

One of the principal outlets for political criticism in Mexico was the newspaper *Excelsior* which operated as a free and distinguished forum and criticized the government rather severely up until July 1976 when it was taken over by a government-engineered coup, an event to which I will return in another chapter. The ousted staff of *Excelsior* created a new weekly journal called *Proceso* which began publishing despite government threats late in 1976. In one of its early 1977 issues *Proceso* carried an article which translates as the "strangulation of the political conscience" and places in bold relief the dilemma of political democracy in Mexico.[29]

The article speaks of fake opposition groups which help the PRI maintain the facade of democracy. These groups like the PPS (Popular Socialist Party) demand legal reforms which can be accomplished quickly and then ignored, but they do not seriously protest voting fraud nor the official violence that is perpetrated against those who criticize the government. The author goes on to say, "we are good at celebrating that which does not exist, we name a few opponents winners to convince ourselves that we are democratic, we celebrate the agrarian reform so as to assure the peasants that they have won the great revolution although they will never have power nor justice . . . we live in two worlds that are contradictory, *it is a schizophrenic life and we are united only via myths and rituals.*"[30] What is the result:

> The PRI proclaims democracy and denounces its own violence and constitu-
> tional violations. The PRI accuses. The PRI investigates. The PRI is judge.
> The PRI is witness. The PRI is jury. . . . The PRI executes. The PRI is the
> court of appeals. The PRI directs and guides. . . . We have had for years the
> same basic leaders of the PRI who are irremovable. These people circulate
> from position to position, from governorships to the national Congress and
> back again. Our theory is perennial rotation. It is the logic of power.[31]

Here, then, are the ingredients of a partial theory of Mexican politics which I shall try to refine in the pages to follow. The people are tied spiritually to an enigmatic past whose symbols of attachment are monopolized but in atrophy; life is schizophrenic and more unbearable as the country grows poorer materially and the myths and rituals become increasingly meaningless; political legitimacy is the monopoly of a single organization; opposition to the regime is readily branded as sedition; political life, indeed life itself, approaches the war of all against all which intensifies the search for protective symbols, panaceas, or messiahs. The Mexican political system is a throne atop a pyramid which has lost most of its basic popular support. Withdrawal of consent is one basic weapon of the poor. Insurgency is another. Power without legitimacy, that is contemporary Mexico. Poverty and repression have thresholds of criticality. When the people can endure no more, political collapse can be expected.

NOTES

1. See his *Sociología mexicana* (Mexico: Porrua, 1969), pp. 203–19. Similar observations appear in the works of Octavio Paz, Oscar Monroy Rivera, and others cited herein.

2. From Carlos Fuentes, "Mexico and its Demons," *New York Review of Books,* September 20, 1973, p. 16.

3. See Kenneth F. Johnson, *Mexican Democracy: A Critical View* (Boston: Allyn & Bacon, 1972), and Luis Spota, *La plaza* (Mexico: Joaquín Mortiz, 1972).

4. The 40-year-old Italian newspaperwoman said, after being shot three times, "I have covered the Vietnam war but I have never seen anything similar to what happened at Tlatelolco . . . I lay on the ground with blood pouring out of my body. Every time I tried to raise my head and call for help a policeman was pointing his gun at me. It was a terrible, unbelievable thing." *Los Angeles Times,* October 4, 1968.

5. Octavio Paz, *Posdata* (Mexico: Siglo Veintiuno Editores, 1970), passim.

6. Fuentes, op. cit., p. 19.

7. See Johnson, op. cit., p. 82.

8. Paz, op. cit., p. 114, author's translation.

9. Ibid., pp. 121–22.

10. Ibid., p. 149.

11. Spota, op. cit., pp. 21–12.

12. Ibid., p. 165.

13. Ibid., pp. 39–40.

14. Ibid., p. 215–16.

15. Fuentes, op. cit., p. 16.

16. Daniel Cosío Villegas, *La sucesión presidencial* (Mexico: Joaquín Mortiz, 1974), pp. 13–18.

17. As photographed by this author.

18. J. H. Elliott, "The Triumph of the Virgin of Guadalupe," *New York Review of Books,* May 26, 1977, p. 28.

19. Ibid., p. 29.

20. Ibid., p. 30. See also Enrique Maza, "Guadalupanismo que libere," *Proceso,* no. 6, December 11, 1976, p. 19.

21. Ibid. The much-lauded work by Jacques Lafaye, *Quetzalcóatl and Guadalupe: The Formation of Mexican National Consciousness, 1531–1813* (Chicago: University of Chicago Press, 1976), ends with a bold claim for the cult of Guadalupe saying that it "is the central theme of the history of creole consciousness or Mexican patriotism. Every study of that subject must inevitably lead to that cult or take it as its point of departure" (p. 299). The Mexican creoles, argues this analysis, had sinful souls and were unsure of their national origins. Identification of Quetzalcóatl with Saint Thomas and, from there, metamorphosing the Virgin Mary into the cult of Guadalupe gave these creoles a passport to respectability, both spiritually and politically. Without these sources of dignity and respect the creoles were doomed to be branded infidels. Lafaye argues that the aspiration to secure dignity was not just a Mexican phenomenon but became a constant that could be identified in other Hispanic-American societies. "It survived long after Independence, as proved by the success in Argentina of Peronist *justicialismo* [alleges Lafaye] whose slogan was 'Perón keeps his word, Evita gives you back your dignity (*Perón cumple, Evita digni-*

fica)' " (p. 303). He argues further that the image a society has of its past may be more revealing of its present state of consciousness than any utopian future vision (p. 306). Mexicans thought they saw the hand of Quetzalcóatl behind Madero's victory in the Great Revolution of 1910–17. They saw him again in Lázaro Cárdenas, the populist messiah-president of the 1930s. No sooner, says Lafaye, does one messiah disappear than another is ready for reincarnation. As Mexicans pass through the throes of this process they are watched over protectively by Guadalupe, over whom no particular political elite class (for example, the PRI) has exclusive control. But the same may not be true for Quetzalcóatl, suggesting a tempting but elusive hypothesis for examination within the modern context of Mexican political life.

22. *Excelsior,* July 9, 1972.

23. From the introduction to Lafaye, op. cit., written by Octavio Paz, p. xvi.

24. Ibid., p. xviii.

25. Fuentes, op. cit., p. 18.

26. Rodolfo Usigli, *El gesticulador* (New York: Appleton-Century-Crofts, 1963), p. 46. This work was first published in 1937.

27. Oscar Monroy Rivera, *El señor presidente de Enanonia* (Mexico: Costa-Amic, 1973), p. 43.

28. Evelyn P. Stevens, *Protest and Response in Mexico* (Cambridge, Mass.: MIT Press, 1974), p. 259.

29. Enrique Maza, "Estrangulamiento de la conciencia política," *Proceso,* January 11, 1977, pp. 40–41.

30. Ibid., emphasis added.

31. Ibid.

Two

The Growth of Revolutionary Mexico: A Historical Sketch

FROM COLONY TO INDEPENDENCE

Following the sixteenth-century conquest of Mexico the process of forming a society began. The spiritual roots that were cited in Chapter 1 may have given Mexicans emotive protection against the vengeful gods but it did not necessarily protect them from each other. A new creole-mestizo class of aristocrats formed with ample wealth that was extracted from the land by exploiting Indian labor. During the seventeenth century this became an idle and degenerate class which sustained itself parasitically in New Spain (subdivided into the *audiencias* of Mexico and New Galicia). Mexico City became one of the great centers of wealth and conspicuous consumption of the then-known Western Hemisphere. The city developed a heavy dependency relationship on the surrounding area with foodstuffs brought by the Indians on mules and across Lake Texcoco in small boats. Yet the creoles developed conflicts with the *peninsulares* (*gachupines* or European-born Spaniards) who held political and religious power. Racial antagonisms, weak law enforcement, and ineffective public protection led to a value syndrome in which the residents of New Spain learned to put individual values before those of the community, that is, to protect themselves first. Quite naturally, this spawned political corruption, the taking of public goods, and the using of public services for the enrichment of one's private self and immediate circle of family and friends. Very early then, corruption became a constant in the political life of Mexico.

By the end of the eighteenth century the Spanish colonial authorities had recognized political corruption as a force to be dealt with and sought to remedy it by imposing on Mexico the system of *intendencias* that was used in Spain. Under this arrangement the territory was divided up into 12 districts (intendencias) whose administrator reported directly to Mexico City. Spaniards born on the Iberian Peninsula replaced the local creoles and mestizos as mayors and administrators of key positions within each of the intendencias. This served to create additional animosities between creoles and gachupines. More significantly perhaps, it deprived native populations in New Spain of government experience with which to replace the Spaniards once independence was won in the 1820s, a dilemma shared by Mexico and a host of other countries. During this period great amounts of wealth (especially silver) were taken from Mexico and shipped to Spain. Most of the natives and commoner immigrants never saw this wealth nor benefited from it, remaining tied to semifeudal agricultural pursuits. Debt peonage and exploitation of Indians under the *encomienda* system (whereby a local *cacique* or boss received a grant of land and rights to the labor of Indians living on it) continued into the nineteenth century, but the scale of such abuses was reduced as the encomiendas were progressively eliminated on orders from Spain.

As the era of movements for independence grew near there was a visibly stratified society in New Spain. A small but powerful aristocracy of peninsulares existed with economic roots in land and mining. By and large this aristocracy was supported by the military and the Church hierarchy. There was also the new class (cited above) of New World Spaniards (creoles) and a mestizo elite, both of whom aspired to the same political power and in many cases became antagonists. The Indians, mulattoes where they existed, and mestizo poor constituted the masses and represented well above 80 percent of the total population. Their illiteracy and extreme poverty was so patent that by the end of the eighteenth century even the viceroy took limited measures to aid them. But few among the elites were seriously concerned about the need for social reform. Those who recognized the need were too few and their voices were raised too late.

The story of today's independent Mexico begins with the early nineteenth-century Napoleonic incursions into the Iberian Peninsula. Napoleon's attempt to dominate the throne of Spain weakened the mother countries' (Spain, Portugal, and France) efforts to hold onto their colonies in the New World. Haiti was the first to break away (from France) in 1804, thereby giving inspiration to others who sought to balance out the structure of power between themselves and the gachupines. As news spread of the fall of the Bourbon crown in the mother country, young generations of New World Spaniards increasingly saw in this an opportunity to separate politically and to create locally managed sovereign states.

In Mexico the governing council of the capital city cajoled the vain José de Iturrigaray, the viceroy of Mexico City, into convening a special junta whose purpose would be to create a provisional government and ultimately declare independence from Spain. The creole ambition to displace the colonists was thinly veiled as was the ingenious sympathy of Iturrigaray for the idea of establishing himself as the ruler of an independent Mexico. The Spanish loyalists responded with a coup that unseated the junta and replaced the viceroy with an infirm old man, Pedro de Garibay, who proved ineffective in suppressing the creole unrest; this did little to bridge the widening abyss between Mexico City and the artificial regime of the French-imposed Joseph Bonaparte in Madrid. The beginning of an indigenous Mexico was at hand. All it needed was a catalyst and a spark of life.

The catalyst was found in the Querétaro Club of 1810, a social and literary circle whose membership included Ignacio Allende, a creole officer of the local militia, and Father Miguel Hidalgo, a creole priest who shared visions of an indigenous Mexicanism while resenting all the while his diminished ecclesiastical status because he lacked true Spanish birth. Padre Hidalgo undertook to recruit clerics to the cause of independence while Ignacio Allende and his companion, Juan Aldama, organized military support for an eventual uprising. But the activities of the Querétaro Club became too overt for the Spanish loyalists to continue to ignore. On the evening of September 13, 1810, the army seized a number of secret arms caches and arrested a small group of followers of Hidalgo. Aldama, learning of the arrests, carried word to the small village of Dolores where Padre Hidalgo's parish was located. Before dawn on September 16, Padre Hidalgo had assembled at his church what would become the nucleus of revolutionary anarchy. Instead of offering sacraments he called upon his parishioners to support him in a march for independence that would be directed against Querétaro. The gullible and downtrodden peasants responded, believing that God had sanctioned the displacement of their foreign oppressors. They marched on Querétaro voicing the famous "cry of Dolores" which in essence meant death to the colonists.

Hidalgo, Allende, and Aldama had unleashed a massive wave of human violence which they were helpless to control. Disaster followed in late September in Guanajuato where Spanish loyalist bullets slaughtered some 2,000 of Hidalgo's fold. With news of this tragedy many enraged poor of the land sprang forth from their slums, spreading blood and hate in all directions about the geographical center of Mexico. Clearly outnumbering the colonists in most of their encounters, the revolutionary army (which at times is thought to have numbered close to 100,000) fell before the withering fire and cavalry tactics of the disciplined loyalist soldiers. Hidalgo's hordes retaliated in a fashion that historians do not easily vindicate. Nearly everyone not openly sympathetic to the revolutionary cause was put to the sword or torch. Multitudes thus perished, most of them innocent, in what clearly had become a fanatic uprising of the Indian and mestizo poor against the dominant upper classes. But the Hidalgo revolt was short-lived. On January 17, 1811, the volunteer army faced a highly skilled force of vastly lesser numbers near Río Lerma. The loyalist army under the superior direction of General Félix María Calleja, himself possessed by a blind fury of revenge against the insurrectionists, ordered wholesale massacres of the revolutionists who in turn fled Guadalajara, leaving Hidalgo and his immediate staff as victims of imminent capture.

Hidalgo was defrocked, disgraced, and executed by the Spanish authorities. Thereafter the charge passed to the more able and temperate hands of another priest, José María Morelos, who earlier had been commissioned by

Hidalgo to undertake responsibility for an uprising in the south. Morelos's superiority to his mentor was both tactical and intellectual. He did not attempt to control more men than was humanly possible and his well-disciplined insurgent units seldom were guilty of wantonness, terror, or outright atrocities. Ideologically, Morelos did not urge vengeance generally upon the non-mestizo. This, in part, had been Hidalgo's error, for in creating an unbridgeable gulf between the Indian-mestizo masses and the creole colonists, he had failed in his opportunity to unite many creoles to his cause. Morelos tried to cajole the creoles but failed beneath the stigma of horror he had inherited.

Morelos called for abolition of religious privileges, for division of land, and, most important of all, he launched a positive appeal for Mexican independence as a general cause; thus Morelos fought for a free Mexico and not merely against Spain. In 1813 he convened a revolutionary convention at Chilpancingo representing the various southern territories still under his control. Out of this meeting emerged Mexico's first revolutionary constitution, which was promulgated at Apatzingán in 1814. Morelos and his supporters carried the haunting specter of Hidalgo's ignominious defeat within their hearts until December 1815. Pursued by the same General Calleja who had ruined Hidalgo, the Morelos movement was gradually driven into the clandestine reaches of the forests and back streets. Forces led by Agustín de Iturbide ultimately captured the rebel priest and later defrocked him. But he could not be made to recant as had Hidalgo. Morelos gave his life as the first real cornerstone of independence, one which could be embraced symbolically and revered without the stigma of treasonable disgrace.

By the year 1819 only two of Morelos's regional chieftains still operated in defiance of the loyalists. One of them, Guadalupe Victoria, more popularly known as Félix Fernández, was driven to living as a mountain cave-dwelling recluse, later to become the object of considerable folklore enchantment. The other, the stubborn and ingenious Vicente Guerrero, continued to fight alone. His guerrillas took a toll of loyalist troops which shocked the viceroy and made it increasingly difficult to maintain publicly that the revolution unleashed by the mad priest of Dolores had come to naught. However, if the Querétaro Club of 1810 had provided a catalyst for revolution, the insurgent wrath of Vicente Guerrero one decade later gave it a final spark. Lamentably, when the spark produced independence it was hardly of the variety envisioned by Hidalgo, Allende, Aldama, and Morelos.

Early in 1820 the government of Spain fell into the control of those who said they favored government by constitution rather than by monarch. The loyalists in Mexico feared that news of this turn would initiate a new wave of independence-minded terrorism by the small remaining patriot forces. The menace of Vicente Guerrero lived on and with it the figures of Hidalgo and others continued to tower menacingly from the past. Viceroy Apodaca commissioned the man who had overcome Morelos, Agustín de Iturbide, to exterminate Vicente Guerrero. He tried and failed. Indeed, he tried many times, to the extent of proving that Guerrero was unquestionably the better of the two men on the field of battle. Then, after stealing money from the loyalists who paid him to eliminate Guerrero, Iturbide launched the Mexican people upon a narrow ideological course whose norm is still a lingering pestilence to this very day: He became a traitor and sold out compatriots and friends. At his headquarters in Iguala, Iturbide invited Vicente Guerrero to the conference table; this was decidedly not the latter's preferred field of battle. When Guerrero agreed to the Plan de Iguala on February 24, 1821, he sincerely thought he had won a victory; in fact, all Mexico had lost.

Incredibly, the Iturbide-Guerrero accord won support of most of the remaining Morelos chieftains: Even Guadalupe Victoria came out of hiding to champion the cause of independence. Creoles too joined the groundswell and on September 27, 1821, Agustín de Iturbide marched confidently into the capital city flanked by Vicente Guerrero and Guadalupe Victoria. A change in government had taken place to be sure, but it was not accompanied by the social and economic reforms envisioned by Morelos. The man who was to rule Mexico briefly as emperor was motivated primarily by personal greed. After all, it was Iturbide who, as military commandant of the agriculture-rich Valle del Bajío, had instituted the insidious practice of monopolizing the sale of grain (and thereby multiplying the numbers of ill-fed and starving in the very midst of plenty) for an attractive personal profit. He undertook to govern the new nation in much the same fashion, naturally to the chagrin of Guadalupe Victoria and Vicente Guerrero. When his congress refused to approve financial measures needed to support his military establishment, Iturbide simply suspended the legislature and ruled openly as a dictator. Putting an army into the field, Iturbide succeeded temporarily in declaring an extension of his empire as far south as what is now the northern half of El Salvador, but he was forced to withdraw in the face of republican opposition throughout what later became known as the United Provinces of Central America. The short-lived empire netted only the southern territory known as Chiapas, a matter still in dispute by Guatemala although it was incorporated as a piece of Mexico at that time.

SANTA ANNA: THE STIGMA OF VENDEPATRIA

Iturbide proved to be a traitor in every sense, even to the point of neglecting his military. Unpaid, and seething with discontent, factions of the military united behind the commander of Veracruz to depose him. Iturbide's final act was fully as treacherous as had been his first. He accepted payment and agreed to leave the country forever.

In February 1823, Mexico entered upon the disastrous era marked by Antonio López de Santa Anna who had learned his style well under Iturbide, and who saw to it that his mentor was promptly executed when he attempted to return to Mexican soil in violation of the agreement under which Iturbide had been exiled. From his estate in Veracruz, known as Manga de Clavo, Santa Anna ruled his nation for virtually 30 years. The era was punctuated by numerous rebellions, interim presidents, and frequent exiles of Santa Anna himself, but until the traumatic end it was a bitter epoch which bore the stamp of a single ruthless hand. Santa Anna left Mexico with the stigma of vendepatria. But it was Guadalupe Victoria and not Santa Anna who became Mexico's first president. He sought to rule under an absurd constitution, patterned after that of the United States, which assumed degrees of political socialization and responsibility nonexistent among the then untutored population. Victoria was opposed by the Scottish-rite Masons as well as by the York-rite Masons. The latter, deeply involved in political intrigues with U.S. Ambassador Joel Poinsett, caused the first republican government of Mexico to be rendered financially impotent.[1] In 1828 when the conservative Scottish-rite Masons succeeded in electing General Manuel Gómez Pedraza to the presidency, Vicente Guerrero rose in arms against the regime. Santa Anna pronounced in favor of Guerrero and thus in 1829 Victoria turned the reins of government over to his former revolutionary partner. The turmoil, and the atrophy of drives toward needed reforms, surrounding these and succeeding events have filled many historical treatises. Their outcome was, unhappily, not one of social progress.

Throughout these events Santa Anna remained in the background. He was soon to emerge as a hero in defending Mexico against an abortive Spanish effort to regain its lost colony and then subsequently came out in defense of President Guerrero, who was overthrown in a military coup in 1830 by Anastasio Bustamante, a mere puppet for conservative boss Lucas Alamán. The latter was a survivor of the massacre of Guanajuato and personified the oligarchic reaction against what Hidalgo and all subsequent revolutionaries had stood for. After two years of military dictatorship and unrest, Santa Anna was finally named president; but he cleverly chose to allow his vice-president, Valentín Gómez Farías, to rule in his stead. Not proving sufficiently reactionary to satisfy the military and the clergy, Gómez Farías was ousted with the treasonable assent of Santa Anna, who had placed him in power. Santa Anna wanted to be cajoled into office so as to more easily justify assumption of absolute dictatorial powers. Nevertheless, he continued to allow the actual governance of Mexico to be handled by lesser figures, all the while remaining skillfully in defensive isolation at his Veracruz estate.

The first great challenge to Santa Anna's cunning began to emerge in 1830 when the question of American settlers in the northern Texas territory generated concern among Mexican nationalists. U.S. Ambassador Poinsett had explored the possibility of purchasing the territory. To unsettle matters further, Stephen Austin was temporarily jailed in Mexico City after attempting to secure independent statehood for Texas—but as a Mexican state—from a hostile Mexican congress. In 1836 Santa Anna led an army north to reaffirm Mexican sovereignty over the territory. After overcoming the dramatic stand of a handful of Texas settlers at the San Antonio mission known as the Alamo, Santa Anna's ill-trained forces were routed near San Jacinto by well-trained American volunteers under Sam Houston. Spared the ignominy of imprisonment upon his capture, Santa Anna was taken to Washington to confer with President Andrew Jackson and made to promise guarantees for the safety of the Texas settlers in return for an American promise not to annex the territory. By returning Santa Anna to Mexico the United States had committed the first in a series of unpardonable acts against her southern neighbor.

By 1845 the attitude of the government had changed from one of hands off Texas (originally dictated by the fear of a new slave state) to one of annexation under Manifest Destiny (in competition with gestures of acquisition on the part of Great Britain). A mission headed by the American diplomat John Slidell, which can best be described as an attempt at international bribery, was sent by President Polk to Mexico City and was rejected promptly by the proudly nationalistic President Joaquín Herrera. The Mexicans then began massing troops in the north to defend their territory, and in April 1846 the United States declared war. The design of President Polk was more the conquest of California than Texas but one could not be had without the other. Border incidents used to justify the war declaration are considered by some historians to be of questionable authenticity. When the war ended, Santa Anna was exiled to Jamaica, thousands of Mexicans had perished, the Mexican treasury had been paid $15 million for the loss of Texas, and Mexico had for all practical purposes lost the most valuable half of its national territory. This was formalized on March 10, 1848, by the treaty of Guadalupe Hidalgo. The irony of this document is that its American negotiator, Nicholas Trist, had previously been fired by Washington for incompetence and at the time of the agreement he was acting without portfolio. The U.S. Congress swallowed its pride and ratified the treaty.

In most nations peopled by proud human beings, the end of the war with the United States would most surely have been the end of a dictator such as Santa Anna. That it was not testifies to the deplorable status of political democracy in Mexico in the mid-nineteenth century. The presidency fell into the hands of a succession of political adventurers, and, however shocking, it is not surprising that the old dictator, now boasting a wooden leg, should be called once again from exile in 1853 to try to impose order upon the resulting chaos. When shortly thereafter Lucas Alamán died, Santa Anna saw no reason to honor the trust of the conservatives who had returned him to power and proceeded to loot the treasury mercilessly. He climaxed the era that bears his name with the epitome of treacherous acts: He sold a piece of Mexico's territory to the United States. The Gadsden Purchase of 1853 gave the United

States a right of way along the southern Arizona border for railroad construction and it gave Santa Anna funds with which to sustain his caprice for another two years. By that time the remnants of the Morelos movement had regrouped into a truly liberal opposition determined not only to get rid of Santa Anna but also to wipe out the landed and clerical oligarchy once and for all. The Liberals proclaimed their Plan de Ayutla in 1854 and the following year Santa Anna left for South America. His era of rapine had ended. But the norm of treason, vendepatria, unfortunately survived and to a large extent would plague Mexico into the twentieth century.

LA REFORMA: SYMBOLS OF HOPE

The Liberal forces under Juan Alvarez, which occupied the capital city following the exit of Santa Anna, brought with them Melchor Ocampo, Miguel Lerdo de Tejada, and, most prominently, the Indian leader from Oaxaca, Benito Juárez. The Liberals were unable to hold the capital permanently and provisional governments were established in the regional centers of Michoacán and Veracruz. The famous Liberal Constitution promulgated in 1857 gave official impetus to the War of the Reform. It soon became a religious war against the Church and its legion of socioeconomic privileges. The constitution embraced the earlier Ley Juárez and Ley Lerdo whose joint effect was to deny the Church all but its purely ecclesiastical functions within a very narrow definition. Marriage was made a civil function, monasteries and other Church properties were confiscated, priests and nuns were proscribed from wearing their habits in public and denied the right to engage in public education. Juárez acquiesced when his followers murdered priests and desecrated altars, but he never allowed the carnage to grow totally out of control as it had in the years following 1810. He occupied the important port of Veracruz and began wearing the Conservative forces down by denying them foreign commerce and customs revenues. With the help of an able general, Porfirio Díaz, the Conservative armies in the south crumbled as had those in the north earlier, and on New Year's day, 1861, Juárez's army seized Mexico City. The war had been won but their reforms had yet to be institutionalized.

To Mexico, the combined cost of the Age of Santa Anna and the Reform was enormous. Although the United States had favored Juárez with guns and financial aid, the European nations and Great Britain now demanded reparation payments for losses incurred by their nationals. Both Liberals and Conservatives had appropriated to their pocketbooks the valuables of foreigners, and to make matters worse, the Civil War in the United States made it impossible for Abraham Lincoln to continue to bolster Juárez logistically. Then in the early part of 1862 England, France, and Spain threatened the port of Veracruz in an effort to collect their losses by force. When it became apparent that

France, then under Napoleon III, really intended to establish an empire in the Western Hemisphere, the British and Spanish withdrew, leaving Veracruz in French military possession.

The invaders were temporarily routed at Puebla on May 5, 1862, making this date into a contemporary patriotic symbol of Mexicans defeating a superior foreign army. Nevertheless, the French invasion continued and President Juárez was forced to move his capital north to Monterrey. Mexican clericals and conservative oligarchs returned from their Paris exile hoping to carry on in the tradition of Lucas Alamán, but they were shocked to find the French busily taking over lands under provisions of the Lerdo Law and the Constitution of 1857; and to make the pill yet more bitter to swallow, Napoleon had in the spring of 1864 imposed the Austrian archduke Maximilian and the Belgian princess Carlotta on the Mexican throne. Their blindness was twice that of Napoleon III, who knew the Mexicans would not love their new royalty but hoped to maintain them by force of arms while the quest went on for the treasures of the Guanajuato gold and diamond mines. These mines, largely ruined and abandoned by 50 years of plunder and abuse, proved to be almost worthless. Maximilian and Carlotta believed that the people would love them and that great treasures were to be uncovered. When both proved to be false hopes, the French withdrew, leaving Maximilian to face a firing squad of Juárez's army, on a hill overlooking, appropriately, Querétaro where the drive for independence had begun in 1810. Carlotta was abandoned to a European exile and eventually to insanity.

Seldom had two cultures met in so irreconcilable a clash. When Juárez reentered the capital city in 1867, the power of the clerics and landed oligarchs appeared broken and aid from the United States again began to trickle in, but he ruled a nation bled of its human and material wealth. It is hard for North Americans to imagine how so much misfortune could be continually visited upon the same nation, and that it should still exist.

PORFIRIO DÍAZ AND THE ROOTS OF REVOLUTION

Desperately lacking in financial resources, Juárez commenced at once to rebuild his ravaged nation. He constructed schools, encouraged railroad development, and sought credits abroad. He was reelected twice to office and seemed to enjoy the confidence of the masses. Notwithstanding, former soldiers-turned-bandits plagued the nation and often intruded into the political arena via attempted coups against state and municipal governments. Increasingly the people looked for a leader, other than Benito Juárez, to bring security to the troubled land. In the elections of 1871 attention turned to one of Juárez's most valuable field commanders in the War of the Reform and in the campaign against the French occupation, General Porfirio Díaz. Since no candidate received a majority of votes, the congress returned Juárez to office over the objections of Díaz, who had campaigned on the pledge of "effective suffrage and no reelection." Tragically for Mexico, Juárez died in 1872 before his new term had hardly begun. Congress replaced him with Sebastián Lerdo de Tejada, who could not quell growing unrest and who fell ultimately to a military coup led by Porfirio Díaz in 1876. At that point, Latin America's longest single dictatorship began.

It has been said that Porfirio Díaz was at once Mexico's most ruthless and most productive president. He governed for 34 years, occasionally stepping out of office to allow a puppet to take over out of deference to his campaign pledge. He cleaned up the violence in the countryside via a commissioned militia of mercenary rogues called rurales who tried and shot criminals summarily and guaranteed the security of the vast legion of foreign investments that now poured into Mexico. In this way Díaz built a gigantic railroad and highway system, thus providing the basic infrastructure the country so badly needed to industrialize. This is the great Díaz legacy to twentieth-century Mexico. As could be expected, it was accomplished with a full measure of blood and brutality, and at the almost total expense of political freedoms and individual guarantees for the masses.

Porfirio Díaz was labeled the inventor of concentration camps for the numbers of countryfolk he displaced from their land in order to create *latifundios,* the great landholdings of which many went to foreigners. Under Díaz's orders some 5 million Mexicans were dispossessed and condemned to debt peonage and slavery. Many large parcels of land went to North American companies and magnates like the newspaper tycoon William Randolph Hearst. Many European and North American industrialists were attracted as well. While mass exploitation was the order of the day, Mexico was, nonetheless, receiving infrastructure investments that would be important to its economic development. The discovery of Mexican petroleum corresponded temporarily with the development of the internal combustion engine; thus the combination of oil and motors made Mexico attractive for foreign investment. Díaz guaranteed the safety of these inventors.

Across the traumatic sweep of nineteenth-century Mexico a collectivity of forces had gathered that would oppose Díaz just as they had fought Iturbide, Santa Anna, and the interim conservative oligarchs. Among the most dedicated foes of the Díaz regime was the Liberal party, a regrouping of previous reformist movements now under the leadership of Ricardo Flores Magón. Toward the end of the Pax Porfiriana, Flores Magón's publication *Regeneración* had become a troublesome thorn in the side of the Díaz oligarchy. In 1906 the Liberal party, largely forced into exile in various cities of the United States, issued a program that was directed against a legion of abuses committed by the Díaz government. The liberals demanded that Díaz honor his commitment to no reelection, the abolition of military conscription, restoration of freedom of the press, increased budgetary outlays for education and school construction, enforcement of the anticlerical provisions of the Constitution of 1857, radical land reforms, and, generally, the disestablishment of the wealthy oligarchy. Not unexpectedly, such entreaties fell on deaf ears in the national government. Although Flores Magón pretended to be heir to the Liberal tradition of Juárez, he was much more radical than the Zapotec Indian from Oaxaca; Flores was bent upon the total destruction of Mexico's socioeconomic fabric, in the fervent belief that a new ideological consensus would somehow be forthcoming. Violent strikes against a U.S.-owned copper company at Cananea and the famous Río Blanco strike of January 1907 brought federal troops into play against the Liberal insurgents and revealed the butchery of which Porfirio Díaz was capable when he felt pressed.[2] Ricardo Flores Magón, at first exiled in Los Angeles, California, then in other U.S. cities, imprisoned while in exile, hounded by the American "yellow" and "jingo" press of William Randolph Hearst (himself the owner of valuable property in Mexico), ultimately became a dedicated anarchist. Flores Magón's writings breathed a spirit of beauty into the violence which he came to worship as a goal of life, whereas formerly it had only been a means to secure justice.

Irony was a lingering trait of Mexican political development. So it was that when true revolution came (not a resignation of cabinet or president, or even a widespread insurgency of national proportions, but rather an uprising that produced lasting and profound socioeconomic change) it was fronted by a meek little man who did not drink or violate women, seldom ate meat, and was not as virile (macho) as most leaders of the Mexican stripe were expected to be. It was not Flores Magón who visited revolution upon his populace but the innocuous aristocrat from Coahuila, Francisco Ignacio Madero. Madero's timid manner belied many of his great skills, but the art of politics was not among them. He had been an early contributor to the Flores Magón movement but broke this tie when it became certain that the Liberals sought carnage first and democracy last. Madero was first and foremost a champion of democracy, as he indicated in his mild-sounding treatise, *The Presidential Succession of 1910,* in which he suggested that Mexicans ought to be free to choose their own leaders.

Interestingly, Madero did not write this treatise via the spontaneous outpouring of his soul as Flores Magón had done. Rather he wrote it after being prodded by an influence from the United States: the publication in March 1908 of an interview by James Creelman held weeks earlier with Porfirio Díaz in which the aging dictator allegedly stated that he would welcome the rise of an opposition (loyal) political movement in Mexico as a measure of the nation's growing political maturity. With this apparent invitation, numerous factions (including Madero's and the followers of Flores Magón) began to declare their candidacies for the approaching elections. Díaz and his brain trust (the "scientists" led by José Yves Limantour) felt uncomfortable. Theirs was a natural reaction. Following publication of the Creelman interview in the Mexican press, a somewhat embellished version to be sure, Francisco Madero announced formation of his Anti-Reelectionist party whose motto also became "effective suffrage and no reelection." Madero demanded that the choice of his party's candidate be made in an open convention and made a speaking tour of the country in which he emphasized that he did not seek to impose himself on the people.

Not only did Madero win his party's nomination, he attracted enough of a following so that in June 1910 a threatened Díaz government had him arrested on false charges of sedition. Later that month the election results were declared to have been overwhelmingly in favor of returning Díaz to the presidency. Madero's family arranged a bribe to free him from prison under his agreement to remain out of the capital city. He honored this pledge, while all the time gathering evidence (it was abundant) that Díaz's election had been fraudulent. On October 25, 1910, Madero and his swelling ranks of supporters issued the famous Plan de San Luis Potosí, whose effect was a declaration of war against the Díaz regime: on Sunday, November 20, 1910, all Mexicans were urged to rebel. Madero by this time was enjoying unofficial sympathy from Washington, and logistic support for his uprising began to cross the Rio Grande. The United States was infuriated with Díaz's apparent favoritism toward European oil concessionaires and annoyed by his aid to José Santos Zelaya, the Yankee-baiting president of Nicaragua.

From exile in Texas, Madero sought to mold U.S. public opinion while at once attempting to lend direction to the now incipient revolution which was bursting forth in Chihuahua and Coahuila under the leadership of such guerrilla fighters as Doroteo Arango (better known as Francisco "Pancho" Villa) and Pascual Orozco. In February 1911, Madero crossed the Rio Grande and shortly thereafter made his famous assault (unsuccessfully) on the town of Casas Grandes. He emerged from the encounter as a man of courage if not of military talent. News came that in the state of Morelos to the south Juan Andreu Almazán and Emiliano Zapata had risen in arms in support of Madero's cause. Venustiano Carranza assumed leadership of the revolutionary forces in Madero's home state of Coahuila. In May 1911 the frontier city of Juárez fell to Madero's forces.

The federal armies, alleged to be some 40,000 strong, were in fact no larger than 15,000 due to the prevalence of the curious greed syndrome developed earlier by Iturbide: the padding of payroll budgets with fictitious names (today's *aviadores*) whose salaries went into the pockets of greedy officers. When it came to battle, the payroll list of fake soldiers was an empty resource. Shortly after occupying Juárez, Madero faced an open confrontation with Orozco and Villa, both intent upon assuming command of the revolutionary movement, and the mild-tempered vegetarian once again proved himself to be a man of courage. Thus his charisma and popular following continued to grow. City by city the country fell to the revolutionaries, and on May 21, 1911, representatives of Díaz and Madero signed a treaty at Juárez providing for the dictator's abdication.

THE GREAT REVOLUTION

Díaz, however, balked at resigning. Late in May, crowds that had gathered outside the national congress building in response to rumors that the dictator was about to abdicate were disappointed and moved on the Zocalo where they were charged by Díaz's palace guard. Before the melee was over several hundred Mexican citizens had been machine-gunned, enough to convince Díaz it was time to resign. By the end of May 1911 Díaz was aboard a German ship bound for Europe and his minister of foreign relations, Francisco León de la Barra, had become interim president, with the promise that he would conduct new presidential elections in the fall and that he himself would not be a candidate. Here was where Madero probably made a serious mistake, one that his country was to pay for dearly and in blood. According to one analyst of the period: "There would have been no hindrance if Madero had seen fit to declare himself President immediately. He might have saved both himself and Mexico much trouble had he done so. Taking power at the high tide of his popularity might have brought peace and stability."[3]

By insisting upon a strict adherence to constitutionality in the succession, Madero gave ample opportunity for separationists within his own ranks, like the Flores Magón group now centered in Baja California, to vie for place and power. To complicate the matter further, Madero naively expected not only de la Barra but the entire federal bureaucracy and army to become loyal to his movement overnight. Compounding the risk, Madero disbanded many of his revolutionary troops, thus denying them a greater share in the spoils of victory and disarming himself of their protection. Many of these disappointed troops became followers of Zapata who openly rebelled against Madero, charging that the process of agrarian reform was going too slowly. Old followers of Díaz like Bernardo Reyes revived their power ambitions.

With chaos threatening from all sides, interim president de la Barra turned over the reins of government to Francisco Madero several weeks early on November 6, 1911. By this time Emiliano Zapata had openly broken with Madero over the failure of the land reform program. Indeed the followers of Zapata had charged Madero with treason: "Mexican citizens: because of the cunning and bad faith of one man blood is being spilled in a scandalous manner; . . . because he is incapable of governing we will take up arms against him for he has become a traitor to the Revolution."[4]

Three major uprisings now threatened: those of Zapata in Morelos, Orozco in Chihuahua, and Félix Díaz (nephew of the exiled dictator) in Veracruz. Madero's Constitutional Progressive party, now headed by his brother Gustavo, sought to cultivate popular loyalty and tolerance but by this time Francisco's charisma had worn thin. Francisco Madero was honest, and brave, but more than that was needed to rule Mexico. Perhaps what was needed was a skilled impostor such as Rodolfo Usigli was later to write in a brilliant play whose insight into the psychology of Mexican politics was keenly penetrating. But this was not Madero; he simply lacked the strength of his opponents. He would lie to no one; he deceived only himself.

The story of Madero's demise unfolds from the fateful trust he placed in General Victoriano Huerta, one of Porfirio Díaz's trusted chieftains who had personally escorted the fleeing dictator aboard his Europe-bound vessel. In February 1913 Huerta undertook to do battle in the center of Mexico City with the forces of Félix Díaz, now stockaded inside an old military arsenal known as the Ciudadela. Ostensibly Huerta was to smash this rebellion against the constitutional government but it is now believed that the action, known as the Tragic Ten Days, was a facade for a pact being arranged between the two men, with the fighting designed, cynically, to decimate the ranks of the government troops. The cruel barbarity of the event has been shown brilliantly by William Weber Johnson, who described the revolution's birth plans in the Tragic Ten Days:

> As a battle it was spurious, fraudulent, a grand deception—like the strategy of a pickpocket who jostles a victim from one side to distract his attention and then picks the pocket from the other side. The purpose, which did not become immediately apparent, was to create a scene of such havoc and frightfulness that any solution, no matter how dishonorable, would become preferable to present horror.
>
> Corpses lay in the street where they fell, bloating in the February sun. Persons dying of natural causes could not be buried; their bodies lay in the gutters, putrefying along with the battle victims. Government troops tried to collect corpses. Some were loaded on two-wheeled carts, taken to Balbuena Park, piled in huge mounds and burned. Others were doused with kerosene where they lay and burned in the street. Still they accumulated faster than these primitive methods could dispose of them. Garbage was piled on the sidewalks. All city services had ceased. No food supplies came into the city and people barricaded in their homes were starving. Electric lines came down in the cannonading and the nights were dark and terrifying, lighted only by the funeral fires and the flames from houses set ablaze by looters or vandals. On the night of the 14th the Madero home in the Calle Liverpool was put to the torch by a group of "aristocratic cretins" as one commentator described them. The Madero family, except for the President, who was in the National Palace, took refuge in the Japanese legation.[5]

When the slaughter ended, Madero and his brother Gustavo were prisoners. The president had tried to repeat the success of the personal confrontation he had had with the rebels Orozco and Villa who earlier sought to depose him at El Paso. This time his defiance failed; the magic of his charisma had waned.

Then came the nadir of shame in the history of Mexican-U.S. relations. U.S. Ambassador Henry Lane Wilson, acting apparently without the knowledge of the president of the United States, offered the U.S. Embassy as the stage from which Huerta and Díaz (the supposed enemies to the death) could proclaim their infamous Pact of the Ciudadela. Huerta would become interim president and in exchange Díaz would be guaranteed the support of Huerta to succeed him via the next "election." Nor did the odious story end there. After Madero and his vice-president, José María Pino Suárez, were forced to sign resignations, they were both murdered under mysterious circumstances while being transported in the "safe custody" of their military captors. The ultraconservative U.S. ambassador, who was slavishly loyal to North American business interests and who viewed Madero's reformist bent with alarm, was inescapably involved in the tragic affair.[6]

American students who ponder the fact that many Mexican intellectuals today dislike us should remember this salient fact: No later than 1913 the United States had succeeded in taking by force the most valuable half of Mexico's terrain, purchased a collateral piece of the national patrimony, and had then sought to ingratiate itself further by presiding over the assassination of the father of Mexico's (and indeed Latin America's) first true revolution. That is a melancholy and sobering truth with which we must live and which our Mexican neighbors cannot easily forget.

The regime of Victoriano Huerta was foredoomed by the very personality of the man who headed it. Huerta was the most inept of dictators. He alienated such regional chieftains as Venustiano Carranza, Pancho Villa, and Emiliano Zapata, who now rose in arms against the Mexico City government. To make matters worse, Huerta began an exchange of insults with President Wilson, after which U.S. marines were ordered to seize Veracruz in April 1914. War between the two countries was barely averted through the good offices of the foreign ministers of Argentina, Brazil, and Chile. In 1914 Huerta resigned and fled to Europe with a generous array of loot taken from the Mexican treasury. In August of that year he was succeeded by General Carranza, who became a de facto president and was later recognized as such by President Wilson. Carranza was forced to flee the capital by an invasion of forces under Pancho Villa and Eulalio Gutiérrez, but returned safely after a major triumph by his trusted general, one of Mexico's truly great military figures, Alvaro Obregón. Carranza sought to repair the injured relations between his nation and the United States, a task made difficult by the border raids of the Mexican Robin Hood, Pancho Villa, during 1916.

Also in that year the state of Morelos (just south of the Federal District) had become a caldron of revolutionary activity. The forces of Zapata held the state in defiance of Mexico City and maintained themselves isolated from the capital. The revolutionaries (at least the Zapatistas) had an internal dilemma: "Precisely because they were sincere revolutionaries and not bandits or vandals they could not derive from the dispute (with Mexico City) alone a motive to keep themselves going."[7] There was disagreement as to whether the revolutionary movement should even continue, in addition to the controversy over goals. It was the charismatic leadership of Emiliano Zapata which, in large measure, held the Morelos revolutionaries together. And it was fortunate also that Zapata had shared power and experience with some able lieutenants, like Gildaro Magaña, who were able to carry on the struggle after Zapata's passing later on.

This period, often referred to as "the storm," is probably the most critical point in the growth of Mexican nationhood. Her political and military leaders now grew aware that the social fabric of the country was almost in tatters. The chronicle of events which led to the month of December 1916 tells little or nothing of the apathy, the naked despair, of the people of Mexico during this horrendous six-year period. The novel *Los de abajo* by Mariano Azuela tells this story in the poignant words of a disillusioned revolutionary who was caught up in the anarchy which swept across the countryside like a plague in the aftermath of the revolution. Perhaps it was the pitiful blindness of those who fought onward to their destruction which ultimately produced a vision of lasting order and the conviction needed to make that vision real. Order was the determination of Venustiano Carranza when he called a constitutional assembly into session at Querétaro at the end of 1916. The following February the assembly promulgated a document which has provided the basic governing format of Mexico to this day.

INSTITUTIONALIZING THE REVOLUTION

The Constitution of 1917 embraced most of the Liberal principles of the Juárez-Ocampo-Lerdo Constitution of 1857. The four key features of the new constitution were the following: Article 3 prohibited clerics from participating in public educational instruction and severely limited the political rights of religious groups (specifically, the article proscribed the use of religious titles in the names of political parties and endorsements by religious groups of political parties); Article 27 deprived the Church and foreigners of landholding and subsoil rights and provided a basis for agrarian reform throughout the republic; Article 33 opened the door for the Mexican president to expel foreign companies and personnel from the land; and Article 123 endorsed the principle of workers' rights, laid a basis for collective bargaining, and recognized the right of workers to organize into unions and to receive compensation in case of accidents. It would be an enormous understatement to say that Mexicans of 1917 were ready for such measures as these.

Carranza recognized the need for the reforms defined in the Constitution of 1917, but he was not eager to enforce them. His own cronies and followers participated generously in the booty that issued from the presidency, but little filtered down to the masses. Thus the populace again came to wonder whether the revolution had been for naught, since it resulted in merely a paper document of reform. Pancho Villa's forces in Chihuahua and those of Zapata in

Morelos and Guerrero still opposed Carranza's rule. Ignominiously—and, it is believed, with the blessing of Carranza—the legendary Zapata was assassinated in 1919, and thus a revolutionary of wide popular following became a martyr. But Zapata, posthumously, may have had his own requital. The following year Carranza himself was assassinated (while attempting to flee the country) by forces loyal to Zapata. Carranza had refused to honor his 1917 pledge of "no reelection" and in April 1920 used federal troops to interfere with a Sonora strike involving Luis Morones's newly formed CROM, the Regional Confederation of Mexican Workers. With organized labor and the followers of Zapata still against him, Carranza recognized the precariousness of his situation and abdicated, only to lose his life in attempted flight.

General Obregón was proclaimed president for a four-year term in 1920. He tried to implement the land-reform promises of the constitution, as his predecessor had failed to do, and carried out an ambitious program of public education under the brilliant guidance of the philosopher José Vasconcelos. Despite an attempted coup by Adolfo de la Huerta, Obregón turned the presidency over to Plutarco Elías Calles, the constitutional president-elect, in 1924. Whereas Obregón had begun educational and land reforms pursuant to the Constitution of 1917, Calles considered as his special province the implementation of the anticlerical provisions of the constitution. To this end he confiscated Church lands, abolished religious instruction in public schools, deported priests, forbade the wearing of religious habits in public, and in general waged a Kulturkampf against religious privilege in all its protean forms. A counterrevolution of Rightists and clerical fanatics, under the banner of the *cristeros,* or defenders of Christ, erupted in defiance of Calles. Despite the shock felt by foreigners over Calles's treatment of the Church, Mexico's relations improved with the United States, largely because of the adept qualities of U.S. Ambassador Dwight Morrow, who sympathetically understood the Mexican dilemma and sought constructive channels to aid it.

Once again, in 1928, the question of the presidential succession threatened to visit another bloodbath upon Mexico, with rival factions of the military seeking to impose their favored candidates. In open contempt of the constitutional prohibition of reelection, Obregón's supporters successfully imposed his candidacy upon the electorate in an election of questionable honesty, as were many of the following elections. Before he could take office, the president-elect was assassinated by a religious fanatic who, anachronistically, was allegedly one of the defenders of Christ working in the employ of Calles. So vigorously did Calles denounce the affair, however, and so determined was his appeal for government by law rather than by passion, that violence of major proportions was avoided. Calles, like other contemporary leaders, was not above enriching himself at the public trough, but he exhibited moments of progressive conviction, as had Carranza and Obregón, which allowed the revolution's paper gains to inch forward toward realization.[8]

Congress named Emilio Portes Gil, an intimate and supporter of Obregón, to be provisional president for 14 months. During this time Calles and his group, which now included Luis Morones, formed Mexico's first revolutionary political party, the PNR, or National Revolutionary party, which held its first convention in 1929 and nominated Pascual Ortiz Rubio to succeed Portes Gil. The latter, in his *Quince años de política mexicana,* described Ortiz Rubio's defeat of José Vasconcelos in a bitter electoral struggle which pitted the reformist thrust of the revolution squarely against the Conservative forces of clerical reaction. Not only was Ortiz Rubio a puppet for Calles, he was also a poor risk. The congress challenged the president's budget, and during the ensuing controversy, Ortiz Rubio saw fit to fire several pro-Calles members of his own cabinet. To this gesture of contempt, Calles, the great cacique, retaliated and forced Ortiz Rubio's resignation, replacing him with a wealthy militarist and landowner from Baja California. Abelardo Rodríguez finished the term faithfully in service to his chief. The elections of 1934 saw the left wing of the PNR erupt in disgust with a situation in which the Mexican presidency was obviously being run by Calles from his villa in Cuernavaca. The new revolutionaries were able to impose upon Calles their own favored candidate for the presidency, General Lázaro Cárdenas, who was promptly elected and assumed office. That Calles had underestimated the general as a potential puppet became swiftly obvious. Soon Calles was in exile in the United States, marveling at the socioeconomic reforms which began to sweep the republic.

CÁRDENAS: TOWARD ECONOMIC INDEPENDENCE

The Cárdenas era (1934–40) was the take-off stage of the Mexican revolution during the postviolence period. Casting aside all remnants of bondage to the Calles machine, Lázaro Cárdenas distributed agrarian lands to peasants more generously than had any other previous chief executive. He did so via the usufructuary device of *ejidos,* or collective farms, regulated by the state. He sought political change internally by scrapping Calles's old PRN in favor of a new party, the PRM, or Mexican Revolutionary party. At the same time the old CROM of Luis Morones was replaced with the CTM, the Mexican Confederation of Workers, which came under the new and vigorous leadership of Vicente Lombardo Toledano. With both Calles and Morones exiled to the United States, Cárdenas governed without serious opposition. His support rested squarely on a broadly based configuration of peasantry, urban labor, and the armed forces.

Among Mexico's true revolutionaries—that is, leaders who were instrumental in bringing about concrete change—Lázaro Cárdenas merits a special place in his nation's quest for the benefits of socioeconomic political modernity. Not only did Cárdenas refuse to become a puppet for Calles's political machine, he was opposed to the exaggerated religious persecution that had led to the cristero crisis. Cárdenas was, to be sure, unsympathetic with fanatical clerics who sought to enslave ignorant peoples via superstition and witchcraft and he lent government support to community reformers who fought to secularize public education; but he would not be a party to extermination of the clergy. To this end he ordered an end to the dissemination of antireligious propaganda in the classroom and encouraged Mexican families to come together around a nucleus of Christian values and practices. In making a limited peace with the Church, Cárdenas had done much to pacify and stabilize Mexico politically. However, this should not be taken to imply that the anticlerical reprisals of the Calles period were without justification. Organized Roman Catholics had emerged from the great revolution clinging tenaciously to a myriad of nefarious economic practices and social evils. The dilemma facing Cárdenas was how to keep a just retribution from becoming ecclesiastical genocide.

Although Cárdenas's quelling of the church-state dilemma was only to be temporary, it was nonetheless an important achievement. He sought to accomplish an even greater step toward modernity in his attack upon the agrarian and land-use structure of Mexico. Upon taking office in 1934 it was painfully clear that previous efforts toward land reform had improved living standards for really very few persons. Cárdenas is said to have spent more time traveling about the country listening to the complaints of the poor and landless than he did in his capital city office. He knew the imperative need for land reform and, perhaps naively and within a somewhat Marxist intellectual framework, believed that redistribution of land would assuage the nation's ills. A vigorously extended and reorganized program of state farms was to be part of his panacea. Cárdenas superintended the reform personally and often from the actual site of a given land distribution. Mexicans have never forgotten this; indeed they should not, for Cárdenas, his naive Marxism and simplistic populism notwithstanding, conquered the hearts of his people, as Madero could not do, for long enough to institutionalize a stable regime. The people loved Cárdenas while the bureaucrats often hated him:

> He created administrative chaos, but he distributed land. In his first three years he doubled the number of heads of family with land to work and the amount of land available to *ejidatarios.* By the end of his term he had expropriated and distributed over 17 million hectares to nearly 8,000 new villages in which over two million people lived. As a result of his efforts and those of his predecessors, by 1941 nearly 15,000 villages accounting for a quarter of the total population enjoyed the use of slightly less than half the crop land and about one-fifth the total land. Twenty-five years earlier almost none of these people had land they could call their own.[9]

At the end of Cárdenas's term the nation was experiencing a somewhat better distribution of wealth than that which existed at the advent of Madero's effort to front the Mexican revolution. But the large landowners, despite all of their egalitarian shortcomings, still were able to demonstrate that private enterprise could produce more food than socialized enterprise. The distribution of the food and its financial earnings was another matter, one that Mexico still must solve. A central, and remaining, fact in this dilemma was that the government bureaucrats appointed to redistribute land, hence wealth, ultimately became a sort of special interest group in themselves, and much of the redistributed land is known to have landed in their hands.

By the year 1921, Mexico produced nearly one-fourth of the world's supply of oil. This part of the territory the Americans had neglected to conquer in the 1840s. The Constitution of 1917 gave the Mexican nation exclusive rights to subsoil minerals. During the Pax Porfiriana, subsoil rights were sold profitably to foreigners. Despite the lip service given to nationalization, little concrete action had really been taken to assure that profits from subsoil exploitation would even in part be reinvested in the Mexican nation or redistributed to her nationals. On March 18, 1938, President Lázaro Cárdenas signed a decree intended to rectify this imbalance. The overall result of his action, in long-range terms, is still a moot issue. What is clear is that before 1938 the majority of Mexico's oil production was destined for foreign consumption. Low salaries and poor living conditions aggravated the complaints of Mexican workers who were forced to labor in the employ of foreign concerns. After Cárdenas expropriated the oil, that is up until about 1951, the quantity of petroleum production destined for local markets almost tripled and thereafter Mexican petroleum products continued to play an important role in the domestic economy (favored, of course, by protective legislation). In this writer's opinion, reached after considerable discussion with informed Mexicans both supportive of the national petroleum firm PEMEX and with some who vehemently oppose it, it is difficult to state categorically that the expropriation has been a success economically. But politically PEMEX, that is Lázaro Cárdenas and others, has been a gigantic domestic success, one that will seldom, if ever, be equaled during the second half of the twentieth century.

Lázaro Cárdenas's reform era was anathema to the forces of the Mexican oligarchy, the same powerful upper class against which all previous reformers had struggled. Wearing modern attire of the twentieth century, the oligarchs arrayed against the reforms were still essentially the same as earlier, but now they were joined by former oil companies and other commercial newcomers (such as U.S.-owned grain farms in Sonora's Yaqui Valley). In his drive for a progressive liberalism, Cárdenas entered into the lineage of Juárez, Morelos, Madero, and Zapata, probably more than any other figure. Cárdenas shaped the image of his PRM as an organized spokesman for popular distress. He instilled securely the notion of public entrepreneurship as a copartner with the private sector in his nation's development and institutionalized the psychology of being revolutionary as a credential of legitimacy (a concept to which we will return at various times throughout this book). It is fair to say that Cárdenas, while a disappointment to Calles, proved to be a delight to the Mexican populace. He combined Juárez's ideological commitment to concrete change with Zapata's ability to reach the common people. He accomplished this without being deposed or exiled as was Juárez and without falling victim to his own violence as did Zapata. At the moment of this writing the late Cárdenas's mystique still inspires the Mexican people; he is, in a very real sense, the father of the contemporary Mexican political system.

In 1940 Cárdenas gracefully stepped aside and was succeeded by General Manuel Avila Camacho, who carried on, though with less urgency, many of the Cárdenas reform programs. Avila Camacho was matched against the independent candidacy of General Juan Andreu Almazán, whose support came from a number of splinter parties including PAN, the party of National Action, which foreshadowed the growth of a permanent political opposition in contemporary Mexico.

The elections of 1946 and 1952 were tranquil compared to the rest of Mexican experience in the twentieth century. The official party, PRM, became the PRI during the regime of President Avila Camacho; and this party supported the successive regimes of Miguel Alemán Valdés and Adolfo Ruiz Cortines. Alemán Valdés's rise to fame set a pattern which was soon to be repeated in Mexican political life. He rose from governor of a major state, Veracruz, to campaign manager for Avila Camacho in 1940, and from that position to secretario de gobernación (secretary of the interior) in the president's cabinet. With the end of World War II, it was felt that Mexico needed a president somewhat to the political right of the Cárdenas tradition who would promote commercial and industrial development. Miguel Alemán Valdés became one of Mexico's most entrepreneurial presidents. During his regime the nation's industrial economy surged forward toward maturity.

The selection of Adolfo Ruiz Cortines as the PRI standard-bearer in 1952 represented only a mild reaction to the conservatism of the Alemán administration. This selection is somewhat paradoxical inasmuch as Ruiz Cortines was one of the more trusted Alemán followers who had pursued exactly the same route of ascent as had his predecessor and mentor. Ruiz had always been distinguished, even within Alemán's orbit, as being impeccably honest, and Alemán is known to have assigned to Ruiz certain financial custodial tasks which Alemán did not even trust to himself. Under Ruiz Cortines, Mexico's public administration was purged of many of its former objectionable practices, and definite strides were taken to expand the state farm program, public welfare, and other needed social reforms.

In 1958, Adolfo López Mateos brought to the presidency a distinguished background as a labor mediator and organizer. His service as secretary of labor in the Ruiz Cortines cabinet and earlier as a troubleshooter for the Mexican treasury had attracted the admiration of ex-president Cárdenas which, coupled with López Mateos's longstanding friendship with Miguel Alemán, served ideally in fitting López for the PRI candidacy. He was unusual in that he enjoyed the unanimous support of not only the three principal emeritus figures in Mexican politics at the time, but also the unqualified support of most businessmen, of organized labor, and of the military establishment.

The election of Adolfo López Mateos in 1958 was significant in several respects. It was the first time in Mexican history that the franchise had been extended to women. Moreover, part of the PRI's campaign pledge was the institution of a sweeping program of socialized medicine, medical and dental clinics, and maternity care centers intended particularly for rural and depressed urban neighborhoods. López Mateos generally made good this pledge and thereby endeared himself to many Mexicans who otherwise might have remained apathetically on the edge of their national political life. The 1958 presidential campaign was one of the most determined, indeed violent, campaigns since the religious riots of the 1920s. The opposition candidate endorsed by PAN was Luis H. Alvarez, an elite-born firebrand who saw Mexico slipping into an abyss of Marxian socialism and ultimately communist dictatorship. Alvarez was openly the spokesman for clerical interests and for some members of the financial aristocracy.

Political stability was the hallmark of López Mateos's regime, a major railroad workers strike in 1959 notwithstanding. This stability continued despite several naval and border skirmishes with Guatemala, international friction over relations with Castro's Cuba, and the problem of salinity in the Colorado River water coming from the United States. Mexico remained a country in which misery and injustice were still widespread. But she had what appeared to be a booming economy, an aggressive trade unionism, and a broad range of social welfare services and an impressive public education system. By 1964 Mexico gave the appearance of becoming a reformist leader among Latin American nations, an image that would last scarcely four years.

DÍAZ ORDAZ: THE DECLINING REVOLUTIONARY AXIS

In the late 1960s there were evidences pointing to what I have chosen to term the declining axis of revolutionary politics. Certainly as the decade of the 1970s opened there were strains occurring in the revolutionary coalition, that is, the PRI, and these were public and visible.

From the discussion of the Tlatelolco massacre in Chapter 1, it should be clear that the system President Díaz Ordaz inherited from López Mateos in 1964 had critical elements that can be labeled entropy, disruptive forces tending to produce dysfunctional behavior and to tear the system apart, to produce disequilibrium. It can be argued that these forces existed during the previous revolutionary regimes (including that of Cárdenas) and that the catalytic element which, combined with other factors, held the system together was in large part the personality of the incumbent president. This, it may be argued, has been true throughout Mexican history. If the president lacked the personality either to electrify the masses or pacify (or deceive) the oligarchies as well as the masses, his tenure of office was gravely insecure. This surely was the lesson of Madero's downfall. Díaz Ordaz, it is felt by many well-placed Mexicans, had an aloofness about him, much as if he were the director of a large bureaucracy in which there was little need to reach out to the operatives at the grass-roots level.

Mexico, like all Latin American (indeed all Western) nations, suffers the baneful consequences of a severe generation gap between the young and old. The most serious manifestation of this gulf occurred during the student riots in Mexico City in 1968. Pressures of the young, the poor, and the wretched and the internal politics of a giant organism itself forced Díaz Ordaz into defensive actions which former presidents with other personality structures might have been able to obviate. It is critical to point out that President López Mateos was widely loved and was regarded as a great compromiser. He was a popular figure despite being widely rumored to be involved with narcotics, to have a teenage mistress, to have lined his pockets handsomely from the public trough; but these macho traits also meant that many powerful figures were in his debt. He knew how to compromise and often did so. Conversely, Díaz Ordaz is widely said to have led an exemplary personal life (as did Madero). But he did not compromise well. He did not communicate skillfully enough to make the power contenders about him feel that compromise was even viable.

Key events during his administration speak partially for themselves. Following an armed clash between members of rival factions of the CNC (Confederación Nacional Campesina, or National Peasants Confederation), on August 20, 1965, which left upward of 30 workers dead, the head of the CNC, Amador Hernández, resigned under pressure from Díaz Ordaz. The conflict dramatized growing cleavage high up in the national power structure and Díaz Ordaz saw expulsion as more feasible than a negotiated compromise. The reform-minded mayor of the Federal District, Ernest T. Uruchurtu, was fired in the wake of a controversy over his campaign to eliminate vice and corruption. Carlos A. Madrazo (to whose case we shall return variously throughout this book) was ousted in a direct confrontation with Díaz Ordaz over a question of democratizing local elections. Madrazo, as president of the PRI, had been in effect Mexico's second most powerful political figure. Governor Enrique D. Ceniceros of Durango was fired for his incompetent handling of a student strike against foreign mining interests. Saltiel Alatriste, director of Mexico's Social Security System, was fired in the midst of an anticorruption campaign he had launched. Ignacio Chávez, chancellor of the National University of Mexico, was forced to resign for his excessive tolerance of student demonstrations on campus (at one point students had forced him into submitting a resignation with a knife to his throat).

In 1967 and 1968 student protests against fraudulent elections in Yucatán, Villa Hermosa, Hermosillo, and what amounted to an unmasked electoral fraud in Baja California testified to the determination of the Díaz Ordaz-steered revolutionary party to perpetuate itself at practically all costs. The greatest evidence of the declining axis of the revolutionary system came in August, September, and October of 1968 when the police and military brutalized student protesters in a sequence of violence that was described as the worst since the downfall of Madero. Tragically, and perhaps ironically, ex-president López Mateos, whose skills as a compromiser might have been invoked to restore peace, had himself been removed as national chairman of the forthcoming Olympic Games; he was slowly dying in a coma with brain damage and complications following surgery when the disaster of Tlatelolco occurred in 1968. Díaz Ordaz's immediate legacy was an ideological abyss between the regime and the Mexican people which the appeal to patriotic symbols could no longer hide.

Historically, it is worth noting in conclusion that Porfirio Díaz is rumored to have once admonished the aspiring Francisco I. Madero that a man would need much more than honesty to be able to govern Mexico—he would need personal charisma and popular attachment. Clearly leaders like Madero, Zapata, and Obregón had those qualities, but each of them was assassinated under circumstances of severe ideological cleavage. Following the death of Zapata, his detractors (acting on orders from Provisional President Venustiano Carranza) sought to diminish the hero from Morelos by attacking his Plan de Ayala, the ideological statement of the southern revolutionaries. It was said that the Plan de Ayala had become a "cry which Emiliano's followers were taught to repeat mechanically" so as to conceal their ignorance.[10] Ironically, when President Díaz Ordaz stepped aside in 1970 his political legacy was a sullied presidency, bolstered by symbols out of the past which people were expected to honor mechanically so as to conceal the regime's growing illegitimacy in the popular mind. That problem would be carried over into the indefinite future. In Chapter 3 I will treat the presidency of Luis Echeverría (1970–76) and its transition into that of José López Portillo (1976–82) as a case study in the roots and uses of contemporary presidential power in Mexico.

NOTES

1. The various Masonic lodges apparently involved themselves in Mexican politics around 1815 when the insurrection that had been unleashed by Hidalgo and Morelos was seen as potentially threatening to the United States. The Scottish-rite Masons and the York-rite Masons soon became enemies in Mexico's ongoing power struggle. There were no Mexican political parties at that time and the lodges became the basis for the eventual formation of political parties. The Scottish-rite people tended to represent the monied classes and sought to maintain close contacts

with Spain. The York-rite people tended to champion political independence with more popular participation in democratic institutions. It was believed in some circles that U.S. Ambassador Joel Poinsett was behind the York-rite group.

2. During 1906 a conflict broke out between Mexican mineworkers and the management of the Cananea Copper Company in the northern state of Sonora. One William Green, the manager of the mine known as "Oversight," called for mercenary troops and ammunition from the American side of the border. With the additional help of Mexican federal troops (*rurales*) sent by the governor of Sonora the striking miners were decimated, leaving hundreds of dead and wounded. The miners had wanted collective bargaining and better wages. The repression visited upon them was not totally victorious: the same year a group of exiles including the brothers Flores Magón met in St. Louis, Missouri, and proclaimed the Mexican Liberal party. Its program contained the demand for worker rights along with a legion of other reforms, all of which were anathema to the Porfirian dictatorship.

The Río Blanco strike the following year (January 1907) came about as a result of a prohibition by factory owners in Puebla and Tlaxcala against the organization of worker unions. A series of firings occurred and disgruntled laborers converged on the town of Río Blanco in the southern gulf coast state of Veracruz on January 7. They were met by the Mexican army and, again as in Cananea, the streets were littered with corpses of protesters. President Díaz gave his blessing to this massacre and took additional measures to assure the factory owners that security would be theirs in Mexico. These events gave currency to the now thundering cry of Ricardo Flores Magón and others for a proletarian uprising against the dictator.

3. From William Weber Johnson's *Heroic Mexico* (New York: Doubleday, 1968), p. 73.

4. As quoted in Heriberto García Rivas, *Breve historia de la revolución mexicana* (Mexico: Editorial Diana, 1964), p. 112.

5. *Johnson,* op. cit., p. 101.

6. Historical research has revealed that Madero's promises of "Mexico for the Mexicans" made some North American and other foreign investors uneasy. U.S. Ambassador Henry Lane Wilson, acting without formal orders from Washington, took it upon himself to conspire with Mexican adventurers toward Madero's overthrow. In point of fact, Madero and his vice president Pino Súarez were taken to a secluded site in Mexico City and a battle scene was simulated in the course of which the two constitutional Mexican leaders died. One year after the night of the murders, February 22, 1913, an eyewitness swore to what he had seen. Clearly, the United States had begun its relationship with revolutionary Mexico in a disastrous way. *Hispano Americano* 38, no. 968, November 21, 1960, pp. vii-xxxiv (magazine no longer published under this name; private copy in author's possession).

7. John Womack, Jr., *Zapata and the Mexican Revolution* (New York: Vintage Books, 1969), p. 287.

8. A distinctly negative evaluation of the Calles period is found in Juan Gualberto Amaya, *Los gobiernos de Obregón, Calles, y regímenes "peleles" derivados del callismo,* (Mexico: Editorial del Autor, 1947).

9. Charles C. Cumberland, *Mexico: The Struggle for Modernity* (New York, Oxford University Press, 1968), p. 299.

10. Womack, op. cit., p. 329.

Three

Power at the Apex: Mexico's Authoritarian Presidency

HIS IMPRINT IS PERSONAL

From Chapter 2 one may surmise that today's Mexican president is a highly authoritarian father figure. This is true providing he so elects to use his almost limitless power, a force which could also be unleashed for reform toward pluralist participation and grass-roots democratization as well. Several Mexican writers have commented on this latter possibility as we shall presently see. Some Mexican presidents have chosen to be less authoritarian than others. Looking across the sweep of years since independence was declared in 1821, it is possible to array Mexico's presidents on a continuum from the most irresponsible of tyrants (for example, Antonio López de Santa Anna in the mid-nineteenth century) to the most benevolent and populistic of despots (for example, Lázaro Cárdenas del Río in the 1930s). But not all Mexican political despots were necessarily also corrupt.

It has been argued that Porfirio Díaz, who gave his name (the *porfiriato*) to Latin America's longest dictatorship (1875–1910), was relatively honest himself but allowed widespread corruption around him as a device for buying the loyalty of key functionaries. Díaz also used the tactic of creating in the various states two or more rival groups, both of whom were loyal to him, and the dictator acted as arbiter of struggles between them. In his divide and arbitrate approach, Díaz discouraged the formation of real political parties. What he wanted was fragmented groups whose obedience he could command by keeping them at each other's throats, hence not at his. That was in marked contrast to today's presidential successions in which, once the official candidate has been chosen, all rival factions of the dominant party agree to join the winner and support his revolutionary campaign for election.

Importantly, the presidential election every six years must be represented as a great victory for the official party, PRI. It is easier to do this, of course, when the official candidate has an opponent. In 1970 the principal opposition party PAN threatened to withdraw its candidate because of ongoing government repression and a melancholy recent history of electoral fraud. By a narrow vote in a special reunion of the PAN's national assembly the party agreed to stay in the running (PAN candidate Efraín Gónzalez Morfín told me personally that he voted to suspend his own candidacy for president). It is known that the PRI was severely concerned over being unmasked before the world, especially the Third World, as a single-party monopoly. Ultimately, that is exactly what happened in 1976. In that election the PAN did not even field a presidential candidate, partly because of internal disagreement but also out of recognition that the party was lending itself to the facade of democracy by even participating at the presidential level (PAN did compete for lesser seats, and lost nearly everywhere, as will be sketched in Chapter 5). Winning in this way, the man who assumed the presidency in 1976 was under considerable pressure to mold a popular image for himself and for the rest of Mexican officialdom.

Even before José López Portillo was elected to the *sexenio* 1976–82 it was possible for an opposition commentator to write in an internationally read magazine that "only his very death could impede his becoming president."[1] And days after his triumph, the official house-organ of the Secretaría de Gobernación (one of the most powerful cabinet-level ministries and roughly a combination of the U.S. Departments of Justice and Interior) carried on its front page the assurance that "the great electoral process of July 4 has confirmed the democratic vocation of the Mexican people."[2] Inside that edition were photos of long lines of citizens waiting patiently to register to vote beneath large patriotic slogans extolling the significance of voting. Without real opposition, without a genuine win, the PRI must use rhetoric to a maximum as a means of symbol manipulation in the hope that popular allegiance will follow (or at least that people will feign allegiant behavior). As one PRI sympathizer has stated in an economic context, "rhetoric neutralizes dissatisfaction."[3]

Some may ask why even bother to have an election if the results are known in advance (the same PAN candidate cited above told me he had seen official election results on a state-by-state basis for all federal seats that had been printed days *before* the elections of 1970 were held). Partially the election is to win support for the national regime, and partially it is to ensure the winning of state and local candidates whose campaigns are supposedly helped by having the PRI's national candidate visit their districts. Many of the state and local seats are contested by other parties and it is easier to accomplish voting fraud in favor of the PRI when symbolic support is present from the national organization. The irony is, of course, that the PRI could probably win in most districts without fraud, a point to which I return later. What is important is bolstering the emotive attachment of the people to the regime, as if it were a matter of religious demand that the Mexican national consciousness (including the Aztec origins dealt with in Chapter 1) be honored in both its past and present contexts by popular adulation and legitimation. Any public sign that the apex of the pyramid is weakening, such as by conducting a restricted presidential campaign without opposition, could have dire emotional consequences vis-a-vis the popular base. Even though individuals, isolated as human units, may be disaffected toward the regime, this must not be allowed to become a consciously shared experience at the group level, such as at Tlatelolco. That is why a vigorous presidential campaign must be held, even without opposition: to give the public impression that there does exist widespread popular adulation for the regime and its figurehead at the apex of the pyramid. What happens, thereafter, the kind of image that is molded, depends greatly upon the person of the president. I will return to the personal imprints of Mexico's two most recent presidents later in this chapter.

Out of the great revolution of 1910–17 emerged a constitution in the latter year which is Mexico's legal basis for government today. The real, or functioning basis is, of course, the established party customs that have become institutionalized. The constitution and established precedent, plus amendments, give strong governing prerogatives to the president should he choose to use them. Among other things he has the power to intervene in state and local governments, to replace their elected magistrates virtually by decree. He has strong powers of the purse over all levels of government, and although the national legislature has a veto, this power has not been exercised over a chief executive since the late 1920s. The president has the power to expel foreigners and their companies. He is invested with extensive powers to protect the internal security of the nation. Security can have various meanings, including security from verbal assault, thus giving the president de facto censorship powers over the media and press. In recent years the censorship of ideas has become a hallmark of the Mexican presidency further underscoring its authoritarian bent.

Also, the president has power to carry out land distribution via the ejido program of collective farms. In recent years such grants of land took on meaning to the extent that the land had value without introducing artificial means (for example, irrigation) of giving it such value. President Lázaro Cárdenas (1934–40) is remembered for his vast distribution of naturally valuable land to many peasants. More recent presidents have made land distribution into a more symbolic gesture. President Gustavo Díaz Ordaz (1964–70) is said to have distributed land of which some 85 percent was worthless. President Luis Echeverría (1970–76) made a major grant of valuable land in the northwestern state of Sonora only three weeks before his presidency ended, thus leaving to his successor a solution of the bitter fighting that ensued between peasants and latifundistas, the large landowners. Knowledgeable Sonorans have told me that Echeverría deliberately left this mess to López Portillo to create difficulties for the latter, a claim whose larger ramifications will be examined later in this chapter.

The president is also invested with the power to promote collective bargaining among workers, peasants, and private-sector ownership. Since the

Mexican state is also a major owner of key industries (petroleum and steel, for example) the existence of an official party superimposed over the government aids in labor relations between proletariat and the state. On whatever level, the collective bargaining is handled through the three sectors (labor, agrarian, and popular) of the PRI and their affiliated unions. There is, to be sure, extralegal labor organizing and this has posed a threat to the PRI's traditional hegemony in recent years.

Probably no president during the twentieth century used his powers to build populistic support and limit political alienation against the regime so effectively as did Lázaro Cárdenas (1934–40), but he had uniquely favorable historical circumstances in which to work. Cárdenas benefited by tremendous personal charisma, an imprint which has been stereotyped into the kind of image many presidents have viewed with both awe and envy. Cárdenas's land distribution to peasants and subsoil expropriation of oil from foreign companies attracted a wide popular following. Cárdenas was said to have spent more time out with the people than in his office. Today, a major state-sponsored steel complex, intended to make Mexico independent of imported steel, functions in Cárdenas's home state of Michoacán and is named after him.[4] Cárdenas is remembered as the benevolent authoritarian, the word "benevolent" being the key, for this is how his contemporary masses and most upper class followers came to view him.

Cárdenas was also independent. He refused to be a puppet for his predecessor Plutarco Elías Calles and even had the latter expelled from Mexico. Since then presidents have tried to establish themselves as unique entities, as creative revolutionaries with a capital "R." Each has sought to leave his own legacy for history to record, but without outwardly repudiating that of his predecessor as Cárdenas did. This, as we will see, has become critical as alienation against the single-party monolith intensified during the 1970s and as that alienation, in turn, was rewarded with government repression.

An oft-quoted dictum of Frank Brandenburg holds that Mexicans "avoid personal dictatorship by retiring their dictators every six years."[5] This was a part of the denouement of the great revolution, no immediate reelection of the president and, in effect, no reelection at all. One president, Obregón, who sought to violate this dictum was assassinated in 1928. Presidents since Cárdenas have sought to perpetuate their influence through a unique process for choosing successors that will be discussed later. And each president has tried to select a compatible successor just as did Cárdenas. His successor, Manuel Avila Camacho (1940–46) guided Mexico through World War II and engineered significant consolidations within the single-party system. This left the PRI with its contemporary name and its present subdivision into three basic sectors: agrarian, labor, and popular. Next, Miguel Alemán (1946–52) used a hard hand in stimulating postwar economic development, especially in collaboration with U.S. interests. In this way he undid some of the hard feelings left by the oil expropriations of the Cárdenas era. Alemán's successor, Adolfo Ruiz Cortines (1952–58) made notable efforts to professionalize the federal bureaucracy and to instill the norm of honesty into Mexican politics. He seems to have been the last Mexican president to have attempted a serious rationalization of the governing system.

By the time of the presidency of Adolfo López Mateos (1958–64), Mexico was changing from a predominantly rural to an urban nation. Population pressures were increasing on the cities. Rural discontent grew. The inability of the PRI to be all things to all people was showing itself. López Mateos inherited labor unrest. The railroad workers led by Demetrio Vallejo and Valentín Campa attempted to paralyze transportation in the spring of 1959. They were put down forcefully by the army under the president's direction. The leaders of that strike received harsh prison terms of 16 years each.[6] At this point, the image of a benevolent president was weakened while the authoritarian part of the equation was reinforced.

Undoubtedly a crucial point in the further atrophy of the presidential mystique came during the regime of Gustavo Díaz Ordaz (1964–70). It was his fate to play sacrificial priest to several hundred students who died in the government-ordered massacre at Tlatelolco near downtown Mexico City on the night of October 2, 1968. Thousands were injured and the true death toll may never be known. As noted in Chapter 1, Tlatelolco became a symbol of the division between people and regime, between official party and the congeries of satellite parties and outgroups. It was Díaz Ordaz's own cabinet minister Luis Echeverría who shared much of the public opprobrium over the Tlatelolco disaster; and the same Echeverría succeeded to the presidency for the sexenio that ended in 1976.[7]

During the Echeverría sexenio the regime exhibited notable instability in the longevity and turnover of important political actors. This was, in large part, because Echeverría sought desperately to overcome the stigma of Tlatelolco and to win acceptance for himself as a leader of the Third World. Echeverría was aggressive by nature and came into frequent conflict with power figures internal to the PRI. Echeverría had a near mania for the consolidation and expansion of personal political power. In one way or another he came into conflict with powerful (or potentially so) governors in the states of Guerrero, Nuevo León, Puebla, Hidalgo, and Sonora. These governors were all removed, and I will touch on several of these cases later in this chapter. Also there were a number of changes in the presidential cabinet, including several attorneys general in 1971 and the secretary of finance and treasury in 1973 (significantly, the man who resigned, Hugo Margáin, became Mexico's ambassador to Washington in 1977 and the man who replaced him as finance minister, López Portillo, became president). A scandal in 1971 involving the government's use of clandestine paramilitary squads gave Echeverría the pretext to remove the mayor *(regente)* of Mexico's Federal District, Alfonso

Martínez Domínguez, who was considered a lingering figure of influence tied to the power circle *(camarilla)* of former president Díaz Ordaz. Echeverría's own power clique tried to compare the expulsion of Martínez Domínguez with Lázaro Cárdenas's expulsion of former president Plutarco Elías Calles from the party years earlier (again, witness the lingering strength of the Cárdenas prototype).[8]

Echeverría proclaimed a policy of democratic openness *(apertura democrática)* which was supposed to make it easier for opposition groups to win elections. This, as we shall see, was little more than empty rhetoric. There was evidence that the regime actively fomented divisions in opposition parties and in one case, that of the Popular Socialist party (PPS), the PRI was obliged to grant a national senatorial seat to an opposition candidate (the first such win in decades) in exchange for his admission that he had earlier lost the race for governor of Nayarit. In his campaign for popular support, Echeverría embraced socialist-sounding doctrines and branded his critics as emissaries of the past, a posture which put him on a collision course with strong vested interests in the private sector. This conflict was sharpened by Echeverría's pronouncements during visits to a plethora of Third World countries, many of which had socialist or communist governments. Especially notable were his close ties with the socialist regime of Salvador Allende of Chile, his subsequent welcoming of Chilean exiles, and his breaking of diplomatic relations with the Pinochet regime.

Echeverría sought to heal the wounds of the private sector by granting fiscal concessions and growth subsidies in areas calculated to win allegiance. At the same time, he took a repressive stand against independent union efforts to break with official syndicates and confront management with tough demands. Despite his promise of democratic openness, Echeverría came to the rescue of the private sector when so threatened. This was conspicuously true of the regime's repressive tactics against SUTERM, an electrical workers' syndicate which broke with officialdom. At the same time Echeverría sought to bolster support within the official unions with worker housing programs such as INFONAVIT.

More evidence of instability in the regime was evidenced by violence in the countryside and the wave of kidnappings and bombings in cities. Echeverría ordered the army to suppress the guerrillas, a task which it came close to accomplishing. But not before great damage had been done to the regime. Even the PRI's candidate for the governorship of Guerrero, Rubén Figueroa, could not make an acceptance speech in person because he had been kidnapped by a guerrilla band. Later, when the opposition journal *Por Que?* sought to publish a version of the episode that was decidedly unfavorable to the presidential image, the government shut down that publication and jailed its editors. It was clear that the cumulative affect of agrarian policy since Cárdenas had not won support for the regime among the peasants, many of whom were joining or aiding the rural insurgents.

Echeverría's authoritarian image was patent in his creation of a new Military University for the armed forces and the inclusion of military personnel in traditionally civilian governmental roles. This led to speculation about an elite corps of hopeful military administrators referred to colloquially as *los penecilinos,* the name derived from the notion that their special training had equipped them with a unique variety of "penicillin" which could be used in case of emergency to supplant civilian rule. Out of these rumors emerged much speculation of a renascent militarism in Mexican politics and the possibility of a coup toward the end of the Echeverría sexenio. Concern for controlling opposition was also evidenced in the regime's decree of strict gun control, this in a country in which possession of arms was, and continues to be, a strong tradition. One consequence of gun control was to stimulate the existing black market in weapons smuggled from the United States. However, to counterbalance this hard-hand approach, Echeverría decreed an amnesty for a large number of political prisoners in 1976, a measure which drew mixed responses from various sectors of the political spectrum. And whereas the regime increased its subsidies to public educational institutions, it countered this by infiltrating and systematically repressing student movements in a number of important universities. For every plus Echeverría seemed to be able to create a minus.

It is worthwhile looking at the Echeverría regime in greater detail as a basis for understanding the legacy of that sexenio which today's president, José López Portillo, will have to overcome if he is to depart office in 1982 leaving a positive balance on record.

Echeverría added to the existing authoritarian tradition his own personal style as the late distinguished scholar Daniel Cosío Villegas noted.[9] Some of this was the outgrowth of circumstances whose development cannot be blamed exclusively on Echeverría. For instance, there was perhaps more publicly reported violence in Mexico during the Echeverría regime than ever before. Guerrillas led by Genaro Vázquez Rojas formed in the hills of Guerrero and began a series of spectacular kidnappings of elitists and attacks on military and police garrisons. When Vázquez died in 1972 his cause was taken up by Lucio Cabañas, who proclaimed a "Party of the Poor." The kidnappings and assassinations continued. By the time of Cabañas's death in 1974 a plethora of violent groups had formed. President Echeverría was their ultimate goal but many wealthy oligarchs were either kidnapped or assassinated as surrogate targets. While the ultraleft reminded the poor that Echeverría was the assassin of Tlatelolco, the rich accused the president of being soft on the extremists and of contributing to an atmosphere in which terrorism could flourish. Eventually, the terror was visited upon the international diplomatic community; rightly or wrongly, much of this was blamed on Echeverría. His response was to mobilize troops for war against the guerrillas.

The new president had opened the second year of his regime with a violent trauma which he certainly did not welcome. On June 10, 1971, in the San

Cosme neighborhood of Mexico City a student march was disrupted by government supported terrorists called the Falcons (Los Halcones) who were transported in government buses and given police protection. A number of students were killed, many more wounded, and even the national press corps was attacked. The scandal was so open that President Echeverría had to ask for the resignation of several high-ranking officials (including cabinet ministers and the mayor of the Federal District). The bulk of the testimony and evidence indicates that Echeverría knew about the Falcons and approved of them even though he insisted otherwise.[10] The victimized students at San Cosme were protesting, among other things, the continued incarceration of student leaders from Tlatelolco. Echeverría promised the public a full investigation of the San Cosme repression, but when his sexenio ended some six years later no such report had appeared. Presidential secrecy was the prevailing mode. The people, in the end, could not be trusted with their own constitutional right to know. To the Echeverría regime, maintenance of the official image of the state, especially vis-a-vis the outside world, was more important than guaranteeing a free press or the freedom to protest, via peaceful means, what the students perceived as abuses of power.

All of this becomes curious when one considers that much of the Echeverría period was devoted to molding a presidential image of Mexico as a leading nation among the countries of the Third World. Echeverría himself openly sought the secretary generalship of the United Nations as his term came to a close in 1976. Since that post is hardly one for which a public campaign has traditionally been mounted, it was obvious that Luis Echeverría had an intense personal need for the acquisition of deference and status values as well as accumulation of political power. This is a key point because the Mexican presidency is such as to allow its incumbent to make almost anything he wants of it. Constitutional provisions are mere formalities that have been amplified by precedent. The president has practically limitless power. If he should so choose, the president can be a great internal reformer like Cárdenas, or he can try to become an international image-builder like Echeverría.

Luis Echeverría exemplified the degree to which the authoritarianism inherent in his office could be used to fit the personal style of the incumbent, in this case the style of an insatiable power seeker. Since he wanted to impress the world, and especially the developing nations, with his statesmanship, it will be instructive to examine selected external views of the Echeverría presidency as it came to an end in 1976. At one pole of the Western Hemisphere, an editorial in *La Prensa* of Buenos Aires (May 12, 1976) revealed preoccupation in both Argentina and the United States with the leftist direction in which President Echeverría was steering Mexico. Feelings were reported (from both those countries) that Echeverría's regime had modalities comparable to those of the Marxist regime of the late Salvador Allende in Chile as well as to Fidel Castro. Commenting on the president's drive for Third World leadership *La*

Prensa said, "No other Mexican president spent so much time outside his country—ten large journeys in five years extending from the African jungles to Russia and to the deserts of the Middle East." The editorial also noted that while Echeverría preached openness and friendship toward the outside world, his government voted in the United Nations to condemn Israel. In addition *La Prensa* charged that while the Mexican embassies about the world were places of refuge for political refugees, terrorists, and hijackers, at home in Mexico any criticism of the regime was castigated with utmost severity. This is evidence that Echeverría's tough hand in domestic politics had not escaped the attention of other nations, especially vis-a-vis Echeverría's preferred image that was for export. *La Prensa* even reminded the Third World of the Tlatelolco massacre as an example of the Echeverría governmental style.

A great deal of attention about the Western Hemisphere was paid to the Echeverría regime's attitude toward the military dictatorship that emerged in Chile following the overthrow of its constitutional government in 1973. Echeverría sent a personal airplane to bring back Dr. Allende's widow and family. The Mexican embassy accepted dozens of political exiles and ultimately many more were sent to Mexico in response to Echeverría's criticisms of the Chilean junta before the United Nations and the Organization of American States (OAS). Eventually, Mexico severed diplomatic relations with Chile in 1974 as a further gesture of protest against what Echeverría ostentatiously challenged in public as violations of human rights by the Pinochet regime. In 1976 Echeverría announced that his government would boycott a meeting of OAS ministers in Santiago saying that participating would be tantamount to recognizing Pinochet. And later that same year the president seized upon the Chilean theme once more. He denounced certain unspecified "emisaries of the past" in Mexico who were allegedly planning to inspire a military coup against him and cited the recent military intervention in Argentina plus that of Chile as cases in point. According to *Excelsior,* at that time the most influential Mexican daily, Echeverría declared publicly, "There will never be a Pinochet in Mexico."[11] The president then condemned a secret meeting that was to have taken place in the northern industrial city of Monterrey for the purpose of financing a "fascist style" resistance to his regime.[12] He also referred to a "small plutocratic and profascist minority which sought to alter the growing rhythm of the Mexican Revolution."[13]

It is a revealing irony of Echeverría's growing paranoid style that, as his presidency drew to a close, he was consistently preoccupied with authoritarian conspiracies against him, and with authoritarianism (fascism) of one sort or another about the world, while at the same time he was reacting in the most authoritarian way to critics of his own regime at home. This leads to consideration of one of the most fateful decisions of Echeverría's career, one that would leave him open to the most severe charge of authoritarianism, indeed of totalitarianism. Echeverría decided to close the newspaper *Excelsior* during

July 1976. This publication was probably the last bastion of intellectual and press freedom in Mexico. It was a cooperative in which the workers owned shares. Its editors were dedicated to open critical journalism. *Excelsior* was easily one of the three best newspapers printed in the Spanish language (in all probability it was *the* best). During most of the Echeverría sexenio the pages of *Excelsior* were filled with stories of popular uprisings against corrupt government officials about the country plus penetrating investigative reporting on a number of sensitive themes including intra-PRI power struggles, corruption generally, and poverty. It was difficult for Echeverría to continue to promote himself as a leader of the Third World, who merited the secretary-generalship of the United Nations, when he presided over a country with some 40 percent of its work force unemployed and over 70 percent of that work force earning less than $80 per month, a nation in the humiliating position of solving its surplus labor problem by encouraging millions to undertake illegal migration to the United States (and then accusing North America of racism for expelling the wetbacks).[14]

Echeverría's paranoid style was anathema to the image he sought to project to the outside world: He proclaimed Mexico as the land of apertura democrática and also of autocrítica (a form of self-criticism). He denounced U.S. racism and great-power hegemony over the Third World economies. He condemned Israel for its Zionist imperialism. He paid tribute to the populism of Juan Perón and then self-righteously condemned the Argentine generals who overthrew the Peronist regime when it degenerated hopelessly into government by sheer terror after having produced the world's worst rate of inflation in 1976.[15] Echeverría condemned a group of Mexican student critics in March of 1975 as fascists working for the U.S. Central Intelligence Agency (CIA) (the president himself had previously collaborated with the CIA as will be cited later). Finally he closed *Excelsior* and replaced it with a puppet newspaper published irreverently under the same name. Echeverría came to power using the slogan *arriba y adelante,* up and forward. But that did not happen in Mexico in any meaningful sense. As Echeverría's six-year term drew to a close, the image he left behind throughout much of the hemisphere is perhaps reflected by this editorial from the New York *Times* on the closing of *Excelsior,* an indication of just how much "up and forward" Mexico had come under Echeverría's style of presidential action:

> Almost immediately after the presidential election [of 1976], a well-financed rebellion was organized [by the government] within the paper's staff to create a situation in which the editors risked armed conflict if they sought to carry out their normal duties. The editors bowed to the threat of force and quit their employment. The bully boys of Lenin in 1917 or of Hitler in 1933 could not have done a more efficient job of enslaving a once proud and free newspaper. But this act of totalitarian suppression discredits those who now boast of Mexico's stability and democracy.[16]

In point of fact, Echeverría had not fooled much of the Third World, especially not Latin America. An article in the influential daily *La Opinión* of Buenos Aires referred to the Mexican elections of 1976 as part of the ongoing "six-year ritual" and noted the use by the PRI of coercion in bringing peasants to political rallies to create the facade of enthusiasm for the regime.[17] Everyone knew that there was only one candidate on the ballot to succeed Echeverría and that public money was being spent to finance an empty ritual. An appropriate question was raised: "To what extent is democracy possible and popular participation meaningful within a political structure which offers no visible alternatives?"[18]

A balance sheet on the Echeverría presidency must read negatively, this according to José Luis Robles Gleen, president of the National Association of Mexican Corporate Executives.[19] The sexenio was most glaring for its contradictions among which the following stand out. Echeverría pledged his word to publish a final report explaining the June 10 massacre and the Falcons. He promised to return to the National University after a violent encounter there with students in 1975 (discussed later). He repeatedly denied rumors that the peso would be devalued. He accused independent television chains of promoting violence with their choice of films and of overstimulating consumer buying, hence inflation. He promised not to undertake foreign travel during the first three years of his presidency. He publicly opposed birth control (then ended by endorsing it). He equivocated on fiscal policy, especially in the taxing of exports. He promised to reduce the national foreign debt. He promised democratic openness, then took over *Excelsior.* He denied having designs on the secretary-generalship of the United Nations. On all of the above issues, Echeverría did the opposite of what he said or worked counter to the policy he had proclaimed.[20] I shall return to some of these issues variously throughout this book as they have relevance to the presidency and related aspects of the Mexican political process.

HOW PRESIDENTS ARE MADE AND PRESIDENTIAL POWER USED

In his work *La sucesión presidencial,* published in 1975, Daniel Cosío Villegas cites the controversial testimony of ex-CIA agent Philip Agee to the effect that Luis Echeverría knew he had been picked to succeed President Díaz Ordaz as early as 1966, that is, four years before the formal nominating procedure would take place.[21] Agee wrote that Echeverría, then minister of gobernación, had confided this to the CIA station head in Mexico City. Gobernación is a political power center in Mexico and it is a frequent source of presidential candidates. No small part of this power comes from the access to intelligence information that the incumbent minister of gobernación enjoys. The Agee testimony thoroughly supports the widespread belief that the CIA and other U.S. intelligence agencies collaborate closely with gobernación and its subsidiary the Mexican Federal Judicial Police. Agee identified both Echeverría and Díaz Ordaz as former CIA collaborators. It is noteworthy that Cosío Villegas cited Agee as an authoritative source. Cosío Villegas, one of Mexico's most respected political historians, is distinguished for his works on the Mexican presidency and the political system generally. He has known most recent presidents personally, and especially Luis Echeverría.[22]

Significantly, Cosío made reference to the Agee book in the context of demonstrating part of his own thesis about the Mexican presidential succession, that is, that the incumbent president makes his selection fairly early during his term and hides it as best he can until he is ultimately forced by pressures from within the PRI to declare himself.[23] Were he to announce his successor before the final year of his six-year term (sexenio), the incumbent president might progressively lose power and thereby impair his ability to carry out any programs intended to carve for him a distinct place in Mexico's political history. However, the president has an intriguing procedure for testing his power structure's reaction to a potential successor. There is a political folklore in Mexico about "veiled ones" (tapados) who are suspected to be the president's choice of successor. But there is only one real (verdadero) tapado and he is unveiled formally at the official party's national nominating convention.

In point of fact, however, the unveiling may occur in other and quite informal ways. For instance, the name of a given tapado may be leaked to the government-controlled press while the president and his advisors await a reaction from within the PRI. But there is also the external reaction to be considered, that is, that of the United States. Because of the close interdependency of the Mexican and North American economies the Mexican presidential succession becomes a matter of importance north of the Rio Grande. The CIA, as a special "policeman" who protects U.S. interests abroad (as Agee put it), will also be interested in the new Mexican president. Thus if Echeverría did declare himself to the CIA station chief, this was undoubtedly a trial balloon of sorts. It was especially significant in the light of the then forthcoming Olympic Games, considering the CIA's interest in them (as per Agee's testimony), and in view of the fact that Echeverría would be the minister principally charged with defending that international event against any threat of attack (and student protests had already been voiced in 1966). How the U.S. power structure felt about Echeverría was clearly important to the presidential decision in 1970, and apparently the American feedback was favorable.

Early in La sucesión presidencial, Cosío treats the works of several North American scholars who found the selection of PRI candidates to follow certain logical rules explained by pendulum theories or by schemes of requisites of a personal and professional nature in which the final selection is someone capable of balancing opposing forces. Cosío finds it interesting that the North

Americans see the Mexican process so rationally and clearly when the Mexican insiders themselves do not see it that way at all. He questions specifically what he sees as a general North American unwillingness to admit that the Mexican presidential succession is resolved "arbitrarily and capriciously," thereby leading those analysts into the error of creating elaborate schemes of kingmakers and power theories to explain the selection process.[24]

But there is more to the Cosío thesis. He argues carefully that the legendary Lázaro Cárdenas saw to it that his successor was a man like Avila Camacho who would rectify whatever shortcomings that might remain in the outgoing president's legacy, but who would do so slowly and quietly; therefore, the rectification would not bear the stamp of condemnation and Cárdenas's image in history would be preserved as truly revolutionary.[25] Cosío Villegas is one of the best-informed scholars of the Mexican presidency and his wisdom is to be taken seriously. He is saying in effect that the outgoing president follows the tradition set by Cárdenas of controlling the selection process so as to guarantee that he will not be repudiated by his successor; yet, he must choose a successor who will allow residual powers to be retained by the outgoing president and, at once, attend realistically to the glaring needs of the nation. He must make the choice early and then test it informally via the ritual of the tapados.

During 1976 a Mexican journalist from the capital city confirmed to me much of the Cosío Villegas thesis and threw additional light on the antecedents of that year's presidential succession. The story (and I have agreed to respect the confidence of the source) is one that can rather easily be verified or rejected by most any biographical scholar of the outgoing president Luis Echeverría. Throughout Mexico great surprise was felt when it was learned that José López Portillo (treasury secretary), not Mario Moya Palencia (gobernación), would be the next president.[26] Most observers believed that Moya was to be the next president. It seems, however, that Echeverría and López Portillo were close college companions who, sometime in the 1940s, took an ocean cruise to Chile for study purposes. Furthermore, it is alleged that the only nonfamily person invited to Echeverría's wedding was José López Portillo. Moreover, it is said that the most intimate of personal relationships existed between the two during the Echeverría sexenio and that López Portillo was Echeverría's principal behind-the-scenes advisor who was the president's secret choice as successor all along; this while publicly an attempt was made to give the impression that Moya Palencia was the chief mover in the president's cabinet.

It is natural to find observers expecting the secretary of gobernación to succeed to the presidency as occurred in 1964 and 1970. Moya was a major power figure. His ministry has great ascriptive powers. Gobernación, after all, has control over the Mexican equivalents of the U.S. FBI and CIA (although nearly every Mexican governmental department has its own secret police of one ilk or another). Gobernación has the most complete and effective intelligence operation in the Mexican republic; hence, it is the head of that department who de facto becomes one of Mexico's most feared men, and on very much the same basis that J. Edgar Hoover was feared in the United States. It is gobernación that has the files on everyone. If it is necessary to leak something unfavorable to the government-controlled press that will diminish a certain power contender within or outside the official PRI, it is almost surely gobernación that will be called upon to do the leaking. As cited above, presidents Luis Echeverría and Díaz Ordaz were both former secretaries of gobernación.

What is significant is the fact that all Mexican knowledgeables I interviewed in the months following the unveiling *(destape)* on September 22, 1975, confessed that the matter was a mystery. Moreover, Cosío Villegas produced a book following the destape in which he also admits that the matter was then a mystery to him.[27] My Mexican informants told me that "when Cosío Villegas does not know (or is not saying) that in itself is significant." It tends to confirm, of course, that earlier-cited Cosío contention that the selection may very well be made arbitrarily and capriciously.

In his latest and last book, *La sucesión: desenlace y perspectivas,* Cosío related the surprising story of how the unveiling of López Portillo occurred. It was done quite informally and in almost bizarre circumstances (Cosío prefers to call the 1975 unveiling *el corcholatazo,* or the uncorking, which conveys better the element of mystery and surprise). He says that late in the afternoon of September 22 Moya Palencia and some colleagues were lunching in an undefined place but to which reporters apparently had access. Their meal was interrupted by newspapermen carrying copies of *Ultimas Noticias de Excelsior* announcing the unveiling of López Portillo. Apparently, they were all surprised that the news was out but confirmed it while Moya Palencia tried to maintain his composure. Cosío relates further the rumor (which he then discredits) that the president in fact had arranged to have the announcement emerge as a surprise and that he, Echeverría, had selected the weakest of the potential tapados to keep him indebted after the transfer of power in 1976 (note that while Cosío discredits this rumor, he nevertheless repeats it).[28]

It was believed that almost all the governors of the states and the key leaders of the PRI's sectoral organizations (labor, agrarian, and popular) had endorsed Moya Palencia's informal candidacy to become the verdadero tapado. So Echeverría clearly dumped Moya. It is rumored that a power struggle had developed between Moya and Echeverría and that this fight became open during 1975. The most patent aspects of the struggle concerned governorships. In April 1975, Echeverría's handpicked governor of the state of Hidalgo, Otoniel Miranda, was deposed by the state legislature after only 29 days in office.[29] My informants claim that the fall of the Hidalgo governor was the indirect work of Moya Palencia, who may then have been fearing that someone other than himself could become the verdadero tapado and therefore sought a confrontation with President Echeverría to force the issue publicly.

This did not happen but the gubernatorial arena yielded later on a more clearly defined confrontation in Sonora during October 1975. There, under orders from Echeverría, and with the helpless acquiescence of Moya Palencia (who by then had been passed over for the presidency), Governor Carlos Armando Biebrich was deposed by the state legislature and replaced with Sonora's incumbent senator, Alejandro Carrillo Marcor. It was the first time since 1935 that Sonora's state government had been so intervened from Mexico City.[30]

The case of Governor Biebrich appears in a later chapter. Suffice it to say here that Biebrich and much of the Sonora PRI were sullied by scandals involving arms trafficking and narcotics. In addition, in the fall of 1975, Biebrich ordered the assassination of a number of peasant squatters and pretended he had approval from President Echeverría and Moya Palencia (which he did not).[31] Biebrich had been a protege of Moya and it was rumored that should Moya become president Biebrich would be elevated to the cabinet post of gobernación, just a step away from the presidency. The Biebrich scandals, and Moya's continuing efforts to protect him, may have figured prominently in Echeverría's decision to drop Moya, if in fact he had ever been considered. There is evidence in the extradition indictments eventually brought against Biebrich that his abuse of public office had been going on for most of the time (three years) that he had been Sonora's governor.[32] It is not likely that Moya was unaware of this, given the number of public protests against Biebrich emanating from Sonora. If these considerations entered into President Echeverría's decision not to unveil Moya as the next president, one may surmise that he had acted in the best interest of Mexico. Of course we will never know for sure as long as ex-presidents maintain the fiction that the PRI's National Assembly decided the presidential succession.

HIS FORMAL IMAGE MUST NOT BE SULLIED BUT FORTIFIED

Looking at post-1977 Mexico one finds little prevalence of the old taboo against attacking the president, especially past presidents. For instance, in July 1977 former president Gustavo Díaz Ordaz left for Madrid where he would become Mexico's first ambassador to Spain in some 40 years. Asked by reporters if he felt concern over the fact that two of Mexico's most distinguished authors had resigned their posts as ambassadors in protest against him, Díaz Ordaz replied, "I have not read those writers."[33] Subsequently the new ambassador was ridiculed for this statement in several opposition press organs and public protests by students were staged against his being designated ambassador.

Then, some 13 days after arriving in Spain, Díaz Ordaz abruptly resigned. He protested a detached retina of the eye. It is believed, however, that ex-president Echeverría, himself than ambassador-at-large to UNESCO, pressured his lifetime friend President López Portillo into demanding the resignation. Díaz Ordaz, shortly after arriving in Spain, had criticized former president Echeverría's own earlier criticism of the Franco regime for its execution of Basque terrorists, saying that the majority of Mexicans considered those comments by Echeverría to be incorrect.[34] It is also believed that Díaz Ordaz never forgave Echeverría for having expelled Martínez Domínguez from the ruling circle over the 10th of June affair in 1971 and was thus motivated to criticize the former president. Both former presidents then returned to Mexico to try to consolidate the personal power they perceived to be slipping. Such are the machinations of ex-presidential power and images in Mexico.

Both ex-presidents became targets for the public opprobrium of opposition groups. Echeverría himself had been attacked publicly for the 1976 peso crisis and devaluation by Hugo Margáin, once Echeverría's own finance minister and then ambassador to Washington. More criticism of this sort came from another former finance minister, Antonio Ortiz Mena, who served under both López Mateos (1958–64) and the subsequent regime of Díaz Ordaz. Ortiz Mena, then president of the International Development Bank in Washington, stated that in his view "not since the death of General Obregón in 1928 had a new government received a nation in worse financial condition," referring to the legacy Echeverría had left for López Portillo.[35] So it is patently clear that the tradition of not attacking the ex-president in Mexico has undergone substantial modification.

But in considering the roots of presidential power in Mexico one must be aware that the tradition of not attacking the person of the president while he is in office still lingers, at least early in his term, and provided he is not plagued by events like those of June 10, 1971. Obviously, the outgroups and satellite parties are not bound by all the PRI may consider to be traditional, but at least until 1968 there had been a general national taboo against venomous personal attacks on the incumbent chief executive. That was abandoned in 1968 when the protesting students demanded the death of President Díaz Ordaz and his minister Luis Echeverría. Later, when Echeverría as president was denounced in 1971 and assaulted in 1975 it became obvious that both the man and the institution of the presidency had fallen into disrepute vis-a-vis the young intelligentsia. Loss of face before this sector must have wounded a determined power-seeker like Echeverría badly and some of his extreme reactions to criticism as his term came to a close (like taking over *Excelsior*) may have stemmed from the cumulative psychological impact of his clashes with students (in 1968, 1971, and finally 1975). President López Portillo had not yet been seriously attacked during the first year of his presidency.

The president's sensitivity to criticism, and his vulnerability to attack, came to light during March 1975. Echeverría had accepted an invitation to speak at the opening of classes at the National University on March 14 and he hoped to enter into a dialogue with students. The meeting was to be held in the medical faculty's auditorium named after the late Salvador Allende of Chile. The rector Guillermo Soberón tried to introduce the president. He was interrupted with insults and charges that "LEA [acronym for the president's name] is a fascist." The president wanted to speak. There were more insults. The student-body president tried to speak and said something about the need in Mexico for a congressional investigation of CIA activities as recently disclosed by the Philip Agee book. He was shouted down as a traitor and more verbal disparagement was hurled at the president of the republic. Then the violence became physical with gunfire. Bottles and rocks were thrown. One of these wounded President Echeverría in the forehead. Shortly before this the president had shouted that the insurgent students were "pro-fascists, manipulated by the CIA, who emulate the youth corps of Hitler and Mussolini."[36] The student leader Joel Ortega replied that it was Echeverría who was propagating fascism by sending police agents into the university and by allowing labor bosses to impede development of a free labor movement in Mexico.[37]

What is significant in this is that, despite the merits of the various charges hurled back and forth, the president had been forced into a position of retreat from dialogue with the students, and this was covered in the national press. The fact that *Excelsior* criticized the student behavior editorially did not make up for its having printed their words and points of view. *Excelsior* also opened its pages to paid notices by radical student groups who denounced Echeverría and the PRI. Undoubtedly, this contributed to the president's determination to close that publication the following year. We may say, then, that one of the key power roots of the Mexican presidency is its formal image. It matters not if everyone knows that the president sends police agents to harass students, maintains paramilitary squads to beat up them and the press corps, and presides over a regime in which corrupt labor bosses enslave the workers in conspiracy with management. What does matter is the formal image that the public communications media can forge. Perhaps the classic statement of this principle came from one-time PRI President Carlos Madrazo, who was deposed by President Díaz Ordaz in 1965 over the former's proposal to democratize the PRI via a scheme of local primaries to nominate candidates. Just as the fateful holocaust of Tlatelolco in 1968 was building up, Madrazo told a capital-city reporter, "Do you know what one of Díaz Ordaz's ministers told me the other day? He said the people didn't count. What does count is the impression we create with our newspapers."[38] In other words, it may be that the "emperor has no clothes," just don't print it publicly.

PRESCRIPTIONS DRAWN FROM PAST LESSONS

In a book published just prior to the presidential succession of 1970, José C. Valadés set forth some suggestive propositions relating to the presidency which can be compared with the later conclusions of Cosío Villegas. Valadés argues that during the decade of the 1930s the Mexican population felt itself sufficiently submissive to the political system so that presidents could designate their successors with little risk. But 30 years later, with Mexico's demographic explosion, there was a population that would not fit under the PRI's umbrella, not even under its penumbra.[39] There were vast youthful interests, crystalized at Tlatelolco, that were effectively divorced from the official political system. This would be a continuing threat to the PRI and to any and all of its presidents; so would the acute and growing pauperization in urban slums and among rural peasants. Yet, the corruption of private interests underlying the absolutism of high functionaries who surrounded the president made it difficult for him to be a true reformist and respond to critical needs. Indeed, it may not have been in the president's personal interest to be a reformer, for the corruption had spread beyond the limits of officialdom and was part of society itself.[40] Valadés says that Mexico's presidents have an inherent need to keep the people humiliated while pretending to do otherwise, but that a statesman with great heroic valor, prudence, reformist spirit, and true modesty could return the presidential selection process to the people and restore democracy. This would change the authoritarian character of the Mexican presidency, but of course it is easier proposed than achieved.[41]

There are two critical facts that must be understood about the PRI and the presidency according to Valadés. One is that the PRI is a political bureau at the service of the president and that serving him is its primary task. The second is that the PRI is not really a party because, except in its early years, it has lacked a program of concretely definable policies. For this reason, the PRI cannot allow genuine competition from a real political party with a clearly defined program. The PRI is a vast elite class, surrounding an authoritarian president, but the class holds many dissimilar and often contradictory elements.[42] The class may also appear as a kind of army without arms but which employs various mafias (army, secret police, paramilitary squads, and so on) to control others and protect itself. Thus, the undemocratic practice of presidents by *dedazo* and *tapadismo* (personal designation via the secret tapado process) is perpetuated so as to keep the president's authority immune from public accountability, to make it unnecessary for him to enter into public dialogue except at his convenience. Thus the president is responsible only to a handful of kingmakers and camarillas who help him to ignore the needs of society while, as before, pretending to do otherwise.[43]

What Mexico needed in the presidency of 1970, said Valadés, was a leader who met two criteria: that he not be picked by the outgoing president but by a national convention, and that the new president not be indebted to the outgoing president but be forced to win popular support on his own merits.[44] Again, this was easier proposed than achieved given established PRI tradition. But Valadés saw the nation exhausted with presidential successions and the continued use of the PRI as a personal power bureau for the president. The public disgust was visible in popular discredit of the electoral process as a sham, a widespread disheartened feeling of abandon vis-a-vis politics, disdain of deputies and senators, the general helplessness and uselessness of the national congress.[45] Where, he asks, is the legislation that regulates those who make life wretched for the masses both rural and urban? The revitalization of the congress is imperative if Mexican presidents are going to return to the people those prerogatives which were originally theirs. The congress, as it is, is a rubber stamp, a part of the president's political bureau.[46] "It is no exaggeration to say that in only a very few countries do presidents have at their grasp the power which Mexico's president personally enjoys."[47]

Valadés points to the personal designation (dedazo or presidentes de dedo) as one of the chief evils in the system which can and must eventually lead to a grave and erroneous designation of a president who will damage the nation severely. As he analyzed the presidential succession of 1970 he saw the people asking, "Why even vote if only the official candidate can win." Later in 1975 and 1976 this came to preoccupy high officials of the PRI greatly as the legitimacy of the regime was being called into question by the abstention of voters and other forms of repudiation that were cited earlier. Ultimately, the PRI was the only party on the ballot in 1976.[48]

Finally, Valadés clarifies that it is not the PRI which is invincible (because the PRI lacks popular grass roots, what he calls *engranaje propio*) but rather it is the president who is invincible because he controls the PRI. This will continue so long as the president is selected by a handful of men or perhaps by his predecessor alone; that is, the PRI will never become a true party until it has been democratized. This, then, was a plea directly to the new president-to-be in Mexico of 1970 to democratize the party system. Published in 1969, the work does not refer to Luis Echeverría by name. But the image depicted is clearly one of a dominant class, calling itself a party which is really the government in disguise, and of a decidedly authoritarian president who *could* reform things if he wanted to. Valadés saw popular resistance efforts, however justified they might be, as doomed to the failure of disorganized anarchy which cannot triumph over the dominant class which was the PRI in 1970.

Let us now skip to the ambience of the 1976 presidential succession in Mexico. Here are some propositions in light of Daniel Cosío Villegas's key work on the Echeverría presidency, *El estilo personal de gobernar,* as related to other works and evidence.

Is it the Mexican presidency per se, or is it the entire regime, that is inherently authoritarian? Valadés seems to say that the presidency is inherently authoritarian and this, in turn, makes the regime conform to his image. In this regard, the American scholar Evelyn P. Stevens's investigation argued that Mexico's political system was not oriented toward the "formulation and modification of goals through pluralistic participation in the decision-making process. Instead, we see repression of authentic interest groups and encouragement of spurious groups that can be relied on not to speak out of turn. The regime deals with bona fide groups almost as if they were enemy nations."[49] The question, then, is does this characteristic behavior originate in the regime, or in the presidency? Valadés says the presidency, Cosío Villegas seems to be saying the regime, and this writer's personal experience tends to confirm Cosío. Yet there is no doubt about the president's practically limitless power.

What has been the recent thrust of the Mexican presidency vis-a-vis the state's capability for generating and distributing wealth? According to Cosío's analysis, President Cárdenas sought to push the entire nation toward existing wealth, thereby to achieve a more equitable distribution. But since the presidency of Miguel Alemán (1946–52), emphasis has been on creating centers of abundant wealth and hoping that some of this wealth would rub off on the population. The result, of course, has been the underlying motive of the student rebellion of 1968, repudiation of a situation in which 10 percent of the privileged families control 50 percent of the national income.[50] Valadés shares the spirit of this judgment.[51]

What impact has the Mexican presidency had on the myth or reality of governmental federalism? Like his successors, Echeverría extended federal control at the expense of local initiative and autonomy. He even allowed the Sonora legislature to modify the state constitution in 24 hours, thereby reducing the governor's required age to 30 to allow the election of Biebrich who was imposed from Mexico City with the president's acquiescence.[52] This, as we have seen, Echeverría was later to regret because of the implications the Biebrich scandal had for the presidential succession. It further dramatizes what is perhaps the governmental Achilles heel of the Mexican system, that is, the flaunting of federal prerogatives at the expense of local autonomy where the critical social problems await solution. Evidence during recent years shows a high incidence of popular, anomic, and violent uprisings and protests against corrupt local governments (especially as reported by *Excelsior* during 1975–76).

Can major errors in long-range policy conduct be attributed directly to Echeverría? To give one example, Cosío Villegas argues that Echeverría was at fault in urging agrarian reform as a way to greater industrial prosperity, rather than having championed the betterment of the rural ejidatarios as an end in itself.[53] He blames Echeverría for acquiescing in a scheme to dispossess hundreds of peasant ejidatarios in Nayarit to permit building of a vacation center for military personnel and a facility for tourists.[54] Here, development was sought at the expense of those who needed it most.

Is the authoritarianism of the Mexican president to be explained principally in terms of a combination of historical thrust and personal psychic qualities? Translating from Cosío's conclusion, the demand by presidents like Díaz Ordaz and Echeverría for popular veneration owes to psychic and historical factors to be sure, but "it is due also to our political system, whose principal characteristic is a president invested with unlimited faculties and resources. This has converted him fatally into the Great Dispenser of Goods and Favors, even of miracles."[55] Valadés would seem to concur. Note Cosío's use of the qualifier "fatally." This resembles the Tlatoani analogy presented in Chapter 1.

What are the implications of the foregoing discussion of the Echeverría presidency for the conventional wisdom, that is, the established literature on Mexican politics by U.S. scholars? Space will not permit a full review of that literature here, but surely one of the best known of the North American writers in this regard is L. V. Padgett. The second edition of his widely used text says, "The president is a semidivine father figure to the people, inherently good in caring for his children. He is never directly challenged, as for example in the press, because that would shake the very basis of secular government."[56] Clearly, Padgett's vision is utopian in light of the evidence presented earlier in this study. Yet it is correct to say that the president may *try* to appear to be what Padgett says he is.

Each sexenio is prefaced with an extensive campaign in which the president-to-be tours every state in the country and uses surrogates to reach out to the villages (we noted earlier how this technique may appear as an empty ritual to other Latin Americans). The conventional wisdom is that the president-to-be can probe out public sentiment on key issues during his campaign tours and better equip himself to reflect his nation's desires in the policy-formation process he will later direct. True, as Valadés says, the president could do so if he wanted to. Moreover, Cosío pointed to Echeverría's use of the watchword "autocrítica" as a pretense of turning self-criticism into a public function; but as Cosío also noted, Echeverría's use of the term was inappropriate because the people were never really invited to criticize anything of substance.[57] Thus, the conventional wisdom about testing public sentiment via a grass-roots campaign (especially when no real opposition is able to express itself) needs to be rethought.

Another piece of conventional wisdom is that the president must take an intermediate position between the official party's left and right wings and that he can do so because there is a "core consensus of Revolutionary values" throughout all of the PRI.[58] This is probably still sound, albeit tenuous. To be sure, Echeverría clashed frequently with the powerful right-wing Monterrey Group in the area of national security policy and over the question of the government's expanding role in the economy. The Marxist review *Punto Crítico* referred to the Monterrey Group as the principal source of Mexican fascism and cited the conflicts that had grown during the Echeverría sexenio between the group's powerful families and the federal government over monopolistic control of the steel industry.[59] But the same source also pointed out the impressive amounts of state capital that had been loaned on favorable terms to the Monterrey Group as an appeasement device and reaffirmed that for the group's political influence to be effective it was imperative that it operate within the PRI, not as in 1940 when certain members of the group supported the opposition candidate Almazán against the PRI's official candidate Avila Camacho.[60] So it appears that barring a complete rupture between the Monterrey Group and the PRI the group will remain a somewhat disaffected right wing but well within the PRI's penumbra. Selection of treasury secretary López Portillo to succeed to the presidency in 1976 may have done something to appease the PRI's political right. This would support the conventional wisdom's claim that there is a core value consensus of sorts within the PRI. But it is questionable how far this applies to the disaffected left, for example, growing alienation against the PRI's labor magnate Fidel Velásquez led by Rafael Galván and others, similar alienation against the agrarian sector of the PRI led by Danzós Palomino and the Independent Peasant Confederation, plus the congeries of guerrilla insurgents totally outside the revolutionary coalition.

It has been argued that the institutionalization of the presidency is such as to put a premium on "moderation and mildness in the political style" of the president as he seeks to balance competing interests and pressures.[61] Echeverría's forcing his attorney general and others to resign following the San Cosme scandal, his repeated but unfulfilled promises to disclose the true origin of the Falcons, his conflicts with the Monterrey Group and with the students of the National University, his intervention in Sonora over the Biebrich affair (for which the president was partially responsible), and his subsequent takeover of *Excelsior* all suggest that Echeverría found moderation difficult, especially when he was challenged personally. The San Cosme affair was an especially bitter pill to take since even the establishment press of the capital city, normally loyal to the government in any dispute, criticized the PRI and laid photographic evidence at Echeverría's feet demanding that he solve the problem of official terrorism (which, of course, he could not do in any real sense without losing face). It may be that the selection of López Portillo again reflects the perceived need to bring into the presidency an actor more prone to the moderate style that has lent stability to the institution in the past. Presidents beginning with Miguel Alemán in 1946 had been able to moderate conflict before it broke into open disorder, a skill that was less characteristic of Díaz Ordaz and even less so of Echeverría.

Institutionally speaking, there is less need to modify the conventional wisdom. For instance, at the beginning of this study it was noted that much of the constitutionalism surrounding the presidency is mere formalism given the near-absolute decision-making power which has accrued to the president. That is because his formal duties are sufficiently flexible to allow for wide interpretation, hence the accretion of power. The president has a wide variety of ceremonial functions which he can use for symbolic purposes as he chooses. He is commander-in-chief of the armed forces (although in his final two years some of Echeverría's public admonitions suggested that his confidence in his own control over the military might have been weakened). Also, most legislation is initiated by the president, and the congress is little more than a rubber stamp (there is, of course, no effective opposition in the congress). Insofar as justice is concerned, the Mexican president has considerable power to influence decisions of the judiciary via appointment of judges and by initiating removal proceedings through the congress. The president has enormous financial powers over the states and localities via his control of grants-in-aid and because the central government has preempted most taxation prerogatives for itself. In the field of foreign affairs, it is the president alone who decides, although normally his foreign minister will be consulted. Resignation of the foreign minister following the international reaction to Mexico's 1975 anti-Zionist vote in the United Nations makes one question whether Echeverría had undertaken consultation or not. The same question may be raised with respect to the breaking of diplomatic relations with Chile in 1974, an abandonment of Mexico's traditional commitment (the Estrada Doctrine) to recognizing new governments de facto or de jure.

Probably the best way to summarize the importance, and complexity, of the president's power role is to depict him as the nerve center of a legion of demands by interest groups, regional political chieftains or caciques, the three sectors of his party and their subsidiary organizations, the alienated satellite parties and outgroups, and a number of foreign influences (principally North American). As a nerve center, then, the president must moderate conflict and dispense a maximum number of streams of satisfactions in the hope of balancing competing interests so that the revolutionary coalition will not fall apart. Compared to his predecessors, Echeverría may have had less nerve-center capability and the revolutionary coalition was, to be sure, threatened with atrophy during his regime. Yet, in all fairness to Echeverría, it may be that most any other president could have fallen victim to the same dilemmas. With population pressure far outrunning economic expansion, and with less escape-valve potential for desperate laborers north of the border, the pressures on the presidency are likely to grow. And one must underscore the fact that the constellation of alienated groups beyond the penumbra of the PRI is growing because the party is unable to spread its largesse more effectively due to increased demands. Defection is inevitable. This will put López Portillo's nerve-center skills severely to the test during the sexenio 1976–82.

The future of the Mexican presidency may depend upon resolution of a key dilemma or paradox. This has been put well by Padgett; that is, the incumbent is supposed to accept responsibility for all that occurs within the system even though it is not humanly possible that he can oversee it all. Thus Echeverría was sullied by the Biebrich scandal in Sonora (the president had helped to facilitate placing of a governor who later fell into disgrace and had to be removed via intervention). His left-leaning toward Salvador Allende of Chile made Echeverría a target of attack by the Monterrey Group for his having contributed to an atmosphere favorable to terrorism. The protesting students in March of 1975 saw the president as the personification of Mexican fascism and he accused them of the same thing. The list goes on ad infinitum. Padgett states the presidential paradox as follows:

> He is supposed to be a benevolent father. Whatever he does for the masses, he does for them personally—he endows them or gives them public structures, sanitation plants, schools, and roads. By the same token, if he fails to provide these things, he has failed in his vital fatherly role. *It is paternal government, but it is only legitimate if it is benevolent paternal government.* [62]

Obviously, with Mexico's socioeconomic sloth relative to her population pressure, and given competing intra-PRI demands for scarce resources, no president can avoid the wrath of the multitudes who are left unsatisfied. Some, like the poet-philosopher Oscar Monroy Rivera, will depict the president as one who must declare to the world what an exemplary place Mexico is, all the while enriching himself illicitly and hiding his crimes. [63]

But there is always one great unknown that lingers, emerging from the instillment of that benevolent presidential father image in the popular mind, a process that the most humble have learned to invoke as a part of their socialization. Elsewhere I have cited a case in point from a Mexican novel of the political opposition written by a federal deputy who once tried to help the poor of his region. Their struggle was for justice against the entrenched central party bureaucracy atop which the president of Mexico is seated. The novel shows the degree to which the mystique of an omnipotent, thaumaturgical, but benevolent president has been instilled into the minds of the humble masses, even those who had been victims of the president's callous neglect. Pedro Alvidres, a peasant farmer, was driven from his land in Chihuahua by oligarchs of the PRI. He had made the desperate illegal trek north of the border seeking work but fell into the hands of Mexican agents upon returning. His body was later found floating in the Río Grande. Pedro was superstitious, yet religious, and held faith in witchcraft medicines and in mysterious revelations of divine truth. But Pedro, a typical Mexican poor devil or móndrigo, believed in things even more absurd than those:

> He believed, for example, in honor, justice, in love, in labor; he believed, ultimately, in a series of utopias, he had that great faith of the miner. But his belief was a pathology in itself, he was dead serious in putting it forth, serious in respecting the law that was in force, in giving an open road to nature's vital forces; he had faith also, an immense faith, in the benevolent justice of the President of the Republic. [64]

The great unknown, then, is how long Mexicans are likely to legitimize the system through their blind faith in a supernatural father figure—how many groups will decide that they are living in misery unjustly, then organize outside the penumbra of the official party and rebel. Mexicans may not place their trust indefinitely in the benevolent justice of a president who distinguishes himself by gracing the international cocktail circuit, seemingly impervious to starvation and despair at home, and who then employs paramilitary squads and the army to silence those who bring him publicly to task. One day such a president may well find that he is seated atop the apex of nothing.

LÓPEZ PORTILLO: HIS PROBLEMS, COMMITMENTS, AND THE SEXENIO 1976–82

President López Portillo inherited severe problems from his predecessor which were the cumulative result of ineffective policy application, or no policy at all, over a period of several decades. You get different statistics depending upon whom you ask. José Luis Reyna quotes *Excelsior* in 1975 as a source of data on the quality of life in Mexico.[65] The journal *Proceso* (which emerged out of the takeover of *Excelsior* in 1976 and is published by *Excelsior's* former staff) issued its own bottom-line assessment as the Echeverría administration came to a close.[66]

Drawing on both of these sources it seems that the following challenges await López Portillo's skills as benevolent authoritarian. Somewhere near half of the economically active population is either unemployed or underemployed as of 1977, and that is by Mexican standards (which often means that if a man was quizzed by census-takers and said he worked three days the preceding week he would be counted as employed). Unemployment is even more severe in some rural areas and along the northern border. There is almost no more useful land that can be redistributed. People continue to migrate to the cities, making Mexico at least 65 percent urban and probably more, but economic growth in labor-intensive industries has not provided jobs. Of Mexico's estimated 65 million people, at least half are less than 15 years of age and perhaps 70 percent are under 25 years. This means that job acquisition and the hope of socioeconomic mobility become permanent enigmas. Worker flight north to the United States via illegal migration becomes more attractive. The size of the youth population has also created an educational crisis at most levels of training.

More than 30 million Mexicans are without medical attention, largely those who are unable to belong to the PRI's official unions and therefore get no benefits (even though the benefits are supposed to exist for everyone, and are free). *Proceso* estimated that only 10 percent of the Mexican population received sufficient nutrition for good health at the end of 1976. There is a housing deficit of 3 million dwellings. Illiteracy is thought to be 20 percent for the overall population but jumps to 40 percent in the countryside. "More than 70 percent of the economically active population receives less than 30 percent of the national income. Some 27 percent of the Mexican population receives between 15 and 20 percent of the total national income. And a tiny elite, which represents barely 3 percent of the population controls between 50 and 60 percent of the total national income."[67] This seems to confirm my earlier calculations based on Mexico's own census for 1970 which showed nearly 72 percent of the wage earners subsisting on less than $80 per month and .05 percent receiving a monthly income of more than $1,100.[68] Both figures compare meagerly with the annual per capita income in the United States which oscillates between $4,000 and $5,000. Mexico's annual per capita income is in the neighborhood of $600. Herein lies much of the magnetic attraction that produces illegal migration to the north, a highly complex problem with which López Portillo will have to deal.

José López Portillo is an educated man, the author of two novels, a good speaker, and was considered an effective secretary of finance and treasury, replacing Hugo Margáin who resigned in 1973. López Portillo warned the Mexican congress about the country's serious inflation in several memorable speeches during 1974 and expressed concern for the government's deficit. It is not clear whether he counseled Echeverría as to the peso devaluation of 1976, but López Portillo could hardly be blamed for the country's economic woes, having assumed office at mid-term. On September 22, 1975, the ancient (and popularly disliked) labor boss *(charro)* Fidel Velásquez personally endorsed the finance minister for the presidential nomination, and on that same day he was "unveiled." It appeared that the new president would owe traditional political debts to old members of the PRI's upper crust.

It had been the judgment of many observers that despite the equivocations of President Echeverría, some of which were intended to please conservative forces, he left office with the political right substantially alienated from the presidency. During his first year in office López Portillo seemed to be recapturing some of this lost support. However, other fears were expressed that the new sexenio might see the alienation of the left, especially progressive Church elements, students, and extraofficial trade unions. The economic crisis which López Portillo inherited made it necessary for him to seek support from among conservative businessmen, including those of the Monterrey Group. The president abandoned much of his predecessor's Third World rhetoric and outspoken criticism of the United States.

Visiting Washington early in 1977, López Portillo rubbed elbows with a number of conservative figures of U.S. politics and the press. He said he had not come to beg for aid nor to renegotiate Mexico's national debt, and he offered the good offices of Mexico should the United States decide to renew its diplomatic relations with Cuba.[69] He insisted publicly that the problems of Mexico's ailing economy cannot be solved by Mexico in a vacuum, including the dilemma of illegal migration, but must be done in a broader hemispheric context and with direct collaboration from the United States. President Carter told his Mexican colleague that this was the first time in 25 years that Mexican and U.S. presidents had been elected at nearly the same moment and that both could begin with a fresh start at mutual collaboration. López Portillo stated that Mexico did not aspire to become the Third World's leader, thus apparently breaking with the rhetoric of Echeverría. He advanced his "tripod theory" in describing his country's current situation, saying that Mexico had lost two of three supports on which equilibrium depended: It had lost control of price stability and of monetary stability. What remained strong, and would be the basis for Mexican recovery, was the final remaining support, Mexico's political stability.[70]

Domestically López Portillo sought to control inflation by holding down wage increases for organized labor to 10 percent during his first year, as opposed to the 45 percent they had received the final year of the Echeverría sexenio. He also encouraged private reinvestment in the Mexican economy via fiscal incentives and went to Monterrey to sign a major investment program involving state and private collaboration. Foreign investment was newly courted by the president and he sought to rectify some of the hard feelings created by Echeverría's last-hour land expropriations in Sonora by paying landowners compensation for a large part of the land that was given to peasants. Although most of the peasants have, for the moment, been allowed to keep the land Echeverría gave them, López Portillo warned that further *paracaidismo,* land occupation and invasion without legal writ, would not be tolerated by his government.

At the same time, the new president has expanded subsidies for basic food prices through the CONASUPO program. Perhaps a symbolic gesture to the left was the legalizing, formally, of Mexico's Communist party which had de facto been functioning anyway for a number of years using various names including its real one. There has been renewed warfare among right and left in Mexico. Several progressive priests have been killed under mysterious circumstances and the progressive bishop of Cuernavaca, Sergio Méndez Arceo, has been attacked publicly by right-wing elements. The insurgent 23rd of September Communist League is still active throughout Mexico with kidnappings, bank robberies, and attacks on police and military garrisons. Thus a polarization of far right and far left, which López Portillo sought to avoid, seemed to be developing during his first year. The president's campaign promises to end the drug and arms smuggling, and to curb the flight of Mexican nationals illegally into the United States, have yet to materialize.

Opponents of Mexico's single-party system still feel that therein lies the key to Mexico's inability to solve its national problems, that is, the absence of an effective and truly loyal opposition which can expose corruption and would have a vested interest in ending socioeconomic ills via concrete policy changes. Even Mexico's newly discovered oil and gas wealth would solve little if the proceeds were to be siphoned off by corrupt politicians and bureaucrats of the

PRI. López Portillo could use his vast personal powers to bring about such reforms if he wanted to, and as indeed he promised in his electoral campaign.

The issue of political corruption in and around the presidency was raised in the opening to this chapter. It is tempting to argue that corruption of political and economic life is an idiosyncracy of the Mexican people with which they are hopelessly and perennially plagued. But the Mexican historian Enrique Florescano denies that this can be correctly asserted about any people or nation, although to be sure one may characterize a given period in a nation's life as typically corrupt.[71] Throughout Mexican history the majority have lived and died without corruption. It is the current beneficiaries of the economic and political system who have made corruption into a social disease. According to Florescano, the great revolution of 1910–17 failed to root out all the socioeconomic bases for corruption that existed in the Porfirian regime against which the struggle was directed. But even then Mexico did not have the generalized corruption which weakens it today. According to Florescano the present level of corruption began during the presidency of Miguel Alemán (1946–52) and spread to many sectors of Mexican life including the universities and education generally. The president is in a strong position to leave his imprint on the nation and no president after Alemán until the end of the most recent sexenio was able to eradicate corruption, if he even tried.

Many industrial, commercial, and agricultural fortunes were made out of the nexus of entrepreneurs and politicians. That nexus was corruption. The Mexican labor movement was tainted as well because it had become a part of the official single-party system, labor control being an extension of political control. To a lesser extent, said Florescano, this spread to the agrarian sector of the PRI as well. The overall effect of this was to reinforce the corrupt and antidemocratic forms of the system. The legislative and judicial powers, subordinated to the presidency, along with the press, lost all of the autonomy that they may have enjoyed in varying degrees between the great revolution and the regime of President Alemán. The center of the pyramid was corrupt and spread this into the states and localities. The destruction of local economies and corruption of the municipalities is one factor in the displacement of Mexicans out of the countryside and into the slums of the larger cities. The center of the pyramid became the model for the rest of the nation, and corruption was its norm.

Professor Florescano still feels that the majority of Mexicans would prefer not to tolerate or practice corruption if the system allowed them to make a living without it. He sees the existing roots of corruption in two basic factors: the first is the lack of truly democratic politics (where loyal political oppositions can act to expose corruption and have a motive to do so without fear of reprisal); the second is the Mexican economic system which is based upon the exploitation of the majority of the population for the benefit of a minority. If only a few corrupt politicians are castigated it will be just a facade; but if the housecleaning is generalized, the new regime could be on the way to permanent reform.[72] Only president López Portillo can initiate it; he alone can move the pyramid toward change, barring a revolutionary explosion from within or unforeseen pressures from outside Mexico—a possibility that is not totally unreal at the moment of this writing.

NOTES

1. Ignacio González Gollaz, "La posibilidad de JLP," VISION, June 1, 1976, p. 48.
2. Gobernación, July 1976.
3. José Luis Reyna, "Redefining the Authoritarian Regime," in *Authoritarianism in Mexico,* ed. José Luis Reyna and Richard S. Weinert (Philadelphia: Institute for the Study of Human Issues, 1977), p. 160.
4. See Marvin Alisky's *Sicartsa: The Mexican Government's New Complex to Make the Steel Industry Self Sufficient* (El Paso: University of Texas, Center for Latin American Studies, 1975).
5. Frank Brandenburg, *The Making of Modern Mexico* (Englewood Cliffs, N.J.: Prentice-Hall, 1964), p. 141.
6. See Evelyn P. Stevens, *Protest and Response in Mexico* (Cambridge, Mass.: MIT Press, 1974), p. 126.
7. It was widely believed following the Tlatelolco disaster that a clandestine book without author called *El móndrigo* (Mexico: Editorial Alba Roja, 1968) was secretly commissioned by President Díaz Ordaz in order to shed the blame on other members of his entourage including Luis Echeverría. This book alleges that the U.S. CIA was behind much of the student protest trying to sabotage the Olympic Games and divert them to Detroit (see p. 47).
8. *Proceso,* November 1, 1976, p. 7.
9. From Daniel Cosío Villegas, *El estilo personal de governar* (Mexico: Joaquín Mortiz, 1974).
10. The journal *Por Que?* and the National Action party's bulletin *La Batalla* carried complete photos and testimony concerning official support for *Los Halcones.* The PAN even transcribed a tape it made of police radio communications broadcast in support of the Falcons. From first-hand testimony the journalist Gerardo Medina Valdés described how the Falcons tried to rescue and/or silence some of their wounded comrades so that there would be no evidence that they even existed. This is the picture he paints of paramilitary group action in defense of Mexican democracy:

> At six thirty in the afternoon machinegun bursts and pistol fire announce the arrival of those who were sent to rescue the wounded Falcons [from inside Rubén Leñero Hospital]. They use no prudence. Two nurses are clubbed, doctors are roughed up. Lic. Piña and another inspector from the District Attorney's office are taking names of wounded persons, writing them on a blackboard. They cannot disguise their astonishment over the brutality being unleashed by the armed hoods who have violently occupied the hospital. The Falcons go from room to room looking under sheets at men and women, jeering at them after they have found all of their own members. They even jerk transfusion tubes from the arms of innocent patients, laughing profusely and grotesquely before the horrified stares of the helpless medical personnel who can do nothing.

From his limited-edition work, circulated clandestinely, *Operación 10 de junio* (Mexico: Ediciones Universo, 1972), p. 98.
11. *Excelsior,* April 2, 1976.
12. Ibid.

13. Vision, May 1, 1976, p. 14.

14. Arizona *Daily Star,* May 15, 1977. See also Thomas Weaver and Theodore Downing, *Mexican Migration* (Tucson: University of Arizona Press, 1976), passim.

15. See Kenneth F. Johnson, *Guerrilla Politics in Argentina* (London: Institute for the Study of Conflict, 1975).

16. New York *Times* editorial July 13, 1976. See also an article in the Washington *Post* by Terri Shaw on July 14, 1976, which credits the takeover of *Excelsior* to both Echeverría and his former secretary, Fausto Zapata, who was in the process of building a media empire for Echeverría to use in perpetuating his rule once out of office. Significantly, the chief of *Excelsior*'s Washington bureau, Armando Vargas, stated that the future president López Portillo was a distant blood relative of *Excelsior*'s ousted director Julio Scherer García and that the president-elect would most likely turn out to be another Cárdenas in the sense of undoing some of his predecessor's deeds. Thus, there was some hope that the new sexenio (1976–82) would see a renewed freedom of the press in Mexico, but this would depend almost entirely on the character of López Portillo as political actor. Should he prove to be unable to accept public criticism as was Echeverría, there would be little likelihood of change. An additional footnote on the takeover of *Excelsior* is that Echeverría prevented news coverage of this action in Mexico. By and large, Mexicans had to learn of it from the outside. According to Armando Vargas's testimony communicated to this writer, Echeverría even threatened Julio Scherer García with the charge of treason if he accepted an invitation to speak in New York about the *Excelsior* affair and the latter is said to have declined for fear of his own safety. One of the more bitter ironies is that in 1971 at the beginning of his sexenio (and two days before the June 10 San Cosme massacre of protesting students) the president addressed the press corps on "The Day of Press Freedom" and declared, "When governments assume that the state is infallible they lay the basis for dictatorship" (*Excelsior,* June 8, 1971).

17. "Los ritos electorales," *La Opinión* (Buenos Aires), July 4, 1976.

18. Ibid.

19. *Proceso,* November 1, 1976, p. 11.

20. Ibid., p. 9.

21. Daniel Cosío Villegas, *La sucesión presidencial* (Mexico: Cuadernos de Joaquín Mortiz, 1975), p. 144. See also Philip Agee, *Inside the Company: CIA Diary* (London: Penguin Books, 1975), p. 509.

22. Cosío Villegas, *El estilo personal de gobernar,* op. cit., p. 13.

23. Cosío Villegas, *La sucesión,* op. cit., pp. 144–45.

24. Ibid., p. 18.

25. Ibid., p. 145. It bears repeating the belief in some Mexican sectors, cited earlier, that López Portillo might turn out to be another Cárdenas and undo much of the legacy of his predecessor.

26. One of many examples of formally published affirmations that Moya Palencia would succeed Echeverría is found in Gastón Rivanuva R. (pseudonym), *El PRI: El gran mito mexicano* (Mexico: Editorial Tradición, 1974), p. 79. There is always the possibility that this very publication was a trial balloon sponsored by the government to test reaction to Moya Palencia and to gauge reaction to a number of regime abuses cited therein. Part of the psychology of the Mexican presidency, as told to this writer by informants well located in the presidential secretariat, is to use pseudonyms under which deliberately disparaging commentaries are published about the regime so as to create the facade of revelations of which the government is not afraid and which it can correct. A pseudonym can always be discredited, however. Not so *Excelsior* where editorial responsibility was clearly fixed.

27. Daniel Cosío Villegas, *La sucesión: desenlace y perspectivas* (Mexico: Cuadernos de Joaquín Mortiz, 1975), passim.

28. Ibid., p. 94 and p. 103.

29. *La Batalla*, May 1975.

30. *El Imparcial* (Sonora), October 26, 1975.

31. Based upon this writer's interviews with colleagues from Sonora during 1976 and also on the account given in *Onda* (Sinaloa), November 12, 1975. The account by *Onda* also involves governor Biebrich and Moya Palencia in the international narcotics traffic.

32. Document in this writer's possession (*Consignación*, Hermosillo, Sonora, January 20, 1976). This is a legal indictment prepared by the Sonora government's attorney general (Procuraduría General de Justicia del Estado de Sonora).

33. *Proceso*, July 18, 1977, pp. 24–25. The writers in question figured prominently in Chapter 1 of this book. Octavio Paz resigned as ambassador to India in 1968 in protest against Díaz Ordaz and the Tlatelolco tragedy. Carlos Fuentes resigned as ambassador to France in 1977 to repudiate Díaz Ordaz's appointment as Mexico's new ambassador to Spain. Carlos Fuentes, it is known, had made his peace with Echeverría and was even on record as having defended the latter's involvement in the Tlatelolco affair, trying to heap blame exclusively on Díaz Ordaz. Most observers feel that Fuentes was somewhat less than honest with himself and with his intellectual followers in adopting this position.

34. *Proceso*, August 8, 1977, pp. 14–17.

35. *Proceso*, August 1, 1977, pp. 6–7.

36. *Excelsior*, March 15, 1975. See especially testimony on page 12-A. Considering that Echeverría came to power with the image of the new and younger generation it is strange that some of his worst problems were with students. Echeverría had served briefly as a law professor at UNAM in 1947. When he was being promoted through the tapado ritual and groomed for the presidency the Young Revolutionary Economists of Mexico (a subgroup of the PRI's popular sector or CNOP) produced a brochure extolling Echeverría's dedication to youth called *Ideario político y social* (Mexico, 1969 [mimeograph]). This was the early image Echeverría gave to the outside world, that is, the "new generation in a country where 60 percent of the population is under 20 years of age" (from Jean-Claude Buhrer's article reproduced from *Le Monde Diplomatique* (Paris) by *Excelsior* on September 17, 1972.

37. *Excelsior*, March 15, 1975.

38. As quoted in Kenneth F. Johnson, *Mexican Democracy: A Critical View* (Boston: Allyn & Bacon, 1972), p. 164.

39. See José C. Valadés, *El presidente de México en 1970* (Mexico: Editores Mexicanos Unidos, 1970), pp. 51–52.

40. Ibid., p. 55.

41. Ibid., p. 74.

42. Ibid., pp. 82–83.

43. Ibid., pp. 100–02.

44. Ibid., p. 125.

45. Ibid., p. 148.

46. In the 1976 elections the PRI broke almost a half-century of tradition. It allowed Jorge Cruickshank, leader of the Popular Socialist party (PPS) to win a senate seat from Oaxaca state. Reportedly, this was to compensate for the fact that a PPS candidate for the governorship of Nayarit had been the victim of official fraud the previous year and Cruickshank, as leader of his party (which traditionally endorsed the PRI's presidential candidate), mediated the dispute which could have grown to public proportions that would have seriously embarrassed the PRI (according to an account in the St. Louis *Post-Dispatch*, July 18, 1976). The results of the 1976 election gave to the PRI 194 seats in the chamber of deputies, 19 to the PAN, 9 to the PARM, and 8 to the PPS, thus assuring the PRI's hegemony once again. According to this writer's testimony the PAN and the PPS would undoubtedly have won more seats had it not been for widespread electoral fraud.

47. Valadés, op. cit., p. 150.

48. According to a letter written to this author from Raúl González Schmal, one-time provisional president of the PAN and a high-ranking member of his party's hierarchy, the PAN suffered a severe internal crisis during 1976–76 and ultimately decided to abstain. This is discussed in Chapter 5.

49. Stevens, op. cit., p. 259.

50. Cosío Villegas, *El estilo personal,* op. cit., pp. 49–50.

51. In all fairness to Echeverría, one must cite as examples of attempts during his regime to deal with poverty and economic stagnation such ventures as SICARTSA (state sponsored steel production) and INFONAVIT (public housing for workers). Their impact remains to be seen.

52. Cosío Villegas, *El estilo personal,* op. cit., p. 57.

53. Ibid., p. 58.

54. Ibid., pp. 60–62.

55. Ibid., p. 128.

56. See L. V. Padgett, *The Mexican Political System* (Boston: Houghton Mifflin, 1976), p. 187.

57. Cosío Villegas, *El estilo personal,* op. cit., pp. 112–14.

58. Padgett, op. cit., p. 196.

59. *Punto Crítico,* July 1976, p. 18.

60. Ibid.

61. Padgett, op. cit., p. 197.

62. Ibid., p. 214 (emphasis added).

63. Oscar Monroy Rivera, *El señor presidente de Enanonia* (Mexico: Costa-Amic, 1973), p. 43.

64. Carlos Chavira Becerra, *La otra cara de Mexico* as cited in Johnson, *Mexican Democracy, A Critical View* op. cit., p. 96. To a certain extent the accretion of power in the U.S. presidency as revealed by the Watergate and intelligence investigations tells the story of the enormous centralization of power in the Mexican presidency; but in Mexico the press and congress are helpless.

65. Reyna and Weinert, op. cit., p. 160.

66. *Proceso,* November 6, 1976, p. 11.

67. Ibid.

68. See Kenneth F. and María Mercedes Johnson, "Human Sacrifice in Mexico: The Modern Aztec Style of Development versus Despair," *Intellect,* March 1975, p. 363.

69. *Proceso,* February 19, 1977, pp. 20–22.

70. Ibid., p. 22.

71. *Proceso,* August 1, 1977, pp. 14–15.

72. Ibid.

Four

Single-Party Democracy and the Rejuvenative Psychology of Control

HOW ESOTERIC DEMOCRACY WORKS

From mid-century, and looking beyond the 1970s, we can entertain an oft-heralded platitude that Mexico has experienced Latin America's first and most lasting revolution (the revolutions of Bolivia from 1952 to 1964 and Castro's Cuba are also frequently cited). There is no doubt that Mexico *had* a revolution, one with a capital R. It killed millions, threw out (temporarily) oligarchs both foreign and domestic, disestablished the Church politically, spawned within society a permanent fear of anticlerical kulturkampf, and eventually removed the military from politics. These accomplishments (although all of them have been substantially eroded away with time) must qualify as profoundly basic changes that can be considered genuinely revolutionary. The Mexican revolution (1910–17) produced a constitution (1917) that is the nation's governing document to this day. Notice that I say document, not institution. The governing institution came later, approximately 1929, and after several name changes it entered the decade of the 1970s as the PRI. Most of the substance of Mexico's political life has to do with the PRI, its adherents and opponents, its traumatic origins and underpinnings, its joys and tragedies, its treacherous internal politics that may lead it toward atrophy and which could even menace the existence of Mexico (as we now know it) during the second half of the twentieth century.

By the decade of the 1970s the PRI had ceased to be a distinct political party that could be treated analytically as a homogeneous ideological group. It was more accurate to call PRI an organized dominant class, having at its apex an official family or coterie of privileged elites. At its base the PRI claimed some 10 million members and many more sympathizers and fair-weather friends. Party stalwarts fanned out their influence, patronage, and coercion via a complicated network of organizational linkages which can be called the formal structure of esoteric democracy in Mexico. Immediately beneath the president in the political hierarchy was the National Executive Committee known as CEN (Comité Ejecutivo Nacional).

I have embraced the terms "organized dominant class" to characterize the PRI. Yet to view it as a single monolith glosses over a legion of organisms, structures, arenas, and even certain defiantly independent participant movements that cluster, often precariously, under the ever-expanding revolutionary aegis. That the PRI has been able to command as many loyalties for over half a century is a remarkable accomplishment in itself. It is possible for some workers and peasants to move up (and down) the socioeconomic hierarchy via participation in the PRI. If one stays in good graces with his benefactors he may greatly improve his material circumstances. But the competition for scarce resources during the 1960s and 1970s has stunted the PRI's ability to distribute largesse and to confer upward mobility.

Most Latin American nations offer certain avenues of succor and reward, but what has been strikingly unique about Mexico is the breadth of coverage and the popular availability of such participatory incentives. The PRI has created a "trickle up and trickle down" system whose benefits, in years past, have been shared on a remarkably wide basis (relative to most Latin American political systems). Whether Mexico's political system can generate sufficient quantities of such material rewards to forestall a repetition of the violent protests of 1968 and 1971 and the terrorism of the late 1970s is yet another question.

Since 1946 when the old PRM of Lázaro Cárdenas was renamed PRI there has been a continuing domination of the party by the presidency of the republic. I detailed the machinations of presidential power in Chapter 3. However, in formal terms the National Assembly is the most authoritative collective organ of the party. Its primary function is the selection of candidates for national president. The National Assembly is charged with creating rules for membership and party conduct and has a lesser function of ratifying occasional policy stands that the party wishes to express outside of the congress.

Also, the National Assembly ratifies the party president who presides over the CEN. A second national organ of the PRI is its National Council or Grand Commission. This body is intended to represent the party organizations of the 29 states and gives representation to special delegates selected from each of PRI's basic membership sectors—labor, agrarian, and popular. The National Council differs from the National Assembly in that it represents regional and functional groups while the latter is meant to represent the people, albeit on a state-by-state basis. Finally, there is the PRI's National Executive Committee which, along with the National Council, is expected to perform a sort of watchdog function on an interim basis between meetings of the National Assembly. The CEN exercises influence in state party affairs via the National Council and it is this nexus that often gives the PRI the appearance of a tightly knit monolith.

The CEN is clearly the most powerful of the three national organs of the PRI and is instrumental in the overall party control exercised by the president of the republic. The CEN convokes meetings of the National Assembly and controls the admission of delegates to such meetings. Great power comes from the following CEN prerogatives: party discipline on a personal and group basis; special investigations; control over state and municipal party-nominating conventions; power to intervene in the affairs of state and municipal party organizations, including the power to remove members of these organizations (the power to remove elected state and local officials belongs formally to the president of the republic); and responsibility for propaganda and recruitment to expand PRI ranks and socialize the people politically into PRI participation. In the above-mentioned list of powers, the control over the municipal party organizations became critical in 1965 when CEN president Carlos A. Madrazo campaigned to create local party primaries in which the choice of party delegates and candidates for public office would be democratized and not dictated from above as had been traditional. Madrazo, in effect, sought to weaken the powerful CEN over which he presided. He was fired for this by President Díaz Ordaz late in 1965.

The CEN president calls meetings of that body along with those of the National Council and is the presiding officer in each case. He controls the CEN budget (which is known to be considerable) and names, with approval of the National Assembly, a general secretary for the party. The general secretary has control over important channels of information and his nomination is an important patronage device for the president of the CEN. There are seven members of the CEN: president, general secretary, and secretaries for agrarian affairs, labor, popular action, political action representing the national senate, and political action representing the national Chamber of Deputies. Key posts in the CEN are those of labor, agrarian affairs, and popular action which usually are held respectively by top leaders of the PRI's labor sector (CTM), its agrarian sector (CNC, National Confederation of Farmers), and the popular sector (CNOP, National Confederation of Popular Organizations). Whereas the primary function of the National Assembly (perhaps in a ritual sense) is the representation of the people, and that of the National Council is representation of local and regional party organizations, the primary function of the CEN is representation of the PRI's functional sectors (discussed later) and the PRI's congressional delegation. Since the CEN virtually controls the National Council, its powers over the grass roots are enhanced significantly. Clearly, the CEN stands at the apex of Mexican *priista* power and pays homage only to the presidency of the republic itself.

Central to the power of the CEN is its control over finances which are destined for informational (propaganda) and educational functions and which may be used to promote individual candidacies of PRI leaders in the various states and localities. It is said that CEN funds come largely from dues-paying members of the rank and file; but informed sources have told this writer that generous subventions come from the federal government. Withholding of these monies prefaced the downfall of CEN president Carlos A. Madrazo's campaign for democratization of local elections. This had the side effect of forcing the CEN president to rely more heavily upon state and local membership contributions which, in turn, was sure to lead to friction between the CEN and its regional affiliates.

With its own funds CEN is able to assist candidates for office in the poorer districts where local sources of financing may be severely limited. This often has a curious side effect that is unfavorable to opposition parties and is cleverly exploited by the PRI, namely, the opposition is often forced to choose a wealthy candidate who can afford to put up a campaign aginst the local priista who enjoys the support of foreign funds. This has produced an especially anomalous position for the opposition left whose candidates are frequently taunted as rich Marxists. Skillfully, thus, the PRI often forces its opposition into the image of a privileged elite while the PRI masquerades as a movement of the people. The financial prerogatives of the CEN are of critical importance in this process. But the basic fact remains that the PRI and the government are one and the same. No other political party in Mexico enjoys such de facto financial support. PRI functionaries, called aviadores, are paid as phantom bureaucrats out of public funds but who, in fact, work for the official party.

Surrounding the party structure discussed above are the three broad membership sectors of the PRI: labor, agrarian, and popular. The labor sector is integrated around the giant CTM, itself divided into regional and local components. The CTM may be considered a functional group specializing in organizing and promoting the cause of labor. Frequently, labor leaders hold at the same time a party office and elective public office. Such an arrangement makes possible attractive opportunities for duplication of reward and serves the cause of intraparty discipline, especially at the state and local levels. The CTM has a long tradition of involvement at all levels of Mexican politics. Labor disputes have recurred and renegade groups have splintered away, but the CTM continues to be the most powerful voice of organized labor in Mexico today and, as such, is a major bulwark of the PRI. Labor magnate Fidel Velásquez has ruled the CTM for much of postrevolutionary Mexican history.

The agrarian sector is shaped around the CNC. Organizationally, the CNC is easily as complex as the labor sector with its grassroots support originating in a myriad of peasant and rural labor leagues that are frequently integrated with the state collective (ejido) farm program. The CNC is charged with mobilization of rural support for the PRI and represents itself as a defender of the interests of rural folk vis-a-vis the government and large private landholders. That it has been unsuccessful in the last-mentioned role is evidenced by the rise of anomic protest movements of rural farmers and peasants against governmental and private land-tenure patterns. Nevertheless, the CNC has made many Mexican peasants into something that they had never been historically, that is, a political force to be reckoned with.

Not unexpectedly, splinter movements have broken with the mother body. Even within the CNC, conflict has at times been severe. Witness the slaughter of some 40 copra workers near Acapulco in 1967 as a result of a conflict involving not only the agrarian sector but labor and members of the national congress as well. Formally at least the CNC is expected to represent its constituents before such organs of government as the Ejido Bank (intended to finance the agricultural development of the state farms) and the Department of Agrarian Affairs and Colonization (DAAC). Padgett has written extensively on the capacity of the Mexican peasants, the state farm leagues, and groups of farmers to make themselves felt within the agrarian sector of the PRI[1] and of the corruption in local agrarian politics that frequently causes unrest about the countryside.

In the late 1950s the UGOCM (General Union of Mexican Workers and Peasants) under the leadership of Jacinto López carried out a number of spectacular protests against the official agrarian sector, invading the lands of the Cananea Cattle Company in Sonora and carrying out land invasions (paracaidismo) in other parts of northwest Mexico. Once again in the 1960s and before his death in 1971, Jacinto López attacked the Cananea landholders and achieved some distribution of land for his extraofficial rebellious peasants. López spent time in a Sonora prison for his challenge to officialdom. Following the death of Jacinto López the UGOCM split into rival factions, some of whom merged with the CCI or Independent Peasant Confederation that had been created in 1963. There have been two rival CCIs in recent years, the most radical of which is led by Ramón Danzós Palomino who ran for the presidency of Mexico in 1964 even though his party (FEP, People's Electoral Front) was denied official registry. Danzós has been a fiery and charismatic figure, in and but of jail, and has considerable rural following in Puebla to the south of Mexico City. Marches and demonstrations by his peasant followers have frequently been seen as a threat to the regime. It would seem that there is more articulate disaffection toward the official CNC than toward the CTM of the labor sector, a theme to which we shall return.

The final and perhaps most amorphous sector of the PRI is the popular sector whose principle integrating device is the CNOP. Whereas in the cases of the labor and agrarian sectors there is a legally prescribed relationship and control between the national government and those sectoral organizations, the CNOP has been allowed to develop with relative independence since the group was founded in 1943. (PRI's former military sector was abolished in 1944 and an effort was made to blend its membership with the newly created CNOP.) Nearly all Mexican communities have a municipal CNOP affiliate that participates in a statewide league and ultimately with a national organization. Like the labor and agrarian sectors, CNOP is represented on the PRI's CEN via the secretary for popular action. Also attached to CNOP are organizations of small private farmers, small businessmen, professional and social organizations, skilled workers (not usually affiliated with CTM or its components), teachers, and public service employees. The merger of such diverse groupings gives CNOP its heterogeneous character. This umbrella experiment has worked well and relatively few splinter movements have occurred to seriously challenge CNOP leadership and hegemony.

Indeed, in recent decades, CNOP has tended to grow in power and prestige while the labor and agrarian sectors were experiencing discord. CNOP claims the federal bureaucrats' union, FSTSE (Federation of Syndicates of Workers in the Service of the State), and is believed to command the allegiance of most of Mexico's organized teachers and professors. Lacking a specific functional orientation that is directly rooted in a policy area (for example, such as labor or agrarian affairs), the CNOP is first and foremost a political movement and as such is one of the principal support-mobilizing arms of the PRI. CNOP banners are conspicuously displayed at all offcial party celebrations, often in greater abundance than those of other sectors. Some observers of Mexican officialdom comment that CNOP holds the potential for becoming a separate political party were it not so closely wed to PRI and therefore subservient to it.

Two cardinal facts distinguish the CNOP from the other nucleus groups. First, because unlike the labor and agrarian sectors, membership in the CNOP or its subdivisions is not controlled by federal law, its members must be continually courted and cajoled into allegiance. This gives a premium to the political skills of the CNOP leadership and creates pressures for efficiency and effectiveness that often are missing in the other sectors. Second, because of the relatively high politicization of the CNOP (via its key role in the CEN) it has become a recruiting ground for high public office at the ministerial and congressional levels. Of all three sectors, CNOP probably has the greatest access to the top levels of planning and decision making in the federal government.

All three PRI sectors operate through an informal system of camarillas or political cliques. This is central to understanding the creation, maintenance, and transfer of power within the various sectors of Mexico's PRI. As seen above, there is a formal power structure in terms of those who have the ability to allocate values, influence events, and bring to bear a near monopoly of coercive pressure upon those who *appear* to be violating formal dicta for political behavior. The formal structure operates, or breaks down, according to the functioning of the political cliques that lie at the heart of Mexico's esoteric democracy. In Mexico the informal structures are likely to take priority over legal ones. Throughout the development of the contemporary Mexican political system, the creation of pressure groups of one sort or another has been crucial to the exercise of power. Whether we refer to them in English as cliques or brotherhoods is unimportant if it is understood that we refer to tightly knit nuclei of loyalty and influence, usually founded about the power of a given individual whose ability to control behavior and allocate rewards makes him the catalyst which gives the group a singularity of purpose and an informal loyalty web that could be called a latent structure.

The beginnings of Mexico's recent political life may be traced to the gigantic supercamarilla that formed around first the powerful figure of Plutarco Elías Calles and second his intended protege Lázaro Cárdenas del Río. From his villa in Cuernavaca, Calles controlled the destinies of Mexican politics for over ten years, both from within and from outside the presidency. This he accomplished by means of a well-heeled brotherhood of patronage and influence. Violent coercion was always a useful tool of recourse. In the shadow of the relatively uncultured but charismatic personality of General Calles a series of lesser, but potentially great, personalities was nurtured: Emilio Portes Gil, Abelardo Rodríguez, Pascual Ortiz Rubio, and Lázaro Cárdenas del Río —all became presidents of Mexico, and all were from the original clique of Plutarco Elías Calles.

The camarilla has been the basis for political life within the PRI ever since the Calles era of the 1920s. Politics, the struggle for power, has been between camarillas. The democracy that the PRI afforded has been controlled democracy among the competing camarillas. The unanointed were to be outcasts, nonparticipants. In the long run that has become the problem: There were more outcasts than could fit within the PRI cliques. Many politically relevant Mexicans wanted in. Some despaired and became violent, as we have seen.

How do these political cliques operate? The camarilla is a political brotherhood. It is also a political family, having multiple linkages and interdependencies with other subgroups of its ilk. These groups form a circular system in the sense of their competitive interaction with the revolutionary coalition (PRI). But within themselves they have an additional circular aspect. There is an original boss who normally will be someone with a known reputation for political and economic power. Following him, immediately below, are collaborating members of the inner circle who are tied to the boss (*jefe* or cacique) for reasons of political godfathership or personal intimacy on a social or economic basis. Here, as in all political systems, the kinds of socioeconomic ties that form the bases of political power must be legion and practically unknowable.

Later the group splits into two circles of intimacy which may multiply. Each of the circles extends its sphere of influences via the location of key persons in places of responsibility among the syndicates, the professional associations, and within the ranks of formal party organs that belong to and depend upon the PRI. As spheres of influence extend, a broader subcircle of influence comes into being and is held together by the common fabric of desire, on the part of individual ideologues, to better their station in life via the rewards that come from support of the next echelon upward. Surrounding them is a penumbra of anomic and diverse groups which can hardly be called brotherhoods. They are the aspirant satellite groups which seek to become cliques; their membership is fluid as is the changing pattern of their ideologies.

BUILDING A CAMARILLA

Here, from the original edition of this book (plus embellishments) is an anecdote, or if you prefer, a simulation, of the road to power within the revolutionary coalition for one who is a relative unknown. This is a true story and I have omitted names for reasons that should be obvious to the reader. The case is one of a young Mexican who aspires to a career in his country's political life. Like many Mexicans he is basically supportive of the PRI although he is aware of many of its failings. The accoutrements of a political career seem attractive to our neophyte, especially money, power, public honors, and social deference. But the young man lacks family or primary group ties on which to base his rise to fame; he needs a formula. Here, then, is a likely sequence of events through which he might pass.[2]

1. He would join the PRI. This is indispensable.
2. He must participate in party affairs, beginning at the grass-roots level, and above all he must attach himself to the coattails of some prominent politician whose orbit of success is already firmly established. He will do this through intermediaries already having contact with the politician himself; such access has great symbolic value and is shared sparingly by those who possess it.
3. In making this attachment he will have joined a camarilla. This is a point of some considerable risk, for should the camarilla fail to grow in power and wealth our young aspirant will have to seek admission to another one and this could be both embarrassing and costly. The camarillas combat each other and the young man and his colleagues must become vehement loyalists to the camarilla and its leader if they are to confront their competition. The leader's cause becomes that of the group. There is a kind of internecine warfare among competing camarillas that often leads to acrimony, something the PRI seeks to cloak from public view.
4. Once a final commitment to a camarilla is made, the young political hopeful must direct himself to carrying out a legion of mundane and highly pedestrian tasks for his group and for the PRI at large, for example, arranging youth meetings, distributing propaganda, answering correspondence, all of which can be done in his spare time and without pay. Our political neophyte has yet to be permitted to live from his politics.
5. If our hypothetical candidate is intelligent, capable, and performs his tasks well, his immediate boss will most likely reward him with a better spot,

perhaps that of private secretary to a deputy who belongs to the same camarilla. This will be a full-time paid job in which the neophyte will learn how to resolve minor political problems and will undertake special missions about the republic in connection with electoral plans and propaganda. He will undoubtedly be handed the task of writing minor political speeches, and in general he will have become initiated into Mexican politics. He will learn the art of covering up the mistakes of his mentors, and doing so without outwardly using the term "mistake."

6. Having shown promise in this role for several years, the young politician (probably living on a salary of around $400 per month) will naturally aspire to greater position; that, after all, was why he entered the arena in the first place. At this point he must pass successfully the tortuous throes of a crucial series of ordeals; he must keep himself on ice cautiously and patiently; he must perform a range of trying but essential ritual functions varying from political breakfast to greeting party dignitaries, all the while molding an image favorable to his silent candidacy for greater fame and higher place. Playing this game skillfully results in his being elevated to the role of secretary for political action within the Youth Committee of the PRI for the Federal District. This is a test of his political sensitivity and an important one. Unfortunately, this position is only honorific, not remunerative, and he must arrange another salary to sustain himself. This, he finds, can be accomplished by means of a special sinecure which is little more than a fake salary (called *aviadora*) paid to our young politician for work he does *not do* in an office that he seldom or never visits. Often the office itself will not exist. This is not unusual, for among the ingroup of the PRI there are many persons who receive five or six phantom sinecures of this sort. In this way the PRI can subsidize its political figures with salaries from the public budget while leaving them maximum freedom to work full time for the party. This, incidentally, is how paramilitary enforcement squads (Los Halcones) are financed.

7. As secretary of political action in the Youth Committee our young man performs well and wins for his camarilla certain honors that qualify him for two more fake salaries and the promise of more to come. He now earns well over $1,000 per month, which is excellent in peso equivalents.

8. At this juncture the young politician has become somewhat seasoned and, feeling secure, he gradually begins to form his own camarilla. He enjoys having younger men look up to him with dreams of future reward. His power is limited but he has some of it nonetheless. He can, for example, recommend a young aspirant of his own camarilla for a special although minor post; he can convene special political meetings based upon his own new circle and can begin to attract a following by doing a legion of minor favors for friends and acquaintances. He is beginning to be successful in the game of politics. By this time he receives a salary of nearly $2,000 per month (thanks to his several sinecure paychecks) and has his own loyal constituency whose members obey

his every command. He even offers an occasional political breakfast, the sign that one has arrived. His supporters want him to rise, as the coattails effect of this will surely benefit them when the power and related largesse are distributed.

9. Our hypothetical politician still has not taken over as head of the larger camarilla which he joined originally at the grass roots. But he remains in the good graces of the man who continues as boss and thereby it is arranged that our politician is named alternate deputy for the PRI in the Federal District. This is a second-rank post as positions of federal power go, but it carries its privileges and credentials which enable one to jump from stone to stone in the upward spiral of trails and trials which constitute the quest for national power in the Republic of Mexico.

10. As an alternate deputy in the Federal District our aspirant welds a series of providential relationships in the upper circles of the federal government. He gains favor with the PRI's top echelon, the CEN, which in turn names him electoral delegate for the State of Guanajuato. He must travel there to represent CEN on the official team in the PRI's coming campaign for governor of that state. It becomes our man's personal charge to appoint special CEN representatives in the various electoral committees about Guanajuato for purposes of liaison with the national party organs. First and foremost in his portfolio, however, is the imperative that the PRI win in Guanajuato, preferably by legal means, but in the last analysis by any means at all. These he is free to invent. But public image and revolutionary symbolism must be preserved unsullied at all costs.

11. Here is where our politician's career is damaged by partial defeat and considerable public disgrace. PRI wins the elections in Guanajuato to be sure, but at the expense of being caught by a vocal opposition with an impressive cache of false ballots, an incident the opposition is able to inflate into proportions of national scandal. Certain organs of the national press carry the story in detail. Federal executive power is necessary to quiet the public storm via the promise of an investigation. Our political hero is blamed by the opposition press for the fraud and his own superiors chastise him for ineptitude. This is a setback and he will have to wait for an opportunity to overcome it.

12. As a result, not unexpectedly, of his failure in Guanajuato, our exemplary politician loses favor with his former boss (of the camarilla) and his political privileges and salaries remain frozen for a time. Nonetheless, he continues to work quietly, organizing a special student group inside the National University and in this endeavor he makes good use of his own small camarilla which is still together. He knows that the university will be a fertile breeding ground in which to reingratiate himself with his boss. Some accuse him of organizing *porros,* student goon squads that act in paramilitary fashion inside the university.

13. For a considerable time the name of our hypothetical politician remains forgotten in the spiderwebs. Then one day in the very bosom of the

university a serious conflict explodes, one which the government fears it will not be able to control. The PRI and the government are one and the same vis-a-vis a common helplessness of not knowing how to proceed. There are groups of rival porros at each other's throats. The government is already under a stigma for sending police into various universities. The president himself seeks a way to avoid another bloody university intervention. This case is worse yet because a university employees' union is involved.

14. It is then, during these moments of crisis, that our disguised personality becomes suddenly very optimistic and ventures to tell his boss: "I can control these students by way of my movement and the extreme loyalty they feel for me. But there is a price tag. The government and the PRI will have to name me as principal candidate for federal deputy in the next elections, and assign several of my followers to positions within the Youth Committee of the PRI." Here he is placing members of his camarilla as an insurance factor.

15. This offer is quietly accepted. With government backing our politician and his camarilla succeed in squashing the student effervescence that surely would have led to a university-government conflict. Out of such a test of strength no one could possibly win, but the PRI would be a sure loser. The conflict subsides and our man is named candidate for deputy along with new positions for his followers. His name has been cleared, the stains of the Guanajuato campaign are forgotten. He has achieved success, he is now invited to political breakfasts, and the press begins to laud him. (Its members form lines to receive their *embute,* a monthly gratuity paid to reporters in exchange for their efforts to create a favorable public image for a given person.) At the top level of the PRI our man is now being discussed for assignment to the CEN. He has made it from the unknown to a high place in the PRI. He has lived within the system, he has honored the sacred dictum, "Live not in error."

REJUVENATING "BURNED" CHARISMA: THE CASE OF ALFONSO MARTÍNEZ DOMÍNGUEZ

Here is an additional example of the rise and fall of political fortune and power in Mexico, one which can be identified by name. In point of fact, this is a case study of a Mexican "Watergate." Alfonso Martínez Domínguez was leader of the PRI Majority in the chamber of deputies from 1964 to 1967 during the regime of President Díaz Ordaz. He was known as an intimate member of Díaz Ordaz's camarilla (in a case such as this the name of the leader —Díaz Ordaz—is made into an "ism" in Spanish, *diazordacismo*). Later Martínez Domínguez served as president of the PRI's CEN during the preelectoral campaign of Luis Echeverría. The head of the CEN, as noted earlier, is considered by some to be the second most powerful position in Mexican politics. Martínez Domínguez did not achieve this easily. Indeed, he had been opposed by Fidel Velázquez, powerful leader of the CTM and one of Velázquez's rivals, Francisco Pérez Ríos of the electrical workers, had placed in nomination the name of Martínez Domínguez at the 1968 meeting of the PRI's National Assembly. All the infighting over this key spot had been done privately and the ritual of unanimous acceptance of the candidate for president of the CEN proceeded as usual. This was a case of dedazo, or imposition of a candidate by the president of the republic over the objections of others in his power hierarchy. Ironically, Martínez Domínguez would later be sacrificed or "burned" as a remnant of the Díaz Ordaz clique during the early years of the Echeverría administration. As of 1968, however, the PRI had unveiled a new strongman, a potential kingmaker of the future, provided he did not make any grave errors as in the anecdote on camarilla-building above.

It was unlikely that Martínez Domínguez would err. For many years he had cultivated his own camarilla from which the political roots of national power could spring. His antecedents tell much of the story of how a competent politician may gain ascendency within the revolutionary coalition. Martínez Domínguez was for years an obscure politician holding varying bureaucratic appointments at lower echelons in the government and in the PRI. Here it is important to repeat that government positions frequently are phantoms, aviaduras, and go to persons whose principal role is political and limited to the PRI, and who rarely are expected to perform in a bureaucratic role although they are ostensibly being paid to do so (a Latinized version of the Anglo-American sinecure). Martínez Domínguez first gained national attention as part of the political clique of Lic. Adolfo López Mateos who was a leader of the public bureaucrats' union FSTSE in the early 1950s. Following the inauguration of Adolfo Ruiz Cortínez as president of the republic in 1952, López Mateos was named secretary of labor and all the members of his clique including Martínez Domínguez were generously rewarded with government sinecures. When López Mateos became president of the republic in 1958 Alfonso Martínez Domínguez was accelerated abruptly to the prestigious position of secretary general of the CNOP, one of the most powerful mainstays of the PRI.

At this point it is correct to say that Alfonso Martínez Domínguez had graduated from membership in the clique of López Mateos and had formed one of his own. Once in command of the CNOP his chief dedication was the placing of his own people in key positions throughout the party and governmental structures. One of these appointments was Pedro Luis Bartilotti, a talented and aggressive right-hand man of Martínez Domínguez. With the support of the people he had placed in key positions, the political star of Martínez Domínguez continued to grow, first as a national deputy under the new regime of President Díaz Ordaz and shortly thereafter as floor leader of the PRI delegation in the Chamber of Deputies, a position considered to be equivalent to cabinet membership. From there Martínez Domínguez built an even greater base of power by promoting the loyal Pedro Luis Bartilotti to the rank of federal deputy (ostensibly via the electoral process but one in which nomination is tantamount to winning) and ultimately to coveted membership on the CEN.

The political trajectory of Alfonso Martínez Domínguez was calculated and progressively upward, conspicuously unsullied by the scars and smears of public scandal or malfeasance of duty. His story exemplifies one of the keys to personal political power in Mexico: He had cultivated a faithful coterie of friends who stuck by him through the recurring uncertainties of the political game in which positions and offers were bartered and exchanged like grabbag prizes. Martínez Domínguez had even been offered the secretariat of the party by Lauro Ortega in exchange for the latter's continuation as head of the CEN (or so this author was informed by usually reliable sources). But surrender to the then provisional president of the CEN would have severely restrained Martínez Domínguez from achieving future mobility, so he made the calculated risk of holding out for all or nothing within the National Assembly. This was a considerable gamble because Lauro Ortega, the principal challenger, enjoyed the powerful support of labor leader Fidel Velázquez. It was said that if Lauro Ortega had convened the special session of the National Assembly one year earlier he might have been able to command a sufficient majority to win the informal power struggle, but this was impossible for reasons of party discipline. By delaying the National Assembly, the Martínez Domínguez clique had time to consolidate its forces and recruit external support for their chief. When the informal power struggle had been resolved, staff members of the presidency of the republic began to leak out rumors of a great wave of popular support for Martínez Domínguez and that the CNOP leadership had gone to his side. This was a typical, and fruitful, machination of political power within the higher echelon of the revolutionary coalition.

Alfonso Martínez Domínguez assumed the reins of the PRI at a time when the entire revolutionary party structure was suffering from multiple ailments: the desertion of the intellectuals, the abandonment of the young, and the increasing alienation of patriotic egalitarian citizen groups who saw PRI as an exclusive, albeit gigantic, club that formed an avenue toward elite privilege. When the National Assembly met in 1968, PRI had two recent thorns in its side: the municipal victories of the opposition party PAN in Hermosillo (Sonora) and Merida (Yucatán), both of which dramatized the popular decline of confidence in the PRI as a mechanism for articulating demands for change. The PRI was still a party open to workers and peasants as Martínez Domínguez took command. The officially sponsored CTM and CNC were effectively organized to give the common masses a broad appearance of political belonging. Martínez Domínguez told the Assembly that the PRI would continue to oppose the privileged status of elites (despite the obvious fact that he himself belonged to one). But he had no plan for the burgeoning middle class, estimated at around 30 percent in 1968, that was producing leaders of satellite movements opposed to the PRI. This tendency toward atrophy and related anomic political reactions against PRI would constitute one of the greatest challenges of Martínez Domínguez's political career.[3]

But it was impossible for Martínez Domínguez to remain president of the PRI's CEN into the next presidential sexenio. This was according to internal PRI rules. Therefore, during the first six months of Luis Echeverría's presidency, Alfonso Martínez Domínguez functioned as the mayor or regente of the Federal District (Mexico City). The new president had seen to it that the succession to the CEN presidency went to one of his own trusted lieutenants. This required a demotion for Martínez Domínguez in hierarchical terms, but it was no public disgrace as he remained in the capital city, in a powerful position, with his own camarilla essentially intact. Besides, it is well understood within the PRI that a new president will name members of his own personal camarilla to key posts, while at once trying not to repudiate the outgoing president by throwing out all harbingers from the previous regime. It was, thus, correct intra-PRI politics to appoint Martínez Domínguez as regente of Mexico City, leaving him with power, position, and face-saving. The face-saving aspect is of critical importance. In all likelihood Martínez Domínguez would have remained as mayor of the Federal District throughout the Echeverría administration or been given some better position had he not gotten himself "burned" in an event which should have turned out to be a Mexican Watergate and, to some extent, did. This event, referred to briefly in the previous chapter, is known variously as Jueves de Corpus, or the June 10th affair. It occurred on that date in 1971. (See the Appendix to this chapter for the complete story of this event.)

Lost in the congested midst of Mexico City, in a neighborhood named San Cosme, not too far from Tlatelolco (and suspiciously so for those given to mystical political interpretations), the religious fiesta Jueves de Corpus was to be celebrated on June 10 in 1971. At 4:30 p.m. some 8,000 students formed in front of the National Polytechnic Institute and began a march that was intended to end in front of the National Lottery building near the center of downtown Mexico City.

The students had marched less than a block when they were confronted by armed riot police wearing breast plates and helmets. They were told by Captain Emanuel Guevara that without a permit their march was illegal; they were also told that whatever means necessary would be used to detain the march. Some distance later Colonel Angel Rodríguez approached Marcué Pardiñas, who then appeared to be leading the march, and informed him that the activity was illegal; the students replied that, in their belief, the constitution guaranteed them the right to demonstrate peacefully without a special permit. They claimed that in fact the interference of the government was illegal. At that point orders were given by radio in the name of Colonel Manuel Díaz Escobar that other special groups were to begin their action. This radio transmission, and many others, were recorded by the PAN and subsequently made available to journalists. A series of actions and transmissions (using code names) followed during which the student marchers and newspaper reporters were savagely attacked by a paramilitary police organization called Los Halcones, the Falcons. Police and troops looked on, doing little except to block traffic so that as few spectators as possible should see what was developing into an officially sponsored massacre.

The upshot of this was a furious public scandal requiring that someone be sacrificed. Clearly Martínez Domínguez knew of the existence of the Falcons and his jurisdiction was paying their salaries. The usually progovernment press corps had been assaulted and made a thorough public expose of what had happened. President Echeverría could not ignore this. Martínez Domínguez was forced to resign, along with his chief of police. Too much evidence had been made public implicating the regente in the San Cosme massacre. This also served the power-building purposes of President Echeverría, since he could eliminate Martínez Domínguez and other remnants of the Díaz Ordaz camarilla from high spheres of power. The president gave the impression that he meant to undertake a large-scale clean up of the entire regime. Indeed, Echeverría appeared on the popular Zabludowsky television news program the evening of June 15 and promised publicly that if any members of his administration were involved on June 10 they would be punished. Thus, the high priest had ordered that the pyramid be purged; there must be face-saving, symbol-saving, pyramid-saving. Political penance (or the appearance thereof) would be one answer. Echeverría was also implicated in the scandal, but he used Martínez Domínguez as his scapegoat.

Alfonso Martínez Domínguez, had come to what then appeared to be the end of the political power cycle as it operates in Mexico. His letter of resignation thanked President Echeverría for having originally honored him with the post of mayor on December 1, 1970, and stated that he did not want anyone to think that his continued presence as head of the Federal District would in any way influence the investigation which the president had ordered the attorney general to carry out.[4] Having succeeded Lauro Ortega as head of the PRI in 1968, Alfonso Martínez Domínguez had nearly become a kingmaker in Mexican politics.

For Martínez Domínguez the nearly six-year period between June 1971 and March 1977 was a long stretch of relative obscurity. Almost needless to say, the promised investigation of the June 10th affair never took place, or at least it was never made public. Several other high figures including attorneys general resigned from the Echeverría government in the aftermath of the scandal. A true public disclosure by the regime as to who was responsible would have ipso facto meant admission by the regime of its own culpability and illegitimacy.

But after Echeverría passed from office in December 1976 it was possible for Martínez Domínguez to surface again. He did this in a symbolic fashion, by being invited to the ceremony at which former governor of the state of Mexico, Carlos Hank González, took office as regente of Mexico City and again when Carlos Sansores Pérez assumed the presidency of the CEN under the new government of President José López Portillo. Since Martínez Domínguez had held both those posts, his being invited to sit among the dignitaries at the head table was significant and went beyond a symbolic gesture; it was an endorsement by the new regime which needed to repair hurt relations with the Monterrey Group, political allies of Alfonso Martínez Domínguez. Reports were that Martínez Domínguez received special personal attention at that public resurrection from Manuel González Cosío, the personal representative of President López Portillo. Martínez Domínguez was quoted as saying that he was there to lend support to his "central," meaning the CNOP which he also once headed.[5]

Later in May 1977 Martínez Domínguez appeared publicly in the Chamber of Deputies at the invitation of its PRI leader, Augusto Gómez Villanueva (a position which Martínez Domínguez had also held). He commented then that he favored the organization of a major opposition party on the left as it would oblige the PRI to select its own candidates with greater care.[6] By introducing Martínez Domínguez into the public view once again, and in the power context of exactly those political positions he had once held, the regime was saying that the once-burned politician had maintained a legitimate continuity after all, and that the crack in the pyramid once created by his exit had now been cemented over. Martínez Domínguez was then ready for new camarilla-building, for another opportunity to share power.

THE HANDLING OF DEVIANT CHARISMA: CONCLUSIONS ON THE GENERAL PREDICAMENT

Mexico's esoteric democracy is led by a dominant class formed out of circles of intimacy which in turn stem from a number of political camarillas, the most basic membership units of power. The principal dilemma of the esoteric system is that its self-perpetuation is hampered by the increasing financial and political demands made upon it by those to whom the PRI has become committed. This is partly because its principal cliques have multiplied and overlapped with groups whose ideological base may be hostile to the revolutionary coalition. The premium placed upon maximizing individual values fosters the proliferation of cliques and tends to dilute the power of the PRI's national organs; at the same time, however, this proliferation is a means of political socialization. On the success of this process much depends. It has certain critical implications that we must mention here.

One of these relates to the ability of the PRI to contain the phenomenon that I will term deviant charisma and which is inevitably generated by the camarilla-based structure of power. As the foregoing anecdotes illustrate, a premium is paid for the aggressive, but dutiful, promotion of one's image as a true revolutionary within the PRI. This requires the neophyte to run certain risks and rewards him for a behavioral style that is commonly described as machismo, the aggressive instinct of the male for conquest. But he must not overdo it or let his subordinates get out of hand as in the June 10th affair. It has been suggested by one analyst that the PRI, "with its hierarchical structure and its virtual monopoly of effective political activity, its overwhelming victories at the polls and its control of elective and appointive offices, provides an emotionally satisfying symbol of masculine aggressiveness and omnipotence."[7] The secret to the PRI's inner psychology would be, therefore, that it allows the participant to indulge his need for macho satisfactions (politically speaking) while still making it possible to carry on certain other compromise-dependent functions that the society requires and by nonmacho styles of behavior, that is, "the current practices of 'petitioning' and maneuvering behind the scenes would seem to display characteristics of what is regarded as feminine behavior."[8]

Following his ouster as president of the CEN in 1965, Carlos A. Madrazo confronted the PRI in a belligerent style strongly resembling the macho behavior described above. In May 1968 he issued a confidential letter to political functionaries of the PRI and other parties who were generally below the level of a nationally known political reputation. He asked them to state which they would prefer, a national front composed of existing parties and groups (basically within the revolutionary coalition), or a totally new party (presumably to be headed by Madrazo) as the solution to the list (which Madrazo presented) of critical problems then afflicting Mexico. The latter option, a totally new party, would have been a radical gesture meaning a closing of the doors to the present revolutionary coalition and denouncing its leadership as petrified conservatives. The national-front proposal, however, admitted of an internal restructuring and revamping of the PRI. It was a compromise which Madrazo seemed to favor while still holding out the possibility of a total split with tradition, thus bringing the crisis of legitimacy directly to a head.[9] Certainly no Mexican politician of the aggressive stripe of Carlos A. Madrazo would admit to being anything less than totally macho; but here was a crossroads situation in which criteria more rational than machismo were needed to avoid what could very well have become a disastrous collision. Madrazo had to be purged by president Díaz Ordaz.

I interviewed Madrazo at some length in June 1968, following the issue of his confidential letter. He expressed hope that the revolutionary coalition could be saved, but he stressed emphatically his disposition to bolt the PRI and to try to regroup the satellite left about his leadership in a new party if there were no other way. Madrazo's tragic death one year later leaves doubt as to the direction in which he would have resolved his unavoidable decision. But this much is clear: Madrazo frightened officialdom, he frightened them into blaming him for the Mexico City riots of 1968 and even, it has been argued, into ordering his assassination via the airplane accident of June 1969.[10] In short, Madrazo tested the reconciliation capacity of the PRI, perhaps as it had never been tested before. Significantly (as treated in Chapter 5) a major regrouping of the left involving PRI dissidents was again under way as José López Portillo's regime began.

Deviant charisma of the Madrazo variety tests the ability of the PRI to reconcile a breach between itself and an individual renegade. The PRI is also called upon to be a co-optation system as described in another analysis published shortly after the election of 1964.[11] Included is an especially good discussion of the experience of the CCI, which began to challenge the PRI's agrarian sector during the early 1960s. Although CCI factions split over the very issue of co-optation, that is, collaboration with the PRI, and rebel leader Danzós Palomino was imprisoned in the ensuing discord, it is argued that the PRI essentially co-opted the CCI into the revolutionary coalition. But in the 1970s Danzós was again heading CCI peasant demonstrations against the regime. It is certainly true that Vicente Lombardo Toledano, founder and titular leader of the PPS and intellectual mentor of the CCI, was co-opted as was the firebrand peasant leader Jacinto López whose squatter-invader movement variously known as UGOCM suffered organizational chaos when Díaz Ordaz took office in 1964. Here is an important principle: "If co-optation of dissident groups fails, then repression is likely to occur."[12] It is crucial to remember that Lombardo and López fell into severe disrepute with a large majority of their followers for having collaborated with the PRI. Danzós Palomino, on the other hand, became a popular hero and his prolonged encarceration helped build his revolutionary mystique. Lombardo and López were seen outside the revolutionary coalition as sellouts. Within the PRI there is evidence that both (they have now passed away) were distrusted for their earlier counterrevolutionary activity. Reconciliation and co-optation may appear to be the same process where individual leaders are concerned, but no matter which term is used, the process may win over leaders and alienate vast masses. My own interviews with popular leaders strongly support this contention.

I would stipulate that the process of co-optation, if indeed this is the best label for the capacity of the PRI to stultify its opposition, is intimately related to the cliques as functional nuclei of power that give meaning to the PRI's structural forms. This is to say that for dissident groups to be integrated (co-opted) into the PRI, there must be at least one clique of significant prestige that is willing to grant them membership. The same must hold true for the reconciliation of individuals like Madrazo who are deviant charismatics. Both Lombardo Toledano and Jacinto López had group ties allowing for co-optation. Madrazo had his own clique which was large and powerful enough to make him a prize sought after by many elements of the revolutionary coalition.

Danzós Palomino, the ex-rural schoolteacher, had few such ties. He was a dogmatic ideologue who would not compromise his revolutionary Marxism and was repressed coercively.

Other dissidents who could not be co-opted have gone full turn from right to left but always in dedicated opposition to the PRI. Lic. Raúl Ugalde, whose political career began as a militant juvenile leader of the PAN, abandoned this for a brief flirtation with the PPS and ultimately helped to found the marxist and violence-oriented MRP (Movimiento Revolucionario del Pueblo). I interviewed Ugalde in the spring of 1969, shortly after his release from prison. Suffice it to say for now that his testimony, and that of his supporters, casts valuable light on the co-optation thesis as applied to the revolutionary coalition. It is likely that the political costs of self-preservation are on the increase in Mexico. The PRI may well reconsider the implications of its own power system of cliques and it may ask itself how many more traumas of the Madrazo variety are likely to result and how many of these it can really afford.[13]

However, the quest for internal reform (restructuring and value change) is more a matter of verbal rituals than of fact in Mexico of the 1970s. That is why President Echeverría's administration at mid-term came to the point of crisis confrontations with organized guerrillas (physical violence) and with the powerful economic camarillas, for example, the Monterrey Group (ideological cleavage). Co-optation, which seemed to work until the late 1960s, has not worked well into the decade of the 1970s, but López Portillo is trying to make it work. However he has other nonpolitical forces to contend with. For instance, demographic pressures: Mexico's population growth has been out of control for too long. Injustice has been the social reality of the day. There have been too many isolated massacres following those of Tlatelolco and Jueves de Corpus, too much guerrilla violence and political alienation. And surrounding all of this has been burgeoning wretchedness and poverty.

The PRI stalwarts learned to say informally, *que no vivas en el error,* don't make the error of living outside the informal rules of the PRI and especially outside its budget. Thus, *not* to enrich oneself at the public trough becomes de facto a crime among priistas, members of the PRI. The main stricture is that the largesse be shared among the members of one's camarilla. That is what it means not to live in error. But what about the millions who are forced by demographic circumstances of birth to live in error, that is, to resent officialdom and to live on their own? It is from these miserable beings that the surplus value, which becomes the PRI's largesse, must be extracted.

Here I must embrace both normative and empirically based analytic postures. Joining the two modes let us say that the wretchedness of human life in Mexico today (glaring evidence that the goals of the great revolution have not been achieved) is a fact that should not be. It should not be because the afflicted masses say so. Yet, the single-party governing institution has distributed enough of the public largesse, until the late 1960s and 1970s, so as to avoid another major revolution; but that is changing. The PRI has been successful (until 1968 perhaps) in requiring conformity to certain thought and overt behavior patterns. The process has been authoritarian and within it were the seeds of frustration and aggression. These reactions are nurtured by poverty and repression which in turn result in deficiencies in human psychological freedom. Deficiencies in psychological freedom, as Christian Bay has noted, may conduce toward authoritarianism. But I would add that these same deficiencies, when perceived at catalytic historical moments (like Tlatelolco and Jueves de Corpus), may conduce to antiauthoritarian rebellion and to anarchy.

Bay has observed that in the more modernized societies parents have the "double role of being the source of love and tenderness and the source of restraints and sanctions employed in trying to direct the socialization process."[14] In Mexico this double role has its emphasis on the repressive side. Because of enormous wife and child abuse, children in Mexico must learn to repress great hostility toward their parents. They must also repress hostility toward the socioeconomic and political system which, in large part, prevents their parents from being good in Bay's terms. If this dual hostility is repressed it is not always sublimated. Given proper accelerators it may explode; the overreaction of an oppressive elite may enable the downtrodden to erupt temporarily in violence. Since the great revolution the Mexican people have been taught progressively to acquiesce in a status quo that was without material or social justice. Modern communications have made the masses aware, however, that there is a better life elsewhere, to the north. Modern medicine (death control) has multiplied the masses to the imposing figure of 65 million in the late 1970s, a population which Mexico simply cannot feed. She must export her wetbacks to die on U.S. deserts, highways, and railways while desperately searching for illegal employment. Mexico must deport foreign scholars who write about such things. The PRI finds it unpleasant to look in a mirror, an honest mirror.

Finally, let me add another important observation of Christian Bay: "No complex society can do entirely without political authority to supplement institutions, and the exercise of this authority, or of power in its support, is likely to be much more ruthless in a non-democratic country in which opposition more easily becomes treason or subversion."[15] These are the issues we must come to grips with to understand what is happening in Mexico during the 1970s and 1980s. Why is opposition forming? How does it organize? What is its ideology? How well equipped are the rebels to guide the country to a better life, assuming their endeavors should succeed? What is the threshold of criticality on which criticism becomes subversion or treason? Later I will address these questions with commentaries on poverty, despair, guerrilla terrorism and heroism in the face of enormous odds, and of the futility of trying to make the system work. Ultimately the reader will have to decide for himself just who it is who has been living a life of error, and who, on the other hand, has reaped a harvest of despair.

APPENDIX

Because the Jueves de Corpus affair took on proportions of a Mexican national Watergate and revealed the violence-prone and irreconcilable interests which rend the PRI from time to time, it is worthwhile telling more of the story in detail. This exemplifies the depth to which corruption has penetrated the Mexican political system and its vulnerability to atrophy from within.

The opposition journal *Por Que?* (closed in 1974 by the government for its criticism of human rights violations in Mexico and for exposing frauds committed by the PRI) stated that before the march got underway groups of Falcons had congregated along the nearby boulevard Calzada México-Tacuba and were ready to go into paramilitary action by 5 p.m. (*Por Que?* June 24, 1971, p. 7). It also reported that the Falcons were being transported in Mexican army vehicles (grey busses) and that they enjoyed the backup presence of antiriot troops. This journal alleged that only as a last resort would uniformed personnel enter into the battle. The government intended to give the appearance that what happened was a fight between rival student groups (to identify themselves the Falcons wore shirts outside their trousers so as not to be confused as students in case the police and military would ultimately be forced into action).

It should be repeated that the radio communications which directed the attack were being recorded by the opposition party PAN. When several of the Falcons were injured, the police radio reflected concern that the identity of these casualties might become public. When the Falcons seemed to be gaining the upper hand the police radio said, "Only the Falcons are in action now" (*La Batalla,* June 1971, p. 2). Red Cross ambulances attempting to take the wounded to Rubén Leñero Hospital were attacked. Some of the Falcons' own comrades-in-arms were picked up and carried to the hospital, but they were taken by force from the doctors, condemned by their own colleagues to die rather than to compromise the group by the presence of their wounded bodies. Some of these bizarre details were cited earlier in Chapter 3 (see note 10).

Photographic evidence was widely circulated of armed Falcons taking aim from behind parked vehicles and firing openly, wantonly, gleefully, from their sheltered positions. The student marchers were wounded by the hundreds. No evidence was presented (at least not graphic evidence) that any of

Much of the material in this appendix is based on Gerardo Medina Valdés, *Operacíon 10 de Junio* (Mexico: Ediciones Universo, 1972).

the student marchers were armed, not even with sticks or bottles. Instead they carried banners and posters challenging the government. (Conspicuous among the banners held aloft were demands that the government free the "68's" or prisoners still held from Tlatelolco.) When the battle was won the Falcons were loaded into grey military busses and whisked away.

A photographer of *Por Que?* gained entrance to the National Teachers Institute where many of the wounded had taken refuge and asked one of the student victims, apparently near death, if he would allow his picture to be taken. The reply was "yes providing you are not from the *prensa vendida*" (controlled press) (*Por Que?* June 24, 1971, p. 14). An incredible series of pictures was published by *Por Que?* in its June 24 edition (an edition that was, for the most part, confiscated by the government) identifying members of the Falcons beyond doubt and showing government troops standing by watching the massacre. Many of these pictures appeared in other Mexican publications. The conservative international review *Visión* even published one of the more damaging pictures which clearly implicated the government in the affair (see *Visión,* July 3–17, 1971, pp. 14–15).

Why did the government plan in advance to have the Falcons waiting near the Casco de Santo Tomas where the march was to begin? Roger Menéndez, editor of *Por Que?*, told me that the decision was purely and simply a tactical one. Its purpose was to isolate the demonstrators from the public and to prevent the march to the center of Mexico City where surely the students would have been joined by thousands of sympathizers. Had the march progressed to that point, another Tlatelolco might have ensued; as it turned out, some 50 persons died. The figure of injured, most of them innocent bystanders, will never be known, but is well into the hundreds. The government did succeed in squashing the manifestation at its point of beginning; but it probably did not count on Falcons attacking the Mexico City press corps and foreign correspondents, one of the errors that the police and troops themselves had committed at Tlatelolco in 1968.

Following the assault the press corps presented a denunciation and graphic evidence to President Echeverría. This was June 12, the same day that the then-free *Excelsior* began publishing exposés on the Falcons, who they were and where they were headquartered and trained. The PAN charged that bulldozers worked all night near the community of San Juan de Aragón behind runway number 5 of the Mexico City International Airport in a desperate effort to obliterate the Falcons' headquarters (*La Batalla,* June 1971, p. 4). The pro-Echeverría (but not always pro-PRI) publication *Semana Política* denied government complicity stating the alleged headquarters area was covered by occupied housing (*Semana Política,* June 1971, p. 3).

On June 10 and immediately afterward, the nexus of Mexican political power and corruption was exposed publicly in a way that perhaps had not occurred since the Calles era of the 1920s. Not only did the conscious public, as in 1968, unite again in sympathy for the students who were victims of military (or more accurately paramilitary) brutality, but most of the Mexico press corps joined in open opposition to the government as well. This latter fact represented a significant first in recent decades of Mexican politics, the press challenging the Tlatoani.

Serious complaints and charges were presented to President Luis Echeverría on behalf of the reporters' and photographers' organization (SNRP) of Mexico City. Some excerpts merit scrutiny here:

> José Luis Parrá, Secretary General, SNRP: ". . . the existence of this fascist group is not something that occurred over night . . . we know, Mr. President, that it is a perfectly organized group well trained in the use of weapons . . . and as you can see from the photographs were protected by the police, a fact which cannot be considered congruent with the patriotic and revolutionary government which you, Mr. President, now direct" (*El Dia,* June 12, 1971, p. 4).

Mario Aguilera, photographer for the daily *Excelsior:* ". . . we wanted to give you, Mr. President, these photographs which show quite clearly that *Los Halcones* carried heavy calibre arms and clubs and you can see them laughing in pleasure as they beat up the people . . ." (Ibid).

President Echeverría joined the press corps in expressing his indignation: *"Si ustedes estan idignados, yo estoy mas"* ("If you are indignant, I'm more so") (*Excelsior,* June 12, 1971, p. 1). In effect, Echeverría played the game of political symbolism quite well and thus singlehandedly disarmed some of his critics. This was in contrast to President Gustavo Díaz Ordaz, who granted no interviews during the 1968 student disorders. President Echeverría not only asked the reporters to turn their evidence over to the attorney general (*procurador*) but also ordered him to undertake a complete investigation.

When Procurador Sánchez Vargas met with the press, the conference was carefully staged. A minor official told those reporters holding the officially recognized questions to rehearse their performance. One reporter asked whether "unedited" questions would be entertained from the floor. Here the official hesitated, embarrassed, and then replied "naturally" with obvious discomfort.

Imagine the scene: The procurador arrives. The sequence of rehearsed questions begins. Then someone motions frantically to the procurador that the tape machine is not working. They need an official record to protect themselves against misquotes in the press. So the ritual is repeated verbatim. Then a furious reporter, himself victim of the June 10th brutality, intervenes and plants aloud a question that was neither approved nor welcome. "Will criminal action be taken, Sir, against General Corona de Rosal and Mr. Alfonso Martínez Domínguez for having maintained these paramilitary conflict groups?" The procurador has a frog in his throat and gulps saliva. This question was not to be asked; no one was even to think out loud along such lines. He looks at the reporter intensely, nervously, and says, "we have no comment on this." But quickly thereafter the procurador turns to his assistant and adds, "Why don't you take these gentlemen of the press to eat now in a good restaurant!" Later, an official version of the procurador's press conference is issued. The incident described above was not mentioned. The tapes had been erased correspondingly. Officially, still, the existence or not of the Falcons was moot. The government would keep it that way although everyone knew the truth. (See Valdés, pp. 144–46.)

Then, unexpectedly, more outward cracks emerged in the base of the power pyramid, big cracks. The presidentially appointed mayor (regente) of the Federal District and his chief of police resigned. Too much evidence had been made public implicating Martínez Domínguez in the San Cosme tragedy; the unfriendly press question put to the procurador had been answered in the minds of the people. The resignations gave the impression that the president meant business and would begin prosecuting the guilty from the top down.

Several observations are in order concerning the "firing" of Martínez Domínguez. More than likely, Echeverría considered him a threat and took advantage of the Jueves de Corpus affair to eliminate a power contender. This explanation of the mayor's resignation becomes highly probable when one considers the following facts. First, it is incredible to suggest that Alfonso Martínez Domínguez and Luis Echeverría were not aware of Los Halcones, who had been functioning since 1968. The former was an intimate political friend of Corona del Rosal, the reputed founder of this paramilitary group. Echeverría, as former head of Gobernación, which among other activities is in charge of a vast intelligence network, had access to all types of information. The government's spies constantly infiltrate opposition sectors, especially student groups. The president and the mayor both had prior knowledge that a student demonstration was in the making and thus had time to plan official strategy. Presumably the government wanted to avoid numerous strikes and disruptions, with snowballing public sympathy, as occurred in 1968. In fact, informants argue that Los Halcones went through extensive drills one day before Jueves de Corpus. Moreover it is highly unlikely that the Falcons would have been used on the first day of a student demonstration without high-level approval from the government of the Federal District, that is the regente Martínez Domínguez.

At 10:00 on the evening following the violence, Alfonso Martínez Domínguez held a press conference. He told reporters that his police, with army support, had preserved the public order. The disturbances, he continued, occurred because rival student groups within the Polytechnic Institute had used public thoroughfares to stage a sort of gang war (*El Día,* June 11, 1971, p. 4) and that the students were armed and looking for trouble. He also said the march was unlawful because the students had no permit from his office.

When asked by a reporter for the daily *El Universal* (who said he had been beaten and his camera damaged) about the Falcons, Alfonso Martínez Domínguez stated categorically that no such group existed and that the government of the Federal District maintained no paramilitary groups (*El Día,* June 11, 1971). It is incredible to suggest that this shrewd politician would have made such statements if he did not expect presidential support. At some point he lost it. It is unclear as to when Echeverría decided to fire his regente. Perhaps after the mayor's press conference it was only too obvious that he had lied and thus the president had to get rid of him. At the same time, however, it was obvious that Echeverría himself had hedged on certain questions put to him by the press. One suspects that Echeverría could have saved Martínez Domínguez if he had wanted to.

The protesting Mexican reporters were perhaps more aggressive than they had ever been because so many of their members were victims of the aimless brutality of Los Halcones. In addition, American correspondents representing, among others, NBC news and the Washington Post were victims of the aggression. For a few days afterward, all the major newspapers in the capital published articles and editorials which were particularly critical of the government. These are the principal charges as reported by *Excelsior* on June 13, 1971:

> The Falcons consist of more than one thousand young men between the ages of 18 and 22 and they are under the command of a colonel by the name of Díaz Escobar. The Falcons have their headquarters and training grounds in an area known as La Cuchilla del Tesoro, located behind runway number five of the Mexico City International Airport and near the community of San Juan de Aragón. This group was formed as a special riot control squad following the student disturbances of 1968 [Tlatelolco] and subsequently was used by the Federal District government to drive prostitutes and illegal street vendors from certain sectors of the city. Initially, the Falcons were paid 60 pesos [4.80] daily but today they earn five pesos more. Those who have distinguished themselves with their aggressiveness earn up to 120 pesos per day ... they receive extensive training in judo, karate, and the use of firearms. A prime requisite is that of perfect health. The Falcons are always on call in case of any emergency and use special code names *(perejil y naranja)* to identify themselves.

The procurador responded that an investigation was underway, that a search was being made for Manuel Marcué Pardiñas and Heberto Castillo. The former was a discredited leader of the Mexican Communist party and the latter a leftist engineer turned journalist and polemicist. Both men had been recently released from prison and were on parole, a circumstance resulting from their alleged involvement in the riots of 1968 and because (according to my testimony) both men made deals with the government to achieve their freedom. Heberto Castillo immediately set about forming a new political movement which at the time of this writing is known as the Mexican Workers Party but whose future is uncertain. Castillo is rumored to have made a deal with the government for his freedom in 1970 but this is only an allegation. His freedom was allegedly granted in exchange for Castillo's promise to create a false opposition party on the left that would be an official puppet. By the late 1970s, however, it appeared that Castillo's party might be a true opposition. As far as Castillo's being released in 1970 is concerned, it has been pointed out that other political prisoners at that time, like the journalist Mario Menéndez Rodríguez, who refused to sell out to the government remained in jail indefinitely (Menéndez was ultimately ransomed free by a guerrilla organization and flown to Cuba). Photographs showed that at one point Pardiñas did appear at the head of the student march but reliable sources informed me that he was not invited to do so and took this action as a desperate move to capture lost public attention. The students were said to have booed Pardiñas, and his presence did nothing to help their cause. Castillo apparently had nothing to do with the affair but his name was deliberately inserted into the procurador's press release to divert attention away from the real challenge that was embarrassing the government, that is, official responsibility.

Subsequently, the attorney general's office issued a statement saying that they had investigated several more times the alleged location of the Falcon's headquarters and had found nothing. Casting about desperately for a scapegoat the Federal District's local PRI leader, Everardo Gamiz, placed the blame on the right-wing group MURO. At the same time the national youth leader of the PRI, Jesus Medellín, demanded an open public dialogue intended to determine who were the people who served "unconfessable interests." He carefully chose to limit his dialogue to the PPS, which is little more than the official left wing of the PRI.

Procurador Sánchez Vargas was also forced to resign on August 19. All of his vast intelligence-gathering mechanism claimed it could not locate a trace of the Falcons and public pressure from opposition political and civic groups still continued. A new procurador appeared in his place but he too eventually resigned, caught on the horns of the same dilemma. There were definite holes in the government's case, and some of these were uncovered via respectable sources. For instance, the semiofficial publication *Siempre* called the situation incredible: "The Falcons were in the street, they were photographed, everyone knew that such a paramilitary squad had to be carefully trained, that it could not improvise itself. If the Falcons did not belong to the government of the Federal District then to whom did they belong . . . to the CIA?" (*Siempre,* August 11, 1971, p. 25). The upper echelons of Mexican officialdom had been discredited and torn by the affair. The attorney general's only recourse was to resign as the mayor had done before him. The above-cited article (by Juan Duch) in *Siempre* revealed how the pyramid could be shaken by popular opprobrium:

This was no simple matter of words but of deeds. The case of Mr. Alfonso Martínez Domínguez—vis-a-vis the politics of Mexico which are so subtle and complicated in their implications—is ample proof of this. His resignation was accepted without regard to whether it was offered voluntarily and spontaneously. He was separated permanently from his position, ostensibly to facilitate the investigation, when normally the granting of a leave of absence during the inquiry would have been sufficient. He was replaced by a man of the upper echelon who would not be likely to accept a merely interim appointment. The resignation of Mr. Martínez Domínguez must be understood as the end of the line for him. And his removal—this is the most important part—went to satisfy the public demand.

Undoubtedly, this article was commissioned by anti-Martínez Domínguez camarilla of the PRI, perhaps by Echeverría himself. But its prognosis on the political end of Martínez Domínguez was premature and hastily drawn.

Each successive procurador was faced with an impossible situation: It was very much like Nixon's first special Watergate prosecutor in the United States. Each procurador was told to investigate the unconfessable, that which would surely lead to the presidential palace if carried to a thorough and impartial fruition. It was also apparent that key individuals involved in the scandal had given contradictory statements in public at distinct times thus embarrassing the administration further. Medina Valdés notes a great incongruity between the testimony of Colonel Díaz Escobar, alleged leader of the Falcons, and that of the procurador. Díaz Escobar was heard to admit publicly that organized paramilitary groups had existed up until November 30, 1970, just before Luis Echeverría took office as president. He said these groups were disbanded on that date. The procurador was forced by the bare reality of what happened on June 10 to admit that indeed "some groups" still existed (Medina Valdés, pp. 209–10). Medina Valdés then cites one of many historical precedents for such armed groups working on behalf of the PRI and I translate his commentary as follows:

> Mexico is not the only country in the world where the government taps the telephones illegally, places spies in political organizations, student groups, religious and industrial associations, and maintains repressive gangs of hoods to keep control of whatever eventuality that may occur. Some years ago [probably referring to the late 1950s] on the occasion of the railroad workers and petroleum workers conflicts, certain individuals identified themselves with a special credential bearing the national colors and reading "Police of the PRI." No, ours is not the only country where these things occur, but on the basis of the June 10 affair it would seem that this form of maintaining "social stability and peace" has gone entirely too far.

Out of this old and well-established tradition of maintaining conflict groups *(grupos de choque)* emerged Los Halcones, who attacked the students at San Cosme and later dragged their own dead and wounded mercilessly from

Rubén Leñero Hospital. Medina Valdés says it is curious that at the very time, so the government alleged, that certain armed revolutionary groups in northern Mexico (the MAR, Movimiento Armado Revolucionario) were being trained in North Korea, Colonel Díaz Escobar was himself on an official visit to South Korea where he was instructed in the paramilitary arts that he would need in organizing the Falcons (Medina Valdés, p. 213). Clearly the regime's involvement was deep.

Although some analysts of the San Cosme violence believe that President Echeverría was innocent and ignorant of the existence of the Falcons, the preponderance of the evidence gathered by this author is to the contrary. There is a nearly unanimous conviction, even within official circles, that Alfonso Martínez Domínguez and the top echelon of the PRI in the Federal District were directly responsible for Los Halcones. The graphic evidence and oral testimony is simply too overwhelming. *Semana Política,* practically President Echeverría's personal news bulletin, showed Martínez Domínguez wearing a swastika and clutching a bird of prey in the same arm. Below the drawing was this caption, *se esfumaron los sueños de Halconso.* (This expression became a sort of watchword in the form of a derogatory political joke. The term "Halconso" is a corruption of Martínez Domínguez's first name [Alfonso] and the Falcon's name in Spanish, *Halcones.* The finished expression then reads, "the dreams of Halconso vanished.") Other writers threw a measure of blame on the students and on pseudo-leftists like Marcué Pardiñas who, apparently, tried to head up the march without student invitation as a publicity device. Nor was there serious doubt about the existence of the Falcons in the minds of many responsible writers and observers. One article went so far as to suggest that the Falcons had grown into a superpolice that went about on its own looting and robbing banks in its off-duty hours (*Excelsior,* June 18, 1971, p. 8A).

The final chapter of Medina Valdés's *Operación 10 de junio* merits special attention. It presents a penetrating thesis about Mexican political life that goes far toward explaining both Tlatelolco and San Cosme. Succinctly put, Medina Valdés argues that between Tlatelolco (October 2, 1968) and San Cosme (June 10, 1971) the regime learned a fundamental lesson about how to protect its image (or at least Echeverría learned it). President Echeverría, it should be remembered, was secretary of Gobernación during the regime of Díaz Ordaz and to a great extent the blame for Tlatelolco was unloaded on Echeverría. Echeverría tried, according to Medina Valdés's analysis, to preserve his image as he saw the San Cosmo confrontation approaching. Thus certain errors of Tlatelolco were not repeated at San Cosme: the movement was not allowed to grow to an unmanageable size; the public forces (army and police) were not directly used; the regime did not refuse to purge itself internally (at least, in ritual form); because the foregoing classes of errors were avoided, the president was able to escape much of the stigma of what happened at San Cosme. Díaz Ordaz, on the other hand, was forced to accept blame for Tlatelolco.

This is crucial; let us look at it in slightly more detail. The movement of 1971 (San Cosme) grew out of the protest (in part) over the student turmoil in the state of Nuevo León. Echeverría kept this from getting out of hand, and partly deprived the Mexico City students of their cause, by deposing Governor Elizondo and temporarily resolving the Nuevo León student crisis. So that when the march of June 10 began, the Mexico City students were in effect protesting something that had almost ceased to exist, except for the continued incarceration of the "68's," leaders of the 1968 movement. Ideologically, therefore, the movement was weakened at the start. Next, even though army and police units looked on and kept spectators back, the basic assault on the student marchers was by Los Halcones, and once they had disappeared into their ambulances, hearses, and grey police busses, it was easier for the government to claim no involvement and to blame the affair on rival student groups. Moreover, the movement was stopped physically within several blocks of its start. Had long processions gotten underway as in 1968 another Tlatelolco would surely have occurred. Third, the resignations of the regente and the police chief served to provide scapegoats and to allow the president to focus critical attention upon others in his entourage who (he could claim) sought to sabotage him. Thus, finally, Echeverría did not have to take public responsibility as Díaz Ordaz felt forced to do in 1968. This face-saving was of psychological importance to the regime, critical to the pyramid.

There was one major difference between 1968 and 1971, a governmental error committed at San Cosme. The Falcons were allowed to attack the press corps without discriminating friends from foes. Attacks on the press which occurred at Tlatelolco could plausibly be made to look like accidents. But the photographic evidence from San Cosme made such a defense impossible as far as the June 10th affair was concerned.

Who are the guilty? Valdés stresses that it is one thing to blame the institution of the presidency and another to blame the incumbent president. In both cases Valdés shares the general consensus that the president knew and he must be held responsible, tricks and scapegoats notwithstanding. Importantly, however, he does not want to undermine the presidency as an institution. Valdés is one of Mexico's few, I stress very few, opposition politicians who sees himself as loyal to Mexico above and beyond his particular political party or any advantage he can personally draw therefrom. Thus he phrases his accusation carefully. Echeverría is guilty in one of two ways. If he knew all the details of the June 10 aggression in advance, Echeverría has essentially a personal guilt but one which cannot help but affect the office he occupies. This is grave. Worse, however, is the institutional guilt if the aggression was planned and carried out without the president's knowledge, for this would mean that the formal maximum authority in Mexico is, in fact, not the real authority. Thus the presidency would indeed have been undermined in Watergate fashion.

Many Mexican political analysts agree with Valdés on another critical point, that at Tlatelolco the army was on the verge of reasserting itself in Mexican politics, not just of regaining its status as a PRI sector which was lost in 1944, but of taking over the government via a coup d'etat. Valdés and others comment that a coup did not take place in 1968 for two essential reasons: the personal following of President Díaz Ordaz among high-ranking officers (especially the defense minister General Marcelino García Barragán), and because of the consensus within the military that it would be more fruitful to remilitarize the country gradually and through institutional channels.

Here it is necessary to take notice of a key group of officers, a special inner-circle camarilla of privileged graduates of the Mexican War Academy (Escuela Superior de Guerra). These men have come recently to be known as Los Penecilinos, whose name is derived from the Spanish word for penicillin. The implication of the term is that this elite corps of officers (a sort of camarilla in and of itself) has a unique brand of medicine (their War Academy training) which can cure all the country's ills. Thus, Los Penecilinos are patiently awaiting the correct moment to enter Mexico's political arena and administer, perhaps, something like what has come to be called the Peruvian solution, that is, progressive military management of government. This inner circle reputedly feels it is above the formal law of the land. Defiantly it operates a notorious political prison near the capital known as Campo Militar Número Uno. There, even purged members of the PRI have been detained, interrogated, tortured. This I have in the form of direct testimony written to me from a prisoner then in Lecumberri (the PRI's formal political prison) and who spent time in Campo Militar Número Uno. Moreover, Valdés and others cite their own evidence (Medina Valdés, p. 256). Those military elitists, Los Penecilinos, who are now rising to the forefront of military politics in Mexico, are taught more than just the trades of war. They have, in recent years, been given special courses in "how to manage the government of the nation" (Medina Valdés, p. 257). It is believed that such courses were instituted shortly after Tlatelolco and as an outgrowth of discussions within high military circles as to the pros and cons of a military coup in 1968. The courses in government management were an institutional compromise. In this sense government management is a reflection of an incipient yet metamorphosed political militarism in Mexico.

If the military had become the "power behind the throne" in Mexico during the Echeverría regime, this would help to explain why the investigations of San Cosme by officials appointed by the president were always frustrated. The military high command would not allow such studies to come to fruition, certainly not publicly and probably they did not want any such studies per se. Thus the regime as a whole, the PRI with its government bureaucracy, its economic oligopolists, and its renascent military politicians, is responsible. But, Valdés argues, there is even yet a more profound responsibility for Tlatelolco and San Cosme. It is a collective responsibility of all Mexicans. Valdés does not say so but this may relate to one psychological thesis of Octavio Paz. No matter how the Mexican decries his corrupt government, he tolerates it; no matter how loudly he cries "corrupt press" *(prensa vendida)*, he does not boycott it (Medina Valdés, p. 264).

> What is lamentably normal in Mexico (remember that during the massacre of Tlatelolco a prominent leader of the student movement drank coffee with two government agents) is that the student movements leave as a result little more than victims, personal hatreds, and a fleeting conscience that something is wrong somewhere and that it must be fixed somehow. But too many of the one time leaders can be bought off with government jobs, "plugged" into the budget [*enchufado en el presupuesto*] (Medina Valdés, pp. 265–66).

If indeed it is true that the military is taking over Mexico while constitutional institutions atrophy, then all Mexicans are responsible. Frustrated at this specter many have now taken to the hills and joined guerrilla organizations both rural and urban. Valdés concludes that revolution must come but that a violent catharsis will not save Mexico. He calls for a change of values, a, new conscience, and a new consciousness beginning at the personal level and extending up through the PRI and the subordinate institutions of government. How to effect this change he does not say. Octavio Paz says do it with constant open criticism, the word against the gun.

NOTES

1. L. V. Padgett, *The Mexican Political System* (Boston: Houghton-Mifflin, 1966), pp. 185–201. See also his second edition of 1976.

2. Kenneth F. Johnson, *Mexican Democracy: A Critical View* (Boston: Allyn & Bacon, 1972). I remain grateful to Lic. Manuel de la Isla for his advice in the construction of this anecdote which is based upon a true life story, one that is (at this moment) the opposite of his own.

3. The description of the succession of Martínez Domínguez to the CEN presidency and of his earlier career development is based on confidential interviews by the author.

4. *El Día,* June 16, 1971, p. 3.

5. *Proceso,* March 5, 1977, p. 26.

6. *Proceso,* May 23, 1977, p. 22.

7. Evelyn P. Stevens, "Mexican Machismo: Politics and Value Orientations," *Western Political Quarterly,* December 1965, p. 853.

8. Ibid.

9. A confidential Madrazo letter (in my possession) carries with it a slip to be filled out and returned to Madrazo by the given respondent. Requested is that person's preference for a coalition-type *frente* or the formation of a new party, plus personal data and group affiliation. The document required the respondent to sign, thus making a de facto pledge of support for one of the alternatives Madrazo posed (continuing with the status quo was not included).

10. An allegation concerning the airplane accident which claimed Madrazo's life is contained in *Voz Nacional,* June 25, 1969. Although many still believe that Madrazo was killed on orders

from high up in the PRI, his son, Carlos Madrazo Pintado, told me personally that he believed it was an accident and no more.

11. Bo Anderson and James D. Cockcroft, "Control and Cooptation in Mexican Politics," in *Latin American Radicalism,* ed. I. L. Horowitz (New York: Vintage, 1969), pp. 366–89.

12. Ibid., p. 380.

13. There is a growing literature based upon survey research data which seeks to distinguish "specific support" and "diffuse support" for the regime in Mexico. In the opinion of the present writer these data have questionable validity because of the way they were collected, that is, contracting via research firms having especially close relationships with the PRI. There is also the question of whether Mexican respondents in poor neighborhoods, many of whom are land invaders, would give reliable answers to any strangers out of fear of reprisals given the authoritarian nature of the regime. It is argued in one such study that "specific support" derives from direct governmental actions and "diffuse support" is more general, an orientation toward the political system and its symbols. Accordingly it is argued that there is an "ambivalent Mexican" who believes in a government whose representatives he distrusts. See Wayne A. Cornelius, *Politics and the Migrant Poor in Mexico City* (Stanford, Calif.: Stanford University Press, 1975), p. 53. Reverence of symbols and disgust toward government functionaries is hardly a new finding. It is a well-established theme in some of the humanistic literature to be cited herein, for example, the works of Rodolfo Usigli, J. Rubén Romero, Carlos Chavira, and in the various anthropological works of Oscar Lewis and others.

14. Christian Bay, *The Structure of Freedom* (New York: Atheneum, 1968), p. 193.

15. Ibid., p. 317.

Five

Government, Economy, and the Quality of Life in Mexico

ON THE CRITICALITY OF ADMINISTRATIVE REFORM

Sloth may be the best term to characterize most of Mexico's internal governmental process, that is, the administration of its public policy (where definable policies even exist). I shall treat in the pages to follow a selection of problem areas which are of critical importance. The selection is by no means exhaustive. Nor do I always try to present a neutral view of each area. The focus is instead on those aspects of government ineptitude which contribute to depressing the quality of life in Mexico. I will also examine the critical nexus of political alienation with unfulfilled revolutionary promises contained in PRI rhetoric. This is offered as an accurate, truthful view. Yet, as in the original version of *Mexican Democracy,* the focus here is deliberately negative. This is for essentially two reasons. One is that a great deal of space has been devoted by North American scholars and the PRI government itself to presenting a rosy picture of Mexico.[1] Second, on the basis of my investigations, the negative view is characteristic of *most* socioeconomic-political life in Mexico. As the noted Mexican scholar and member of the PRI establishment Pablo González Casanova has noted:

> Our successes deceive us and they fill us with a parochial satisfaction; this makes a tabu of all profound criticism of the national policy of Mexican development, and converts into heretics and delinquents those who enunciate and sustain such ideas, even if they do it sincerely to promote development. But the structure of dependency and inequality continues and permits us to move ahead only slowly with an enormous toll of miserable human beings.[2]

He is not alone in this pessimistic outlook. Mexico's president José López Portillo is quoted as having said, "We Latins, by our Mediterranean heritage, what I call superstition, are prone to believe that social and political problems can be resolved by passing new laws ... but this is not so, we must organize and work."[3] And a skeptical analyst in López Portillo's own budget bureau admitted that as long as the vices of corruption and incompetence permeated the public administration no reform would have a meaningful effect.[4]

Administrative reform was one of the initial sweeping promises of the regime that would rule Mexico during the sexenio 1976–82. It was ventured that the success or failure of López Portillo's regime would rest upon the outcome of his administrative reforms. The president himself had worked on an advisory commission on public administration between 1965 and 1970. Some of his collaborators in that era were eventually to become cabinet members in the López Portillo administration; for example, Julio R. Moctezuma Cid became treasury secretary. It was presumed that these men who had studied the problems of Mexico's vast bureaucracy of 1.5 million employees (including regular government employees and those of the state-controlled industries) would be well equipped to assist in a major bureaucratic reform. The reform itself perhaps cannot fairly be judged until 1982 when López Portillo's constitutional term ends. Suffice it to say that a great number of laws were passed during 1977 decentralizing Mexican public administration, giving more formal powers to the states, and setting up budgetary control mechanisms to avoid waste, incompetence, and graft. Certain bureaus and state-controlled industries were taken from one ministry and placed in another. This was noted as a potential problem area because it required a redistribution of power that would inevitably create conflicts between those who gained and those who lost.[5]

Overall, some 799 entities were regrouped into sectors. Each sector would have a coordinator located in one of the cabinet-level ministries. He would be responsible for planning and for guaranteeing administrative efficiency, that is, "to guarantee that public functionaries separate their own (personal) economic interests from their professional functions."[6] It is significant to note that Gobernación, generally thought to be the most powerful cabinet-level ministry, retained control of some 22 entities (government-owned or-controlled industries are referred to as *paraestatales*) including PIPSA (the newsprint monopoly), Channel 13 television in Mexico City, a radio chain, and a series of theatrical and artistic enterprises. Gobernación also remained the home of the Federal Judicial Police and of most other intelligence-gathering operations. López Portillo's own words to the effect (quoted above) that changing the law and the structure does not ipso facto mean a change in values and practices again come to mind. The regime did not propose anything like (to use the U.S. example) a multipartisan watchdog committee to oversee the efficacy of its administrative reform. It merely passed laws and reorganized structures.

Because of the major role played by the Mexican state in the economy, the outcome of these proposed administrative reforms could have major importance.[7] It is doubtful, however, that either the state or private capital (or a mixture of the two) can readily solve Mexico's unemployment problem. It is uncertain whether administrative governmental reforms like those sketched above will change anything. Hopefully they will. Insofar as unemployment is concerned, however, the estimate of 50 percent of the total labor force being either underemployed or unemployed is frequently given.[8] A more conservative estimate focuses on the economically active population (EAP) and claims that 23 percent of this sector is unemployed.[9] Projections into the 1980s are not hopeful either vis-a-vis the ability of the Mexican economy to create labor-intensive industries that will absorb the growing population and consequent labor force. As Mexicans trek north to the border seeking illegal employment in the United States (and who can blame them), the unemployment and resultant social conditions on the border deteriorate, making those areas just as desperate for reform as the already-plagued center zones of Mexico.

It is important to stress that a major theme of this work is the baneful influence of corruption which impedes Mexico's socioeconomic and political systems from solving acute problems.[10] For that reason, the administrative reforms proposed by President López Portillo are a hopeful sign, providing they are converted into value and behavioral change as well.

POLITICS AND THE ECONOMIC AMBIANCE

Ever since President Cárdenas expropriated major foreign enterprises during the 1930s the PRI has promised that Mexican industries would be state-controlled and in the interest of Mexicans.[11] In the last decade, however, this rhetoric has faded before the increasingly patent truth that major foreign enterprises (principally North American) have returned and are in control of much of Mexico's economy. It has become fashionable, therefore, to blame foreigners for many of Mexico's ills. It would make little sense politically for the PRI to take the blame publicly for the nation's maldistributed wealth. Anomalously, Mexico (more than any other Latin American nation) has a direct economic dependence upon the United States via the tourist industry plus the remittances of illegal Mexican aliens employed in the United States who send an estimated $10 billion a year back to Mexico.[12] One study showed Mexico to have the most favorable "balance of tourism" situation of any Latin American republic.[13] This tourism has been, and continues to be, predominantly from the United States. Such is Mexico's dependence upon the tourist dollar that it has become a commonplace to hear that "Mexico hates the gringo precisely because she depends upon him so much." And it is quite within the realm of possibility that *should* the tourism be stopped for any reason (that is, plague, insurgency, discriminatory taxation, monetary devaluation, boycott, and so on) Mexico could collapse economically and, shortly thereafter, politically. A strategy for revolutionaries might be to make Mexico unsafe for the average American tourist; the murder of a number of Americans in Mexico during the mid-1970s increased tourist fears. There have also been attacks upon the captains of industry, kidnappings of top managerial personnel, leaving basic rank and file employees relatively untouched.

Revolutionaries claim that one of their prime justifications for political violence is social injustice. Guerrilla leaders like Genaro Vázquez Rojas and Lucio Cabañas adopted violent roles out of despair over the socioeconomic situation in which they and their families found themselves and out of frustration and aggression over the inability of society to alter the scenario using legal means. Thus the kidnapping of the wealthy Jaime Castrejón Díaz late in 1971 produced a considerable sum of ransom money for the guerrillas and gained the liberty of a number of key members of the revolutionary movement. The kidnap victim was a key figure in Mexico's Coca-Cola operation, that is, a Yankee imperialist.

Here then is part of the crux of the matter. There is a popular tendency to blame Mexico's ills exclusively on the United States. Many Mexican analysts trace the causes of their nation's poverty to international phenomena, one of which is the flight of capital to the United States. President Echeverría told his people that Mexico must recoup its dwindling economic sovereignty which has gravitated toward the United States. In 1972 he urged the United Nations to adopt special protocols guaranteeing the economic rights of nations in the Third World. In the same year he addressed the U.S. Congress and stated unequivocally that many of Mexico's ills stemmed from the salt-pollution problem caused by discharges from the Colorado River that have damaged Mexico's northern cotton production to serious proportions. He also made it clear that he expected more favorable trade relations with the United States.

Perhaps to underscore his determination in these matters, Echeverría flirted with Chile's socialist president Salvador Allende, lauding the accomplishments of the Chilean peaceful revolution with lavish public attention. Steps were taken also to increase commerce between Mexico and Japan. Significantly, however, Mexico took no concrete steps to end its alleged decapitalization in flight profits and capital going to other countries.

Echeverría's trips to socialist Chile and capitalist Japan may have greater significance than his North American visit. Mexico has moved toward more nationalization and state regulation of commerce and industry. At the same time, it has indicated its willingness to test the theory that somehow all capitalists are not alike, that is, a fairer shake might be had with the Japanese, Germans, and French than with the North Americans. Such an attitude is not an unexpected consequence of Mexico's recent economic history. In this context, therefore, it would be well to examine briefly some of Mexico's experience with mixed (state-private) capitalism.

One of the best-known efforts is the Plan of Ciudad Sahagún. This refers to an industrial complex in the state of Hidalgo some 35 miles northwest of the Mexican capital. This experiment was initiated by the government of President Miguel Alemán in 1952 and carried on by his successors with the goal of providing work for the inhabitants of slum zones on that edge of the Federal District. In the specific area where Ciudad Sahagún was erected the existing population lived under a subsistence hand-to-mouth economy producing small grains and a few vegetables. It was hoped, moreover, that Cuidad Sahagún would attract some of the urban proletariat from the Federal District, thus lessening demographic pressures in the central city area.

Cuidad Sahagún is best described as a complex of three integrated factories which ultimately became the property of the government (via its development bank, Nacional Financiera). In the beginning, however, it was a mix of capital. SIDENA (Siderúrgica Nacional S.A.) was initiated with Japanese capital but later was absorbed by the government (1960) when it suffered financial losses in the existing steel production market. DINA (Diesel Nacional, S.A.) was founded with a combination of Mexican private capital and funds from Nacional Financiera, but this too ultimately passed to governmental control. CNCR (Constructora Nacional de Carros de Ferrocarril, S.A.) was a government-founded industry for the production of railway coaches. These core enterprises of Ciudad Sahagún produce a range of capital goods from textile equipment to diesel automobile engines, some of which are done under a foreign-owned franchise (for example, Ford, Renault, and others). Among the more ambitious plans for Ciudad Sahagún was the development of a revolutionary aluminum motor especially suited to Mexico's widely varied driving conditions. Also planned was the fabrication of special containers for transporting crude steel products.

There is considerable disagreement in Mexico as to whether Ciudad Sahagún has been a successful experiment in dollar and cents terms, but there is no doubt that it fits within the growing image of state capitalism that President Echeverría tried to project to the world. In Latin America alone, Ciudad Sahagún won international recognition. Cooperative ventures were planned with state-controlled enterprises in various of the Andean Pact countries, beginning with Colombia and Chile. Mexico intended to send its experts to these countries to help set up satellite industrial cities like Ciudad Sahagún and, through joint ventures, enter into the hemispheric industrial competition with the private sector. How much of this came to fruition is not entirely clear.

Although Ciudad Sahagún is now totally capitalized and operated by Mexicans, a significant part of its activities has depended upon technology whose use is rigidly controlled by North American interests and patents. These franchises require licensing and payments to the parent firms (for example, Rockwell Standard, Westinghouse, several European firms) along with export-import limitations. It should be noted, also, that some plants at Ciudad Sahagún have undertaken management experiments similar to those being tried in Sweden and elsewhere by creating worker councils that participate in some management decisions. In addition a new program was piloted in Ciudad Sahagún that was intended to spread to all of Mexico and achieve construction of low-cost worker housing. This program is claimed as one of the hallmarks of the Echeverría administration and is called INFONAVIT (Instituto del Fondo Nacional de la Vivienda para los Trabajadores). I have been reliably told that INFONAVIT achieved significant early successes. Additional attention has been focused on Ciudad Sahagún by plans to establish a branch of Mexico's National University nearby.

Beyond what the Mexican government is willing to reveal publicly, however, the real success of Ciudad Sahagún, after two decades of operation, is still a moot issue and perhaps another decade must pass before a definitive judgment can be reached. Critics charge the enterprise with graft, waste, and call it a haven for useless government bureaucrats who do little or nothing while the public treasury foots the bill. It has also been alleged that the labor unions of the CTM are the real powers behind the "throne" of Ciudad Sahagún and that the government continues to invest its money there to please the official labor sector of the PRI. Another frequently voiced complaint is that every president brings to Mexico his own favorite auto contractor and many of these franchises have landed unceremoniously at Ciudad Sahagún. An example is the German Borgward franchise favored by the López Mateos administration (1958–64) which for a time became the Renault of Mexico (that is, Mexico's state-owned car), failed commercially (as did Renault in those same years), and has now virtually ceased to exist. Under President Díaz Ordaz (1964–70) the favored auto industries were Renault and Chrysler (AUTOMEX) and these cars were also produced at Ciudad Sahagún. During Echeverría's government, official favor and emphasis went to Volkswagen (used for Mexico City's mini-taxi system), whose principle plant is not at Ciudad Sahagún but in Puebla. López Portillo has yet to declare a favored vehicle.

The Echeverría government spoke of its commitment to Mexicanization of major facets of its commerce and industry, this in reaction against what was claimed as excessive foreign control. In 1972 the president set forth a controversial legislative proposal intended to regulate foreign-owned patents, the importation of technology, and to limit the contractual obligations that foreign concerns could impose on a Mexican subsidiary. The projected legislation meant the gradual, and in certain cases rapid, subjection of foreign interests to previously nonexistent controls. It should be noted that along with the new control law Mexico nationalized its telephone system in 1972 (promising consumers lower rates for 1973) and took over major parts of the country's radio and television industry. But let us consider here only the project law that would Mexicanize patents and technology, for it was this proposal that generated the greatest storm of controversy, one López Portillo will have to come to grips with.

In October 1972, U.S. Ambassador McBride spoke at a public meeting of the Mexican-North American Businessmen's Committee in Acapulco. His words were taken as a thinly disguised threat of some undefined U.S. reprisal against Mexico were President Echeverría's reform law passed by congress and put into effect. Specifically, the ambassador was disturbed over provisions that would prohibit a foreign company from requiring its Mexican subsidiary to restrict its sales to the domestic market after having received production technology imported from the United States; that is, many Mexican subsidiaries of North American firms were then being forbidden by the parent firm to sell their products in neighboring Guatemala. Echeverría's proposed reform would eliminate that type of restraint. The restrictions obviously favored the parent firm which would itself sell freely in Guatemala, thus helping the U.S. balance of payments but potentially curtailing Mexico's. Equally offensive from the Mexican point of view were the foreign-imposed controls over patents and new discoveries made by Mexican subsidiaries. Speaking for Mexico, Undersecretary of Industry and Commerce José Campillo Sáinz complained:

> We are against any stipulations which require that Mexican inventions tied to foreign technology should belong to a foreign enterprise. Such contractual clauses militate against the possibility of our creating our own technology and limit our possibilities for autonomous growth. Besides, it is absolutely inequitable that if one pays to receive technology he should have to surrender freely the fruits thereof.[14]

Campillo Sáinz also denounced the practice of requiring the Mexican subsidiary of a foreign-owned firm to purchase its primary materials for manufacture from the foreign home office. He cited evidence based on a United Nations study that the parent firms often charged their Mexican subsidiaries up to 500 percent in excess of the actual market price of these goods. Such practices would, understandably, contribute to a higher consumer cost for the manufactured product in Mexico, inhibiting thereby the subsidiary firm's competitive domestic posture and stultifying its opportunities for expansion. Furthermore, he opposed production limitations that were imposed contractually on subsidiary firms as well as price fixing and he condemned compulsory arbitration of commercial disputes in foreign courts. He added that Mexico would not oppose fixed international arbitration under, perhaps, United Nations auspices (this ignored existing international machinery for the resolution of such disputes). Finally, and categorically, Campillo Sáinz stated, "You will probably say that there are really few such discriminatory contracts . . . be that as it may, we intend to see to it that not a single one exists from here on out."[15] In all fairness, an impartial view would be sympathetic to most of these Mexican complaints.

A recent good survey of the involvement of specific North American firms in Mexican business and industry has been presented by Richard S. Weinert.[16] One of his fellow analysts, Lorenzo Meyer, contends that

> in general terms, foreign capital (not just American) accounts for less than 10 percent of the gross national product, but if we look at key sectors the situation is different. In 1970, about 70 percent of total manufacturing

output came from the approximately 800 enterprises in which foreign capital was present. In sectors such as the automobile industry, the capital-goods industry, or the chemical industry, foreign participation is around 100 percent. The rate of growth of foreign vis-a-vis national enterprise is astonishing —60 percent higher or more.[17]

Another statistic frequently mentioned is that some 80 percent of the patents used in Mexican industry are U.S. owned. Thus, the picture of involvement by multinational corporations and foreign corporations in Mexico is complex and economically significant to the life of that nation. All of this is in addition to the degree to which the Mexican government has mortgaged itself to foreign lending agencies: that is, the Mexican development bank Nacional Financiera will be loaning money which it has borrowed abroad. The amount of this indebtedness is considerable and Mexico is thought to be mortgaged to the hilt.

For these reasons, it becomes somewhat ironic when Mexican industrialists and bourgeois ideologues embrace the Echeverría rhetoric of blaming the failure of their economy on foreign interests. To some extent it is foreign lending concerns which have kept Mexico afloat, a process which was somewhat interrupted when the peso had to be devalued in 1976 for the first time in some 20 years. Exploiting its own labor force with the miserable wages that are paid in many sectors has also helped to keep Mexico's economy moving. Nevertheless, it is possible to see the Mexican side of the dispute also, especially in terms of the patent controversy and the forcing of Mexican manufacturers to import raw materials at outrageous prices. This certainly contributes to the decapitalization of Mexico, a phenomenon which merits brief scrutiny here. Because of the disparity of views and of statistics on the Mexican economic dilemma, it is often hard to separate fantasy from reality. Like electoral results in Mexico, many data are spurious.

According to the economist Sergio Mota Marín, the 1970 figure of foreign investment in Mexico represented 4 percent of the total (state and private) and 8 percent of the private sector investment.[18] This might seem a small degree of external involvement (ignoring the fact that almost 80 percent of that foreign investment is of U.S. origin); however, the crucial fact is that many key sectors of the economy fall within this small percentage of foreign control, as noted earlier. At the end of the Porfirian dictatorship in 1910 some 80 percent of Mexico's foreign investment was in extractive activities and primary materials; but by 1968 foreign investment had become concentrated almost exclusively in the manufacturing sector.

Protectionist tariff policies have aided the growth of this industry and the lack of policies to promote independent Mexican industry have led to a reduced export capacity. It should be noted that in 1975 Mexico's protective tariff structure was changed with the number of tariff items reduced drastically.[19] Foreign controls over what Mexican industry produces have resulted not only in a low export capacity, hence poor expansion and domestic employment potential, but these controls affect the growth of other secondary sectors which are in Mexican hands. In other words, foreign control of 4 to 8 percent of the national total investment has had a stultifying effect upon the remaining 90 percent. From this Mexicans derive the oft-quoted expression that 80 percent or more of the total Mexican economy is, in fact, controlled by foreigners, for the most part North Americans.

During the middle 1960s the state acquired 51 percent control of all mining operations; an important case in point was the sulfur industry which was one of the world's largest. Earlier in the century the state had acquired exclusive control over petroleum, electricity, railroads, and many communications. It is now required that Mexican capital alone may finance radio and television, transport using the federal highways, gas distribution, and the elaboration of forest products. An investment of at least 51 percent Mexican capital is required in the areas of credit and banking, insurance, bonds and securities. There is an additional and impressive list of economic activities (petrochemicals, rubber products, glass, fertilizer, cement) in which at least 51 percent of the investment must also be Mexican. But often this ostensible Mexicanization has not worked, due to the controls that the foreign investors still exercise via their restrictive clauses on the use of technology and the ownership of patents and high investment levels as mentioned above. Again, a distinct minority of the total investment picture has been the controlling factor in recent years.

Whereas the average investment profit earned by U.S. investors within the United States was 10.1 percent during the decade of the 1960s, it has been estimated that U.S. investments in Mexico yielded three times that percentage. Mexican investment policy allowed this to happen by granting special tax privileges to firms which could show they were in the process of Mexicanization, an illusive and easily violated concept. In addition, Mota Marín estimated that the foreign-owned enterprises in Mexico pay on the average no more than half the taxes they rightfully owe the state.[20] This fact, in and of itself difficult to ascertain with precision but generally believed, makes it likely (in the view of Mexican economists) that foreign investments may be generating a profit greatly in excess of 30 percent annually and the majority of that, they sustain, is *not* reinvested in the nation.

Also according to Mota Marín, the Banco de México figures show minimum profit levels of 20 percent which are in conflict with the early 1972 statement by Frank B. Loretta, president of the American Chamber of Commerce in Mexico, that the total profit earned by North American investments in Mexico during the decade of the 1960s was 8.8 percent.[21] Why, he asks, would U.S. capital remain in Mexico with a profit of 8.8 percent when the average profit in the United States itself is 10.1 percent and carries with it ostensibly safer investment guarantees and better credit terms? The answer given by Mota Marín is that year by year the investors have taken out more than they put into Mexico, leaving an economic deficit. "In 1970, for example, the new foreign investment was 210 million dollars and the flight of capital to the exterior was 343 million, a situation obviously affecting our balance of payments and decapitalizing the country."[22]

Seeing themselves favored by the protection of governmental tariffs (secured by political payoffs) and defended by their own contractual safeguards, the foreign enterprises embraced much existing technology with little original contribution (during the 1960s) and tried to adapt themselves to favorable local conditions, that is, primitive construction methods wherever possible using cheap labor. They did not take advantage of economies of scale and deliberately kept prices high and production low through the creation of oligopolies. The case most often cited of this sort of large-scale diseconomy is the automotive industry.[23] The automotive industry was still protected by a 100 percent import tariff on cars assembled abroad in 1977.

Mexicans have looked toward nations of the Andean Pact which have taken steps to control the decapitalization of their respective countries. Chile, Peru, Ecuador, and Colombia have at times focused attention upon eliminating overpricing of the importation of primary products for manufacture and the stranglehold of foreign investments on locally produced exports. These related phenomena have been a traditional channel for the flight of capital to the exterior (some of the Andean Pact nations, for instance, have found that the basic products imported for the pharmaceutical industry were overpriced by as much as 300 percent vis-a-vis the free market price). Looking elsewhere, Japan is cited as the example of a nation that has learned how to control foreign capital so as to make that investment contribute to the national economic growth by capturing foreign technology instead of being subjugated by it.

Mexican economists are aware, by and large, that foreign capital operates successfully and without conflict in Japan. But that country offers a particular commodity that most Latin American nations generally cannot: honest public administration and political stability. So despite the efforts of the Mexican bourgeoisie to lay their economic problems at the door of Uncle Sam, there is still the concomitant element of internal corruption and waste plus political violence and other forms of instability that are not conducive to a progressive business ambience. It is precisely such factors that generate discontent, alienation, violence, and which lead toward system atrophy.

SPECIAL INSTANCES OF GOVERNMENTAL ENTREPRENEURSHIP

The Mexican government is so thoroughly enmeshed in the national economy via its system of state enterprises or *paraestatales* that it often becomes difficult to distinguish governmental and private sectors. One report at the end of 1976 showed that for the preceeding year there were 26 principal paraestatales, and of this number only 8 showed a profit. Among those were the national petroleum monopoly PEMEX, and the fertilizer agency Guanos y Fertilizantes. In the loss category were 18 enterprises ranging from the Federal Electrical Commission to the railroads and airlines to CONASUPO (Companía Nacional de Subsistencias Populares), a staple-goods distribution system in the form of shopping centers and mobile vending stores designed to subsidize basic goods acquired by low-income families. In 1975 alone CONASUPO lost 5,197 million pesos.[24] It is not necessarily correct to conclude that the CONASUPO program, for instance, was a failure because of this deficit, given that it is intended as a popular subsidy in the first place. To the extent that CONASUPO or the railroads provide needed services to the public they can be called successful. To the extent that their losses are due to mismanagement and corruption, however, they are fair game for criticism. Elsewhere I have dealt with some of the controversial issues surrounding CONASUPO.[25] Its problems plague other state enterprises.

In the 1975 reporting year there was a new governmental venture which could not be definitively evaluated as it was just getting underway. This was SICARTSA, a major entrepreneurial venture for the production of steel. SICARTSA, a Spanish acronym for Siderúrgica Lázaro Cárdenas Las Truchas S.A., makes little sense when translated literally, but it was well-described by Marvin Alisky as "the Mexican government's new complex to make the steel industry self sufficient."[26] Launched in the early 1970s, SICARTSA had both economic development goals and those of political symbolism. Economically it was a government corporation intended to complement the private sector so as to achieve import substitution and end Mexico's dependence upon imported steel by the late 1970s. It was also meant to provide thousands of new jobs, that is, it would be a labor-intensive industry. Ultimately it was intended that the Mexican federal government would dominate Mexico's steel industry.

Politically and symbolically the project was the brainchild of a former president, the late Lázaro Cárdenas who lobbied effectively with the Díaz Ordaz administration for location of the project in his home state of Michoacán. The location was blessed by the presence of good hydroelectric sources, rich iron ore deposits, and the availability of abundant labor. Indeed, Michoacán traditionally had been one of the principal states from which Mexicans migrated because of chronic unemployment there. Symbolically, then, SICARTSA became the aging *caudillo's* legacy to his home state. Cárdenas hardly needed to improve his symbolic capability, having been perhaps Mexico's most charismatic president since the great revolution of 1910–17. But the legacy of a Mexico independent in steel, and done in the name of Cárdenas, was a politically useful tool for the PRI. The coastal village where the steel complex was to be located was renamed Cárdenas City as well.

The venture captured the imagination of both governmental and private entrepreneurs, and in the case of the latter some envy and resentment. It was supposed to be functional by 1976 when President Echeverría left office. Part of SICARTSA was in fact operating, but not all of it. Plans had been for the complex to generate 10 million tons of steel annually by the end of the century, hopefully making SICARTSA the largest such complex in Latin America. But early in his presidency José López Portillo suspended some of the construction on the project. Both he and outgoing president Echeverría had inaugurated SICARTSA shortly before the transfer of power in December 1976. They announced that the equipment needed to run SICARTSA had been acquired in 13 distinct countries so as not to tie them to any one source of capital goods and replacement parts.[27] Of the SICARTSA investment, 40 percent was made by the Mexican government and the remainder was financed through international loans via Nacional Financiera. The overall investment at the end of Echeverría's term had exceeded original estimates by some 24 percent. SICARTSA might be symbolically Mexican but there was a considerable external debt underlying it. Because the foreign loans were made in dollars, the 1976 devaluation of the peso almost doubled Mexico's cash indebtedness. Eight months after its opening, SICARTSA was operating at only 30 percent of capacity, a fact which its director, Adolfo Orive Alba, explained in terms of a natural breaking-in period necessary for both men and machines. Other steel experts charged that the low output was due to incompetent management.[28]

Shortly after the opening of SICARTSA the same Orive Alba had been quoted as having said, "We live today in the civilization of steel and steel is a thermometer to use for measuring the development of a people."[29] A critical analysis likened SICARTSA to a "black elephant" and called it a bureaucratic monstrosity of managers and submanagers with little to do but look important. It was argued that there were a total of 40 managerial positions at SICARTSA of which only 15 were necessary, the remainder being expensive *aviaduras*.[30] This was in contrast to quality-of-life conditions for the proletarian classes whose labor had contributed to the building of the SICARTSA complex.

Affected were some 17,000 common laborers who came for the initial construction phase of SICARTSA and who, once it was completed, were discharged as unneeded unskilled laborers. They and their families were attracted from various parts of the country, lured by the myth of permanent opportunity. They came in such quantities as to depress salaries to the advantage of the construction contractors (who apparently passed little of this saving on to the Mexican government). The majority of the migrant workers remained in squatter settlements, slums *(asentimientos ilegales)* surrounding Cárdenas City. This was hardly in keeping with the symbolism the late president had envisaged. SICARTSA was supposed to provide poverty relief. Instead, it had created new slums, vast concentrations of poverty surrounding the steel complex, a bitter testimony to the expendability of Mexican humanity. When reporters asked the management of SICARTSA about the misery of their former employees a spokesman replied, "Anyone in Mexico is free to choose his place of residence as he pleases."[31] The final word on SICARTSA is, of course, not in. By the end of the López Portillo sexenio it may well have achieved the goals for which it was intended.

Not all entrepreneurial ventures of the Mexican government have the potential promise of SICARTSA. One such recent effort had an early and politically damaging demise. During the Echeverría sexenio an extensive building plan was launched in the state of Nayarit whereby popular tourist attractions, upper-class homes, and a recreational facility for the military would be developed. In Chapter 3 I alluded to Cosío Villegas's criticism of President Echeverría for allowing peasants to be dispossessed of their landholdings in connection with this development scheme. It was known as the Bay of Flags trust *(fideicomiso Bahía de Banderas)*. Some 87 miles of beaches and interior properties had been taken from peasants. By mid 1977 only a golf course was functional, built on what had formerly been peasant-owned agricultural land. There was also a hotel, but it had no tourists. Plans to relocate the peasants and to convert many of them into fishermen (against their will) had also failed. Several packing industries were installed in nearby areas but were able to absorb only a few of the displaced peasants and functioned at minimum capacity.

Two ex-governors (Francisco Medina Ascencio of Jalisco and Roberto Gómez Reyes of Nayarit) were among the principal early promoters of this venture. They originally planned to relocate the peasants who would be displaced from Nayarit and sent to the state of Chiapas, far to the south on the Guatemalan border. The peasant ejido owners (ejidatarios who possessed collective farms) tried to organize against this move during the 1960s but the pressure became too severe. Governor Gómez Reyes sent men to beat up the peasants who opposed the resettlement.[32] In 1969 a team of officials from the Department of Agrarian Affairs and Colonization headed by Aguirre Palancares appeared in Nayarit to deliver titles of the peasant lands to the two ex-governors, but there was more peasant resistance. They fought rather than leave their land. Yet in late 1970, before leaving office, President Díaz Ordaz signed a decree of expropriation against the Nayarit peasants. The peasants were promised one nominal payment (4,000 pesos per hectare) and the rest of what they were due when the expropriated lands began to generate a profit. It was never clear what guarantees the peasants had of ever receiving any other remuneration for their lost land. In January 1971 President Echeverría authorized the creation of a federal trust *(fideicomiso federal)* in which the Mexican government would invest capital along with the ex-governors and their associates. On that occasion Echeverría is quoted as having said, "I am a disinterested partner along with the other members of the trust."[33]

So disinterested was President Echeverría that he must not have ordered controls placed on the management of the funds which the Bay of Flags trust was to administer. In June 1977 the former director of the trust, Alfredo Ríos Camarena, and some of his colleagues were accused of fraud by the new managers of the trust named by President López Portillo and by the attorney general's office. The fact that the new regime of López Portillo was willing to formally prosecute members of the outgoing regime for corruption was seen by some as an encouraging sign that someone in Mexico was waking up to the reality of resources being squandered and desperate needs going unmet. Others saw it as another ritual purge of holdover members from the previous regime. This investigation would have implications for former president Echeverría, considering that he had arranged to have a branch of his Center for Third World Studies (which he created during his last year in office as a power base for the future) located at the Bay of Flags. This location was to be an oceano-graphic institute dedicated to studying cultivation of food from the sea. Echeverría was, then, hardly a "disinterested" party to the endeavor. It was reported in 1977 that only a single Japanese researcher was working at the Third World Studies branch of the Bay of Flags.[34]

Although the master development plan that was published in 1973 showed government and private enterprise splitting the investment nearly 50-50, there were strange financial machinations involved. On the one hand President Echeverría's wife had presided over a dedication ceremony in her capacity as president of the National Institute for Infant Protection in which she declared that the ejidatarios of the area themselves had made a gift of the lands for the benefit of Mexico's youth (some of whom would presumably use the tourist facilities when completed). But apart from this "gift" (one sort of transaction) the fraud charges against Alfredo Ríos Camarena et al. alleged that some $2.5 million of government and private investments were bilked, hardly a gift-giving situation.[35] Some of these funds had derived from a loan of $7.5 million which the trust received from the Panama branch of the First National Bank of Chicago.[36] The loan carried what were described as exorbi-tantly high interest rates and contained a clause under which the guarantors of the trust would be responsible (that is, the Mexican government would be responsible) for payment to the bank in case Ríos Camarena and his partners defaulted. The loan of $7.5 million had a peso value of 93.8 million when it was taken out before the devaluation of 1976. By late 1977 the peso debt had doubled because of the declining value of the peso which was left to float and find its own level on the international market.

Additional charges were made by the new director of the trust, Federico Martínez Manatóu, ostensibly on behalf of all interested parties concerned. They included that the Chicago bank had been made to believe that the shares to be sold by the trust would have, within a year, twice the value of their actual sale price and on the basis of this erroneous belief the bank loaned the trust much more money than was justified.[37] In July 1976, two months before the peso was devalued, the Chicago bank presented a demand of nearly $8 million (including interest) to the Mexican national bank which had received the liability for the Bay of Flags trust failure to pay (this was the Banco Nacional de Obras y Servicios Públicos).

The Bay of Flags scandal reached deeply into the ranks of the PRI. At the moment during the early 1970s in which the bulk of the fraud apparently was committed, the head of the Ministry of Agrarian Reform, and also president of the Technical Guidance Committee of the Bay of Flags trust, was Augusto Gómez Villanueva. By June 1977 Gómez Villanueva had been elevated to the presidency of the national Chamber of Deputies under the López Portillo administration. It appeared that he had earlier approved the transactions in question but it was not clear at first whether Gómez Villanueva knew that fraud was being committed or if he personally benefited by it.

Since the investor groups that received the Chicago loan had insufficient funds to guarantee purchase of shares (which they had pledged to accomplish) in the Bay of Flags investment, the real guarantee consisted in a "purchase contract" which the Banco Nacional de Obras y Servicios Públicos held. These negotiations were the nub of the fraud.[38] Also included was the promise of guaranteed stock values according to an unusual scale under which the shares would double not only their value within the first year but would graduate in value thereafter. This was a violation of Mexican law that was described as monstrous considering that much of the basis for the shares to be emitted would be real estate on which the buildings would not even be completed within the first year, much less be able to double their value.[39]

On the basis of the charges brought by the new director of the Bay of Flags trust, a series of government audits discovered large embezzlements of funds using false expenditure accounting to disguise the flow of funds. The embezzlers were not very skillful, or perhaps they never expected to get audited. They used such transparent tactics as inventing banquets given at nonexistent restaurants and showing enormous promotional parties given for hundreds of persons in cafes where scarcely 30 persons could be seated.[40] All the while the principals to the fraud collected generous salaries. In this way, much of the funds from the Chicago bank loan were eaten up. There were political expenditures as well.

Ríos Camarena was arrested in Miami, Florida, during July 1977 by FBI agents under legal provisions of the extradition treaty existing between the two countries. Mexico had requested the arrest and sent documentation to support its demand that the fugitive be returned to face justice. Gómez Villanueva, still president of the Chamber of Deputies, told reporters he favored a full investigation and disclosure of all public functionaries involved in the Bay of Flags fraud, apparently having nothing to fear himself.[41] But Ríos Camarena had a great deal to fear. When he was apprehended in Miami he mistook the FBI agents for Mexican secret police and upon learning in whose custody he was he demanded to speak with U.S. Immigration authorities. He begged that they grant him political asylum saying, "I don't want to fall into the hands of Mexican justice."[42]

It appeared that there would be little justice for the peasants who were dispossessed of their land via the Bay of Flags scandal. Nor were the funds involved, running into the millions of dollars, used to benefit the needy or to stimulate the economy. Such corruption-based failures of the Mexican government's entrepreneurial schemes cannot help but be seen as an administrative style which benefits the few and alienates the many. In the process, there is no change in the overall quality of life. The people are wretched as always.

MEXICO'S POVERTY: STATISTICS AND VIGNETTES

Political alienation stems from poverty, among other things. Surely the direct victims of poverty are alienated toward the regime, provided they sense their relative deprivation.[43] Intellectuals seize upon poverty conditions as a cause for political movements designed to subvert what is perceived as an unjust social order. False expectations such as those generated (at least temporarily) by SICARTSA or scandals like that of the Bay of Flags are likely to increase frustration and aggression toward the wrongdoers (and toward those who protect them). Much of Mexico's governmental style does alienate those who are capable of knowing that a better life is possible were not scarce resources wasted. The acute violence perpetrated in the late 1970s by terrorist groups reflects the desperation of certain segments of the society toward a status quo which is not likely to be changed via playing the formal rules of the game. This was attested to by the growing menace of extremist groups like the 23rd of September Communist League and other terrorist organizations of its ilk. Let us examine here some of the apparent socioeconomic roots of such rebellion via a series of statistics and vignettes.

Roughly a million persons live in Delegación Alvaro Obregón, one of the Mexican Federal District's 16 urban administrative subdivisions. Some of these people live in material splendor, in neighborhoods called San Angel and Pedregal. Also located in Delegación Obregón is the National University with its world-famous murals and mosaics. Combined, the university community, San Angel, and Pedregal make up something approaching 30 percent of the total delegación population. However, a classified study, to which I became privy, indicates that the other 70 percent live in wretched poverty.[44] We might call this unpublished document the "Pentagon Papers of Mexico City," for it dramatizes in bold relief the pathos of the culture of poverty placed side by side with the culture of affluence and conspicuous consumption.

At the other end of greater Mexico City, beyond the Zaragoza exit of the subway, there lies another great human wasteland. Its name is Ciudad Netzahualcóyotl. Over 100,000 wretched souls live in this *colonia* alone, largely without sanitary services of any kind. There is no justice, scant education, little trash and garbage collection, most drinking water is polluted, few of the shacks have electricity, and the majority of those which do enjoy this luxury have dangerous wiring that is spliced illegally into a power line. By and large medical care is homeopathic or by witch doctors. The government's health services are reserved, generally, for members of the favored unions that belong to Mexico's official government party, the PRI. There is a welfare system for the poor, but corrupt officials frequently sell the medical services and food staples provided thereby. This means in fact that there is true welfare for almost no one. The paucity of employment opportunities for these people is just about as desperate.

If we return to Delegación Obregón in Mexico City, and the classified study with which I "absconded," we find a similar horror story. The air is among the most acutely polluted of any urban area in the world. At 7,500 feet the air is also short on oxygen. Several samples from this officially conducted (and later deliberately classified) study illustrate the fate of some 70 percent of the inhabitants of Delegación Obregón. The delegación is divided into colonias whose lines are defined arbitrarily or in accordance with socioeconomic and geographic characteristics. In the colonia Barrio Norte there is no public health service of any kind. Dirty water pours down from Juárez Avenue above, the streets flood with sewage, garbage and human refuse are thrown in the street. It rots there if the rats do not eat it first and what they leave children play in. In the colonia Bejero people have erected crude huts beneath large sewer conduits which frequently leak a fetid poisonous liquid that runs down the sides of the *barrancas* or canyons and whose pestilence escapes no one. Even though it is known that people live at the bottom of the barranca, those on the hillside throw their trash and feces onto the cardboard roofs of their less-fortunate neighbor's huts. There is a total absence of public services in this colonia. There are not even any paved roads for a garbage truck to enter. This is typical of some 70 percent of the colonias that make up Delegación Obregón.[45]

Conditions of life in the poor colonias such as Bejero would have to be reflected in an honestly administered census. Although any figures on the quality of life emanating from within the Mexican government must be used cautiously, I have reason to believe that the most recent census was taken as accurately as possible. Earlier I cited the 1970 census (published in 1972) as being semiclassified (because of the grim picture it paints) at the time I acquired a copy. It shows that nearly 72 percent of the total wage-earning population of Mexico subsists on less than $80 average per month. About 0.5 percent of the same population receives a monthly income of more than $1,100. These are niggardly figures when compared with the United States whose average per capita income fluctuates somewhere above the $4,000 mark while that of Mexico is nearer $600. Within that tiny peak of the Mexican wealth pyramid (that is, the 0.5 percent) there is much wealth. In Mexico's capital city alone, a junior bank officer told me, off the record, there are some 14,000 millionaires and at least half of them began without a nickel in their pockets. How did they make it? Through politics of course. At whose expense did they make it? Well, that is a different question. There is a saying I cited earlier in Mexican officialdom that one must not "live in error," that is, live outside the public budget if he is to be considered truly a success. Indeed, feeding at the public trough is a mark of success in Mexico. And as the above figures show, success is a very scarce quality, one to be prized, fought for, and held tenaciously once won. Of course, there are cases like that of the Bay of Flags which place a system winner into a loser category when he must be sacrificed like Ríos Camarena, in order to purge the system of its impurities.

But let us examine other indexes of who gets what, a question obviously related to poverty and to one's purchasing power. In all 32 of Mexico's federal subdivisions, only the Federal District (Mexico City) and the state of Baja California Norte (bordering on San Diego, California) have an average monthly income that is predominantly in excess of $80. This is to say that with the two mentioned exceptions (and the Federal District is a borderline case, 47.07 percent) none of the Mexican states can claim that over half of their wage earners receive more than $80 average per month. Another interesting fact emerges from inspection of these data. The 11 states having the lowest per capita incomes also have the highest concentration of relative affluence.

Here is still another indicator of poverty, taken from the official census data. Throughout the entire republic 13.08 percent of the total housing units (not population) were found to subsist without ever eating eggs, milk, meat, or fish. This we will label acute poverty. Given the numbers of persons who, on the average, occupy edifices that can be identified as housing units in Mexico, this figure has horrendous implications. Looking only at the question of milk, experts estimated that out of Mexico's approximately 52 million total population in 1972, there were some 17 million who normally were unable to drink milk at all and at least 3 million who scarcely knew what milk was.[46] On the other hand, if we seek an indicator of relative affluence, the 1970 census shows that in the entire republic only 1.29 percent of the total housing units were characterized by the consumption of eggs, milk, meat, and fish from four to seven days per week. And I stress that this is relative affluence because the census does not tell us anything about the nature of the distribution of this consumption; that is, does the father gorge himself while the wife and children starve? Yet the census takers may count his dwelling as within the category that I have defined as relatively affluent. Using this criterion still, the federal subdivisions range from Zacatecas in which nearly 33 percent of the housing units are in the status of acute poverty vis-a-vis food consumption to the Federal District with less than 3 percent in this category.

Finally, let us look at footwear as an indicator of Mexican well-being. The data show that for the entire republic 20 percent were without any footwear whatsoever (sandals, huaraches, and shoes being lumped together). The range of this indicator runs from Oaxaca where 55 percent of the people went barefoot to the Federal District where only 1 percent were so unfortunate. It should be kept in mind, however, that in some tropical areas of Mexico there may be a social tradition of going barefoot and in such cases the absence of shoes is not necessarily a sign of poverty—but the fact that one does not even possess sandals may be such a sign.

On all the evidence that I have seen, these poverty conditions have not changed significantly in the late 1970s. If the Mexican population in fact triples during this century as has been predicted, it would seem that unspeakable penury and human sacrifice will result; indeed, it now exists. Added to the population pressure has been the impact of rural-to-urban migration, largely as a result of an impoverished peasantry seeking the enigma of opportunity in the larger cities. The concomitant growth of gigantic slums is seen today in every urban area. This situation has been largely ignored by Mexican governments until the Echeverría regime which decided, too late perhaps, to break with tradition and support birth control.

The Mexican government took notice of the demographic prophets of gloom in December 1972 and promulgated an anti-Malthusian document known as the Program of Family Planning. The striking feature of this move was that Mexico's 80 Catholic bishops endorsed the document, abandoning their previous resistance (not all bishops had previously opposed), declaring that the circumstances of the majority of Mexican families were so inhumane as to make family planning a matter of human mercy.[47] An Episcopal Letter was also issued ordering all priests to prepare young couples to accept a moral responsibility for determining the size of their families. It left to each individual the decision as to methods. This, it was stressed, would not cause a Christian believer to lose grace in the sight of God.

The irony of the Mexican government's decision to offer family planning is that many of the people who need it most are illiterate and in such marginal socioeconomic conditions that they cannot take advantage of what is offered (even when it is offered honestly and efficiently).[48] For millions a bus trip to a distant family planning center is costly to the point of being an economic hardship. It is especially important that North American readers grasp the poignant circumstances of life in which these people find themselves. Poverty conditions not only underlie political alienation, they lie behind illegal migration to the United States, a phenomenon which is very much a part of the failure of the Mexican political system to solve its internal problems. Here are some anecdotal insights.

1. In the northern desert of Coahuila bordering Texas, on the ejido Puebla, Ofelia Arroyo de Rosales says goodby to her husband Urbano: "Let's

hope our daughter Dolores has her baby well without bad luck."[49] Urbano is a bent, twisted man whose hands are bloody from scraping a living out of the desert, looking for *lechuguilla,* a kind of wild lettuce with thistles. His wife also hopes no wicked person will put the evil eye on her daughter so as to ruin her delivery and place a hex on the child if it survives. Ofelia tells the reporter that her life has been filled with misery, that three of her ten children died because God wanted it that way. While she talked her husband Urbano would be hunchbacked for 14 hours doing the stoop labor that scraping the desert for a living demands. He works 14 hours a day to be able to eat tortillas and beans every evening. Ofelia had urged Urbano to give up scratching the desert, she had begged him to do so for the past 25 years, but he seemed glued to the land and would not leave it. The reporter entered the crude hut made of desert stone and mud. These people were well off compared to many in Mexico, they had two rooms for nine people and were able to eat bean tacos at least once a day. The roof of the hut was thatched with wooden rafters, next came palm leaves, and on top of this were assorted pieces of cardboard. Covering the entire roof was a seal of mud clay.

Ofelia is thin but her stomach protrudes for she is sick. She covers her head with a black veil to hide the effects of the sickness. She makes tortillas and bean soup all day, the only nutrients the family is able to enjoy. This also describes the caloric intake of approximately 100,000 surrounding families who occupy some 20 million hectares of desert land that extends into the neighboring states of San Luis Potosí, Zacatecas, Nuevo León, and Tamaulipas —in other words, much of Mexico's northeast. The only recent day that Ofelia has eaten meat was over a year ago when her daughter, now expecting, got married. Meat is for fiesta days, and then only the most rare ones at that. "Look at that little pig that we are fattening" she says, "we are saving it for January 6 which is the day of the Holy Kings; then the children will eat meat." Ofelia has four hens which seldom lay eggs but when they do the whole family has a feast on eggs fried with beans.

Their ejido is some 30 miles from Saltillo where the husband of Ofelia's expectant daughter works as a manual laborer whenever there is work. She speaks of one of her sons who died of a stomach infection that could not be cured by the local homeopathics. She offers the reporter a glass of water after relating that death. He looks at the color of the water and Ofelia says "it is rainwater, there are some little worms in it but they won't do you harm." Then she adds, "The third of my children died at the age of 15 days, also of a stomach infection." Ofelia presses on her stomach from occasional pain. The public health service gives her a prescription of medicine, but no pharmacy will honor it without cash. So Ofelia remains ill as have most of the members of her family.

The reporter hears tales of horses that have died from encephalitis despite the vaccinations they received from government veterinarians. The people of the ejido believe that their own witchcraft is a better cure for horses and that the injections given the horses were, in reality, intended to kill them so as to drive the people from the ejido—or it was a case of the evil eye once again. Various peasants had cured their horses with herbs. The reporter gives 10 pesos to one of Ofelia's younger children who immediately runs to buy corn meal for his mother. The reporter asks, "Why haven't you abandoned this desert?" The reply is, "Because it seems that this land sticks to the feet and the heart of my husband and he always says to me, 'You wait and see, this year it will rain and then we will no longer be poor.' "

Someone asks, "When will don Urbano return?" "Well, when the sun begins to point toward evening he'll come home exhausted, eat a few tortillas and beans, and fall asleep in that crude bed." The children by and large sleep on the floor using rag mattresses. Ofelia shows the reporter the record book of produce that her family has generated for La Forestal, the government agency that buys wood and desert products. She asks, "After this much produce is it fair that they give us no medicine whatsoever?" "We even took Marcos out of school to help bring in a little more and our pay is almost nothing, these tortillas you see here." With the reporter's gift of money they would buy meat in Saltillo and invited him to eat with them the following day. There would be a fiesta in ejido Puebla.

2. Puerto Escondido, Oaxaca, April 1972. The people of this village eat peelings, roots, tree leaves, birds, iguanas, snakes, and rats. Often they eat them raw when in desperation. It is rare for them to enjoy tortillas and beans. When there is nothing, as is often the case, the children suck their fingers to forget their hunger. Jacinto Sánchez Ventura, his wife, and three children live in the most squalid misery. They, along with numerous other peasants, have been forced by the state government to leave their food-producing lands under threats of violence. The state simply expropriated their lands and now these peasants live in a slum called colonia Lázaro Cárdenas, named, ironically, after the Mexican president who distributed probably more land than any other and for whom a giant steel mill would soon be named as a promise of better times to come.

It is almost two miles to the center of Puerto Escondido where they must take their children for schooling and go in search of work. Lázaro Cárdenas looks like a concentration camp where people live jointly with animals.[50] In its center is a giant ditch where the people throw their refuse. Sanitary facilities (other than the ditch) do not exist. The shacks are palm-thatched huts. People seldom take to the street after midday for fear of sunstroke. In this torrid zone the sun falls like a lead weight. Naked starving children sleep listlessly under the few trees that grow there.

Why did the government take Jacinto's land? His wife, carrying their tiniest child in a *rebozo,* says, "No one can resist the government and we poor don't dare complain or things will be worse for us even yet. Most people here are afraid to talk about it, but not don Hilario Cortés who lives over there; go talk with him!" Hilario Cortés, ex-peasant landowner and now slum dweller, tells the reporter, "It was a good life, I worked my land hard, like a mule, and we were happy. One day government officials arrived and told us they were going to relocate us so as to improve our life. Now look at us as a result. This is all I can tell you. I have already lost my land. I don't want to lose my life as well."

Hilario calls to an ex-fisherman, Andrés Bautista, who was also expropriated who comes over. Once the ice is broken in the conversation, and he does not fear the reporter, Andrés says that he was expropriated without a cent of payment and now they want to move him out of his slum dwelling, again without payment. Hilario interjects, "But the gringo Jones, who else?" Andrés responds, "In my case this Jones was accompanied by a group of policemen to my house and they threw me out and took me to jail for the rest of the day. Then Jones came to see me in my cell and said I had been one of the most troublesome peasants in the area. He said that I would have to 'sell' my land if I did not want harm to come to my wife and nine children. I had to leave to protect my family." Andrés, Hilario, Jacinto, and the other slum dwellers near Puerto Escondido, Oaxaca, cannot eat beans and tortillas every day. But the gringo Jones is willing to have them eat snakes and rats.

3. Aztecas 49 is a barrio in Mexico City's zone known as Tepito in which the inhabitants were threatened with expulsion for their inability to buy the land from slum landlords. For them an ideal solution would have been government-financed mortgages.[51] These people were born in this neighborhood and are certain that there will be no place for them to go if real-estate speculators begin a construction project. Juan Espinosa, a small merchant in barrio Aztecas 51 told the reporter, "I live here with my wife and eight children in two rooms without bath or toilet, but where else are we going to find a house this cheap." His concern was prompted by the tactics of slum landlords aimed at forcing their tenants to sign new leases that would avoid Mexico's frozen rent law that applies to poor housing. The landlords will not repair the huts they rent as dwellings. One tenant who admitted repairing his own shack pointed out, "But look there, the house of Señora María Luisa Vargas Rodríguez with her eight children—the little house is falling in on top of them but she is in desperate financial condition and can do nothing." Another lady has lived in Tepito 20 years and now pays almost $9 per month rent. She has to do her own painting and repairs.

The people claim that, poor as they may be, there is no delinquency problem in Tepito, "We are all good people working in small shops like shoe repair, but because we must work long hours we cannot care for our children of which there are too many." The testimony continues: "In this area there are 52 dwellings, many occupied by two families, and the smallest of the families begins at five children. Recently a second kindergarten was set up here by the government but it does not meet our needs." Doña Mariquita González is 80 years old and has lived in Tepito 70 of those years. She is considered the *portera* or caretaker of barrio Aztecas 51 and lives there free as representative of the landlord who, in this case, is a lady from Spain. The people complain of many such landlords, and of the water that ruins their possessions when the city floods. They dispatched prayers via the reporter that President Echeverría would help them.

4. Had Mexico's circumstances of poverty and hunger changed for the better as López Portillo's presidency got underway? It did not seem so. Inflation had hurt the poor people severely. The peso devaluation affected the economy adversely. Manufacturing, agriculture, and other so-called labor-intensive sectors were functioning at low levels. In 1977 President López Portillo admitted that his nation was passing through an economic crisis. Figures of 50 percent unemployment were being cited for various sectors of the available labor force.

In this atmosphere the journalist Ricardo Garibay did a three-part series on hunger in Mexico during 1977. He wrote there are at least 5 million desperately poor people in greater Mexico City (total population somewhere near 12 million), they are all about us, he said, just around the corner, but most of us never see them.[52] But, he told his friend Margarita, the future crush of humanity is on the gallop rapidly approaching us. Garibay invited Margarita the anthropologist (who had somehow not seen the real poor of the city in which she lived) along with a sociologist and a photographer on a tour of Mexico City's slums to see the millions of paracaidistas or squatters who lived in precarious zones. These are people who have brought with them from the country their own methods of survival.

The government may align their streets and pave the principal ones, it sells them cheaply a grey wall-making material made of pressed sand, but they still live in mud huts with metal and cardboard tops, often no windows; inside live fathers and daughters, aunts, uncles, nephews, dogs, hens, and pigs, all scrambled up together. The area about each house is strewn with excrement, vomit, rotting garbage; cockroaches, flies, and spiders are everywhere; life inside the shacks is often one of drunkeness out of despair—men, women, children all drunk—and there is much incest. From these hovels come thousands of nighttime thieves, prostitutes, and muggers. The metropolis is surrounded by them.[53] "Don't you see," Garibay quizzes his companions, "we are surrounded by nearly half the population which lives in a way that you would not wish on your dog, and to a certain extent we who are better off owe our condition to the suffering of these poor whose services and salaries we consume."[54]

The reporter and his friends were accompanied by some women of the barrio. They said that during the presidency of Luis Echeverría and the governorship of Carlos Hank González in the state of Mexico (where the slum extends out of the Federal District) an effort was made to "varnish over" the misery of this zone and thereby hide the scandal. But they left it as it was. Echeverría went on to better things and Hank González became regente of Mexico City where he could continue to ignore the scandal of poverty.[55] They also commented that the new president López Portillo had made a speech saying he was sorry for living conditions here and that something would be done. But he never said what would be done in any precise terms that the people could understand. The women expressed cynicism predicting that the same governmental crooks as before would siphon off any funds that could be used for welfare and deposit it in the banks to the north of Uncle Sam.

Mounds of trash and garbage build up everywhere. They are covered with health-infecting flies and bloated rats. One of the girls accompanying Garibay asks why doesn't the public authority simply come with bulldozers and remove this fetid mess. Because, the reporter replies, it would take from many people their only way of living. Some of the trash is brought from the city and may contain things the poor can use and sell. Others simply eat the garbage, rotten though it may be. And, he adds, don't forget that the real problem is that there is little or no demand for the labor of these people.[56] The stench of the slum is overwhelming. Nausea overcomes the reporter's friends. They begin to understand, and to fear, what life in the slum must be. They speak to Pablo Romero who came to the slum five years ago from Michoacán. He is a *pepenador,* a scavenger in the trash pile, his only employment. Pablo's personal filth is such that the reporter holds a handkerchief over his nose, pretending he has a cold.

Pablo is willing to talk. There are 13 people in his family. If he has luck finding articles of value in the trash dump he earns two U.S. dollars (peso equivalent) every three days. On this and garbage scraps his family subsists. When asked if his children eat meat and eggs or drink milk he only smiles, sadly, but does not reply.[57] Pablo says he and his people are very bad off. Then he opens his shirt and displays a gangrenously infected side. The reporter becomes ill and cannot continue the interview. He leaves saying, *que mierda somos. Te aseguro que somos una mierda.*[58] Still in some of the homes he sees the national flag pasted to the wall and the image of the Virgin of Guadalupe, watching over her 5 million wretched beings.

A woman from Guanajuato tells of life in the urban slums versus life in the rural slums. She says the air was much better in Guanajuato and one often had a nicer view, but there one would surely die. The rain was scarce and crops were few. Although the economic circumstances in Mexico City were bad, once in a while they sold something, they ate poorly, but they ate. She was cooking a stew made of tripe as she talked to the reporter. Her husband would carry this to a nearby street to try to sell cupsful to passers-by. She assured the reporter that everything was clean in her kitchen and feared he might be someone from the Health Department (about which she had heard but not seen). Looking about the reporter saw pestilence everywhere, rabid dogs, diseased children, and no sign that anyone in modern Mexico knew or cared. Garibay wrote that perhaps the best one could do was to forget about these miserable people surrounding the well-to-do other half of Mexico City:

> . . . five million humans who will erupt one day, what doubt is there, even though tomorrow they will have forgotten you too; but they will erupt, or disappear in the final condition of human beings in this society: they will be erased, liquidated, to exist no more, and will become shadows beneath the splendors of rifles and clubs of the coming dictatorship which is almost inevitable.[59]

What seems also to be inevitable is the continuation of this poverty. Mexico in the late 1970s does not show signs of being able to absorb its excess humanity through economic growth and this will likely be a problem into the 1980s, perhaps forever. And economic growth is unlikely to come as long as political corruption impedes it. Corruption also impedes research efforts to gauge the extent of poverty. Thus, when the reporter cited above declared that 5 million people lived in the slums of Mexico City as of 1977, one might correctly ask on what he bases his estimate. But the formal census data can be revealing. Classified studies, such as the one from Delegación Obregón cited earlier, also tend to uphold the 5 million estimate. Informal communications I have received from scholars in Mexico suggest that on a nationwide basis the problem is likely as severe, and even more so in many places, as was the case depicted by Garibay and his interviewers.[60]

CONCLUSIONS ON GOVERNMENT AND THE QUALITY OF LIFE

One recent study of employment (and the lack thereof) in Mexico contends that it is not quite so serious as had often been alleged but admits findings that between 37 and 45 percent of the available labor force was un– or underemployed in 1970 and that the unemployment of women was nearly double that of men. This study attributes most of the problem to technological change as a human displacement factor and admits that having a labor surplus tends to depress wages across the board. It also cites the problem of disguised unemployment, which includes such circumstances as unpaid family workers in a family-operated enterprise. The study further concludes that Mexican unemployment was somewhat alleviated between 1940 and 1950 and then worsened thereafter. The cited period of alleviation comprehended World War II when millions of Mexican workers were welcomed into the United States.

The worsening period to 1970 corresponded to harsher U.S. efforts to stem such migration, which by then had been made illegal in most instances. The problem of such migration is taken up in Chapter 7. But by the late 1970s Mexico's unemployment crisis was manifest both by illegal migration to the United States and by slum concentration in Mexico's major cities, as described in some of the foregoing scenarios. It may be difficult for researchers to come to agreement on the correct statistics of poverty in Mexico, but it is somewhat easier, as I have tried to show above, to reflect the pathos of the phenomenon as found in the great slums.

One of the great unknowns during the decade ahead is the impact of Mexican oil on the nation's economy and as a potential source of relief for the nation's severe poverty conditions. Probably a key consideration here is that petroleum development is generally considered to be capital intensive with strong export potential. What Mexico seems to need most are labor-intensive industries; however, proceeds from a successful oil-export operation could, if not wasted by corruption, be used for critically needed welfare purposes in Mexico.

During 1972–74 Mexico actually imported oil to satisfy its internal needs. But also during those years major oil discoveries were made in the southern states of Chiapas and Tabasco along with some impressive off-shore finds. The so-called Reforma Fields now put Mexico in the position of an exporter nation that can use its scarce commodity as a diplomatic tool. According to a study surveyed in the *Wall Street Journal* (October 26, 1977) the nationalized Mexican oil monopoly PEMEX could be producing from 4 to 6 million barrels per day by 1990, an increase from 1.1 million in 1977. That would put Mexico roughly on a par with Iran given a continuation of the current Iranian output rate. The U.S. production in 1977 was approximately 8 million barrels per day and this is expected to decline over the years barring major new finds. Mexico also has major natural gas reserves and plans are already in motion to import this scarce commodity into the United States. In short, by the end of the López Portillo sexenio in 1982, Mexico hopes to be exporting more than $8 billion annually of oil, natural gas, and related petrochemicals and it is anticipated that most of this will go to the United States. Thus the dependency relationship already existing between the two nations is likely to become all the more critical. Given that Mexico has some 40 percent unemployment in the late 1970s and a heavy foreign debt to service (much of which is owed to U.S. banks), it will be easier for the Mexican politicians to pressure the United States for a liberal immigration policy (relieving Mexico's population pressure) in exchange for favorable terms of trade on petroleum products.

This may not meet with unanimous approval in North America. The Mexicans are demanding a price of $2.60 for 1,000 cubic feet of natural gas, significantly above the $2.16 that has been paid to Canadian producers.

Domestic producers, especially in Texas and Louisiana, may object to the Mexican competition. If Mexico does win generous terms of trade, and channels these funds to pay off the some $25 billion of foreign debt it had in 1976 when Luis Echeverría vacated the presidency (and about half of that is owed to U.S. banks), it will have met the International Monetary Fund's austerity terms for stabilizing the economy and preserving Mexico's good credit overseas. But the costs at home will be limits on domestic lending, reduced purchasing power, wage ceilings, a pinch on the consuming masses, and a range of unpopular symptoms which accompany austerity. This, in turn, may be accompanied by increases in profit-related crimes and political violence as well. It will almost certainly mean that more and more Mexicans will seek income north of the Rio Grande, regardless of changes in the immigration laws that the U.S. Congress may enact.

During the last year of the Echeverría sexenio there were jokes floating about international banking circles that the long-range strategy of the outgoing president had been to mortgage Mexico completely to the United States, then default, and turn the country over to whatever Wall Street might decide as a proper fate. It is also said that for the first time in twentieth-century Mexican history that nation has as president a former finance minister in the person of López Portillo. Perhaps he will provide the genius needed to solve Mexico's economic malaise. But it is intimately linked with corruption, a social and political malaise. If Mexico's suffering millions are to have a glimpse of hope within the next decade, the politics of plunder and poverty will have to undergo radical and lasting changes in their operating norms.

NOTES

1. One of the best-known texts in this category is L. V. Padgett's *The Mexican Political System* (Boston: Houghton Mifflin, 1966 and 1976). His work, while for the most part sympathetic and even apologetic toward the PRI, is still rich in formalistic detail and will be a useful research source for many scholars.

2. Pablo González Casanova, *La democracia en México* (Mexico: Ediciones ERA, 1965), pp. 137–38.

3. *Proceso,* January 22, 1977, p. 13.

4. Ibid., p. 11.

5. Ibid., p. 12.

6. Ibid., p. 11.

7. A useful recent survey of the Mexican government's role in the economy is found in José Luis Reyna and Richard S. Weinert, eds., *Authoritarianism in Mexico* (Philadelphia: Institute for the Study of Human Issues, 1977).

8. José Luis Reyna, "Redefining the Authoritarian Regime," in ibid., p. 160.

9. René Villarreal, "The Policy of Import-Substituting Industrialization, 1929–1975," in ibid., p. 75.

10. Corruption is the illegal use of public power to serve private ends. Political modernization may contribute to corruption by creating new sources of wealth and by making the acquisition

of wealth tantamount to acquiring power. It has been argued that in some cultures corruption may be most acute during the more intense phases of modernization. See Samuel Huntington, *Political Order in Changing Societies* (New Haven, Conn.: Yale University Press, 1968), p. 59.

11. In addition to expropriation of the foreign oil interests operating in Mexico in 1938, Cárdenas undertook an agrarian reform program that the country had never witnessed. In fact, during his first three years he doubled the number of heads of family having land to work. Twenty-five years before, none of these people had land they could call their own. See Charles C. Cumberland, *Mexico: The Struggle for Modernity* (New York: Oxford University Press, 1968), p. 299.

12. These estimates by U.S. Immigration and Naturalization officials are impossible to document given the obvious problem of taking a census among members of an illegal population.

13. As published in *Visión,* November 4, 1972, p. 19.

14. Translated from ibid., p. 15.

15. Ibid.

16. See Richard S. Weinert, "The State and Foreign Capital," in Reyna and Weinert, op. cit., passim.

17. Lorenzo Meyer, "Historical Roots of the Authoritarian State in Mexico," in ibid., p. 17.

18. *Visión,* December 2, 1972, p. 12.

19. Villarreal, op. cit., p. 97.

20. *Visión,* December 2, 1972, p. 12.

21. Ibid.

22. Ibid.

23. See the treatment of the case of AUTOMEX in K. F. Johnson, *Mexican Democracy: A Critical View* (Boston: Allyn & Bacon, 1972), pp. 98–101.

24. *Proceso,* December 11, 1976, p. 30.

25. In the first edition of *Mexican Democracy* I dealt at some length with the complaints which have been made against CONASUPO. Most of these occurred during the 1960s when Carlos Hank González, later governor of the state of Mexico and more recently the mayor of the Federal District, served as director of CONASUPO. The charges ranged from swindling countryfolk out of the profits from their grain harvest, to elevating the price of bread consumed by the poor, to an indirect subsidy of foreign nations through selling of grains at a loss on the international market. More recent testimony indicates that some of these abuses have been corrected. At any rate, the PRI seems permanently committed to maintaining CONASUPO as a contact mechanism with the masses, one that is intended to have a welfare function as well.

26. See his monograph by the same name published by the Center for Inter-American Studies at the University of Texas at El Paso, November 1975.

27. *Proceso,* June 20, 1977, p. 16.

28. Ibid.

29. Raul Prieto, "Elefantes negros," *Proceso,* December 11, 1976, p. 46.

30. Ibid.

31. Ibid., p. 17.

32. *Proceso,* June 20, 1977, p. 7.

33. Ibid., p. 9.

34. Ibid., p. 11.

35. Ibid., p. 8.

36. Ibid.

37. Ibid.

38. *Proceso,* June 27, 1977, pp. 8–9.

39. Ibid.

40. Ibid.

41. *Proceso,* July 25, 1977, p. 29.

42. *Proceso,* August 1, 1977, p. 12. Later, on August 10, 1977, it was announced that President López Portillo had named Gómez Villanueva as ambassador to Italy. He was thus removed from his leadership position in the Chamber of Deputies and placed in a sort of diplomatic exile from which it would be hard to involve him further in the Ríos Camarena scandal. In making this appointment the incumbent ambassador to Italy, Fausto Zapata, a key member of former president Echeverría's camarilla, had to be bumped. Fausto Zapata had been instrumental in the takeover of *Excelsior* in 1976. As these events unfolded, new evidence was made public implicating Gómez Villanueva in the Bay of Flags scandal, but official PRI statements tried to make it sound as if he were leaving the Chamber of Deputies because his real profession was diplomacy and that Gómez Villanueva was simply following a patriotic call to "revolutionary discipline" (*Proceso,* August 15, 1977, p. 8). It appeared that Gómez Villanueva had been burned by the scandal but he could not be sacrificed via public disgrace as was done with Ríos Camarena, the former being too powerful in the PRI hierarchy and the leader of his own influential camarilla. It could be argued that the Bay of Flags scandal had provided López Portillo with the opportunity he needed to purge holdovers from the previous regime just as Luis Echeverría had done when the June 10th affair presented him with an opportunity in 1971.

43. Relative deprivation is understood to mean the discrepancy between a political actor's value expectations and his perceived value capabilities. See Ted Robert Gurr, *Why Men Rebel* (Princeton, N.J.: Princeton University Press, 1970), passim.

44. This study of Delegación Alvaro Obregón was titled simply *Investigación de Campo* and was made available to this writer, and to his colleague Robert Bezdek, by Carlos Madrazo Pintado, the administrative head of the delegación in 1972.

45. Ibid.

46. *Visión,* November 4, 1972.

47. *Diario las Américas* (Miami), December 16, 1972.

48. See Marvin Alisky's "Mexico versus Malthus: National Trends," *Current History,* May 1974, especially p. 203.

49. *Excelsior,* October 31, 1971.

50. *Excelsior,* April 16, 1972.

51. *Excelsior,* October 1, 1972.

52. *Proceso,* August 8, 1977, p. 7.

53. Ibid., p. 8.

54. Ibid.

55. Ibid., p. 9.

56. *Proceso,* August 15, 1977, p. 14.

57. Ibid., p. 16.

58. Ibid. Translated loosely, this means "What rotten crud we are. I assure you, that's all we are."

59. *Proceso,* August 22, 1977, p. 16.

60. A study by Wayne A. Cornelius (*Politics and the Migrant Poor in Mexico City* [Stanford, Calif.: Stanford University Press, 1975]) has some valuable observations about poverty in Mexico. However, it suffers from the contamination that is inevitable when one must depend for research input upon those who are "in" with the party regime. Cornelius argues that the basic aim of the study is to understand how specific kinds of urban dwelling environments affect the political attitudes and behavior of selected urban poor, but he infers, not proves, that given environments condition attitudes. He has no causal connection between the expression of attitudes and differing physical environments. The study is full of self-fulfilling prophecies like the assertion that those having had good experiences with the regime will be more inclined to support the political system (p. 218).

Six

Forces and Parties
of Political Opposition

One lesson from the previous chapters is summarized in a statement by Edward Williams, one which grasps a key root cause of Mexico's political and socioeconomic malaise. He writes:

> The Mexican elites (over the years) quite consciously chose to initiate a headlong dash to industrialize and fashioned nationalistic ideology and power centralization to facilitate that goal. Measurable, indeed remarkable, progress has been achieved over the past several decades, but beginning in the late Sixties and early Seventies stresses and strains began to emerge in fairly clear form. The injustices wrought by the system eventually evoked opposition which, in turn, explains the signs of increasing repression.[1]

But socioeconomic development did not yield an equitable wealth distribution and, as we have seen, more Mexicans grew increasingly desperate. On top of that more and more Mexicans were added to the population, mouths which the system could not feed. Political pluralism did not increase either; indeed on all the evidence the numbers of bona fide political forces and interest groups which could participate meaningfully in national decision making have been on the decline. Only intra-PRI democracy or official pluralism remained. Those outside the penumbra of officialdom were continually ostracized and persecuted.

In the original version of *Mexican Democracy* I attempted to construct a kind of spectrogram depicting the range of political opposition groups in Mexico according to sectors of ideological tendency, for example, the Marxist sector, the restorationist sector, and so on. The years have shown that such a typology has only ephemeral value. Parties change internally. Outgroups are suppressed and eliminated. But the politics of protest continue. During the last 50 years of Mexican political life there have been at least six major opposition movements which can be identified and whose efforts can be traced to lingering influences in today's opposition circles. These are the following:

The cristeros, crusaders against the perceived communist and atheistic tendencies of the Calles era, were Christian guerrillas, numbering perhaps as many as 25,000, who fought against federal troops three times that number. In 1929 the Vatican negotiated a cease-fire and most of the cristeros turned in their weapons, knowing that they would probably be slaughtered. Out of their martyrdom grew today's *sinarquista* movement.

The sinarquistas, formally the Unión Nacional Sinarquista (UNS), organized a struggle against the socialistic thrust of the Cárdenas regime. Led by Salvador Abascal and others, the sinarquistas created a "spiritual militia" which unsuccessfully sought in 1941 to take over the city of Morelia and attempted the colonization of part of Baja California. This group remains active today and is the foundation of one aspiring opposition political party (discussed later).

In the elections of 1940 a conservative and reactionary force bolted the official party and supported the independent candidacy of General Juan Andreu Almazán. He had support from the recently formed National Action Party which is today's principal opposition party with legal registry. Almazán (*almazanismo*) also received support from what is the now-powerful Monterrey Group which was just then being organized. Almazán's party (Revolutionary Party of National Unification, PRUN) disappeared but some contend that his influence lingers in right-wing groups both within and outside the PRI. Almazán became a symbol of advocacy for bourgeois interests.

Toward the middle of 1958, as Adolfo López Mateos's presidential campaign was well underway, the railway workers' union erupted in defiance of the official unions that had consolidated their grasp on Mexican labor since the presidency of Miguel Alemán (1946–52). One of the principal complaints was poor living conditions. The workers were guaranteed housing under law but it was being denied. The writer Renato Leduc alleged to have evidence that the United States intervened using the CIA to help López Mateos break the workers' strike with force.[2] Under the Mexican Penal Code, Article 145 (*delito de disolución social,* a variety of sedition) strike leaders Valentín Campa and Demetrio Vallejo remained in prison for 11 years along with the painter David Alfaro Siqueiros (whose captivity is said to have been one of special treatment out of deference for his world-renowned status). Valentín Campa was a symbolic presidential candidate for the Mexican Communist party in the elections of 1976.

The student protest movement of 1968 which culminated in the massacre of Tlatelolco has already received ample attention in previous chapters.

In 1976 the Mexican teachers' organization known as MRM (Movimiento Revolucionario del Magisterio) had come to be a potentially revolutionary force which sought to group around it certain progressive relief forces within the Sindicato Nacional de Trabajadores de la Enseñanza which is part of the PRI's popular sector, the CNOP. In its quest for an independent teachers' syndicate, the MRM experienced violent conflicts with police and army units during 1976 and 1977. Many members of the MRM are known to be active in the opposition politics of various leftist parties without official registry. The MRM ties its struggle to that of the working classes and identifies with opposition worker and peasant organizations.

In addition to the six movements cited above, the American writer Evelyn P. Stevens treats the doctors' strikes of 1964–65 as a major opposition movement, one which evoked repressive tactics from the government of President Díaz Ordaz and left little doubt of the regime's unwillingness to enter into negotiation and compromise for the resolution of differences with bona fide interest groups in the society.[3]

The discussion to follow of opposition politics in Mexico stresses the principal legal opposition party, the PAN, and develops some insight into its internal troubles during the late 1970s. Later a range of opposition groups without official registry are surveyed, most of them to the Marxist left of the political spectrum. It should be kept in mind that the official PRI enjoys two fundamental advantages over all of these groups. The first is that since the PRI and the government are one and the same the public treasury is drawn upon to finance the perpetuation of the PRI, including electoral campaigns, its image-building rituals, and its repression of rival groups which threaten it (including the denial of newsprint to the opposition press). The second is that the PRI controls the political registry and can make the rules for establishing one's political bona fides as easy or as difficult as seems convenient. These are major considerations in evaluating the potential of any opposition party in Mexico.

LEGALLY REGISTERED PARTIES
Partido Acción Nacional

Recent scholarship has traced the roots of Mexico's PAN, the principal legal opposition party, to the Christian movement which supported Madero's revolution. PAN has been linked to the cristeros who fought Calles during the 1920s and to the campaign for the presidency of José Vasconcelos in 1929. It has been pointed out that the Vasconcelos movement died out because it failed to move out of the limitations of personalism and to create an institutionalized and lasting political movement with a definable program and ideology.[4] This was also a failing of Madero as we have seen in the historical sketch of Mexico's political development in Chapter 2. The early founders of the PAN sought in 1939 (the year in which the party was formally launched) to create a more lasting political entity. It is also noteworthy that the PAN's founding coincided with the end of the Lázaro Cárdenas presidency. Many early members of the PAN reacted to the anticlericalism of both Cárdenas and Calles before him. Much of their reaction was toward the official prohibition against religious teaching in the public schools and the formal endorsement given during the Cárdenas years to socialism as a fundamental part of public education in Mexico. Many conservative Catholics feared that Cárdenas was leading the nation down the road to Communism.

The struggle between socialists and Christians during this epoch pitted the socialist leader Vicente Lombardo Toledano (who enjoyed the sympathy of President Cárdenas) against Manuel Gómez Morín, founder of the PAN. In 1933 Gómez Morín was elected rector of the National University of Mexico. He demonstrated that the university could be run by nonsocialists, without constantly increasing government subsidies, and without forcing socialist teaching on students. When the PAN achieved formal government registry in 1940 it was the first time since the PCN (National Catholic Party) of Madero's era that the conservative Christian right had a political organism with which to identify (it should be noted that the Constitution of 1917 prohibited use of religious words in the title of a political party).

The PAN, despite its early conservative trappings, was essentially pledged to support the revolutionary program of Madero just as much as any other group, thus the PRI has no unique basis in historical fact for claiming that it alone is the true heir to Madero's legacy. Also noteworthy was the relative absence, during most of PAN's development, of personalistic camarillas such as are found to dominate the PRI. As we shall see later, however, personalism did have an adverse effect on the internal unity of the PAN in the years 1975 and 1976. Both von Sauer and Mabry have provided historical sketches of the PAN[5], and this material need not be repeated here except to point out that there is some disagreement among scholars as to whether the PAN today is a Catholic, conservative, and reactionary party or if indeed it is a truly popular and reformist party vis-a-vis the PRI's monopoly. It is von Sauer's argument that the PAN's founders faced a situation of political monopoly in 1939 that was analogous to that which Madero had confronted in 1911. He contends that the PAN's true goals have been those of political pluralism via civic organization, responsible education, and the creation of legitimate and accountable institutions. This requires that the single-party system allow a loyal opposition to become effective, that is, that it have a share in the making of public policy and have the ability to hold governmental officials accountable. This, today, the PAN does not have.

PAN also seeks to restore to the Church the rights of religious education and political participation which were taken away from it by the Constitution of 1917. In fact, most of these rights have been de facto restored through increasing toleration by the official regime. There are those within the PAN who have seen Catholic religious unity in Mexico as a major goal, especially so when confronted with Protestant infiltration of the country. Such pronouncements were more characteristic of panistas during the 1940s and 1950s than is the case today. That the PAN is a version of what in other countries is called Christian Democracy seems to be a reasonable assessment, although formally it remains nonconfessional. PAN leaders frequently cite Madero's historic belief that the state should not interfere in one's private religious life. But they also hold the conviction that the Church can and should play a revolutionary role in the development of the Mexican state. Most of Madero's supporters were not, of course, in agreement that the Church could be revolutionary and most of them opposed its continued role in political life.

Since 1952 the PAN has normally competed with the PRI for national and regional elective offices and has usually fielded a presidential candidate. The PAN's presidential candidate in 1970, Efraín González Morfín, told me he had voted to withdraw his own candidacy in a special national assembly that was convened due to the repression that officialdom was visiting upon various of that party's state and congressional candidates. By a narrow margin the convention voted to continue the race. Even José González Torres, the 1964 PAN standard-bearer, also told me he had voted to withdraw from the race, leaving the PRI unopposed. In the 1976 campaign this is exactly what happened, a point to which I will return. PAN has stressed publicly and repeatedly the open nature of its internal procedures for candidate selection. Reputedly there is no *tapadismo* or back-room nominating of candidates in the PAN; all is done openly and the party is wont to remind the public of this fact so as to cast the official regime in an unfavorable light by comparison.

Many American scholars (including myself) have been led to believe that the PAN is and has been a distinctly reactionary or right-wing party. Some of the anticommunist pronouncements of PAN candidate Luis H. Alvarez in 1958 and those of José González Torres in 1964 did give the outward appearance of Mexican John Birchism. But during the early 1970s when I got to know González Torres personally I found him to be quite progressive, even to the point of defending the integrity of the pro-Marxist journalist Mario Menéndez Rodríguez who was then being persecuted by the government. González Torres's anticommunism seems to come more from his profound religious dedication. He expressed affinity toward Christian Democratic movements about the hemisphere. Quite rightfully, therefore, von Sauer called me to task for having once equated González Torres ideologically with Barry Goldwater in the United States.[6]

Von Sauer gives thorough treatment to the various instances of electoral fraud that have been committed against the PAN, just as I did in the first edition of *Mexican Democracy*. In particular, von Sauer was disturbed by the PAN decision not to participate in the 1973 elections in Baja California, given that state's past history as a PAN stronghold. Indeed, he argues that just because the majority of voters abstain from voting for the PRI doesn't mean a de facto vote of confidence in the PAN. This may, in fact, be evidence of overall Mexican disillusionment with the political system generally. Speaking of the 1973 elections, he raises these questions:

How does one explain that 16.5 percent of Mexicans chose to censure PRI by voting for PAN in 1973? What about the 38.4 percent of the electorate which showed preference for PAN over PRI in the Federal District? Or, more significantly, what about those 10,840,814 alienated voters that chose to remain home rather than vote without a voice?[7]

This should be considered against the fact that, on the basis of my own investigation, the majority of PAN leaders at the national level believed that PAN had really won in the Federal District and that the PRI allowed publication of such a large losing percentage only because the real overwhelming vote against it rendered a more lopsided figure unbelievable. The prevalence of electoral fraud throughout Mexico, and the awarding of a handful of deputies-at-large (*diputados de partido*) to PAN and to a couple of minor parties that are attached to the PRI for use as a democratic facade, was behind some of the disillusionment which ultimately led PAN to abstain from the presidential contest of 1976. It may be, however, as von Sauer concludes, that the PAN would be best advised to concentrate its forces at the municipal level in the hope of building a national organization from the grass roots on up. "Today the free, competitive *municipio* offers Mexico the most immediate prospects for an effective multiparty system."[8] Without this base, higher levels of competition will merely serve to reinforce the PRI's democratic image. And building such a base will depend importantly upon PAN ideology, its ability to communicate its interpretation of political life to the populace, and on the PRI's being forced to relinquish its hold on the localities.

A major difference of interpretation involving the PAN's ideology appears if one examines the analyses of Mabry and von Sauer. The former argues that PAN became increasingly identified as a Catholic party as its founder Gómez Morín had intended from the start.[9] But von Sauer quotes his own interviews with Gómez Morín to the contrary, that is, in the context of the potential affiliation of PAN with the international *confessional* movement of Christian Democracy, this following the visit of Venezuelan Christian Democratic leader Rafael Caldera to the PAN's national convention in 1962. It is von Sauer's contention that, yes, a certain group within the PAN (perhaps led by González Torres) wanted to affiliate with the international Christian Democratic movement.[10] That was my own impression from talking with González Torres personally. But Gómez Morín told von Sauer in 1969 that PAN was divided over this matter (not to mention the legal impediment in Mexico of using a religious word as part of the name of a political party) and that he, Gómez Morín, opposed the Christian Democratic affiliation. Being affiliated with Christian Democracy would make PAN a confessional Catholic party. And this, essentially, is what Mabry claims it is, without, of course, formally declaring itself as such. Although my own experience in knowing panistas confirms that they are mostly ardent Catholic believers, I have not been told that the party considers itself to be a Catholic party as such. However, I cannot honestly say that Mabry is wrong, as I have never deliberately researched the matter as he did in depth. And Mabry's evidence is impressive.

A good deal of testimony has been accumulated by Mabry, and in my own earlier research, linking PAN and the definitely religious UNS in various local campaigns throughout Mexico. But on the other hand there is evidence of PAN's having declared its sympathy even for causes embraced by communists (but never communism itself) such as the plight of the railway strikers in 1958.[11] Yet there is no avoiding the fervent anticommunism of PAN leaders like Adolfo Christlieb and José González Torres. Acting to moderate the PAN's extreme right wing have been Christian socialists like Luis Calderón Vega and Efraín González Morfín, the latter serving as PAN's presidential candidate in 1970. Adolfo Christlieb, PAN's president during the 1960s, tried to please the several factions within his party while not running a direct collision course with the Mexican government. As Mabry puts it, "Although PAN also quietly maintained relations with Christian Democratic parties, particularly in Latin America, Christlieb repudiated the Christian Democratic label because Mexicans would always believe that such a party was really an instrument of ecclesiastical power. To him, religious parties led to totalitarianism, and the Church should stay out of politics. . . ."[12] But still, according to Mabry, PAN remained close to the Christian Democratic label and was (and is) a progressive Catholic party. Christlieb, notes Mabry, was a friend of the progressive bishop of Cuernavaca, Sergio Méndez Arceo, and without formally using a Church label other panistas have adhered to this progressive, reform-oriented, sector of the Church.

PAN's official doctrine or ideology is called political humanism. It focuses upon bettering the life style of the individual in his total cultural context and rejects the narrow concept of man as an atomized being.[13] Man is seen as having been created in God's image and has inviolable and inalienable rights to life, liberty, to control his own destiny, and to be free of repression. Man must also respect the rights of others; he must, in effect, live the good Christian life. Politics is to enhance man's self-fulfillment, not to subordinate him to the state or class as in fascism or Marxism. The local community is seen as the foundation of the good life and forms a basic part of the nation. But the nation and the governmental apparatus are not one and the same nor should they be. Thus since the PRI's apparatus and the nation are treated by officialdom as practically synonymous, the PAN and the official party are seriously at odds. Any regime which puts the good of an elite before the good of the individual is rejected. The PAN defends the right of private property so long as it serves a useful social function and is not achieved by leaving others in economic misery.[14] Political participation, for the PAN, is a moral duty. As we shall see, that dictum is easier proclaimed than achieved.

Whereas von Sauer's analysis views PAN as a historical outgrowth of Francisco Madero's revolutionary visions, Mabry sees it as a force to propagate Catholicism and to save the revolution from becoming socialist or, worse, communist. These are distinct points of view but not necessarily self-excluding. Both agree that PAN was formed out of a reaction against the Cárdenas era of the 1930s, but one detects in Mabry's analysis a more pejorative evaluation of the Cárdenas reforms than is the case in von Sauer's work. Both seem to agree that the goals of the great revolution were essentially good but that PAN saw the revolutionaries as taking the wrong road to achieve those goals. Mabry then suggests an ironic analogy between the PRI and the Church, both espousing official truths and both decrying as heretics those who challenge that truth. The irony, according to Mabry, is that today "a Catholic-oriented party has had to compete against an anticlerical, secular government which uses the techniques of the Catholic Church to maintain itself in power."[15]

The central dilemma for the PAN is that by accepting a participant role as the PRI's key opposition it contributes to the very facade of democracy which the PRI wished to perpetuate. When PAN accepts the "gifts" of deputies-at-large it most assuredly contributes to the facade of democracy. The PRI, of course, is afraid to give the PAN those seats it genuinely won on a district-by-district basis. That would contribute to strengthening PAN at the grass-roots level and undermine the PRI. However, if the PAN refuses the "gift" deputies it then leaves Mexico with virtually no legal alternative to the PRI. And there is also a risky probability that the PRI chooses to recognize as elected those PAN deputies whom the PRI feels it can most successfully manipulate, thus giving more basis to the charge that PAN is a "kept" party. Yet my own field investigation supports those of von Sauer and Mabry, that is, that the PAN is not kept financially or otherwise by anyone and that it seriously aspires to become a loyal and progressive opposition in Mexico.

The works cited above plus my own earlier published investigations tell the story of the electoral frauds and other repressions which the official regime has perpetrated against the PAN. The intensity of such repression, especially in the campaigns for governorships and mayoralty races, has progressively demoralized the PAN. This raised, as noted earlier, the possibility in 1970, and the actuality in 1976, of PAN's not contesting the national presidency so as to deprive the PRI of its desired international image as a popular and revolutionary party that repeatedly won sweeping electoral victories against the emissaries of the past. One great unknown was the impact of such national abstention on the PAN's state and municipal roots.

Since little has been written about the PAN's abstention from the 1976 presidential campaign, I will present one insider's version of that story here. It is well to remember that both of the PAN's last two presidential candidates (González Torres in 1964 and González Morfín in 1970) told me personally that they had voted in the PAN's special national convention of 1970 to withdraw from the presidential race against Luis Echeverría, so the notion of abstaining was not new. It came about in 1976, however, in an unanticipated way. Here are excerpts from a letter written to me by a high PAN official and which are offered with his permission.[16]

Concerning the questions you have raised about the PAN I shall try to present a synthesis of the origin and development of the events which produced the most grave crisis in the party's history.

During the presidency [of the PAN] of José Angel Conchello [1972–75] the party began gradually turning toward rightist and frankly conservative positions, abandoning thereby the great lines of socioeconomic thought which previous presidents like Christlieb Ibarrolla and González Morfín had instilled in the party's platform and doctrine. The progressive ideas of the PAN's founders dating from 1939 were abandoned by Conchello and substituted for a thesis which was clearly of the "Liberal Manchesterian" variety, a thesis which the PAN has always opposed. On the other hand, the internal organization of the party suffered a gradual splintering, owing in large part to the ideological confusion which Conchello created by making wild declarations to the press, a demagoguery intended to attract followers from middle class sectors outside the party.

Then came the moment for the party's presidential succession in March of 1975. Against the intentions of Conchello to have himself reelected president, I and a number of other party leaders including Luis H. Alvarez, Calderón Vega, Rosas Magallón, Fernando Estrada, and Javier Boesterly [leader of the PAN's important university student sector] took action in favor of the candidacy of Efraín González Morfín, our party's candidate for the presidency of the republic in 1970. González Morfín was elected and I was designated the party's secretary general. Conchello was profoundly resentful at not being reelected and undertook to form a parallel organization with himself as leader whose goal it was to create fissures within the PAN and to foment regional divisions. The Conchello group became an "antiparty" which tried to win our new recruits away and spread the impression that the party was dichotomized between the "elites" (that is to say the elected leadership) and the membership. The goal was to convert the PAN into a tool for the most reactionary interests in the country.

As part of this surreptitious undertaking Conchello and his group, in flagrant violation of our party statutes, proclaimed at a press conference that Pablo Emilio Madero would be the PAN's "presidential" candidate for the presidency of the republic. This occurred several months before PAN's national convention which had exclusive powers to nominate our true presidential candidate. With a public display of propaganda, paid for by funds from who knows where, Madero began to tour the country for several months in an effort to win over convention delegates who would meet in November to name our party's candidate. Madero's informal campaign was supported by writers and groups of the far right wing which, until then, had been the PAN's enemies; these were fascist movements such as MURO and Integrismo Nacional and such openly pro-Nazi writers as Salvador Borrego and Victor Manuel Sánchez Stenpreis.

In these conditions and with the presence of *agents provocateurs* sent by Conchello, the PAN celebrated its national nominating convention during November of 1975. The atmosphere was one of great tension. Amidst multiple hints of violence the candidacies of Pablo Emilio Madero, Salvador Rosas Magallón, and David Alarcón Zaragoza were presented. On the first ballot Madero had a simple majority but not the 80 percent to be nominated as required by our bylaws. In each successive vote Rosas Magallón increased his percentage of the vote and Madero lost, but neither was Rosas Magallón able to reach the 80 percent figure. In these circumstances, and after more than 12 hours of voting without electing a candidate in an atmosphere threatening physical violence, it was decided to suspend the convention and reconvene it in February of 1976.

It is very important to point out that the November convention did approve the political platform for 1976–82 of which Efraín González Morfín was the principal author and whose content was vehemently opposed by the Conchello-Madero group, especially in the socioeconomic and educational aspects. This placed in bold relief the fact that the abyss within the party was ideological between the ultraright conservatives and the legitimate leadership which advocated social change and progress.

Since our National Executive Council did not give a vigorous and ample condemnation to the "antiparty" group, González Morfín resigned as party president in December 1975. In my role as secretary general, I assumed provisionally the presidency of the party and convoked the National Executive Council in order to designate a new party president. One of our former party presidents, Manuel González Hinojosa, was thus elected unanimously.

Then, in February of 1976, we convened the second national nominating convention in the hope that we could reach agreement on a presidential candidate. This meeting featured larger numbers of conflict groups [*grupos de choque*] who were partisans of Madero and who sought to intimidate the delegates pledged to Rosas Magallón. After numerous votes no one had the required majority, although Madero led in the voting due to the fear that had been instilled in many delegates that the party might be forced into electoral abstention. The convention reached an impasse and the party president, with approval from the majority of the delegates, declared that Acción Nacional would not offer a presidential candidate in 1976. His pronouncement was the key for violence and, loyal to their mission, the troublemakers [*porristas*] of the Conchello-Madero faction set about to assault the party's leadership physically, including González Hinojosa, leaving a toll of many persons beaten and injured.

Never in the 36 years of the PAN's existence has anything so humiliating, so out of keeping with our democratic tradition, taken place. This was not a PAN convention where one always could participate with absolute liberty, responsibility, and respect for the rights and ideas of other colleagues. Always the delegates came seeking the best interest of the party and that of Mexico. But in February of 1976 many delegates came pledged to do the work of niggardly interests. At the moment of this writing [1976] we are striving to reconstitute ourselves, to overcome the crisis which Acción Nacional has suffered, so that the party will not lose its identity and its *raison d'être*.

The impact on public opinion of our decision to abstain from presidential competition and to offer only congressional candidates was something rare; for days the press and the people spoke of hardly anything else. We gained much public sympathy we did not have before and certainly much interest. One thing remained clear: that the PAN is the only opposition party capable of creating an electoral vacuum in Mexico. From then on, the first ones to "tear their clothes" [pull their hair in panic] were those of the government and its official party. I do not consider that the other so-called parties of the opposition, the PPS and the PARM [Partido Auténtico de la Revolucíon Mexicana] have benefited by our abstention since they are appendages of the official party and endorse its presidential candidate, López Portillo.

Never before has the expression *apertura democratica* [democratic openness] been so meaningless. It is clear the government fears the PAN as evidenced by the electoral frauds committed against us in the most recent municipal elections, even after some PAN victories had been signed and certified by local PRI officials. The army was brought in to steal ballot boxes. The PRI wants us to "run" for office so as to create a facade, but not "win" office. Political liberties in Mexico are restricted to members of the oligarchy.

I pray that I am wrong, but I believe we are at the threshold of grave social convulsions and with the generalized public inconformity such as it is, an outbreak of major violence is not hard to imagine. The public debt has reached a disproportionate level with the capacity of the country to pay it. Agricultural production has fallen to the point that the once exporters of beans and corn are now importing these essential products. Despite all the rhetoric from our president, the distribution of wealth in Mexico during his six-year term has been worse than during the previous regime. We are all becoming paupers while our president makes expensive international trips to promote himself as "leader" of the Third World. Governmental corruption and inefficiency have passed all tolerable limits.

Possibly you will think me too pessimistic with respect to the future of Mexico, but the objective facts are so overwhelmingly impressive that optimism in these circumstances becomes a form of intellectual desertion.

It is noteworthy that the PAN candidate Madero in the events just set forth claimed to be a descendant of Francisco I. Madero, the father of Mexico's great revolution. It is that revolutionary legacy with which the progressive forces within the PAN today would like to identify. Clearly, the contemporary panista Madero represented forces of reaction, the very emissaries of the past whom President Echeverría had been denouncing. Also noteworthy is the fact that the writer quoted above, Raúl González Schmal, does not blame PRI agents for the internal disintegration of the PAN. He blames camarillas within the PAN, even though traditionally PAN had been relatively free of camarilla politics as noted in von Sauer's analysis. Also, the above testimony seems to place PAN ideologically to the progressive left of the political spectrum, at least insofar as most of the principal leadership elements of the party are concerned. On the basis of my own experience over more than a decade of knowing ranking panistas, I would accept this testimony as an accurate view, albeit the perception of one inside and well-placed participant.

Researchers wishing to do further analyses of the PAN's doctrine and political activism should consult the regular press bulletins which are issued, the magazine *La Nación,* and the intermittent handbill *La Batalla.* In a press release in September 1977, PAN's president, Manuel González Hinojosa, made a resumé of 38 years of PAN. He stressed the Christian commitment of the party, its fervent opposition to the antidemocratic conditions prevalent in

Mexico, and characterized the official regime using terms such as corruption, egoism, and hedonism.[17] An earlier bulletin had characterized the PRI deputies in congress as *levantadedos* (finger-raising yes-men) who approve automatically everything that comes from the president of the republic.[18]

Partido Popular Socialista

This party, founded by the Marxist intellectual Vicente Lombardo Toledano in 1947, has grown into little more than the left wing of the PRI and, therefore, merits only brief attention here. The PPS normally endorses the PRI's presidential candidate and many of its gubernatorial candidates. It receives a handful of deputies-at-large and in 1976 became the first opposition party in decades to be awarded a senate seat. This is because the PPS leader in that year, Jorge Cruickshank García, agreed earlier in 1975 to recognize the PRI's win in a disputed gubernatorial election in Nayarit in which the PPS candidate, Alejandro Gascón Mercado, apparently won. It should be noted that the family of Gascón Mercado is a traditional and powerful family in Nayarit and one of its members had previously been governor there. PRI's voting fraud was so visible that PPS leader Cruickshank's decision to recognize the PRI's victory labeled him clearly as a puppet of the regime. In return, Cruickshank was allowed to win a senate seat from the state of Oaxaca. This was especially odious in that the PRI's winning candidate in Nayarit was none other than Colonel Rogelio Flores Curiel, the man in charge of government troops during the June 10th massacre in Mexico City and who had to be moved elsewhere because of his resultant unpopularity in the capital.

It has always been a professed goal of the PPS to become the nucleus of the Mexican left. Only once did the party have enough independence to offer its own presidential candidate: This was in 1952 when the founder Vicente Lombardo Toledano himself campaigned. From then until 1976 the party was virtually an appendage of the PRI, enjoying a handful of deputies-at-large in the lower house since the electoral reforms of 1964 made that possible. In 1977 the PPS confronted a major internal crisis in that the defeated Nayarit candidate Gascón Mercado and a number of ranking PPS leaders bolted to form the PPM (Mexican People's party) which did not have legal registry. The new PPM declared that it would serve to regroup the left, probably in collaboration with the Mexican Communist party (PCM) and that it would seek legal registry. This schism cast doubt over the future of the PPS in the late 1970s.[19]

Partido Auténtico de la Revolución Mexicana

Like its so-called leftist counterpart, the PPS, the slightly right-of-center PARM (or Authentic Party of the Mexican Revolution) is an appendage of the PRI. The PARM is the newest of the legal parties having achieved registry in 1954. At its inception it consisted principally of a nucleus of old militarists who had served in the great revolution following 1910. Its original directors were Jacinto B. Treviño and Juan Barragán who dominated the party until the latter's death in 1974. In 1975 the presidency of the party was given to Pedro González Azcoaga. It is fair to say that the PARM is simply a conservative extension of the PRI, endorsing most PRI candidates, never offering an independent presidential candidate, and receiving deputies-at-large in greater proportion than its popular vote merited under the existing electoral laws.[20] The PARM has little political relevance.

Key Provisions of the Electoral Registry Law

The electoral code that took effect in 1973 was intended to further democratize the Mexican political system by reducing the voting age to 18 and reducing the age for deputies to 21 and that of senators to 30. In addition it provided that for a political party to secure legal registry, hence a place on national and state ballots, it would have to show at least 2,000 bona fide members in each of at least two-thirds of Mexico's 31 states and that the total number of such members would have to be at least 65,000. It further required legal certification in each of the states by a judge, notary public, or designated government functionary of lists of local party members affirming that these members understand and subscribe to the program of the party in question. That document would be accompanied by the name, address, electoral identification card number, and signature (or fingerprint in case of illiterate persons) of each party member. This process of certification at the local level could be initiated with only 5 percent of the total state membership represented but ultimately all members would have to register. There are additional requirements that public assemblies be conducted in the various municipalities and other red tape designed, formally, to guarantee the honesty of the certification procedure.[21]

Not unexpectedly, many political organizers and aspirants saw these detailed procedures as an impediment to party organization. One of the most frequently cited problems was the requirement that all members have an electoral credential. Few Mexicans living outside the large cities have such credentials and getting them often requires political influence or a bribe. Also criticized was the requirement for convening local assemblies, a costly process which few beginning parties could afford, not to mention the ever-present threat of police repression if a meeting was held without a permit from the local government (which would also require a bribe or political influence). If a PRI-controlled local government wanted to prevent a certain group from securing electoral credentials or from celebrating a reunion it could easily do so. Again, democratization from the grass roots up emerges as a difficult yet critical goal, an indispensable one, for opposition parties. President López Portillo promised electoral reform early in his term. One way to gauge the seriousness of his intentions would be to determine how many of the aspiring opposition parties actually achieved registration during his regime. Changes in electoral procedures could also be important.[22]

PARTIES WITHOUT LEGAL REGISTRY AS THE LÓPEZ PORTILLO SEXENIO BEGAN

Of the various parties and groups without official registration in the late 1970s there were at least six which appeared to enjoy some possibility of becoming legal. Of these six, five had a Marxist orientation and proposed radical changes in Mexican society along socialist lines. The one exception to this was the sixth party known as PDM (Partido Demócrata Mexicano, or Mexican Democratic party). This organization emerged out of the UNS, a right-wing theocratic party. It is unrealistic to consider the program of the PDM without also examining its relationship to the sinarquista movement. I will examine this ideological grouping first because it is the principal deviant case in the Mexican out-group spectrum.

Partido Demócrata Mexicano and Unión Nacional Sinarquista

Formally, as has already been noted, one may not use religious titles or symbols in Mexican politics because of a constitutional prohibition. Thus, as we have seen, the PAN could not formally declare itself to be a Christian Democratic party without losing its official registry. This stricture, indirectly, has kept the UNS out of formal participation for years. The expression *sinarquismo* or *sinarquista* is a union of two words, *sin* (without) *anarquía* (anarchy), or stated positively, "with order." The key term is order, *orden,* as the name of a noted sinarquista publication implies. Order is the hallmark of UNS. It is an order of Christian theocracy, first under God, then under a God-fearing state. This formal religious nexus is too overt to allow UNS to participate as a political party. All UNS members are ardent Roman Catholics. They are disciplined soldiers of a theocratic faith. The movement was founded in León, Guanajuato, in 1937. One of its founders, José Antonio Urquiza, was assassinated in 1938 by agents which the sinarquistas claim were in the employ of President Cárdenas. Sinarquista documents note that the movement was a reaction to the dangers of socialism and communism which, allegedly, were overtaking Mexico during the Cárdenas era.[23]

The sinarquistas collected other early martyrs which are used symbolically by the movement today. For instance, on July 11, 1939, in Celaya, Guanajuato, a woman sinarquista named Teresita Bustos was murdered (allegedly also by agents of Cárdenas) while performing in a public rally. Today, when national conventions of the UNS are held in the city of León, each outgoing president passes to his successor the blood-stained flag which this woman carried to her death.[24] A past president of the UNS, José Trinidad Cervantes, once showed me this flag and explained that it has major symbolic value, even to the extent of mysticism, for the sinarquista movement. He also said that attempts have been made by detractors of UNS to steal the flag. The sinarquistas have been likened by some Mexicans to Nazis because of their use of armbands and the way in which they give salutes during public ceremonies. León, where the movement was born, has been given the menacing epithet Sinarcópolis, where every three years a major pilgrimage is held to witness the installation of a new national president. In conversations with UNS members (which were difficult to arrange due to the secrecy the group practices) I was continually impressed with the sinarquistas' conspiratorial interpretation of history and of contemporary politics. They were prone to blame Jews, Masons, communists, and foreigners generally for the woes of Mexico. They also were unanimous in condemning the single-party regime as inhumane and atheistic. The sinarquistas favor restoration of Church privileges and are known to have ties to the reactionary Opus Dei organization. I was told that earlier in the 1970s the sinarquistas (or at least some of them) were implicated in the right-wing terrorist group MURO (Movimiento Universitario de Reformadora Orientación) which has been centered in the state of Puebla but with ample penetration of social and academic institutions throughout Mexico. MURO, it will be noted, was one of the principal conflict groups which intensified the student disorders leading up to Tlatelolco in 1968. It is also believed that financial support for all the above-mentioned right-wing organizations comes from the conservative Monterrey Group.

When the UNS sought to enter the political arena at the beginning of the López Portillo sexenio, this had to be accomplished in such a way as not to run afoul of constitutional strictures about religious parties. Thus the formation of the PDM was done carefully so as to avoid legal pitfalls. The PDM contends that its doctrine is humanistic and democratic within constitutional requirements. Although it is widely known that PDM is a political arm of the UNS, this fact is never mentioned formally and overt association with religious entities is carefully avoided. One of its principal leaders, Ignacio González Gollaz, is a long-time militant in the UNS and sought to gain registry for PDM in 1976, even before the end of the Echeverría sexenio.[25]

Additionally, PDM claims that the primary mission of the state is to guarantee an atmosphere which will protect and honor human dignity and preserve the family as the basic unit of society. The PDM doctrine asks that Church and state work together for common goals such as material abundance for all and freedom of intellectual inquiry and religious belief, but urges that the state not curtail the privileges of the Church. The PDM stresses the right to private property and is concerned (as were its forebears during the Cárdenas era) over governmental encroachments into the realm of private enterprise.

The party calls itself "populist," which is understood to be neither extreme individualist nor communist. Its doctrine endorses ideological pluralism and calls for a profound educational reform in which distinct groups could participate and educational policy not be dictated by the state. All of this presupposes electoral reform and a responsible government that will make such reforms meaningful.[26]

Parties of the Marxist-Socialist-Trotskyite Spectrum

Partido Revolucionario de los Trabajadores (PRT) belongs to the Trotskyite Fourth International and seeks to conquer both state and private capital via the kind of worker and peasant militancy (using violence) that occurred in Russia during 1917. This group, known to be very small, believes that it cannot triumph in a strictly national context and identifies the class struggle along international lines as did Lenin and Trotsky. The party's chief focal point at the moment is to create an independent movement of worker syndicates that will be free from manipulation by the labor bosses of the PRI. In this way the PRT intends to absorb the means of production and guarantee an equitable distribution of wealth for the masses.

Less militant is Partido Socialista Revolucionario (PSR), which wants to implant a truly socialist system in Mexico. Along with Marx, this party sees the evolution to socialism as the outcome of inevitable historical forces. The PSR argues that its very existence, even without overt militancy, will be a factor in hastening the crumbling of the corrupt edifice of the Mexican state and its capitalist partners. Avoiding the endorsement of violent civil war, the PSR does foresee coordinated uprisings of workers to take over factories when the objective conditions are right for this to happen. General strikes are also endorsed. The party recognizes that now is not the time to take over the state and urges transitional planning and a unification of the various socialist groups into a potent nucleus. In this respect the PSR differs from the PRT in that the latter prefers a more isolated posture, hoping that other groups will join with it when its example shows success.

The PSR advocates progressive nationalization of private property by the incumbent regime, somehow hoping that it will be able to share in the decision making once everything belongs to the PRI. The party has a long list of labor reforms including a 40-hour week and 30 days of paid vacation for every 11 months of work. There is also a demand for radical agrarian reform including elimination of *latifundismo* (great landholding) and replacement of the ejidos with genuinely collective farms or cooperative communes. Also on the PSR's policy list are elimination of landlords and rent controls. It calls for jail terms for speculators (in land, money, nearly anything), and complete state control of the means of communication (this last, the PRI has nearly accomplished on its own).[27]

154 / Mexican Democracy: A Critical View

Mexico also has a Partido Socialista de los Trabajadores (PST), or Socialist Workers party. It calls for a socialist proletarian-governed state, free from exploitation, in which the workers will enjoy full benefits of their toil. Again, most everything would be nationalized. The PST declares itself to be the true vanguard not only of the workers and peasants but of students and women plus all those who are exploited. The PST declares that its socialism is scientific within the context of dialectical materialism and admits that a broad-based national front may be necessary to achieve its goals.

In this context it is not unlike the Mexican Communist party which promises most of the same socialistic goals and tactics. In fact, much of the program of the PCM concerning human dignity and the right of each individual to develop himself was not unlike that of the rightist PDM cited earlier. However, the PCM insists that only communism is the road to achieve these goals. The PCM preaches a democratic revolutionary process avoiding calls to overt violence but accepting the general strike as a tactic. Care for people from cradle to grave is promised by most of the socialist parties including the communists.

The party which seemed to be emerging as a nucleus around which the entire left might group itself temporarily was the Mexican Workers party, PMT (Partido Mexicano de los Trabajadores). This party, founded by Heberto Castillo in the early 1970s following his release from prison (a holdover from Tlatelolco), responded to President López Portillo's pledge of electoral reform calling for the abolition of the deputies-at-large, calling this a device for corrupting and subjecting opposition groups. The PMT also claimed to be the vehicle for socializing Mexico and ridding the country of exploiters both domestic and foreign. It identified strongly with intellectuals. Heberto Castillo's regular articles for *Excelsior* and, after its takeover in 1976, in *Proceso* gave the PMT a broad audience on which to draw. Early in the López Portillo sexenio Castillo's rhetoric was carefully phrased so as to avoid direct attacks on the president, but it did challenge the PRI generally and many of its traditions (including that of monopolizing legitimacy).

Quite specifically, the PMT advocated strict electoral reforms that would simplify the task of getting opposition parties registered as legal. It demanded the creation of a popular mechanism to avoid electoral fraud that would force the PRI to honor the results of secret balloting. Also the PMT argued that the Federal District (essentially Mexico City but not including its suburbs which overlap into two states) should be given regular status as a state with the regente becoming a governor who would be popularly elected. It called for the abolition of the Federal Judicial Police and "other unconstitutional police organizations."[28] This was a daring and specific program point which distinguished the PMT program from most other parties on the left. By calling for federal police reform the PMT had, in effect, gone on record as cutting away the base of Gobernación, one of the power centers of Mexican officialdom. The

PMT called for amnesty for all political prisoners and endorsed a sweeping program of economic reforms affecting industry and agriculture, much the same as those championed by other organisms on the left.

The PMT was also unique in the specificity of its other proposals. It advocated fiscal reform with a graduated income tax intended to penalize the wealthy. It called for municipal governments to take over all business, the implantation of truly democratic worker syndicates, and publication of the names of stockholders in those enterprises not to be nationalized (it was not clear just where the PMT drew the line between what was to be nationalized and what would remain private). Pharmaceuticals, banks, steel and coal, and many major industries were to be nationalized but not all private enterprise would be wiped out by the PMT. In this way it appeared to be the least extreme and, perhaps, the most potentially successful, of the leftist opposition parties. The PMT called for the usual agrarian reforms with special attention to be given to indigenous communities, recognizing in the Indian a great human resource that was growing extinct, pledging that lands and agricultural assistance be destined for the Indian population. The party strongly defended free speech, human rights, and emphasized the critical social and political role of an independent university system. The PMT may have a better chance than most of setting itself up as a genuine opposition party of the left because of the intellectual prestige and popular following of Heberto Castillo. Of course, there are still the lingering charges that Castillo is a bourgeois communist who lives in luxurious Pedregal and who negotiated his release from prison in 1970 by agreeing to create a fake opposition party, charges which Castillo and his supporters vehemently deny.

The PMT venture appears to have been well thought out and planned. In collaboration with Francisco Paoli Bolio, Heberto Castillo himself prepared a book of political analysis and protest which began to circulate openly in 1975, thereby laying a basis for his party's off-ballot participation in the electoral campaign of 1976.[29] The book begins with a resume of previous attempts to form leftist parties in the early twentieth century including those of the brothers Flores Magón and Luis N. Morones. Paternalism and caudillismo are cited as principal impediments to the growth of rival parties. Castillo stresses the failure of Carlos Madrazo's new party attempt in 1965 as depending too heavily upon one man. Madrazo argued unsuccessfully for a grass-roots democratizing of the PRI. When Madrazo died in an airplane crash (which some still doubt was accidental) in June 1969, his party died with him. Castillo and Paoli Bolio charge that the Mexican political system cannot be reformed or even modified from within. This owes, they say, to the innate urge of those who, once in power, acquire an insatiable taste for power and the wealth that goes with it.

The PRI, they say, is a mafia of *charros,* corrupt manipulators of the working class like Fidel Velázquez who has been in control of the official

Mexican Workers Federation almost forever. The bureaucrats, the congressmen, all have their camarillas, and it is the internal value structures of these groups that direct the PRI, not concern for the revolution or policy issues of major import. Castillo claims, as one might expect, that the CIA and other North American influences are deeply involved with officialdom so as to keep Mexico enslaved for the benefit of the Anderson-Clayton Company and other imperialist exploiters. He blames the PRI's labor and peasant leaders for selling out to the imperialists. Finally, Castillo seeks to discount the charge that he has been commissioned to create a fake party, saying that those who play this game are simply entering into the business (*negocio*), which he says is the most correct word to describe the PRI. The secret, says Castillo, is to start poor and build a party on socialist principles plus human honor. It is not exactly clear just how this is all to come about except that everyone will be required to surrender something of himself unto the collective whole (on a Rousseauian-sounding basis).

OPPOSITION BY VIOLENCE: THE PEN AND THE SWORD

Guerrilla insurgency as a political skill has increased in Mexico since the student riots of 1968. Movements have come and gone as have their leaders, men like Genaro Vázquez and Lucio Cabañas in the mountains of Guerrero. In northern Mexico the government claims to have eliminated a guerrilla front called the Revolutionary Armed Movement (MAR), and in the south the legendary Zapata's name was invoked to designate the FUZ, Urban Zapata Front. In the late 1970s the principal guerrilla movement appeared to be the 23rd of September Communist League. None of these movements seem to have a major lasting power and some of them have even allegedly been created sub rosa by officialdom, a point to which I will return. But guerrilla violence continues to escalate in Mexico. Let us survey here some of the recent high points of Mexican guerrilla politics.

Following Tlatelolco a few underground press organs kept up a steady attack on the government's guilt over the massacre and continued to dramatize Mexico's socioeconomic penury. Much above-ground criticism came from the PAN. The most severe criticism, however, was printed in the weekly journal *Por Que?*, which had been Mexico's principal opposition organ since it began in 1968.[30] *Por Que?* was founded by Mario Renato Menéndez Rodríguez and his brothers Roger and Hernán in 1968. I interviewed Mario concerning his exploits the previous year in Colombia with the guerrilla movement there.[31] His goal was to create a journal that could maintain itself with commercial advertisements plus subscriptions and street sales. *Por Que?* was to be a magazine of political and social criticism with a section on literature and the performing arts, much like *Ramparts* in the United States. But it was meant to be a commercial success and to be self-sustaining without the government embutes, which are paid to many Mexican publications to keep them going while they print the government's official line.

Although it became fashionable to refer to *Por Que?* as a communist magazine, its founders and editors were far from it; it is questionable, on the basis of my knowing Roger Menéndez personally, that even intellectually are they genuine Marxists, but that is not critical here. All three brothers are U.S.-educated scions of a wealthy conservative family in Merida that operates the *Diario de Yucatán,* one of Mexico's few truly opposition papers, one that most would call conservative. The brothers split with their father ideologically although they all were opposed to the PRI monopoly. *Por Que?* was, like the Menéndez brothers, a publication of the ultraleft in the sense that it became a voice for student protest leaders and guerrilla movements. This commitment was antiregime and not tied (as far as I could determine on the basis of frequent personal contact) to any domestic or international ideology. *Por Que?* was also bitterly anti-United States. Thus, like so many revolutionary movements in Latin America, the Mexican rebels of the second half of the twentieth century had secured collaboration from upper-class intellectuals plus the allegiance of downtrodden poor devils, *los móndrigos.* Potentially it was a volatile combination. *Por Que?* was their pen and press.

The regime reacted defensively. In February 1970 Mario Menéndez and a number of alleged rebel leaders were taken into custody by federal police.[32] They were accused of belonging to a Revolutionary Struggle Committee called CLR whose alleged head, Ignacio González Ramírez, conveniently confessed to authorities that he had undertaken guerrilla training in the states of Tabasco and Chiapas under the orders and guidance of Mario Menéndez. This committee was alleged to include such onetime PRI stalwarts as former Baja California Governor Braulio Maldonado and the Marxist writer Heberto Castillo (often called a wealthy bourgeois Marxist).

Still more significantly, however, Mario Menéndez's name was linked to that of Genaro Vázquez Rojas, a once-humble schoolteacher who had formed his own guerrilla movement in the mountains of Guerrero. Mario Menéndez was detained indefinitely without being brought formally to trial. He was accused of various acts of terrorism, including the bombing of the offices of the PAN. Officials of the PAN denied these charges saying, to me, that off-duty police of the Federal District put the bombs in their offices. José González Torres, 1964 presidential candidate of the PAN, spoke to me of Mario Menéndez as an honorable, albeit left-wing, journalist. His brother Roger told me in 1972 that the guerrilla charges against Mario were fake and that the real crime committed was a series of exposes printed in *Por Que?* of the electoral fraud several months earlier (November 1969) when the PAN had clearly won the governorship of Yucatán and the PRI intervened to falsify the election with armed force. In addition, *Por Que?* had published some embarrassing revelations of tortures and Mexican military and police collaboration with the CIA. But the government did not want Menéndez in court defending himself on such charges, so he was held indefinitely on sedition and subversion. They had no real proof against him and dared not fabricate any for the moment.

It should also be noted that since the appearance of *Por Que?* in 1968 the government had applied indirect censorship upon it via the newsprint monopoly called PIPSA. This meant that while the officially tolerated press could get good-quality newsprint imported from Scandinavia, partially subsidized by the government, the underground press, that is, *Por Que?*, had to buy its newsprint on the open market for several times the official price. Thus the glossy print for advertisements that originally appeared in *Por Que?* in 1968 rapidly disappeared. So did the advertisements. They were replaced by editions printed on paper that was little better than toilet tissue. The government threatened advertisers into not buying space in *Por Que?* and it came to be an underground tract subsidized by its readers. However, *Por Que?* did not fold as had other publications. Indeed, it increased its national circulation to approximately 100,000 weekly in 1972. This, in and of itself, was a significant measure of the willingness of the Mexican people to read bitter attacks upon the PRI, bolstered by signed testimony and photographic evidence. I do not deny, however, that *Por Que?* had its tabloid aspect of sensationalism. But the case of *Por Que?* and the government's campaign against it via PIPSA became an international scandal and was even denounced as far away as Argentina by the respected conservative newspaper *La Prensa* of Buenos Aires.[33]

On the basis of my field investigation, combined with the fact that the government never dared to bring Mario Menéndez formally to trial, it is doubtful that he was even the intellectual author of the formation of guerrilla movements. However, there is no doubt that his magazine sympathized openly with the guerrillas, both urban and rural, and that its pages were used to promote public sympathy for the guerrillas and to disseminate their communications and propaganda. This was not an abuse of freedom of speech under Mexican law, yet official terrorist groups frequently machine gunned the offices of *Por Que?* at night. I stress the case of *Por Que?* and its editors here because they relate to the genesis of the recent Mexican guerrilla movement.

The incarceration of Mario Menéndez in 1970 became a *cause célèbre* for certain student nuclei of the National Strike Committee who themselves were forming urban guerrilla organizations. In addition, the rural guerrillas under the leadership of Genaro Vázquez Rojas and José Bracho Campos had combined with their urban counterparts to form Acción Cívica Nacional Revolucionaria (ACNR, the National Civic Revolutionary Action Movement). The ACNR became a nominal umbrella under which a congeries of guerrilla groups could relate and occasionally merge. One of these was MAR, centered in the northern border state Sonora. The government periodically claimed to have decimated (and, curiously, redecimated) the MAR. It was alleged officially to have been trained by communist infiltrators from North Korea. A myriad of such groups appeared, often with student-peasant collaboration, thus blurring somewhat the distinction between urban and rural insurgencies.

It is not necessary to repeat the details of all the kidnappings and acts of terrorism which the Mexican guerrillas carried out during the years of the Echeverría presidency. From the standpoint of forming an insurgent opposition, and guaranteeing optimal freedom for its intellectual directorate, the most critical detail is that Mario Menéndez was converted de facto into a guerrilla leader in exile. This took place suddenly on November 28, 1971, when he and a handful of other political prisoners were flown to freedom and exile in Cuba. The ACNR, and specifically the guerrilla band of Genaro Vázquez Rojas, accomplished this by kidnapping Jaime Castrejón Díaz, rector of the University of Guerrero and wealthy elitist who held the Coca-Cola franchise for that state. The guerrillas had reached into the upper echelons of political power, taken a hostage. Then they told the government to release a select list of prisoners plus pay a generous ransom.

Here the credibility of the Echeverría leadership first came to be seriously questioned; the industrialists began looking to the military (Los Penecilinos) for safety guarantees. Echeverría gave in to the guerrilla demands; this was neither the first nor the last such capitulation. But if the country was not safe for the elites they might move to replace the president. This became a national rumor. Although unthinkable in recent decades, this was now a distinct reality and no one was more aware of it than Luis Echeverría Alvarez (and that is why the assassination of industrialist Eugenio Garza Sada of the Monterrey Group in late 1973 placed Echeverría in an especially precarious position; the government was given no ransom opportunity in his case). Mario Menéndez began to write articles in *Por Que?* from exile in Cuba, scathing attacks on the government which deepened its credibility crisis.

Then, Genaro Vázquez Rojas, founder of the rural component of ACNR, was killed on February 2, 1972, when his car hit a bridge abutment on the Toluca-Morelia highway to the west of the capital city. At least that is what the government alleged. But it was learned that despite the complete demolition of his auto, and the fact that he allegedly died after being flung through the windshield, the photos of his cadaver showed the face to be nearly unscarred. No one was allowed to see the rest of the body. His widow and family alleged that Genaro was not in a car accident at all but that he was tortured and shot by the army. This, for now, must remain moot. Suffice it to say that the widow's story had credibility among the alienated opposition sectors of the militant left. Genaro became a martyr, a symbol of revolutionary self-sacrifice. Guerrilla brigades were named for him. The name Genaro Vázquez took its place along with that of the legendary Emiliano Zapata, whose memory was invoked the year of Genaro's death with the formation of FUZ. Genaro, some said, would become Mexico's Che Guevara. At graveside in Guerrero no one bothered to denounce Echeverría as would be done the following year in Monterrey when the industrial magnate Garza Sada was buried. With the passing of Genaro Vázquez, Mexico had lost a soldier of the people. His cousin, Daniel Vázquez Rojas, said in eulogy: "Your life was certain, your ideas transcendental. Your attitude was generous, clean, honest. You have fought for the poor and weak, for the peasants, and for this people will never forget you."[34]

Among the ironies of Genaro Vázquez's life was his service as a primary schoolteacher; until he was fired for his subversive ideas, he taught school in the late 1950s in the captial city's outskirts, in a district known as San Juan de Aragón (later to gain notoriety as the training ground for the right-wing official terrorist organization, the Falcons). Next, Genaro moved to his home state Guerrero where he founded the Guerrero Civic Committee to resist government abuses and to fight the caciques. He also helped to establish the renegade peasants' organization CCI (see Chapter 7). His organizing and leadership skills culminated in the ACNR and in his death. But the humble schoolteacher had threatened and physically shaken the power pyramid. President Echeverría knew it. Castrejón Díaz, the Coca Cola magnate, knew it also.

With the passing of Genaro Vázquez, leadership of the rural portion of the ACNR passed into the able hands of Lucio Cabañas.[35] One of Genaro's lieutenants, José Bracho Campos, was captured shortly thereafter. Early in 1973 Bracho Campos and a number of his companion cellmates in the prison at Chilpancingo issued a declaration that was published by Por Que? eulogizing Genaro Vázquez on the anniversity of his death and ending with "long live the ACNR."[36] Publication of such a document by political prisoners obviously carried the risk of grave reprisals. There was abundant testimony in Por Que? and in the publications of the PAN as to the incidence of political torture throughout the country. Bracho Campos was tortured; photos of this found their way into print.

Several months thereafter Lucio Cabañas and others in the mountains of Guerrero declared that ACNR would found a political party (perhaps it would be a party in name only). It would be called the Party of the Poor. In one of its early declarations the Party of the Poor, which I will refer to hereinafter as PDLP (Partido de los Pobres), dichotomized Mexican society into two classes, oppressed and oppressors, and called for class warfare. The communique then revealed:

> Be it known that the PDLP [also calling itself Brigada de Ajusticiamiento del Partido de los Probres] takes responsibility for the kidnapping of Mr. Francisco Sánchez López, member of the Mexican exploitive bourgeoisie, agricultural magnate who exploits and dominates vast coconut plantations in the state of Guerrero, who owns part of the oil and soap factory known as "La Polar" and who loans money to the peasants at such high interest

rates as to eventually take away from them their garden plots when they cannot pay on a fixed date. He pays his workers miserable wages and extracts a life of conspicuous consumption from their toil.[37]

After calling for students, workers, intellectuals generally, and peasants to rise up against their oppressors the document concludes: "to execute a corrupt labor leader [charro] or a plant foreman means there is one less enemy of the people. Our fundamental method of battle is with arms. We will win or die trying."[38] This was signed by Lucio Cabañas and others.

The operating principles and ideology of the PDLP were these: Destroy the bourgeois society by violence, abolish capitalism and private property which is its base, eliminate class exploitation and antagonism, expropriate all industries and businesses except for the smallest of private concerns (street vendors, and so on, may be allowed to operate), nationalize all the land, socialize medicine and all means of transport and communications, implant an effective legal system that will guarantee equality of opportunity for all and prevent the emergence of new elites, and identify the revolutionary struggle in Mexico with that in all other lands where there are oppressed peoples.[39] These declarations of the PDLP were followed by similar proclamations in other states, many of which identified themselves as members of, or in solidarity with, the PDLP. One example was the announcement of the Brigada Campesina Emiliano Zapata which boasted that it had put into motion plans to exterminate key members of the landed gentry in the state of Oaxaca.

A reading of Mexico's underground press gave the distinct impression that President Echeverría arrived at the midpoint of his presidency facing the threat of a nation risen to arms. Public evidence of turmoil and violence suggested this. Here it should be noted that as a sequel to the kidnapping of Francisco Sánchez López, as acknowledged by the PDLP, he was tried in a people's court style and executed about one week following the communique that was cited above. This led to reprisals by the army against suspected accomplices and resulted in the execution, without trial or legal due process, of a number of peasants in the village of Piloncillos in Guerrero. Lucio Cabañas called it a "little Viet Nam." He pledged an "eye for an eye" campaign of attrition against the regime and the privileged classes.[40]

Perhaps the most spectacular of Lucio Cabañas's exploits did indeed involve a member of the privileged classes, the kidnapping of federal senator Rubén Figueroa in June 1974. Figueroa was also the PRI's candidate-elect for the governorship of the state of Guerrero, the scene of major rural guerrilla activity since the great revolution. The first communique of the PDLP advising that Senator Figueroa had been sequestered was signed on June 3 by Lucio Cabañas and received nationwide publication. On June 14 came a second communique stating that Figueroa had been tricked into a meeting with Cabañas (just like the great revolutionary Emiliano Zapata had been tricked into his death in 1919, boasted Cabañas).[41] A third communique appeared on June 26 and detailed the conditions for the release of Senator Figueroa: that the government retire all troops from the mountains of Guerrero, that all political prisoners be freed, that a ransom of 50 million pesos ($4 million at that time) be paid to the PDLP, that the government publish and broadcast a number of guerrilla manifestos throughout the country, and that a list of labor and peasant complaints be attended to immediately. A demand was also made on the governor of the state of Guerrero that prisoners be released, that peasant debts to several local caciques be formally canceled, and that reprisals be instituted against several named police officials for their alleged acts of brutality against the poor people of the state.[42] The government's reply was given by Procurador Pedro Ojeda Paullada, "We make no deals with criminals."

Then, surprisingly, the father-in-law of President Echeverría was kidnapped on August 25, 1974, while Senator Figueroa was still captive. Responsibility for the kidnapping of José Guadalupe Zuno (83 years old) was laid to the FRAP, Revolutionary Armed Forces, who were believed to be collaborating with Lucio Cabañas. This strange event has been the subject of a multitude of interpretations including that the incumbent PRI government (or high-ranking persons therein) engineered the kidnapping to generate public sympathy for Echeverría personally whose security forces were being discredited by the yet unsolved Figueroa kidnapping. Others argued it was a trick by militarists hoping to force Echeverría to resign. On September 7 the daily *Excelsior* carried a communique from the FRAP guerrillas and the text of a taped recording in which the kidnapped Zuno said that he favored the PDLP and that he personally admired Lucio Cabañas. Some observers urged that this was more proof of the government's complicity; others recalled that Zuno, in his younger years, had been a Marxist and urged that the tape was the product of senility. The next day Zuno was released unharmed in Guadalajara and his kidnapping remains moot to this day, despite several allegedly definitive revelations to the contrary.

What makes the kidnappings of Figueroa and Zuno so curious is that both men reportedly were released on the same day, September 8, 1974. Various accounts allege that Figueroa was released after the government in fact paid the 50 million peso ransom and Cabañas dropped most of his other demands.[43] I also have it on good authority that the opposition journal *Por Que?* was about to publish photographic evidence of the ransom being paid to Cabañas and documents signed by Figueroa to this effect, but that same month (September 1974) government agents invaded the offices of *Por Que?*, smashed the presses, confiscated the edition in question, and arrested Roger Menéndez and his staff. Some of the evidence allegedly to be published in *Por Que?* was that the Mexican army had staged large troop concentrations and convoys deliberately to create the facade of a major operation which resulted in Figueroa's rescue. Later, pictures were published of Cabañas, pictures which had been taken by Figueroa himself during his captivity.[44]

If the freeing of Figueroa (who ultimately assumed the governorship of Guerrero despite being kidnapped during part of his electoral campaign) had murky aspects to it, so did the ultimate struggle of Lucio Cabañas who died months thereafter on December 2, 1974. Mexican authorities claimed to have smashed the Cabañas guerrillas in a valiant military encounter. Yet, only official photographers were permitted to see Cabañas's body. Questions have been raised (perhaps deliberately in the desire to build mystique) as to the authenticity of the government's report, including the suggestion that Cabañas may have shot himself. It is known that Cabañas was ill and under medical care during the last months of his life.[45] What is certain is that all of this doubt lends itself well to martyr-building in the style of Che Guevara. By leaving the issues moot the government surely discredited itself.

Lucio Cabañas had been a rural schoolteacher in the village of Atoyac, Guerrero. During those years, on October 18, 1967, a group of parents met in that village's square to protest the firing of Cabañas and his replacement with a puppet for the state's governor who opposed Cabañas's subversive teaching and his involvement in Marxist circles, just as Genaro Vázquez had been ostracized. The parents and some children were massacred by police when they refused to disperse. These were poor people, Cabañas's people, and he never forgave himself for being involved in their massacre. It was then that he took to the hills, later to join forces with Genaro Vázquez, and ultimately to found his PDLP with its peoples court and justice brigades.[46]

While a plethora of guerrilla fronts, movements, groups, and commands have proliferated in Mexico, it seems that the names of Genaro Vázquez and Lucio Cabañas are invested with the greatest symbolic revolutionary potential. It is often hard to distinguish truly political revolutionaries in Mexico from commercial revolutionaries who steal for profit. The evidence seems clear, however, that Vázquez and Cabañas were not the common bandits which the regime would like to claim they were. Their extortions and robberies, of which there were many to be sure, were designed to support revolutionary activity along the lines of the Cuban or Guevarist models. Their motive was popular liberation and social justice, this much I have been told by admittedly anticommunist Mexicans who disapprove of guerrilla insurgency themselves, but who still share the goals of social justice that were held by Vázquez and Cabañas. The platform of the PDLP, then, summarized a broad spectrum of problems which Mexico's esoteric democracy has not solved and which many opposition groups see as justification for violent rebellion against the status quo. The document, as promulgated in 1972 and signed by Lucio Cabañas and other members of the PDLP, not only promises to lift the Mexican masses out of their wretched existence but specifically identifies their struggle with that of oppressed minorities in North America as well.[47]

Late in the 1970s Mexico appeared on the verge of replacing Argentina as Latin America's most violence-prone nation. Just as in Argentina, it was often difficult to know who in Mexico was acting in the name of whom and which supposedly left-wing terrorist group might be a government paramilitary squad in disguise. It is not possible at the moment of this writing, nor within the scope of this work, to attempt an ideological or functional identification of all such groups. But as the decade comes to an end it is well to look briefly, but prophetically, at one of them: the 23rd of September League (Liga Comunista 23 de Septiembre). Press reports during those years made it difficult to tell whether the League was simply a mercenary band of commercial communists or whether it had revolutionary ideological goals. Numerous kidnappings and encounters with police seemed to suggest a profit motive.

A political novel published in 1977 and offered as a requiem to the League gave a somber interpretation.[48] Here is one key scenario, its setting a movie theater in Mexico City.

As hundreds of innocent spectators watch the screen, the projection is suddenly interrupted and a propaganda film, "Atzlandia hoy y mañana," appears depicting a montage of symbols reflecting what Mexico is and what it might be. Significantly among the symbols are Cuauhtemoc, Tlatelolco, the Supreme Court, a cadaver, jails, Daniel Cosío Villegas, human suffering, and deputies of the Chamber sleeping in their seats. Shortly the screen goes black. Machine guns open up from behind the audience, creating a prism of deadly blue and green lights. Over 500 people die. The 23rd of September League has been hired by certain members of the government to conduct unofficial terrorism which will permit maintenance of a state of seige, accompanying opportunities for elite enrichment, and justify the use of national security as a cover for their grafts. It will also serve as an excuse to persecute enemy camarillas within the establishment.

The guerrillas in this fictitious scenario speak of Genaro Vázquez and Lucio Cabañas as having been idealists. They are told that the massacre at Tlatelolco put an end to one police chief, and that Jueves de Corpus got rid of the mayor. Perhaps the theater massacre would bring down the president, along with his cabinet. There were those within the official party who wanted to precipitate just such a happening (by this time it is abundantly clear that the country called Atzlandia in which this tale unfolds is really Mexico, and the transparent pseudonym for President López Portillo is Gómez Gordillo). The idealistic Guevarism of the ACNR struggles in Guerrero has vanished. A real tragedy must occur as a goal in itself. Then the government will fall and a group of intellectuals who are better prepared to guide the destiny of Mexico will assume power.[49] But the League guerrillas are mercenaries, some doing it for a perverted love of killing, others to escape their former misery, all of them in it for money. They are paid by a government official who later betrays them. Betrayal is the norm throughout these traumatic moments. The guerillas are not loyal rebel patriots, followers of Morelos and Zapata, as were Genaro Vázquez, Lucio Cabañas, and their fighting mountain men. The

League's trigger men are shabby hired killers, only a few of whom need to rationalize their acts.

The scandal of the theater massacre precipitates the resignation of the president, but he is no fool and he does it in a way which reveals the rotten timbers supporting the corrupt edifice on which his state's political system is erected. The president goes on national television and resigns. He does not use the controlled Channel 13, the government's channel, but uses private facilities. The president interviews two young men on the live broadcast, men who were brought to him by a courageous reporter who had penetrated the police secrecy and revealed to the president the true enormity of the theater affair. These men recount their story of going to the movie with family and friends who were killed by the machine-gun fire. Surviving miraculously, these men were later accused by the police of complicity in the affair. The president then interviews the arresting officers on live television and publicly deposes them for having forced the two men to sign confessions under torture.[50]

Later, in the presence of congressional leaders and Supreme Court justices, the president confronts the police officials who investigated the theater massacre with the journalists' evidence. The police admit they lied to keep the body count low and avoid a scandal. They confess to having tried to keep out all reporters and also to having robbed the bodies of the dead. Before the president, livid with rage and shame, officials are made to empty their pockets revealing watches, money, women's rings, assorted jewelry. The subordinates implicate their superiors.[51] This is a tale of high-level public administration in Mexico; even a cabinet minister got his share of the booty.

The massacre was not supposed to be *such* a massacre in the first place. It was meant to weaken the president and perhaps even force his resignation in the face of an uncontrollable guerrilla problem that would require a military government to preserve the social order. The affair was not intended to unmask the cruel and corrupt barbarity of the system, any more than Tlatelolco or Jueves de Corpus had been planned to end as they did. The theater massacre is traced to key persons working around the president himself, one Sedas Peñalva who ends out winning nearly everything by betraying nearly everybody. The president will not reconsider his abdication. What, he muses, is the use of working for the nation when no one cares about anything except his own self-aggrandizement, when everyone is egoistic and corrupt. In the end the League members begin to liquidate each other. Betrayal is the constant norm which guides conduct. What the author depicts is a political system in atrophy, peopled by nihilists, egoists without ideals, or idealists whose goals are base and irreconcilably in conflict with each other. The novel is a likely reflection of the internecine warfare within Mexico's political system today. The fears of many Mexicans had come true, for the institution of the presidency itself had been undermined. Alone, the president could not be a benevolent authority figure. An intimate nexus between the official regime and a terrorist out-group had ended this traditional imagery. The president himself was a prisoner of the political system.

Of course, we cannot pretend that fiction in the form of a transparent political allegory is predictive theory or empirical evidence. But that is not the issue here. What counts is that Mexican intellectuals who write such literature are analyzing (in their own way) their political system and foreshadowing its denouncement, albeit using nonscientific techniques. The visions of political novelists need not be presumed ipso facto to be accurate. But it is a fact that the given writer, himself a product of the political system or a student of it, sees the system in a given way. The fact of his vision, then, becomes important for its very self; let us say it is evidence of the soft variety, but potentially revealing.

A CRYSTAL BALL: OPPOSITION POLITICS IN 1988

Suspend your beliefs again temporarily: What will Mexican politics be like in another decade? What if the PAN should really win in 1988? That is a concrete question, one which invites speculation; yet speculation can have a sound cultural anchoring. Consider a political novel circulating in Mexico during the presidential campaign year of 1976.[52] Its English title would be *The Day the PRI Lost*. The author asks his readers to suspend their beliefs only slightly, assuming they have read, or have been told, about the norms, styles, skills, and arenas that make up the Mexican political culture (told, that is, by someone who is not a paid apologist for the regime). The novel appeared, coincidentally, at the moment the PAN issued a statement by its 1970 presidential candidate, Efraín González Morfín, that referred to political corruption almost as if it were an innate characteristic of the Mexicans which impedes any drive to instill truly democratic norms.[53] Innate corruption and resulting PRI atrophy are dominant themes of the novel; indeed the PRI falls apart in 1988.

In the fictional account, many characters have transparent pseudonyms tying them to great figure of the past. Others use true-life names. The values and practices depicted are real; the denouement is imaginary, but within the realm of the possible. The novel is provocative and highly instructive.

A charismatic figure named Zapata takes over control of the opposition party PAN and rallies multitudes around an anticorruption and promoralization campaign.[54] The PRI defenders during the 1988 election year are forced to admit that corruption is rife, yet they defend it as a wealth-distributing mechanism, one which pacifies the people and avoids the adventure-lust of military coups so characteristic of South America. The PRI theorists argue among themselves that it is cheaper to allow bribes (*mordidas*), phantom bureaucrats (*aviadores*), extortion (*coyotaje*), than to pay the salaries needed to enforce honesty. Besides, they add, ending corruption in Mexico would destroy the socioeconomic mobility aspirations of the entire middle class. This is a crucial and profound observation by the novelist, that is, governmental accountability and honesty become barriers to socioeconomic mobility.

But PAN disclosures of public abuses attract millions to the opposition campaign. The North American Chicanos give their support to the PAN rebels in the form of printing and broadcasting facilities, plus financial contributions. Enormous corruption is disclosed, paramilitary squads (Los Halcones) disguised as a Department of Public Protection, bank tellers who demand bribes to accept deposits, and so on. Preelection polls begin to show that the PRI will lose the election. The PAN organizes its own paramilitary organization to defend itself and to stage a military coup should electoral fraud occur. This organization is called the Guardia Tricolor and it engineers popular uprisings directed at voracious government bureaucrats about the country.

Now the anticommunist instincts of U.S. interests (which have invested heavily in Mexico) are aroused. It is believed that both the PRI and the PAN are flirting with communism. The CIA tries to intervene and succeeds only in alienating both groups vis-a-vis the United States. The PRI tries to bribe the PAN presidential candidate Yañez into defecting and denouncing the PAN's intellectual leader Zapata as insane. But the PRI gets taken at its own game. The millions of dollars used for the bribe are deposited in a foreign bank to finance the PAN's campaign. Their Chicano-supported newspapers reveal the entire scandal. Now the PAN reemphasizes that its primary target is the bureaucracy, called a growing cancerous caste. The bureaucracy is like a theocracy: Its only goal is to increase its size indefinitely and surround its members in maximum comforts with minimal labor.[55] This is not an unreal description of what the PRI had actually become in 1976 when the book appeared.

The tale closes following a near public sex orgy staged by high PRI officials. Then comes a rare admission from the outgoing Mexican president, that the PRI has served its historic usefulness and must be dissolved and restructured to better serve the people. So as not to appear to go down without a fight, the PRI hierarchy tries to make victory out of defeat. They will use their own agents to encourage the insurrection the PAN already has planned. They will trick both the CIA and the communists into involvement; the PRI will say the insurrection is occurring out of desperation, led by a minority which fears losing and, importantly, that its culmination will be a fascist dictatorship to which both the CIA and the communists shall have been unknowing contributors. Thus, the constitutional order will have been altered and the PRI can use its army to put down what will have become a civil war. But since the CIA will be convinced of the likelihood of a socialist-populist-communist win (this erroneous perception has been spread quite deliberately), there will be no more support permitted for the PAN from Chicanos in the

United States. It will be a bloody war which the PRI can win, *but,* says the incumbent president, the PRI itself will also lose in a very real sense:

> Naturally, at the moment of our triumph we will have to make important changes in order to recapture the good will of the people, and we will do this. This is humiliating, but we must recognize that the opposition has forced us to introduce changes which, since many years past, we ought to have imposed ourselves.[56]

And the president is then asked, "What if, in fact, the opposition actually wins the civil war?" He replies that in that case *they* will have to make the changes, to clean up the corruption. At any rate, he admits, it is Mexico the nation that will win. That was the day in July of 1988 when the PRI knew it had lost. The next day, riots erupted throughout the country. This is fiction, yet it is potential reality.

No one can say that the PRI will meet its end as the foregoing scenario depicts, but none of the constituent elements in that scenario are beyond the realm of possibility (with the very probable exception that it would be some opposition group other than the PAN which would serve as catalyst). Nor is it unreasonable to assume that out of the PRI a truly enlightened despot might emerge who would carry out his own campaign of rationalization and moralization. That is the prescription contained in the work of José C. Valadés who viewed the Mexican presidency critically as the 1970 sexenio began. He argued that the PRI really should not be called a party because it lacked clearly defined policies to distinguish it from other groups; all the PRI had was historical symbols and watchwords to manipulate. He also saw the PRI as a personal power bureau for the incumbent president, one that he can use for real change should he see fit during his term, one that he can use to perpetuate his power thereafter.[57] Enlightened leadership may, indeed, emerge from within the PRI. There are those who argue that President Luis Echeverría, with his electoral reforms, his INFONAVIT housing program, and his land reform attempts, has been the most leftist reform president since Cárdenas (1934–40) and, at once, the most effectively anticommunist leader the nation has ever had.[58] Others still await enlightened leadership.[59]

ON THE FUTURE OF MEXICAN OPPOSITION POLITICS

The scenarios presented in this chapter do not augur well for the future of Mexico's political opposition. Whether or not 1988 materializes it is doubtful that it will be the PAN which acts as revolutionary catalyst. This can be inferred from the testimony about the PAN's internal disintegration that was given earlier. However, much could change if the PAN finds it possible to build itself a strong organization from the ground up, that is, capturing municipal offices (mayorships) about the country. There is evidence that the PRI recognizes that local politics may be its Achilles heel. It is at the community level that the contrast between citizen needs and governmental sloth is most conspicuous. Chapter 7 offers a microview of one such explosive local situation. But the vulnerability of the PRI at the local level has led it to resist even more furiously the efforts of opposition groups to spread local roots and gain real power. The device of giving opposition parties a handful of deputies-at-large in the national congress is merely a device to perpetuate the facade of democracy, while at once guaranteeing that no opposition deputy has a real constituency. That is to say, the PRI does not fear deputies-at-large who represent no specific geographical district that can be used for building a power base. In recent years, the few mayorships that the PAN has won, such as in Sonora and Nuevo León, had to be retaken by the PRI as such examples of opposition fortune could grow to proportions that would be difficult to control. It is hard for the single-party regime to admit that a defined piece of land "belongs" to the opposition, be it land won for the PAN by votes or won by Lucio Cabañas with guns.

The PRI does not fear political pluralism, then, so long as it does not have precise geographic limits, so long as no opposition party or group can stick pins in a map and say, "These districts are ours." Efraín González Morfín called pluralism in political life the fundamental base of the democratic attitude and charged that he who cannot tolerate complexity and ideological diversity in political life is in essence a totalitarian[60] To this we can add the observation of Evelyn P. Stevens that Mexico does not have a

> political system oriented toward the formulation and modification of goals through pluralistic participation in the decision-making process. Instead, we see repression of authentic interest groups and encouragement of spurious groups that can be relied on not to speak out of turn. *The regime deals with bona fide groups almost as though they were enemy nations.*[61]

Mexican leaders have come to the absurd point of making speeches against the party of abstentionism, the fear that the people will stay home and not give PRI its desired legitimacy by going to the polls to participate in rigged elections[62] In expressing such fears the PRI orators admit ipso facto that political pluralism is almost extinct in Mexico. This will be dramatized further by the microview of opposition politics and corruption in Chapter 7. Real political pluralism would require the PRI to practice the art of compromise. That it refused to do so is evident even in the composition of the Federal Electoral Commission which, as Cosío Villegas pointed out, represents the executive and legislative branches of government, but not the judiciary, "that power obliged by the Constitution to investigate electoral fraud."[63]

Exclusion is built into the system and exclusion breeds enemies. As Kenneth Coleman aptly puts it, system legitimacy (for the PRI) will be harder to maintain as the PRI's enemies become more numerous.[64] And the PRI's enemies are now doing more than just abstaining from voting, they are looking the other way while irresponsible terrorists like the 23rd of September Communist League assault an odious officialdom and disrupt society. In the face of such realities it is difficult to maintain the facade of legitimacy. Coleman foresees that get-out-the-vote campaigns may not necessarily reinforce system legitimacy for the PRI. He argues that "urban protest voting will be likely to increase in Mexico, especially in nonpresidential elections."[65] I would add to this that urban guerrilla warfare is likely to escalate as well, as long as the PRI's legitimacy rituals fail to cloak the neglect or ease the suffering which the Mexican citizenry continues to endure at the hands of the revolutionary coalition. One will be well advised to watch the development of local protest movements in Mexico to evaluate this prediction insofar as opposition politics are concerned.

NOTES

1. See Edward J. Williams, "Mutation in the Mexican Revolution: Industrialism, Nationalism, and Centralism," in *Secolas Annals,* March 1976, p. 41.

2. *Excelsior,* July 4, 1976 (*Magazine Dominical,* p. 11).

3. Evelyn P. Stevens, *Protest and Response in Mexico* (Cambridge, Mass.: MIT Press, 1974), pp. 127–84.

4. Franz A. von Sauer, *The Alienated "Loyal" Opposition* (Albuquerque: University of New Mexico Press), 1974, p. 31.

5. Donald, J. Mabry, *Mexico's Acción Nacional: A Catholic Alternative to Revolution* (Syracuse University Press), 1973.

6. Von Sauer, op. cit., p. 125.

7. Ibid., p. 138

8. Ibid., p. 148.

9. Mabry, op. cit., p. 50.

10. Von Sauer, op. cit., p. 123.

11. Mabry, op. cit., p. 59.

12. Ibid., p. 74.

13. Ibid., p. 99.

14. Ibid., p. 101.

15. Ibid., p. 189.

16. Letter from Raúl González Schmal, former Secretary General of the Partido Acción Nacional to Kenneth F. Johnson, May 5, 1976. This version is confirmed by Carlos Arriola, "La crisis del Partido Acción Nacional," in *Foro Internacional,* April–June 1977.

17. News bulletin of the PAN's Comité Ejecutivo Nacional, *Información de Prensa,* September 1977.

18. *Información de Prensa,* August 25, 1977.

19. *Proceso,* September 26, 1977, p. 25.

20. *Proceso,* April 23, 1977, p. 15.

21. Ibid., pp. 48–49.

22. Without entering into detail, it is now possible for an opposition party to win deputies-at-large if it wins a certain percentage of the overall popular vote, but the important consideration is that these deputies so won cannot exceed 25 in number and they have no geographic constituency, hence no one could be expected to make direct appeals to them for national solutions to specific local problems that would give a certain deputy a sense of grass roots.

23. This was originally cited in Kenneth F. Johnson, *Mexican Democracy: A Critical View* (Boston: Allyn & Bacon, 1972), pp. 123–24.

24. Ibid.

25. *Visión,* June 1, 1976, p. 48.

26. *Proceso,* May 9, 1977, p. 10.

27. Ibid.

28. Ibid., p. 11.

29. Heberto Castillo and Francisco Paoli Bolio, *Porque un nuevo partido?* (Mexico: Colección Duda Semanal, Editorial Posada, 1975).

30. The year in which *Por Que?* was born saw the death of *Política,* a prominent opposition publication identified with the extreme left but which, under proddings from former president Cárdenas, stopped publication because of the hurt feelings of President Díaz Ordaz who had been severely attacked in its pages. *Por Que?* took up the role vacated by *Política.*

31. Mario Menéndez had been the director of the journal *Sucesos* and in that capacity had lived for a matter of weeks with Fabio Vázquez Castaño and his rebel forces in Colombia. Mario was expelled for this by the Colombian authorities (for life) in 1967. The journal *Sucesos* became increasingly less political thereafter and, despite the historic nature of the revelations in 1967 which make those issues of *Sucesos* collectors' items today, Mario told me in 1968 that the then owner of *Sucesos* blackmailed several Mexican politicians by saying, "pay me so much or I'll send Mario Menéndez to write a story about you." With this, and in light of the demise of *Política,* the Menéndez brothers decided the time was ripe for a true opposition journal of the left to appear. It was my own association with the Menéndez brothers which, in part, resulted in my own expulsion from Mexico in 1972. This was followed by a concerted campaign by the Mexican government (especially Gobernación) to purge all copies of the first edition of *Mexican Democracy* from Mexico City bookstores. Their confiscation of my material also delayed the second edition for nearly six years.

32. *Ultimas Noticias de Excelsior,* February 14, 1970.

33. *La Prensa* (Buenos Aires), April 7, 1973 (editorial comment).

34. *La Batalla,* April 1972.

35. A later account states that the Cabañas movement was actually formed one year prior to that of Vázquez. See Jaime López, *10 años de guerrillas en Mexico* (Mexico: Editorial Posada, 1974).

36. *Por Que?,* February 22, 1973, pp. 3–4

37. My translation from *Por Que?,* May 3, 1973, p. 4.

38. Ibid. This was a part of Cue Guevara's tactical doctrine as well.

39. Ibid., pp. 6–8.

40. *Por Que?,* May 10, 1973, pp. 3–5.

41. López, op. cit., p. 136.

42. Ibid., pp. 138–39.

43. J. Natividad Rosales, *La muerte de Lucio Cabañas* (Mexico: Editorial Posada, 1975), p. 39.

44. Ibid., p. 166.

45. Ibid., pp. 124–25.

46. López, op. cit., p. 68.

47. J. Natividad Rosales, *Quien Fue Lucio Cabañas?* (Mexico: Editorial Posada, 1976), pp. 94–95.

48. José Pérez Chowell, *Requiem para un ideal: la liga 23 de septiembre* (Mexico: Editorial V Siglos, 1977).

49. Ibid., p. 121.

50. Ibid., pp. 135–36.

51. Ibid., pp. 158–59.

52. Armando Ayala Anguiano, *El día que perdió el PRI* (Mexico: Editorial Contenido, 1976).

53. Specifically he says (and I translate), "How can you PAN members [panistas] expect to establish a democracy in Mexico or honesty in the public administration if our idiosyncracy is dishonorableness in such endeavors." From Efraín González Morfín, *El cambio social y el PAN* (Mexico: Ediciones de Acción Nacional, 1975), p. 17.

54. The novelist's version of the PAN triumph should be weighed against the evidence presented earlier that the PAN was in severe disarray into the late 1970s. However, the same scenario could materialize should the opposition groups of the left regroup around an organism such as Heberto Castillo's PMT providing it could become a legitimate and recognized power contender.

55. Anguiano, op. cit., p. 164.

56. Ibid., p. 185.

57. José C. Valadés, *El presidente de México en 1970* (Mexico: Editores Mexicanos Unidos, 1969), pp. 82–83.

58. Based upon comments by Rudolph de la Garza at Arizona State University's conference "On the Future of Mexico," April 23, 1976.

59. That seems to have been the position of the distinguished Mexican scholar Daniel Cosío Villegas in his *La sucesión presidencial* (Mexico: Cuadernos de Joaquín Mortiz, 1974), passim.

60. Morfín, op. cit., pp. 17–20.

61. Stevens, op. cit., p. 259 (emphasis added).

62. Daniel Cosío Villegas, *El estilo personal de gobernar* (Mexico: Cuadernos de Joaquín Mortiz, 1974), p. 78.

63. Ibid., p. 86.

64. Kenneth W. Coleman, *Diffuse Support in Mexico: The Potential for Crisis* (Beverly Hills, Calif.: Sage Professional Papers, 1976), p. 5 (from galley proofs).

65. Ibid., p. 47.

Seven

A Microview of Atrophy and Corruption in a Border Setting

PERSONAGES, VIGNETTES, AND VISIONS

It was common during the late 1970s to see a green pickup truck rumble through the streets of Nogales, Sonora, with the words "Banco de Sangre Y Plasma" (Blood and Plasma Bank) printed on its side. I noted the Mexican license plate number. The man who drove it was known locally as "the Vampire." Much of the blood he bought and sold was taken from heroin addicts then sold to local Mexican hospitals where it was used to create potential new heroin users. Nogales had plenty of such addicts who would sell their blood for money with which to maintain their habit. Thousands had been lured to the border area by the promise of jobs in the *maquiladoras* or twin-plant border industries, a joint Mexican-U.S. scheme for providing economic opportunity on the border. The myth of opportunity had simply raised the unemployment rate to around 50 percent of the available labor force in Nogales. In desperation many found themselves resorting to drugs, prostitution, and illegal contraband operations (including migration) into the United States. There were, however, good opportunities for people like the Vampire. This was typical of the socioeconomic situation in many Mexican border communities.

Also in Nogales was an enterprising druggist whose access to narcotics in pill form was practically unlimited. It was possible for North American addicts, residents of Arizona, to make a regular bus trip to Nogales, Arizona, cross over the line as tourists into Nogales, Sonora, and get a fix in the back room of one of his various enterprising pharmacies. This meant that there was an ample supply of persons from both sides willing to sell their blood to feed

---

Some of the material in this chapter has been condensed from Kenneth F. Johnson and Nina M. Ogle, *Mexico's Silent Invasion,* a report to the U.S. Immigration and Naturalization Service and the U.S. Congress on border problems and illegal migration. Selections have also been condensed from Kenneth F. Johnson, "Opposition Politics and the Future of Mexico," in *On The Future of Mexico,* ed. Lawrence Koslow, (Tempe: Arizona State University Center for Latin American Studies, 1978).

their habits. The druggist in question can be referred to as Javier Oslos, a pseudonym he would later receive in a book of testimony and protest by an author who had witnessed the horrors of a drug-infested prison in Nogales.[1]

Oslos had another racket, the creation of young addicts who would eventually become regular clients. Every morning in certain schools the students would find a brightly colored pill in the pen well of their desk. The teachers ignored the pills, they would not say how they got there or what the students were to do with them. The teachers had been paid to take *la vista gorda,* look the other way. Inevitably some of the students would take the pills and, finding that they generated a pleasant experience (relief from hunger or infection), would tell their friends. Ultimately a good number of students were taking the pills. They got turned on every morning for a matter of weeks. Then there were no more pills. But a friendly boy outside the school told them where the pills could be purchased. More money for the druggist. More future clients for the Vampire.

Indeed, it could be said that Nogales, like so many Mexican border towns, was full of vampires. Those who took advantage of their own excess population and, at the same time, offered sexual and psychedelic services to degenerate North Americans, of which there were thousands ready to pay for prurient and lascivious experiences that would not be permitted in their home communities. Unfortunately for Mexico, the act of going to a Mexican border town has become a way of "letting it all hang out" for a multitude of U.S. citizens who almost inevitably will return to the U.S. side and criticize the degradation of Mexican culture (which they have just helped to perpetuate). But it is futile to speculate which came first in the matter of vice, the supply or the demand. What is clear is that degradation is a circular and self-reinforcing process which cannot be easily dichotomized by an international boundary fence. The fence might separate political systems, but it could not divide the culture of vice.

One Mexican who contemplated that fence was an old man, virtually speechless, diseased, the town beggar, and who would die during the early 1970s at what was estimated to be 74 years of age. This sounds vague but since no one knew where the old man lived (usually it was in alleys and doorsteps) neither did they know for sure when he died nor what became of his body. He was called El Bulla[2] and one day he just vanished. Weeks passed before anyone noticed his absence; but one man did. He was the writer-poet-philosopher Oscar Monroy Rivera, himself a native of Nogales, Sonora, who had been educated in Mexico City and returned to his native border town in the hope that he could somehow enlighten the cultural wasteland where he had spent his youth. Monroy would write about El Bulla, of his inability to comprehend the struggle around him which involved humans making each other suffer. Nor could El Bulla understand the strange society to the north on the other side of the border fence, a far-away land from which pale strangers came to look at the old beggar and joke about his cruel society. El Bulla, of course, could not understand their words nor speak any of his own.

In his youth, Oscar Monroy Rivera and other boys growing up in the same Mexican border town of Nogales, Sonora, used slingshots to knock out the lights of the boundary fence which divided his country from the United States.[3] He told me that sometimes boys from the U.S. side would fire back at them with .22 rifles, a costly weapon the Mexicans could not afford. Crossing the line surreptitiously was always a challenge for the *nogalenses,* the Mexican border youth of Nogales. The U.S. city just across the line in Arizona was also called Nogales. There were stores where finery could be had, where it was safe to drink the water, and the policemen usually did not accept bribes. Once young Oscar assembled a group of his friends along the border fence while he and others looted a partially burned department store called La Villa de París. They threw merchandise over the fence to the boys who came from a congested and poor neighborhood. Oscar was delighted in hearing the clamor of so many people receiving unexpected treasures from north of the fence.[4]

Oscar Monroy Rivera was himself born nearly on the dividing line, in a building whose kitchen would later grow into a famous restaurant, although not a luxury one. Named for his mother, the Restaurant Elvira was Oscar's growing up place. Today, it can be seen with a Corona beer sign above it from the Arizona side of the international border. Therein, Oscar and his twin brother plus a host of other brothers and sisters would be raised. In later years, when the family divided socially and ideologically, the Restaurant Elvira fell to one faction and became an issue of resentment among the others. It was difficult for Oscar's mother to raise nine children without a father. Much of Oscar's early care and affection, therefore, came from the maids of the restaurant. He would remember many of them for their kindness and for the education they encouraged him to pursue under difficult circumstances. Yet, the Monroy family was financially in the middle class of Nogales. The children were not deprived when their mother died of cancer at the age of 48. Her passing moved young Oscar to write poetry, he said, to honor her memory with his pen for the many pains she bore so that he would not have to suffer them.

He remembers happily a brief period of primary school which his family was able to arrange for him across the line in Nogales, Arizona. Despite this he never developed an affinity for the English language or the American culture, regardless of the opportunity he had to absorb it. But Oscar mastered *castellano* Spanish brilliantly, a quality which made him stand out in educated Mexican society and especially above those along the border who habitually flaunted remnants of several languages, pretending ostentatiously to be bilingual. When Oscar spoke his voice had an innate charisma. People listened and respected him. But this quality would one day make certain elites fear him as well. Oscar spoke with a brutal frankness. Often this brought him conflicts in school. The bulk of his primary and secondary education was spent in Nogales,

Sonora, and he hated it. Oscar would steal unnecessarily (in the sense that he was not going hungry) but it was his dream to amass a fortune, buy an airplane, and drop bombs on the Sonoran school which he so detested.[5] He told me that his reaction against much of the Mexican public school system led him into an opposition political role in later life. And at the same time he reacted to an unjust social system, one in which it was common (and still is) for fathers to abandon a wife with many children, leaving them all to their own fortune.

In Oscar's case he transferred all filial piety to his mother. Once, when he was either six or seven years old, she called him to her side and pointed to a stranger who passed in front of the door to their restaurant-home. He was heavy set, tall, and getting on in years. "Do you see that man there in the street?" she said. "Yes Mama, I see him." "Ask God to care for him in your prayers every night before you go to bed—he is your father." Oscar was confused. No one had ever spoken of his father and he never felt the need to ask about him. It would be many years before they would have personal contact.[6] His early need for a father image would go largely unfulfilled.

But not so his need for someone to pity. There was still the pathetic old figure El Bulla whose mind had never developed and who could not speak except to scream "mmmaaammmaaaa!," from which his nickname was derived.[7] El Bulla came to be almost a theological symbol to Monroy, one who had the hand of a poor beggar but whose need and wretchedness symbolized that of the entire Nogales community. El Bulla had the ability to forgive the boys who teased him when he stuttered and screamed at them. The maids of the Restaurant Elvira also cared for El Bulla as did many others in the community. Later Monroy would write about this personage for his ability to forgive the society which tormented him; Monroy would make El Bulla into something like a deformed Christ whose only sermon was the lesson of charity implicit in the suffering he endured.

El Bulla was a reflection of his community. As a personage he might come to eclipse the author himself. This, indeed, was foreshadowed by the cultural publication *Apuntes Especiales* when the first edition of *El profeta del silencio* (The Prophet of Silence) appeared in 1972.[8] It was said that Oscar Monroy had been the first to discover that the true name of El Bulla was Carlos Moreno Galindo. The book went into several editions, in many cases appealing to Mexican readers' sense of pity, in others to their desire for bizarre reading, but to most for its intellectual attraction, the portrait of a poor beggar being held up to the world as a mirror of his community and its broader society. At times the three persons are merged, the prophet El Bulla, the beggar Carlos Moreno Galindo, and the writer Oscar Monroy Rivera. Such moments in the book are often those of intense social criticism tied directly to Nogales which, in turn, becomes a microcosm of the greater universe which is Mexico.

It is El Bulla who contributes nothing to the usury of the banks and commercial businesses, nor to the U.S. tourist trade. He received nothing from the nuns who were nurses of charity but served only the well-to-do.[9] And Monroy says that because El Bulla has died he cannot know of the shameful fact that under the pretext of constructing an additional Social Security office in Nogales the government has used pumps to drain one of Nogales' few remaining fresh water springs and has poured the precious resource down the sewer. In a city with more than 100,000 people lacking water to flow into their meager homes, the local government of Nogales takes six months to pump out a spring and dry it up. This is a profitable business venture for those who later will sell water, and for those who will collect rents from the new building. El Bulla, were he living, would wish a merciful revenge upon those who destroyed a gentle stream, the source of life which God has provided for both man and tree.[10]

Monroy received acclaim for his works on "the Prophet" from such distinguished Mexican scholars as the philosopher Porfirio Miranda and from the poet and one-time minister of education Jaime Torres Bodet. But in his community the Prophet was scorned by many who thought him unsightly. He surely died wearing the same dirty white shirt and black tie as always, his legs swollen, infected, and moving only with the aid of a cane. In a second edition El Bulla posed with Monroy for a series of photographs. El Bulla survived more than 50 years of his life in Nogales, sleeping outside during the oven heat of desert summers and the cold snows of winter. No one knew exactly where he came from or when he came to Nogales. But, says Monroy, El Bulla lived because of those who cared for him, those who had discovered that "the true love is that which learns it is wrong to let a fellow being suffer. . . . El Bulla, so long as there was a breath of life inside him, was the other fellow-being who reflected the community about him."[11] He was more than an incarnate condemnation of suffering: "El Bulla is the complete pious geography of those who form the basic [moral] context of this city . . . because it is piety [charity] which creates cities out of peoples," but it goes also in reverse, for the vain pretense of charity causes a city to atrophy into its selfish human units.[12] To Monroy the overall health of his community was a vital concern, and through the person of El Bulla Monroy castigates the wrongdoers about him.

Although he cannot speak it is El Bulla, the Prophet of Silence, who accuses with his piercing glance the system in which Mexicans live. One day Monroy was writing about El Bulla. Below he heard sirens of fire trucks as they lurched onto the narrow street to seek out a disaster. There watching them was El Bulla. Monroy told me, "Here I had my personage directly below me at the very instant in which I was trying to capture his spirit with my pen." There was El Bulla, with the eyes of a child, watching the fire engines and hearing the scream of their sirens, and he might be thinking that these men dressed up in uniforms only on fiesta days when a game was played. He did not know, perhaps, the service which these men rendered to the unfortunate of Nogales when fire should be visited upon them. El Bulla was innocence, so who could be his enemies? They are those who abuse others, practice fraud and accept bribes, abuse widows and orphans, men of violence who lack charity.[13]

For reasons as yet unexplained, the Prophet seemed to know when someone was in trouble, when someone was about to die, and he would show up at a respectful distance as a funeral cortege moved toward a distant cemetery. Perhaps his built-in silence gave him a spiritual clairvoyance. The Prophet arrived in front of the house of a godless personage of the community, a wrongdoer. Only his expression changed and his hands trembled as he removed his hat, looking on with glances of disrespect that chilled the wind. "Because wherever the impious and godless one lives the Prophet will be there watching, accusing with his marble-like silence, whatever time of year it may be."[14] Silence is the language of El Bulla. He has seen it all, the cries of the abandoned children, the names of travelers and wetbacks seeking to cross the border illegally, the disenchanted priests, the weeping prostitutes who did not get paid, the flowers in gardens bordering on dirty streets, the clock above the customs house, the students who never returned to Nogales for there was no future there except one of vice, the nicknames of the local dogs, peddlers, and pushers. He knew it all in his silence. He contained it all inside him, but the perceptive writer Oscar Monroy Rivera saw it as a reflection of social and political reality in the eyes of El Bulla, the Prophet of Silence.

Knowing all that he had witnessed and absorbed in Nogales, the author asks what was it that the Prophet did not know.

El Bulla did not know how to traffic in marijuana, live from abortions, sell copper calling it gold, defile temples of worship, extort the weak, sell human flesh [prostitution], profit by contraband, create monopolies, rig scales to overcharge customers, violate the honor of others, assassinate characters with false rumors, spit on the poor, defame the widow, commit tax fraud, cause hatred among others, rob his brother or betray his friend.[15]

These things the Prophet witnessed but never did. They were reflections of the socioeconomic-political reality of the community in which he lived. Monroy constructed the memory of El Bulla, Carlos Moreno Galindo, as a reflection of all which the author disapproved of in his society, of all that he had dedicated his life's work to undoing. He wished that El Bulla could have been proclaimed candidate for political office. Surely he would bring honor and charity with him. It would be a new and revolutionary experience for Mexico, giving power to one who made silence into a political skill. In this way all society would be reminded of the atomization of individuals that has affected Mexican life adversely, draining the richness of its cultural heritage. It is an atrophy which reaches into the halls of government at all levels in Mexico and stultifies life for everyone.[16] Had the people looked deeply into the eyes of the

Prophet they would have seen their social and political disarray, but they would still have received his Christ-like absolution.[17]

This is my own interpretation of one of Monroy's principal works, and he has confirmed most of it to me personally. His writings go on, however, much beyond the scope of this chapter. Monroy spent some 20 years studying and writing in the Mexican capital. When he returned to Sonora it was with the hope of entering into that state's political life. His frustrations at trying to work within the revolutionary coalition, that is, within the PRI, ultimately drove him into the role of a lawyer of the poor and to challenging the regime with his pen. *The Prophet of Silence* is one of many such challenges and, perhaps, it is the best from a humanistic point of view. His written portrait of El Bulla helps to engrave in the minds of at least some Sonorans the tragedy of one who everyone saw, few really knew, and who nearly everyone despised until the moment of his death when he simply disappeared and was seen no more. Then, claims Monroy, the people of Nogales sensed that they had lost a messianic figure whose pitiful life had been silently interwoven with their own.

SONORA AS A POLITICAL MICROCOSM

The political thought and civic activist career of Oscar Monroy Rivera can best be understood within the context of Sonora, his native state. A number of studies have been made of the electoral frauds which were committed in Sonora and of the frequency of protest voting there against the PRI's hard-fisted monopoly. The works of von Sauer and Mabry cited in Chapter 6 touch on this. Also available is an especially intensive study of the Sonoran protest voting of 1967 by Robert Bezdek.[18] The following background is necessary to understand the political career of the writer-activist Oscar Monroy Rivera as a microreflection both of Sonora and of Mexico's greater political reality.

In the year 1967 the PRI decided to impose a gubernatorial candidate on Sonora, a wealthy agriculturalist named Faustino Felix Serna. He also happened to be the favored successor of the incumbent governor, Luis Encinas Johnson, who was notorious for his corrupt administration and repressive tactics. The dedazo which was employed to impose Faustino Felix provoked such resentment that during the two months before the election in July many of the state's schools were paralyzed by strikes and police were used to repress demonstrators. A great deal of evidence has been assembled to support the charge that unnecessary brutality was used under orders from Governor Encinas. Entry of the PAN into this election produced a record voter turnout (nearly 50 percent according to the Bezdek study) and had it not been for officially engineered fraud, the PAN's candidate for governor, Gilberto Súarez Arvizu, would have won.

Indeed, the voting for the PAN as an antiregime protest was so over-whelming that the PRI-controlled electoral commission was forced to recognize that the PAN had, indeed, captured the mayorship of Hermosillo, the state capital. Jorge Valdez Muñoz became the first opposition mayor of a major Sonora city in recent history. Bezdek suggests that the PRI allowed the mayorship to go to the PAN in order to hide the fact that their own gubernatorial candidate had lost, a great blow nationally. It should be noted that wherever the PAN came close to winning a governorship in recent decades the PRI has intervened in one way or another to annul the election (for example, Yucatán in 1969 and Baja California in 1968). Governorships are considered a major part of the power pyramid in Mexico and to lose one would disgrace the PRI. Again, this recalls the implications of *The Day the PRI Lost* as cited in Chapter 6.

It is extremely serious when a governor falls into disgrace and has to be deposed from within by the PRI itself. This kind of situation developed in 1975 in Sonora. When Faustino Felix was replaced in 1973 by Carlos Armando Biebrich, this was another dedazo but with less popular reaction. This governor, in turn, was replaced before his term had expired, but in full public disgrace which the PRI could not hide. Biebrich was a young man in his thirties, in whom many people had placed great hope for leadership and reform in Sonora. Instead, he proved to be more avaricious and repressive than either of his two predecessors. When he was deposed (forced by Mexico City and the state legislature to resign), and replaced on October 25, 1975, by Sonora's incumbent senator, Alejandro Carrillo Marcor, it was the first time since 1935 that Sonora had witnessed such a change of chief executive.[19]

The most immediate reason for his demise was the assassination of eight peasants by state police acting under orders from Biebrich. In reaction, more than 10,000 peasants representing such official groups as the National Peasants Confederation (CNC) and the extra-official Independent Peasant Confederation (CCI) converged on Ciudad Obregón, near where the massacre had occurred, and demanded the governor's destitution. Forces within the PRI were openly condemning other forces within the PRI. There was no way to blame outsiders or the PAN for this affair.

Mexico's tabloid press was quick to point out that Biebrich was a product of Sonora's multimillionaire class and that he had become governor in open violation of the law (he did not meet constitutional age requirements that were subverted).[20] The story of just why Biebrich fell is critical to this analysis as it sheds great light upon the internal corruption and atrophy of the PRI monolith. The following resume is made on the basis of interviews which I carried out during 1976 and 1977 with key Mexican political knowledgeables from Sonora, and also upon an account published by the semiunderground review *Onda* of Culiacán, Sinaloa.

The massacre of San Ignacio Río Muerto came about on the night of October 22 and was known publicly on the morning of the following day. Several peasant families and leaders of the CCI had occupied lands belonging to latifundistas who were allegedly foreigners of German nationality and close friends of Governor Biebrich. The tabloid *Alerta* reported that the man in charge of the operation to dislodge the paracaidistas was Francisco Arellano Noblecía, who "ordered his agents to plant weapons on the cadavers of the peasants once they were dead."[21] This version was supported in my interviews. The state police were acting under direct orders from the governor who, in turn, was responding to demands from the latifundistas who dominated the state's power structure.

The governor had coerced the commanding officer of the military zone, General José D. Belmonte Aguirre, into giving assistance to his state police. The coercion took the form of lying to General Belmonte Aguirre to the effect that he, Biebrich, had cleared the matter by telephone with President Echeverría and his cabinet officer (gobernación) Mario Moya Palencia. According to the account published by *Onda,* Biebrich had made *no* such consultations and, worse, he was in a state of intoxication from alcohol and cocaine when he made the demand on the general and gave the orders to the state police.[22] When the peasant protest began the next day, it was the president of the republic and his cabinet minister who got burned; they knew nothing about the incident until it appeared in the national press. Intervention from Mexico City assured that the state legislature would accept Biebrich's resignation in favor of Senator Carrillo Marcor.

The issue of Governor Biebrich's alcoholism and drug involvement has political significance. Widespread efforts had long been underway in Sonora to eradicate the drug problem that was intimately tied to the incumbent state government and its municipal counterparts. In May 1975 the drug issue was dramatized by the Arizona *Daily Star,* which carried a story about the efforts of Mexican federal prosecutor Jorge Villalobos and the civic leader Oscar Monroy Rivera to combat drug involvement among the local police.[23] Villalobos and Monroy had been threatened with death over their public exposes of vice activities throughout the state. Local defense committees were organized to defend both men. Monroy had been instrumental in creating a successful free clinic for the treatment of alcoholism and drug addiction and enjoyed great popular following both locally, because of his civic leadership, and nationally, because of his writing.

It seems that Biebrich's personal style had been anticipated by some within the PRI who sought to avoid scandals. Following the imposition of Biebrich as Sonora's governor in 1973, the PRI's national delegate to that state, Lic. Rodolfo González Guevara, resigned in protest against Biebrich and virtually disappeared from political life until around August 1975. At that moment he ventured to give an interview to national press media criticizing Biebrich for many failures (including the drug involvement) and branding the young governor a reactionary. Biebrich in turn denounced González Guevara as a political nonentity. As a foreshadowing of Biebrich's downfall, President Echeverría is said to have commented to a reporter in Mexico City that González Guevara's comments about the Sonora governor were well founded.[24]

Thereafter, in late September, the presidential destape occurred and the PRI's candidate was López Portillo and not Moya Palencia. Biebrich belonged to the camarilla of Moya Palencia and his mentor's loss of the presidential nomination, plus the public censure of Biebrich by Echeverría over the González Guevara criticism, meant that Biebrich's days as governor were numbered. All that was needed was a convenient pretext to depose him. That came from Biebrich himself who, at the insistence of former governor Faustino Felix and the Sonora latifundistas, took the fateful decision to dislodge the CCI peasants by force. The fact that the governor was under the influence of drugs when he gave the orders seems to have been a matter of public knowledge in Sonora. This sort of personalized political scandal exemplifies the threshold of criticality for tolerance of internal corruption within the PRI. This writer was told that as many as 60,000 peasants converged on Ciudad Obregón, demanding the governor's destitution, and threatening violence otherwise. Thus key sectors of the PRI were shamed and outraged by what had transpired within their own monolith.

The Biebrich affair took on international ramifications when the governor fled to the United States and later, it is believed, to England. Informed sources in Sonora told this writer that two days after he was deposed Biebrich issued a check for some 4 million pesos to his brother, state funds which he, no longer being governor, had no right to dispense. In addition, some two months after he was deposed, the Arizona *Daily Star* reported that Sonora's new attorney general was considering extradition proceedings to bring Biebrich back from hiding in the United States to testify as to some 36 million pesos (close to $3 million) that were missing from the state treasury.[25] These funds, according to the news story (and corroborated by trusted informants interviewed by this writer) were spent on public works contracts awarded to Biebrich's brother. According to my testimony, most of the contracts never even existed on paper and almost none of the public works were even begun. This financial scandal seemed also to be public knowledge throughout Sonora and again the question of thresholds of criticality is raised. It is tempting to hypothesize that a scandal grows dangerous to the PRI and can provoke internal instability, as in the Biebrich case, to the degree that it becomes a matter of public knowledge with no scapegoat possibilities available. When the scope of the issue becomes international as well, the pressure on the PRI is even greater. This is probably what caused Biebrich to begin to lose favor with Mexico City early in his governorship, that is, reports on both sides of the border that state prison facilities in Sonora were used as fronts for narcotics traffic and other vice activities which, ostensibly, had the governor's blessing.[26] I am in possession of a sensitive report made by Sonora state investigators of the Biebrich case which throws additional light on its national ramifications.[27]

At this point, consider the Sonora civic leader and poet-philosopher Oscar Monroy Rivera whose life was surveyed above. Monroy was then one of many still clinging to the penumbra of the PRI who believed it might yet be possible to reform the system from within, to save it from itself as it were. Monroy, the political actor, was convincing evidence that honorable civic-spirited political leaders did exist at the grass roots in Mexico and that it was possible for them to bring reforms to fruition without joining the violence-prone satellite groups. Oscar Monroy's civic action campaigns against narcotics abuse and vice activities had won him prestige on both sides of the border. In January 1975 he was invited by the University of Arizona to participate in an important conference devoted to international problems of the border,[28] and in 1977 he took part in an international conference on drug abuse held in Texas.[29] Monroy has also been active in championing the cause of political prisoners.[30]

When protest and reform action does occur within the PRI the leadership reacts by trying to funnel the protest through what one analyst has termed the narrow neck of selective repression.[31] The dominant class always produces a compensating device to try to keep its public image unsullied. Obviously, in cases like that of Governor Biebrich this was impossible. In trying to deal with Monroy and the federal prosecutor Villalobos the regime had an equally difficult problem in that the two men enjoyed widespread respect in Mexico City, in Sonora, and in Arizona.

The death threats reported in the Arizona press were real, of course. Monroy told me that paid assassins had been sent directly by the secretario de Gobernación, Moya Palencia (upon request from Governor Biebrich who was a key target of Monroy's civil action attacks), but that the people of his local community made it clear to the governor that any such attempt would result in a popular uprising.[32] Unlike the poor campesino victims whom the governor's agents killed, Monroy had access to communications media on both sides of the border and made his case public before the governor could move secretly against him. Public exposure became a defense. Obviously, then, the news of Moya Palencia's defeat in the internal power struggle to succeed President Echeverría was reassuring to Monroy and Villalobos. Equally so was the fall of Governor Biebrich. Both Monroy and Villalobos thought they enjoyed access to the entourage of the president-to-be, José López Portillo. When he took office both men felt sure there would be genuine reforms forthcoming throughout the PRI and that there would be a real apertura política or democratizing process in Mexico. But this was misguided optimism as we shall see presently.

Attempted image-control and repression as practiced in Sonora and throughout Mexico had a marked impact on Oscar Monroy Rivera. One of his earlier works deals exclusively (in a mix of poetry and prose) with the repressive political traumata of his native state and with his outrage over the behavior of the then governor Luis Encinas.[33] Ironically, as that work was being published an event occurred which propelled Monroy across the threshold (within the penumbra) from PRI participant to PRI critic and reformer.[34]

In the wake of the violent repression of the Sonoran students in 1967, Oscar Monroy resigned his administrative position at the University of Sonora and devoted himself to legal practice and teaching as a way of furthering his study and writing. He never forgave Luis Encinas Johnson for the way he had profaned the University of Sonora, wounded its distinguished rector, and abused its worthy students. His hatred of Encinas led him to a crisis of choice, either the route of the violent revolutionary who joins a satellite group, or that of the writer devoted to social protest. Monroy chose the latter, and therefrom comes an outpouring of literature which merits sampling here. Governor Encinas internalized both physical and mental deformities which evoked from Monroy a single pejorative concept, that of "moral dwarfishness." Probably his most widely read book is *El mexicano enano* (The Mexican Dwarf), which has sold thousands of copies to the outrage of many Mexicans in and outside of the regime.[35] Later there appeared *El señor presidente de Enanonia* (Mr. President of Dwarfland), which is an onslaught against President Echeverría. It has also sold thousands. Much of the distribution of these books Monroy has had to arrange himself due to the reluctance of many distributors to handle such material. *El profeta del Silencio* was not an indictment of specific powerful figures and therefore was sold more openly.

In these works Monroy sought to develop the concept of dwarfishness as a social, economic, and political malaise of the Mexican people which is central to understanding much of his nation's political behavior. Dwarfishness involves the reduction of human beings to avaricious, corrupt, selfserving, heartless, and often bloody robots who are motivated by a lust for pillage and rapine. Always, Monroy stated, the former governor who ordered atrocities against the University of Sonora is in the forefront of the image that surrounds the concept of dwarfishness. The image is a kind of mental inferno for Monroy, a twilight of shame that refuses to recede into the darkness it merits. Dwarfishness is not a unique condition that plagues only Mexico's ruling class; there are many in the broad society who share these attributes. Keep in mind that Monroy is a well-educated Mexican criticizing his own social and political norms and practices. Enanismo is in no way an ethnocentric North American invention.

The essential political workings of enanismo are these. The people are for the most part small enanos, not necessarily because they want it that way, but because this has been foisted upon them by the elites or big enanos. The people, then, are Juan Pueblo (John Q. Public) and are pariah capitalists whom the government must continually drain of most of their wealth. Yet, they must be kept alive so that the gigantic organism which is the PRI will always have some sure source of flowing largesse. But the Juan Pueblos (the small dwarfs) have their own threshold of toleration vis-a-vis the exploitation and repression they receive. The small people can rise up, as at Ciudad Obregón in 1975 against Governor Biebrich, or earlier as at Tlatelolco in 1968. They can depose the big enanos like Biebrich, and even his superiors like Moya Palencia (who, in effect, was deposed in the destape) and maybe, eventually, they can even depose the greatest enano of them all, the descendent of the successors to the Aztec high sacrificial priest or Tlatoani, that is, the president of Mexico.

It is a desperate political game with harsh rules. But the little people are driven onward in their fight by the bizarre daily spectacle they must witness of corruption in political life, and there are always tragic figures like El Bulla to remind them that life is cruel, that those who govern have greed and not mercy. Well before the Biebrich affair became a matter of public record, Monroy had written lines that capture perfectly the governor's dilemma (especially in terms of the account cited from *Onda*) and which I translate freely as follows: "Our magistrates live as inebriated sexual psychopaths in their civic brothel. These are the ones who govern with refined perversion, killing their enemies, castrating them."[36] Monroy could not have known that nearly the exact scenario would appear in the journal *Onda* when it described the physical and moral circumstances in which Governor Biebrich took the baneful decision to dislodge the peasants with military violence, hence, to dislodge himself. From then onward Monroy's writing became increasingly bitter.

In *El Señor presidente de Enanonia* Monroy caricatures the president of the republic in the act of eliminating his critics, a blighted image which can be applied to political chiefs at various levels of power. His key agents are the military and police who do the muzzling and human liquidating. They are instructed to "do a clean and direct job of covering up the crimes that are ordered from the Presidency."[37] But the regime has been, so far, unable to muzzle Monroy. His biggest defense factor is probably his public following and his commitment to the principle of nonviolent resistance. Most difficult for the regime to sweep away was the immense respect for Monroy's life style and his writing that existed among key individuals within the PRI, not just in Sonora but in Mexico City. Honor does have its place inside the great pyramid. For Monroy et al. to save Sonora from Biebrich could be to save all of Mexico from continued atrophy, to save it from collapse.

NOGALES AS A POLITICAL MICROCOSM

The problem for Monroy and Villalobos, however, was that the PRI had ways of silencing its critics other than simply putting out a contract on them. Here it will be well to look in some detail at the power structure of Nogales, Sonora. What follows is based largely upon my own interviews during the spring months of 1977 with trusted knowledgeables on the Arizona-Sonora border. Where possible, citations are offered, but in many cases the names of the informants must remain confidential for obvious reasons. This section has been read by a number of border residents and they insist that it is an accurate account.

According to my informants the development of a power triad of interests (political-business-contraband) in Nogales proceeded through four overlapping stages during recent history. These are:

monopolistic controls over real estate following 1930;
consolidation of the local market (inside Nogales) for the sale of addicting
    drugs during the 1940s;
creation of systems for distribution of contraband merchandise of all varieties
    from the United States (including arms) during the 1950s;
establishment of the twin-plant border industries (maquiladoras) to alleviate
    Mexican unemployment crises following the ending of the Bracero con-
    tract labor program in 1964 and the concomitant rise of international
    contraband in aliens, arms, and drugs as a major business during the late
    1960s and early 1970s.

Key figures in local political life came increasingly to dominate the enterprises involved in these developmental stages.

Real-estate controls facilitated entry of some investors into the local drug-dispensing business. The names of several prominent families in the Nogales power triad were important in the development of the second and third stages, especially after Mexico replaced Europe as the principal North American source of hard drugs early in the 1970s. The real-estate monopolists also branched out into other businesses, the most pertinent of which is pharmacy chains as a natural link with drug trafficking. In the 1950s the man who was to be mayor of Nogales in 1977 set up a chain of pharmacies on properties he owned. Among his chief lieutenants in this business was Jaime Ostler Robles, one of today's principal traffickers in drugs and aliens and who served a brief prison sentence in Mexico during 1975–76 for narcotics violations. Ostler was one of the principal narcotics smugglers cited in the Arizona IRE (Investigative Reporters and Editors, Inc.) report,[38] and his activities have been documented in a widely circulated book dealing with corruption in Nogales.[39] Upon his release from prison in 1976, Ostler was made a member-advisor *(consejero)* of the Nogales Chamber of Commerce, thanks largely to his friendship and working relationship with Nogales mayor Héctor Monroy. The mayor, ironically, is an elder brother of Oscar Monroy Rivera.

Also a major figure (consejero) of the Nogales Chamber of Commerce is Issac Dabdoub. One member of this family (cited below) is alleged to have narcotics involvements. Another consejero is Elias Freig, a personal representative of former governor Carlos Armando Biebrich. It is worthwhile repeating that the formal charges brought against Biebrich in 1976 were mysteriously suspended in 1977.[40] Elias Freig is said to have been a major smuggler of liquor and other merchandise from the United States.[41] It should be stressed that just because the IRE report or other reliable journalistic testimony may link some or even most members of a given family with corruption, this does *not* automatically mean that all members of that family are so tainted.

The nexus of interests which forms the political-business-contraband power triad in Nogales, Sonora, is easily seen in the relationship between mayor Héctor Monroy and Jaime Ostler Robles. Following their earlier relationship in the pharmacy (licit) business and subsequently contraband plus illicit local drug sales, the two secured advisory positions with important banks. Consultant roles with financial institutions are useful for those who would penetrate and control the Nogales business spectrum as sketched herein. The mayor and Ostler allegedly have ties with narcotics traffickers in Arizona. Real-estate monopolies, contraband, and local drug sales all contributed to the wealth which enabled these figures to penetrate other ostensibly legitimate business and financial institutions. They were aided in this by cooperating with other drug, gun, and alien smugglers.

Any investigation of the relationship between narcotics and other contraband in Nogales inevitably leads to the notorious drug pusher Juan "Johnny" Grant. The Nogales-based Grant, alleged to have had both U.S. and Mexican citizenship and who is known locally as El Negro Johnny Grant, was cited in the IRE report as follows:

> John Grant Gómez. Based in Nogales, Sonora. Major heroin dealer. Supplies cities as far as Washington, D.C. Wanted by the Federal Drug Enforcement Administration [DEA]. Grant's wife, Amelia Barrera Gómez, is a major ounce-or-more heroin dealer. Gómez connected to José Luis Terán's drug organization, one of the biggest in northern Sonora.[42]

The report also details another of the sources of wealth upon which the local regime in Nogales depends for largesse in exchange for law-enforcement tolerance:

> Possibly the biggest organization is headed by a Chinese father-son team, both named Héctor Mar Wong. The youngest Wong has a Chinese restaurant in . . . Nogales . . . he is listed by the DEA as a "known large-scale heroin dealer" who may have connections with Red Chinese drug-smuggling rings.[43]

Thus the contraband has international linkages other than the U.S. connection. This is perhaps more than coincidentally related to the fact that a younger brother of the current mayor of Nogales, Octavio, is known to have involvement in the smuggling of aliens through Nogales from countries other than Mexico; among his specialties, reputedly, is the smuggling of alien Cubans and Chinese. Add another strange irony: Octavio is the twin brother of Oscar Monroy Rivera.

All of these interests have, as can be seen, direct tie-ins to the Nogales Chamber of Commerce and the municipal government whose restricted tax base makes vice an almost natural direction to turn for finances. A documented case in point is that of Elias Zaied Dabdoub whose family name was cited above in connection with the development of real-estate monopolies and the drug traffic. As of this writing Elias Zaied Dabdoub enjoys the public support of Rafael Orduño Reyes, owner-director of the newspaper *El Diario de Nogales,* an influential figure in the Chamber of Commerce and in local politics. It is alleged that Orduño Reyes's newspaper has been utilized to aid in smuggling rip offs, that is, the robbing of smugglers by other smugglers (it is known from the IRE report that this practice is widespread in Tucson, Arizona; thus it should not be surprising to discover the same phenomenon in Nogales, Sonora). Drug dealers moving shipments north from Culiacán will, according to my testimony, sometimes arrange (pay) to have *El Diario de Nogales* publish a bogus news report that such and such a smuggler was apprehended by the Mexican or American police and his load confiscated. In this way the smuggler has a ready-made excuse to try to avoid paying his supply source. Not unexpectedly, this has led to gang wars.

So notorious were Orduño Reyes and Zaied Dabdoub that an entire volume by Monroy Rivera was dedicated to exposing them and to document- ing their activities along the border.[44] It should be kept in mind that the expose reflects activities of a range of individuals tied to both the local government of Nogales and its Chamber of Commerce. In the published account, Zaied Dabdoub and a fellow attorney, Guillermo Barragán Celaya, were cited by members of the Nogales Bar Association for having defrauded clients of a Mexican bank for which the two attorneys worked as legal counsels.[45] When Zaied Dabdoub was subsequently expelled from the Nogales Bar Association, he sought to bribe officials of the newspaper *Acción* into not printing the story (they refused) but was successful in preventing the journalist Marco Antonio Guevara from broadcasting the story on a local radio station.[46] The same Dabdoub and another lawyer, Francisco Javier Peralta, were also investigated by a Mexican federal prosecutor for involvement in gun smuggling with arms intended for the guerrilla movement Liga Communista 23 de Septiembre.[47]

Later in 1975 the owner of *El Diario de Nogales,* Rafael Orduño, was arrested and charged with gun smuggling and narcotics violations.[48] In this case, Orduño was given initial protection by an army officer until the local federal prosecutor, Jorge Villalobos, was able to intervene and arrest Orduño after his involvement in a shootout.[49] Thus the local power structure had its roots extended even into the Mexican national military establishment. It was also reported that the Orduño organization was so well equipped for contra-band operations that it used special automobiles with dual radios to monitor the Mexican and American police and Border Patrol broadcasts.[50]

Orduño was arraigned before Judge José Refugio Gallegos Baeza on September 18, 1975, and charged with a range of contraband violations includ-ing guns, arms, and aliens (it is a crime in Mexico to abet those who emigrate illegally, although this charge is seldom brought by itself against an offender unless he is involved in other offenses that are considered more serious). Commentaries on the indictment tied Orduño and Zaied Dabdoub to massive trafficking in drugs, arms, and a wide variety of contraband.[51] I received testimony that aliens for work gangs had been exchanged for arms in the United States. Ultimately, Zaied Dabdoub was indicted for similar charges after he sought to defend arms smugglers working for the September 23rd League.[52]

One key point to be stressed is that these traffickers are not left-wing political ideologues who might seek to aid a communist guerrilla organization. They are first and foremost contraband businessmen who sell arms, drugs, and anything else they can move without getting publicly disgraced. But even disgrace can be assuaged with money and both men are free as of this writing. Within the power circle (triad) of friends and collaborators it is normal to disregard public arrest and/or conviction as an accident which temporarily interrupts an otherwise smooth business process, reinforced of course by a single-party-dominant political system and highly restricted participatory democracy.

There is no point (and probably considerable risk) in listing exhaustively all individuals allegedly involved in the Nogales power triad of influences. However, I was told that the kingpin for the entire influence network as of March 1977 was the manager for international affairs of the Nogales branch of a prominent Mexican bank. Related to this individual professionally was Professor Fidel García, president in 1976 of the Junta Federal de Mejoras Materiales (a nationwide confederation of local public resource councils) for the border cities of Naco, Agua Prieta, and Nogales. A published critical analysis by Monroy Rivera of the water shortage problem on the Sonora border charges that Professor García has deliberately allowed underground water sources to be improperly utilized so as to enable local politicians to make a business out of selling the scarce commodity.[53] It has also been charged that the public water supply of Nogales, Sonora (which is hopelessly inadequate and reaches homes in most neighborhoods only during the early morning hours), is seriously contaminated with arsenic.[54] Such are the consequences of political corruption in Nogales, Sonora.

Historically the power triad of Nogales demonstrated an impressive abil-ity to withstand threats (for example, criticism) from outside the system. It proved vulnerable to attacks from within. During recent years the operation of the power triad was threatened by local federal prosecutor (Agente del Ministerio Público Federal) Jorge Villalobos Moguel, who insisted on arresting prominent members of drug trafficking organizations as well as those who deal in illegal aliens and gun smuggling.[55] The efforts of these men led to the imprisonment of Jaime Ostler, albeit briefly.

Both Villalobos and Oscar Monroy had been victims of assassination attempts and their families had been threatened (here I must repeat the irony that Oscar Monroy, the reformist civic leader, is a younger brother of Héctor Monroy, the incumbent mayor who is deeply implicated in many questionable activities). Oscar Monroy was instrumental in creating a local drug treatment center which collaborated with the Santa Cruz Guidance Center in Nogales, Arizona, in helping youth with drug problems on both sides of the border. He was supported in this antidrug crusade by federal prosecutor Villalobos, who was clearly a thorn in the side of the Nogales power triad.

When the Mexican national government changed hands the first of December 1976, the Nogales power elite saw their opportunity to rid themselves of Villalobos, who was interfering with their international contraband. It is not known whether they took advantage of the presidential transitional disorganization in Mexico City or whether the Nogales smugglers had the blessing of Mexico's new president López Portillo.[56] What is certain is that lacking other means of removing Villalobos, the local elites brought charges against him of accepting bribes and of drug involvement, the very things he had opposed. There was a new and sympathetic municipal administration in Nogales. Mayor Héctor Monroy apparently was willing to cooperate with those who sought to remove Villalobos.

Two former colleagues of Villalobos, local federal prosecutors Pedro Mireles Malpica and Ernesto Avila Triana, joined with such drug and alien smuggling figures as "Johnny" Grant (El Negro Johnny), Jaime Ostler Robles, and Major Fernando Ramírez (local chief of the federal highway police) and invented the drug and bribery charges against Jorge Villalobos. The accusations against him were not completely signed but contained the initials J.O.R., J.G.G., and F.R. (corresponding to the above names) plus some others, according to testimony given me in private interviews.[57] But, it is believed, it was the leaders of the Nogales power triad who were the movers behind this action. Villalobos was a real threat to the contraband activity and had to be eliminated.

On December 16, 1976, a federal district judge in Nogales, Sonora, ordered the release of Villalobos who had been held prisoner for about a week, ruling that there was insufficient evidence to support the charges that had been filed. Friends of Villalobos immediately spirited him across the border into the United States and he was eventually granted an informal tourist asylum in California with the blessing of U.S. authorities. Next to fall was the judge who had freed Villalobos. In February 1977 it was announced that Judge Gallegos Baeza would be transferred (demoted) to a lesser position in the southern state of Oaxaca. This action was hailed by the power-triad-controlled press of Nogales as a just reprisal for the judge's abuse of authority (in the Villalobos decision).[58] This action was ordered from Mexico City. The opposition press in Nogales defended Judge Gallegos and inquired who would be next, who would be left to fight the smugglers?[59] A perceptive Arizona journalist summarized the issue well:

> Gallegos was the judge who dropped the spurious charges against crime-fighting federal attorney Jorge Omar Villalobos in December. Fellow prosecutors had tried to pin some bribery raps on him for what he had done to the Nogales smuggling establishment's peace of mind. Villalobos countered with charges against his accusers.[60]

That journalist's correct reference to the "Nogales smuggling establishment" equates roughly with what has been referred to herein as the power triad of interests. Threatening one part of the triad as Villalobos had done prejudiced the entire power system, the legitimate businesses, the fronts of convenience, the political largesse. Many of the Nogales money-lending institutions and investment firms depended upon contraband sources of money, be it drugs, aliens, or guns. It is argued by some that without the contraband activity across the border many key financial enterprises of Nogales and of the state of Sonora would collapse (this is easier alleged than proved, but it is believed in many well-informed circles). Even the municipal revenues of Nogales, it is argued, would drop to near zero without the corruption on which businessmen, public officials, and most civic leaders depend. As throughout Mexico, for instance, much of an average policeman's salary comes from the bribes he can collect. This is a basic condition that keeps the contraband moving.

The published IRE report cited variously throughout the preceding pages listed 23 major smuggling rings, most of which were part of the Mexican connection via the "Arizona corridor." The IRE report confirms much of the testimony gathered independently as reported herein. Surely there can be no doubt but that municipal mismanagement and corruption of political and business life in Nogales, Sonora, is a major "push" factor in the drug and alien contraband and in the continuing human rights abuses in that Mexican city. Commenting on Nogales the IRE report said:

> Nogales, Sonora is a crowded city of 120,000, many of them workers who flocked from the interior to find better jobs in this booming border city. It is also a city without enough drinking water, schools, housing, jobs, parks and police protection. Many of the unemployed men and women smuggle narcotics to feed their hungry families.[61]

All of this was what federal prosecutor Villalobos and his civic reform leaders had sought to end by attacking the power triad of interests which benefited from these circumstances. The often-critical publication *Información* of Hermosillo defended Villalobos for his crusade against what it termed the "mafia of drug traffickers," saying that until his arrival several years previously Nogales had been almost the exclusive property of the racketeers who went about the city, guns in hand, "even into the churches."[62] This same publication singled out the notorious Negro Johnny Grant as a key mafioso. El Negro Johnny had been harrassed and detained by Villalobos but never convicted. The article concluded:

> everyone in this "disenchanted Mexico" likes to see a public functionary fall from power but also everyone has some idea of the power of the mafia and for this reason in Nogales it is not strange to hear that the mafia is having good luck with the new regime. People who knew of the successes of Villalobos Moguel in his fight against the narcotics traffickers will understand this. Can we believe, then, that the most fiery combatant against the mafia [Villalobos] was in fact one of their allies?[63]

Until about six months before his detention and false accusation in Nogales, Villalobos had been principally in charge of contraband activities in Nogales. At that point, and presumably in recognition of his favorable record, he was elevated to a higher position in Tijuana, Baja California, where he had control over the entire zone of the northwest Mexican borders. Coincidentally, observed *Información,* the order of detention against Villalobos came just after the national change of government when the Procurador General (attorney general) of the republic, Pedro Ojeda Paullada (who had rewarded Villalobos' antivice campaign) was replaced by Oscar Flores Sánchez, a new appointee of President López Portillo. Flores Sánchez a former governor of Chihuahua, was widely rumored to have been involved in border vice activities between Chihuahua and Texas.

The saga of Villalobos versus the Nogales smuggling establishment ended with the former's temporary exile in the United States and the probable finish of his law-enforcement career. This is just one of many cases in which honest reformers inside the PRI sought unsuccessfully to end corruption within the single-party monolith. There was a similar tragedy in the case of Oscar Monroy Rivera. The axe fell swiftly. Early in 1977 his picture appeared in a binational (English-Spanish) publication which honored Monroy as director of the Nogales Center for Juvenile Integration, a drug-control center for Mexican youth. This was a conference sponsored by antidrug campaigners in Mexico and Texas and enjoyed the official support of Mexico's government.[64] But by August of that year Monroy had been removed as director of the very center he had helped to found and the smuggling establishment in Nogales was doing all it could to end the civic activist career of Oscar Monroy Rivera.[65]

Just as in the case of Villalobos, the racketeers began to circulate rumors that Monroy himself was trafficking in drugs, an enormous charge totally without foundation.

The Monroy defeat had a deep personal aspect, reaching into the writer's home. He and his wife had befriended a deaf and dumb Indian girl and made her a part of their family. One day local agents showed up with her alcoholic father and a warrant for the Monroys to free her or face criminal prosecution. Monroy told me that this poor helpless being would be returned to her earlier fate, that of a forced prostitute to feed her father's alcohol habit, one of the reasons why she had fled in the first place to take refuge in the Monroy home. Oscar Monroy wanted to avoid the creation of a female version of El Bulla haunting the streets of Nogales.

Thus, as of this writing, it appeared that the PRI monolith was incapable of yielding even small concessions in the name of human compassion. Ironically, as Monroy was being deposed on orders from Mexico City as director of the Nogales antidrug center, he was being honored by a young scholar from the University of Sonora (where Monroy had once worked), Maritza Jerez Camargo, who presented an analysis of his works of social protest as her senior thesis. The youth of Sonora knew of the courageous pen, and personal valor, of Oscar Monroy Rivera.

But for him the new regime of López Portillo did not portend much optimism. Contrary to the promises about cleaning up border corruption that López Portillo made as the PRI's presidential candidate in 1976, his new procurador had ordered the deposing of Prosecutor Villalobos and Judge Gallegos Baeza. The directorship of the Nogales antidrug center had been taken from the outspoken and dedicated Monroy. In place of these three men, persons more loyal to the regime had been imposed. Drugs again moved freely. And to make it worse, this coincided with suspension of the charges against the fugitive ex-governor Biebrich. Some observers even speculated that an attempt would be made to reinstate Biebrich as governor.[66]

So if Sonora and Nogales were to be held up as microcosms typical of Mexico, the future would seem to be grim during the remainder of the López Portillo sexenio, this despite the good gestures of Mrs. López Portillo and Mrs. Rosalynn Carter early in 1977 to the effect that the border areas of Mexico and the United States would be turned into places of aesthetic cultural exchange. In my own view, the only exchanges likely to continue regularly along the border would involve guns, drugs, and illegal aliens.

The broad thrust of my argument, drawn from this microview of politics and corruption, is that contraband generally (be it aliens, drugs, arms, assorted merchandise) is part of a socioeconomic system which tends, in Mexico, to be coterminous with certain political power structures. Mexico's single-party democracy allows very little real political participation, and therefore local or even national level reformers are doomed. One study of local politics in Mexico (which extrapolates its conclusions onto a broader national context) suggests that it may be necessary for Mexico to maintain its highly restrictive norms of political participation. For should they be relaxed, "self-interest would soon lead deprived sectors to push harder in the competition for social and economic benefits."[67] Therefore, the resulting scarcity of goods and services would lead to intense competition and political conflict.

There is, of course, vigorous political competition and conflict over control of desperately scarce resources in Mexico's border areas (water and land being only two of the more obvious examples). And the border is precisely where a large quantity of that nation's population has concentrated due to Mexico's internal economic distress and the pull of the United States as an escape hatch from misery. Mexican border cities would be hard pressed to provide adequate welfare and municipal services to their burgeoning populations, even if local administrations were honest and efficient. Add political corruption to the picture, especially that which involves contraband, and the interface between local political power and international trafficking becomes patent. Some have pronounced as dead the legacy of the Mexican revolution (1910–17) which was intended to alleviate such inequities of life. The study of local government cited above asks what does the development of Mexico today have to teach?

> That greed, corruption, and mass manipulation are the earmarks of leadership? That apathy, negativism, and withdrawal are the common condition of citizens? That the expression of grievances ought to be met with gunfire, beatings, and jail when more ordinary controls fail?[68]

Such was the fate of Monroy, Villalobos et al. in Sonora. These observations, then, are directly relevant to our consideration here of political power throughout Mexico and its interface with the United States.

NOTES

1. As contained variously in Alejandro de Galicia, *De visita en la prisión,* 3rd ed. (Mexico: Costa-Amic, 1975) (with prologue by Oscar Monroy Rivera).

2. The expression "El Bulla" refers to an irregular noise or a scream as in the present case since the only speech which this person had was little more than a noise.

3. Oscar Monroy Rivera, *Ayer: recuerdos de infancia* (Mexico: Costa-Amic, 1973), p. 23.

4. Ibid., pp. 72–73.

5. Ibid., p. 33.

6. Ibid., p. 50.

7. The saga of El Bulla is set forth in Monroy Rivera's two-volume work, *El profeta del silencio* (Mexico: Costa-Amic, 1974 and Editorial Diana, 1975). For convenience the first-cited will be referred to as the "brown book" and the second as the "blue book." Despite the dates, the "blue book" first appeared in 1972 but I have in my possession only the 1975 reprint.

8. *Apuntes Especiales* (Nogales, Sonora), October 1972.

9. Monroy, *El profeta del silencio,* brown book, op. cit., pp. 39–40.

10. Ibid., pp. 73–74.

11. Monroy, *El profeta del silencio,* blue book, op. cit., p. 37.

12. Ibid., p. 43.

13. Ibid., p. 80.

14. Ibid., p. 85.

15. Ibid., p. 88.

16. Ibid., pp. 116–17.

17. Ibid., p. 119.

18. Robert R. Bezdek, "Electoral Oppositions in Mexico: Emergence, Suppression, and Impact on Political Processes," doctoral dissertation, Ohio State University Department of Political Science, 1973.

19. *El Imparcial* (Sonora), October 26, 1975.

20. *Alerta,* November 8, 1975.

21. Ibid.

22. *Onda* (Sinaloa), November 12, 1975.

23. See Alex Drehsler's article in Arizona *Daily Star,* May 12, 1975.

24. Confirmation of this version appears in Heberto Castillo's article in *Excelsior,* October 30, 1975.

25. See Bill Waters's article in Arizona *Daily Star,* January 5, 1976.

26. For instance, a report issued by the office of Senator Charles Percy dated October 27, 1975, and one published in the Mexican journal *Sucesos,* No. 2202 (1975), citing both Mexican and U.S. sources.

27. The document (photocopied) in question is a warrant-accusation called a *consignación* dated Hermosillo, Sonora, January 20, 1976. This includes eyewitness testimony as to the amount of silver deposited on behalf of the state treasury in various banks which Governor Biebrich, his wife, and others removed and had flown to Mexico City for private uses. It details the governor's use of federal drought-relief funds for private use, how even the rugs and dishes were stolen from the governor's mansion under orders from Biebrich, plus much more. The document bears the seal of the state attorney general's office (Procuraduría General de Justicia del Estado de Sonora).

28. "A University of Arizona Conference on Mexican-United States Relations," January 17–18, 1975, Tucson, Arizona (panel five).

29. See *Proceedings of the CADAP-CEMEF Bi-National Conference on Drug Abuse* (El Paso, Texas: Southwest Training Institute, 1977), p. 30.

30. Perhaps the most dramatic of such cases was that of Jorge Issachtts Corrales who spent some six years in a state prison in Sonora falsely accused of embezzlement in a state bank in Baja California. The truth was that Issachtts, once a bank accountant, discovered the fraud and reported it to his superiors. The investigation got out of control and involved high-ranking members of the PRI in several states. Their defense was to blame the fraud on Issachtts and have him jailed on spurious charges. He was finally able to buy his freedom in late 1976. Monroy was intimately involved in the effort to free Issachtts, a case to which I will return in Chapter 9 (see note 16).

31. Evelyn P. Stevens, *Protest and Response in Mexico* (Cambridge, Mass.: MIT Press, 1974), p. 11.

32. Some corroboration of this is found in de Galicia, op. cit., which also contains a first-hand account of tortures in Sonora prisons.

33. Oscar Monroy Rivera, *Sonora: en torno al valor de mi pueblo* (Mexico: Editorial Libros de Mexico, 1967).

34. Until the government-sponsored violence against the University of Sonora in 1967, Oscar Monroy Rivera had been press secretary and public relations director to the rector, Dr. Moises Canale R. Dr. Canale was a distinguished medical doctor with great respect in his community and was one of Monroy's mentors. In order to blackmail the rector into resigning and, at once,

to pressure the students into dropping their antiregime protests, the rector was kidnapped on orders of Governor Encinas, this as Monroy told it to me. Before being released, the rector was made to appear before moving picture cameras as participant in a homosexual act (forced upon him by perverted agents employed by the governor). The price for promising not to show this film publicly, in any of Mexico's many porno-houses, was for the rector to resign and to influence the students to end their disturbances resulting from opposition to the PRI's rigged elections that year (1967). Monroy told me that other such bizarre filmings had taken place in Sonora and elsewhere in Mexico. This was the way the PRI kept its own people in line. Defection by PRI's own rank-and-file members, such as the Sonora Students Federation, was feared more than campaign oratory from the PAN. It also tells something of the human perversion which may underly key events in Mexican political life, facts which are seldom uncovered. Governor Encinas's role in this psychological atrocity committed against the rector made Encinas into a prototype for what Monroy would later call el Mexicano enano, the Mexican dwarf.

35. From a humanistic point of view, Monroy's best work is probably *El profeta del silencio,* and from a philosophic point of view his more recent work, *León de Galán* (Mexico: Editorial Libros de Mexico, 1977), is surely one of his best.

36. Oscar Monroy Rivera, *El Mexicano enano* (Mexico: Editorial Diana, 1967), p. 161. It should be noted that the books in the dwarf series have gone through a number of editions that have been widely commented on even in the establishment press, for example, *Siempre,* November 30, 1966, and *Impacto,* October 21, 1970, to cite two early examples.

37. Monroy, *El mexicano enano,* op. cit., p. 43.

38. The IRE Report ran in series for 23 consecutive days ending April 4, 1977, in the Arizona *Daily Star* and was carried by numerous newspapers in other parts of the country. Its general focus was vice and corruption in Arizona and on the Mexican border.

39. See de Galicia, op. cit., which details from press and other sources the involvement of Ostler in narcotics traffic. Significantly, on one occasion when Ostler was in danger of being incarcerated for his physical assault on Oscar Monroy Rivera, the underworld-controlled press carried a letter in Ostler's defense signed by, among others, a member of the influential Kiriakys family (*Diario de Nogales,* April 20, 1974). Ostler was barred from entering the United States in 1977 following the publicity about his narcotics connections in the IRE report.

40. According to an article by Bill Waters in Arizona *Daily Star,* March 25, 1977.

41. According to an article by Alex Drehsler in Arizona *Daily Star,* May 4, 1975, plus corroborating interview testimony.

42. As published in the IRE report, Arizona *Daily Star,* March 31, 1977.

43. Ibid. Subsequently Mar Wong was indicted in Tucson during 1977 for illegal possession of weapons.

44. Oscar Monroy Rivera, *La burgesía y la opresión en la noticia* (Mexico: Costa-Amic, 1976). Additional evidence of the involvement of Zaied Dabdoub, this time the extortion of American citizens, is found in a series of documents collected by Russell Laughead that were made available to this writer. He also wrote a series of articles in the Tucson *Daily Citizen* (see, for example, December 4 and 5, 1974) concerning the American pilot Robert Champion who was held for one year in a Nogales prison while his wife paid excessive fees to Dabdoub who pretended to represent Champion but disappeared once his fee had been paid. When Champion was finally freed, following payment of more bribes, it was clear just how extensive was the interface between private and public corruption on the border, especially insofar as the courts and penal systems were concerned.

45. Monroy, *La burgesía,* op. cit., p. 21.

46. Ibid., pp. 32–33.

47. Ibid., pp. 34–37.

48. Ibid., pp. 74–75.

49. *Acción,* September 12, 1975.

50. *Acción,* September 13, 1975.

51. *Acción,* September 18, 1975.

52. Monroy, *La burgesía,* op. cit., p. 98.

53. Oscar Monroy Rivera, *A la espera del día (frontera sin agua)* (Mexico: Costa-Amic, 1975), passim.

54. This contention is based upon a study made available by the Centro de Integración Juvenil of Nogales, Sonora. Officials of that public-service agency (sponsored in part by funds of the Mexican federal government) stated that the study was done by professional chemists from Phoenix, Arizona, but the document does not contain the names of the researchers. The study shows arsenic, lead, and other mineral content in the water of a series of border cities. Sources in Nogales stated that the arsenic content was high enough to be a health hazard and that local officials refused to spend the money for a filtering system that would eliminate the problem.

55. See articles in Arizona *Daily Star* by Alex Drehsler (May 12, 1975) and by Bill Waters (January 5, 1976).

56. At the end of President López Portillo's first year in office many observers of the border were concerned that the president's campaign promises about cleaning up border corruption were forgotten. Not only were the charges against the fugitive Biebrich suspended but his accomplice in the assassination of the peasants, Francisco Arellano Noblecia, was welcomed in the presidential security forces in Mexico City despite the warrant for him in Sonora and another in Pima County, Arizona. This augured poorly for the cause of border reform during the López Portillo sexenio.

57. *Acción,* January 5, 1977; see also *El Imparcial,* December 17, 1976.

58. This was a front-page story in *El Diario de Nogales,* February 11, 1977.

59. *Acción,* February 14, 1977.

60. From an article by Bill Waters in Arizona *Daily Star,* February 20, 1977.

61. Arizona *Daily Star,* March 31, 1977.

62. *Información,* December 13, 1976.

63. Ibid.

64. See *Proceedings of the CADAP-CEMEF,* op. cit.

65. Monroy's most recent work as of that moment in 1977 was *León de Galán,* op. cit., which reflects bitterness over the cruel turn of the political milieu against him.

66. See this writer's article in Arizona *Daily Star,* May 15, 1977.

67. From Richard R. Fagen and William S. Tuohy, *Politics and Privilege in a Mexican City* (Stanford, Calif.: Stanford University Press, 1972), p. 168.

68. Ibid., p. 171.

Eight

Illegal Aliens and
the US-Mexico Interface

AN INTRODUCTORY PERSPECTIVE

As seen in the foregoing pages, a number of forces coalesce to produce a mammoth crush of unemployed humans concentrated in Mexico's northern border areas. Because the affected local administrations are either unable or unwilling to deal with this problem, it is tempting to acquiesce in (and to encourage) illegal northward migration as a partial solution to what is an increasingly serious threat to both the United States and Mexico. Some observers see the border areas as a human time bomb that is just waiting for the correct moment to explode. Estimates from respected sources have it that as much as 10 percent of Mexico's some 60 million people are living or working illegally in the United States. Mexico is expected to double her population by the year 2000. The implications of this are frightening.

My view is that the problem of illegal Mexican aliens in the United States can be considered properly as an extension of Mexican politics, that is, the inability of the Mexican political system to solve its poverty problems. In the foregoing chapters the connection between system deficiencies in Mexico and political corruption should have been amply demonstrated. Providing that we in the United States do not have another international military involvement, I would guess that the greatest problems the United States will have to face during the 1980s will be energy and illegal aliens from Mexico and elsewhere. The former issue was touched on in Chapter 5 insofar as Mexican oil and gas may be related to North American energy deficiencies.

I am indebted to CBS News and the *Arizona Daily Star* for their collaboration as reflected in this chapter. I would also like to thank the following Immigration and Naturalization Service and Border Patrol officers for their aid: Javier Dibene, Manuel Escobedo, George Geil, Lowell Genebaugh, Dave Gross, Edward J. Gus, Gerald Jacobson, Carl Judkins, Harold Mims, Herbert Walsh, and Gene Wood. The comments and criticism of General Leonard Chapman, Jr., and Michael Nolan are gratefully acknowledged, as is the assistance of Stephen Mumme, Manuel de Jesus Alvarado, Helen Ingram, Linda Garcia, and the Institute of Governmental Research, the University of Arizona, Tucson.

In recent years this writer has devoted considerable time to interviewing illegal Mexican immigrants who have come into the United States, without inspection or proper documents, in search of the economic opportunity which their country does not offer them.[1] These aliens, often known irreverently as "wets" from the term "wetbacks," have given me several general impressions that merit attention. First is the dignity and honest dedication that most of these men exhibit toward their families back in Mexico, this as evidenced by receipts for money orders sent and other written evidence. Second, most of these *mojados* (wetbacks) and *alambristas* (fence jumpers) have a strong and enduring loyalty to Mexico as a social system. While condemning Mexican political coyotaje (corruption), most would prefer to live in Mexico if it were economically possible. A third impression is that the illegal Mexican aliens, by and large, are excellent workers and are preferred by many U.S. employers over other American minorities (true, the distinction between "preferred" and "exploited" may be blurred in many cases). A fourth impression which surprised me is the knowledge of their country's history, and pride in its historical symbols of nationhood, which many of the illegals possess, even some of those without a grade-school education. I suspect that a greater percentage of wetbacks can tell you who Hidalgo, Juárez, and Zapata were than could a comparable sample of American workers respond correctly to similar questions about Jefferson, Lincoln, and William Jennings Bryan.

For those many Mexicans who know something of their nation's history, it is hard to ignore the fact that the United States took by military conquest what was probably the richest half of Mexican territory and then legitimized this with a treaty that was imposed in 1848. Mexican intellectuals often comment wryly that what the United States took by conquest Mexico will one day retake through illegal migration. And there are those today in the United States who fear that the southwestern states plus all of California could become dominated politically by people of Mexican origin and descent, a solid power bloc that could affect vital policy decisions made by the U.S. Congress. Others view such a prospect as welcome.

Not until the U.S. economic recession of 1973 and 1974 did a general public awakening occur to the problem of illegal Mexican aliens in the United States. Much of the credit for bringing the issue to the attention of Congress and civic groups throughout the nation belongs to General Leonard Chapman, Jr., who served as commissioner of the Immigration and Naturalization Service from 1973 until 1977. He is generally felt by veterans of that service to have been the most progressive and effective commissioner the INS ever had. In addition, the American public was alerted to the dilemma by courageous journalists, writers, and broadcasters who, like Eric Sevareid of CBS News, ventured to treat a potentially explosive public policy issue. Sevareid wrote to me that as a result of the following broadcast many people jumped to the mistaken conclusion that he hated the poor.[2] Witness:

CBS TELEVISION NETWORK
CBS EVENING NEWS WITH WALTER CRONKITE (Excerpt)
MONDAY, JULY 15, 1974
6:30–7:00 p.m., EDT

WALTER CRONKITE: The Immigration and Naturalization Service has been under investigation for corruption, and in his commentary tonight, Eric Sevareid suggests there's an even larger problem to be dealt with.

ERIC SEVAREID: It's getting hard to walk about in the federal government without barking your shins on a powder keg. One sitting there for years is immigration—the agency itself, the Immigration and Naturalization Service, and the immigration policies and the enforcement of the policies. There's a deafening silence at the service today about a New York *Times* account of corruption charges—prosecutions allegedly quashed, alleged attempts to compromise congressmen and other officials who go visiting around the Mexican border.

Far more important to the general condition of the country is the truth about immigration itself. Many congressmen and executives have been looking the other way deliberately because they don't want to appear illiberal, deny the American tradition of sanctuary for the poor, or offend organized minority groups already established in the country.

The truth is that so many people from other lands are pouring into the United States each year that no one can do more than guess at their numbers. All we are sure of are the 400,000 who entered last year in legal fashion, and nobody's upset about that. But something around 2.5 million got in illegally, and of that number, only 800,000 were caught and sent back. The estimate at the Immigration Service now is that 6 to 7 million illegal immigrants are living in the United States. Some individual estimates put it around 10 million.

People from the Caribbean region, using Puerto Rico as the escape hatch, are part of this but the critical mass of the problem is at the Mexican border. Only very recently has Mexico tried to do anything very serious about population control. Its population is likely to double in 20 years or so. Unemployment is heavy; millions there are desperate to get across the border. Mexico hardly loses by this; its own problems are relieved and the migrants send earnings back to their families in Mexico—probably around a billion dollars a year. Since illegal immigrants rarely pay taxes, the loss to the federal treasury here is about 100 million a year; about 15 million lost to the states, according to one House committee study. The drain hardly stops there. Cities and counties in Southern California, for example, are losing millions because they can't get federal reimbursement for emergency medical services to illegal immigrants.

One prong of the counterattack would be to impose criminal penalties on employers who knowingly hire illegal immigrants. The House has passed a bill on this twice; it seems smothered on the Senate side.

But a showdown on all this has to come. It's the poor versus the poor, those already here hunting jobs or housing or welfare against those pouring in. In the moral sense, it's the essence of classical tragedy, not right against wrong but right against right. And making decisions on this kind of thing is what separates the men from the boys.

Since that broadcast the figures (or estimates) on the illegal Mexican alien presence and impact have skyrocketed. Estimates were that in the late 1970s some 6 million Mexican aliens (about 10 percent of Mexico's total population) worked or lived illegally in the United States. My own research in St. Louis produced well-informed estimates that some 90 percent of the Mexican illegals were employed while unemployment for the inner-city blacks (U.S. citizens) was between 30 and 40 percent. Because an illegal population will hardly cooperate in census-taking, we must often rely upon informed judgments as to numbers. Other dimensions of the alien problem (like a statistical profile of those apprehended)[3] can be specified more exactly.

WHAT IS THE WETBACK PHENOMENON?

Mexico, in 1978, had some 60 million people, one of the world's highest annual birth rates (3.5 percent), and some 40 percent of her available labor force was either unemployed or only marginally so. There seems little likelihood of major changes in this condition during the decade of the 1980s. Thus, the attraction of unskilled jobs to the north with vastly better pay scales is hard for Mexicans to resist. Rather than acquiesce in a life of penury and neglect at home, many Mexicans choose to become illegal migrant aliens who go north in search of wages with which to support families left behind. Estimates are that in the late 1970s perhaps $10 billion or more annually are returned to Mexico by illegal aliens. Cutting this source of income could have repercussions of major national scope in Mexico. It could also adversely affect many U.S. business interests who feel they cannot operate north of the border without the availability of cheap illegal migrant labor. Contentions such as this are reflections of a system of interlocking or incompatible influences which must be understood if the problem is to be dealt with via pragmatic public policy.

The wetback phenomenon is not without its poignant human aspects as well: like the feelings of border residents in Douglas, Arizona. They charged that the high incidence of assaults and robberies in their area had forced nearly everyone to turn his home into an armed camp against the illegal alien raiders from Mexico. It inspired one member of a private security group to comment, "I think it's safe to say that everyone around here is armed . . . we didn't used to be. It's not a racial thing, not an ethnic thing, not a nationalistic thing. It's just plain and simple fear."[4] In contrast, one scholar has expressed the plight of the Mexican migrant as follows:

> The individual alien himself has the strange experience of leaving his family, friends, community, and country for an undetermined period of time. He lives outside of the law, on the fringes of society, in constant fear of being apprehended. Invariably he leads a life of hardship, and he is at the mercy of those who would exploit him.[5]

Stated in general terms, the wetback phenomenon involves the interests of a poor nation, Mexico, and the needs of a richer nation, the United States.

Prior to the profound social revolution which Mexico experienced following the turmoil of 1910–17, it was possible for a landed oligarchy to control the mobility of the peasant masses which it held in virtual serfdom. The Mexican revolution, and the infrastructure developments (transportation systems) which preceded it, freed the rural proletariat in what became migratory patterns toward the central Mexican cities and toward the economic opportunity that existed in the north. The revolution made mobility possible for many of the previously enslaved masses, that is to say geographic mobility at the very least.

During recent years, however, Mexico's ability to absorb its poor has been stultified.[6] While Mexican economic growth may recently have met the old Alliance for Progress goal of 2.5 percent per year, the nation's birth rate of around 3.5 percent has wiped out most of the distributive benefits that economic progress might have created. Also, due to monopolistic economic practices, expatriation of capital, and excessively corrupt political and administrative systems, the benefits of the alleged Mexican economic "modernity" have been largely reserved for the pockets of the few. Consumers in Mexico have been victimized by inflation and by a range of undesirable monetary effects of the dramatic devaluations of the peso which occurred late in 1976.[7] This also hurt business in U.S. border towns when their regular Mexican customers lost much of their purchasing power as a result of the devaluation (in 1975 one peso was worth eight cents U.S., but at the beginning of 1978 it was worth about half that). Other reports based on Mexican government figures indicate that there was up to 50 percent unemployment in the border areas as of 1977.[8]

To appreciate the Mexican alien problem in its historical context, a brief overview will be helpful. During World War II the United States experienced a severe manpower shortage. An agreement was reached whereby Mexican laborers could cross the border with relative ease. After the war, however, the manpower need declined rapidly and the United States began to impose restrictions that would protect its own labor force. Understandably, many Mexicans and Americans of Mexican descent resented this, feeling that they had contributed to the war effort only to be spurned when victory was won. A virtual wetback culture had developed by that time as former legal migrants now became illegals. By 1946 the struggle to cross the border brought conflict among the illegals themselves and reports of bodies floating in the Rio Grande became common.[9] Farmers, especially in the semitropical lower Rio Grande Valley, had come to depend upon the wets to harvest and cultivate their crops. At times the need for illegals was so great that U.S. authorities bowed to state pressure for illegal entry to be allowed at harvest time. The illegals would earn $.20 to $.37 per hour and would work long hours that North Americans were reluctant to endure. Some farmers insisted they had a right to the illegals and Texans accused New Mexicans of pirating their wets in violation of Texas statutes.[10] Major industries of the southwest had been capitalized, de facto, under the assumption that cheap Mexican labor would be in constant supply. Many American interests looked to the INS and its enforcement arm, the Border Patrol, in the late 1940s and early 1950s as if it were a virtual farm recruitment and labor placement agency. At times the INS could do little else but collaborate.

As the illegal immigration continued the human sacrifice factor became a more poignant issue. The desert sun and the river killed many. Others who were sent back to Mexico were set upon by their own countrymen hoping to reap spoils from another's illegal labor. Some U.S. employers provided decent living conditions for the wets while others exploited them miserably. A high incidence of infant deaths was common throughout the 1950s in the migrant labor camps. Many rural counties in the U.S. border areas complained that the wetbacks constituted an unfair burden in terms of medical services that had to be provided the illegals and their families.

All of this changed somewhat with the advent of the Korean War in 1951. Once again there was a labor shortage and large-scale labor recruitment of workers (*braceros*) began in Mexico. Hourly wages had jumped to an average of $.85 an hour with some side benefits.[11] But the alien invasion which had begun more than satisfied the labor supply. It was reported that, for California alone, whereas in 1940 about 900 wetbacks had been expelled from the country, by 1945 the number was 16,311; in 1950 it was 224,588, and the total for all border states in 1950 was 500,000 expulsions.[12] The peak year for expulsions was 1954 with over 1 million reported.[13] The more the myth of opportunity circulated, and the more U.S. employers contributed to that myth, the more the invasion continued unabated. Moreover, the Mexican illegals proved to be better workers than North Americans in many cases, especially in the agricultural stoop labor which attracted almost none of the U.S. labor force, the protestations of U.S. labor organizations notwithstanding.[14]

Evidence also accumulated during the decade of the 1950s as to the ease with which one could cross the border surreptitiously either on his own or with prearranged help. In 1952 a San Diego journalist named Gene Fuson, who had been covering the smuggling of narcotics and aliens on the border, went to Mexico and turned himself into a "Czech Communist agent" who arranged to cross into the United States illegally twice for the total price of $40.[15]

Poor Mexicans in all corners of the republic had learned of the great demand to the north, exaggerating it greatly in relation to the actual demand. At that time the Border Patrol was equipped with jeeps supported by an 11-plane "air force" to stem the illegal tide. Mexicans, by then, were not exclusively destined for the border states but had found access to industrial and agricultural jobs in such northern locations at St. Louis, Chicago, and Detroit. Many went as far north as Oregon and Washington. Once out of the Border Patrol's reach, and with only an understaffed series of INS field offices to carry out area control operations, an illegal Mexican could live months and even years without detection or apprehension. This was critical to both the individual Mexicans and their nation, for by the early 1950s they were sending back to Mexico an estimated $170 million ($70 million sent by the legal braceros and $100 million sent by the illegal wets).[16]

But Mexico also demanded that the U.S. guarantee decent pay and working conditions for its migratory population. Negotiations stalled at one point in 1953 and Mexico even went so far as to threaten to keep its people at home, that is, to ban U.S. labor contracting.[17] This would probably be the last time that the Mexican government would seriously make such a threat given the population explosion that occurred during the succeeding decade.

The decade of the 1960s saw alien smuggling from Mexico develop into a major international business. By 1971, of the 412,000 illegals apprehended, 87 percent were Mexican. The State of California, under severe pressure from the AFL-CIO, attempted to fine employers who knowingly hired illegals. And other groups had also become concerned over the illegal Mexican. Doctors called them a multihealth problem who, coming from an environment with low health and sanitation standards, melted into the Mexican-American barrios and contaminated them.[18] The illegal often shunned treatment, claimed the doctors, rather than attract attention to himself. Moreover, he might send his children to public school for which he paid nothing. Children undergoing cultural transition often contributed to juvenile delinquency problems. And few school districts wanted the image of turning young children over to INS officials, one superintendent stated.[19] Large illegal, hence voteless, populations in the barrio potentially undermined Chicano social reform causes because the numbers who could participate in the political process were disproportionate to the problems that should be solved by governmental agencies. Those who were able to be active had to carry a greater burden of the representation, so stated Chicano activist Manuel Aragón.[20]

When the United States allowed the Bracero Treaty with Mexico to expire in 1964, the pressure from illegals became even more severe. In 1965 quotas were set for immigration from the Western Hemisphere and the Department of Labor was required to certify that a Mexican entering the United States would not be displacing a North American from a job. This meant that, excepting a handful of scarce and highly specialized occupations, it was very difficult to come to the United States legally to work. Having a family tie in the United States, and subsequently marriage fraud to create such ties, became keys to gaining admittance. Visitor's passes were often used to cross the border and work illegally.[21] But for many Mexicans the hard way, *a la brava,* of the wetback remained the most viable alternative. The law still did not require employers to verify one's alien status and there were many employers who depended upon the illegal Mexican labor.

North American labor unions, to be sure, sometimes informed on the illegals, especially when they were being used as strikebreakers. Also, cases are reported of union leaders who demanded kickbacks in return for helping get jobs for illegal aliens.[22] Vulnerability to deportation often led wetbacks to pay high rents to unscrupulous landlords and high fees to unethical lawyers who promised to arrange residence documents. Smuggling of aliens of various nationalities across the Mexican border turned into a well-organized crime operation. In July 1973 federal agents broke up the biggest ring uncovered to that date, charging 25 persons with smuggling some 15,000 illegal aliens into California.[23] Many of these illegals had pawned all their worldly possessions to raise the $300 to $500 per person that was charged by the smugglers. The same smugglers, known as "mules," often dealt in illegal narcotics and guns at the same time they handled people.

Illegal aliens were found working in practically every phase of the un-skilled labor market. In 1971 it was revealed that President Nixon's appointee as treasurer of the United States, Ramona Bañuelos, owned food-processing plants in Los Angeles that employed illegals. At least one wetback was even found working in the Western White House at San Clemente. The ease with which the illegals penetrated the labor market, especially in California, led that state's legislature to enact a law in 1971 that would fine employers for hiring illegal immigrants. But the law was declared unconstitutional in early 1972 because the state had encroached into the field of immigration and naturaliza-tion which is reserved to the federal government. The California law was followed by a bill introduced in the U.S. Congress in 1973 by Representative Peter Rodino of New Jersey. The Rodino Bill, which was still being hotly debated in 1978, was almost a carbon copy of the California legislation but offered at the federal level.

While the issue of fining U.S. employers for hiring illegals remained moot before Congress, an amendment to the Immigration and Nationality Act (P.L. 94-571) was passed in late 1976. This has become known colloquially as the Western Hemisphere Bill and will be reviewed only superficially here. In essence, the new amendment which took effect on January 1, 1977, cut the legal entries of Mexican aliens (excluding minor children, spouses, and parents of American citizens) from 40,000 to 20,000. A limit of 20,000 alien visas is fixed for each of the noncommunist countries of the Western Hemisphere. This enraged many Mexican-Americans because Mexico was the biggest supplier of newcomers to the United States and many saw the act as an outrage to their perceived ethnicity. Other Mexican-Americans, especially those in organized labor, approved the action as protecting their jobs. The expected impact is to make more potential newcomers into eventual illegals, should they ultimately cross surreptitiously. Estimates in 1977 were that some 1.5 million people, mostly from Mexico, would enter the United States unlawfully in the calendar year. Canadians, of course, were under the same restriction that applied to Mexicans. As a result there is now severe competition throughout the hemisphere for entry visas (the effect on Canada may be minimal as the rate of migrants from that country has dropped radically in recent years).

Principal beneficiaries of the Western Hemisphere Bill of 1976 will be other Latin American countries, especially those in Central America and the Caribbean. This prospect worries officials in New York and Philadelphia which are traditionally settling places of non-Mexican immigrants from Latin America. High unemployment there means that more newcomers could strain the overburdened welfare rolls.[24] The measure will still give preference to those aliens which the U.S. Department of Labor certifies as having scarce professional skills. It is supposed to eliminate much bureaucratic delay in reuniting families who are temporarily separated by visa problems.[25]

SILENT INVASION: KNOWN FACTS AND INFORMED ESTIMATES

In the eyes of some observers, the paradox of U.S. national security policy in the late 1970s is that while it may be directed at countering perceived threats from the USSR, in reality one of our most grave menaces is that posed by illegal Mexican immigration. Thus a pragmatic immigration policy is ipso facto a matter of national defense. This was the goal of former INS Commissioner Leonard F. Chapman, Jr., who is credited with coining the phrase "silent invasion" to describe the phenomenon. Evidence of increasing awareness of the problem at all levels is seen in hearings conducted by Senator James Eastland in 1976 and by President Ford's charge to the National Council on Employment Policy, and to a special cabinet-level Domestic Council Committee on Illegal Aliens in 1975, that a thorough study be made of U.S. immigration policy. In January 1977 the Los Angeles *Times* ran a series of long articles focusing on both the national and local aspects of the dilemma. A reading of that evidence indicates that illegal immigration is, indeed, "one of the murkiest issues of public policy" that must be resolved in the near future.[26]

The Domestic Council Committee called for a basic rethinking of America's historic role of absorbing the external migration of other nations, some 46 million persons in two centuries. The issue becomes most poignant when the principal concern is Mexico, our neighbor which has contributed most of the illegal migrants in recent years. The fact that Mexico is expected to more than double its present population of some 60 million by the year 2000 is a guarantee that the problem will not cure itself. Estimates range that in 1978 there were between 8 and 10 million illegal aliens (perhaps 80 percent or more from Mexico) residing in the United States. The INS assumes that for every illegal alien who is apprehended, probably three or four others remain free. The Border Patrol has nearly 2,000 miles of frontier in common with Mexico and to patrol that it had, in fiscal 1976, 2,975 investigators and patrolmen (this figure is 4,425 less than the authorized size of the Los Angeles Police Department).[27]

In fiscal 1976 nearly 28,000 illegal aliens were deported, a judicial proceeding making it a felony for those persons to return without proper visa or other documentation (illegal entry itself is only a misdemeanor under current statutes). Another 765,000 illegal aliens apprehended during the same period opted for what is known as the I-274 Program or voluntary departure under safeguards. This applied to Mexicans only. Such persons waive their right to legal counsel, to a court hearing, but their potential reentry into the United States, even illegally, would be only a misdemeanor. An A-File is kept indefinitely on persons who have been formally deported. An I-213 form is kept on those who accept voluntary departure, but this form is retained normally for five years and only in that particular office of the INS which made the original apprehension. There is a central record file of apprehensions kept in Washington, but INS officials consider its usefulness to be severely limited. Subsequently the I-213 forms are destroyed.

This creates problems. For instance, under present operating capabilities, an alien who had accepted voluntary departure from the INS office in Kansas City, Missouri, and who returned three months later and was apprehended in St. Louis could easily get away with saying he had no previous record, for there is no central storage bank of computerized information that can be called upon to determine if a given alien is a repeater. In large jurisdictions like Los Angeles and Chicago this is a critical dilemma; identification and reidentification become very difficult to accomplish.

Of the figures referred to above for total deportations and voluntary departures for fiscal 1976 (a total of 875,915), more than three-fourths were Mexicans. Chicago's illegal alien population during 1976 was estimated at nearly 0.5 million, but only some 6,000 were apprehended. The illegal alien population of Los Angeles is estimated at between 1.5 and 2 million, but during fiscal 1976 only 41,275 such illegals were caught. St. Louis has an estimated illegal alien population of around 4,000. In fiscal year 1976 only some 300 Mexican illegals were apprehended. Again, the figures tell the story of a badly undermanned and underfunded Immigration Service and Border Patrol. Entry of organized crime syndicates into the smuggling of aliens during the last two decades has further complicated the law-enforcement problem. The INS has been able to prosecute successfully less than half of the smugglers apprehended and the majority of those get off with misdemeanor charges under existing laws.

It is not known what the cost to U.S. taxpayers is in lost jobs and balance-of-payments deficit terms, but one estimate done for INS in 1976 calculated that some $16.5 billion per year was lost, this on the basis of reasonable estimates.[28] There seems to be little question but that illegal immigration tends to absorb the worst jobs first, but the INS found that at least 1 million illegals (all nationalities) held well-paying jobs during fiscal 1976.

Illegal migration out of Mexico gives that country an escape valve for its uncontrolled population. The migrants tend to establish beachheads for future migration in that they may have children who are U.S. citizens if they are born in this country. It is difficult to determine just who is having what impact and where because the various government agencies do not collaborate fully with each other. Little is done, for instance, by the Social Security Administration to prevent illegal aliens from securing social security numbers, hence jobs. Welfare agencies do not always concern themselves with an applicant's immigrant status when determining his eligibility for benefits. At all levels of government the illegal alien issue is so emotional that everyone expects everyone else to play the role of cops, no one wishing the stigma of turning desperate aliens over to the INS.

When Los Angeles County's Department of Public Social Services started making alien legitimacy checks in 1975, this reduced the number of illegals who gained welfare benefits, but it offended some Mexican-Americans who felt they were being harassed on an ethnic basis. The INS field office in Los Angeles estimated that this procedure saved taxpayers some $5 million in welfare benefits that would otherwise have been paid out to illegal aliens, the great majority of them Mexican. Similar figures were reported on the medical costs of treating illegal aliens. The Los Angeles Unified School District still refuses to identify illegal students and therefore the educational costs are not known. What is known is that the district has about 24,000 students who speak no English and some 59,000 more who speak little English; and these figures seem to be growing steadily year by year.[29]

Looking more closely at the Los Angeles situation, which may be the epitome of illegal alien impact at the local level, a briefing paper on the problem was presented at a meeting of staff officers of the Los Angeles Police Department (LAPD) early in 1977. This paper argued that the illegal population in that city had increased over 200 percent since 1971 and that with current trends continuing there would be a "hidden population" within the city of well over a million by 1981.[30] A principal thrust of the Los Angeles police study was that its officers must be responsible for a population that is 23 percent larger than the officially counted 2,824,828 residents. Instead of the LAPD's official ratio of 2.63 officers per thousand inhabitants it drops to 2.14 per thousand due to the excess population of illegals, around 90 percent of which are Mexicans.

The Los Angeles study also questioned the traditional image of the illegal alien as a servile person who avoids trouble. Even if the illegals committed no more than their proportional share of routine violations requiring police protection this would be costly. It was estimated that illegals cost the city some

$37 million annually. During a test period in 1974 illegals were estimated to have committed 36.6 percent of all felony arrests. During another test period which coincided with a major INS sweep of the Los Angeles area there was a drop of 14.7 percent in repressible crimes.[31]

Los Angeles officials blame the federal government for carrying out a policy they term as benign neglect in that they allow the INS to remain undermanned.[32] This allows the illegals to sneak in and when some of them have difficulty in getting jobs it is not surprising that many would turn to crime.[33] The Los Angeles study also cited the deleterious effect on young children of being raised in an atmosphere of fear by parents who are working illegally and constantly worrying about arrest by federal authorities. That Los Angeles should have an illegal alien subculture dedicated to crime is no surprise to the LAPD, one of many local agencies which must deal with the consequences of the absence of an effective national policy that is vigorously enforced.

Most illegal Mexican aliens do not get caught. The quest for employment brings so many wetbacks across the border that the Border Patrol at its present size can never expect to contain them. In their desperation to find work the stories of tragedies multiply, tales of illegals riding atop 12-foot trucks that passed under bridges with only a 13-foot clearance, of wets found nearly frozen to death in refrigerator vehicles or crushed by heavy crates inside railway cars. Many have perished in traffic accidents or suffocated in tightly locked trailers.[34] A good number have died in fights among themselves.

A study done by the county of San Diego in 1975 revealed a variety of forms of exploitation affecting illegal aliens, including refusal of state and federal authorities to pay workman's compensation to the wife of an illegal alien who was killed on the job (the federal authorities lost this one in court), California notary publics who charged aliens outrageous fees to certify signatures and who profited unlawfully with unfounded promises that legal alien status could be arranged. Illegal aliens were paid a fraction of the going wage in San Diego County for doing landscaping work and then they were charged $10 a week for the privilege of sleeping under a tree or in a hole on the contractor's property. There were reports of aliens being forced to drink water from polluted irrigation ditches—with inevitable illness and an excuse to discharge the aliens without pay.[35]

The full enormity of the human tragedy will never be known. Many of the potential mojados and alambristas never reach the border, having been ripped off en route by their own countrymen. Edmund Villaseñor recounts how innocent Mexican workers were cheated while still within Mexico by crooks known as *coyotes* who promised, for a fee, to arrange rapid work permits with the Americans and to place the workers swiftly north of the border:

And so the men lined up in a line of tens and hundreds and gave their money to these men in suits in the shade of a big beautiful umbrella with the Mexican flag on one side and the American flag on the other side, and these men took three hundred pesos (24 dollars) from each single man . . . for six straight days, and then on the seventh day, they didn't come back. And grown men with callused hands and knives in their belts fell down and cried . . . and began, by the thousands, the long journey home.[36]

A colorful tragic folklore has grown up among poorer Mexicans based upon adventures during the long trek north pitting men against the pitfalls of nature and the treachery of humans. One can demonstrate his machismo or male prowess by doing it the hard way, a la brava, but one can also earn money. Both factors operate in the psychology of the wetbacks and spur them on against difficult odds. Once a foothold north of the border has been made, a man's family may hope to come as well. The competition to go, and perhaps to stay, is fierce. To return to Mexico without money is to lose face among one's peers.

It is difficult to separate the alien problem in the immediate border area from the broader phenomenon of smuggling and vice. It is a south-to-north flow for aliens and narcotics. For stolen American goods and illegal arms the flow is usually north-to-south. All sorts of arms are traded for drugs and for special shipments of aliens to be moved by syndicates for special work commitments. It is not uncommon for border newspapers on the U.S. side to show pictures of enormous caches of arms and marijuana that have been confiscated. On one occasion weapons made in Red China and smuggled from Hong Kong by U.S. syndicates were captured.[37] Border security is so inadequate as to make smuggling relatively easy. The border fence at places like Nogales is a sieve with large holes, some of them large enough for vehicles to go through, going unmended for months at a time. The Border Patrol is now experimenting with large metal plates, used during World War II to set up emergency aircraft landing strips, to patch up some of the more notorious entry points. Photographs taken by this writer give an idea of the extent of the problem and suggest why some Border Patrol officers might privately comment that only a "Berlin Wall" or full-scale military deployment can stop the international traffic.

Following the student riots in Mexico during 1968, that government closed down what had been a relatively open arms industry and commercial distribution of guns within Mexico. Today Mexico requires all privately owned guns to be registered. This favors black-market dealings in the United States and often the same people who smuggle aliens deal in arms and drugs. Because of bureaucratic delays in getting gun permits in Mexico it was reported that even many agencies of the Mexican government—federal, state, and local—deal with the arms smugglers to supply their extraofficial paramilitary operations. This level of corruption in Mexican government leads to the cutting of fences for all varieties of illegal traffic. For example, the head of Baja California's highway patrol was himself charged with arms smuggling in San Diego during January of 1977.

There have been numerous clashes between law-enforcement officers on opposite sides of the border. The San Diego police department reported in February 1977 that Mexican federal agents had followed illegal aliens to the California side of the border and exchanged shots with San Diego police officers sent out as special decoys to curb night raids from Mexico on American homes and businesses. One Mexican agent was wounded in the exchange and his government claimed the crossing had been accidental. American residents charged that the Mexican police often use hot pursuit as an excuse to commit robberies in the United States.[38] Chicano groups in San Diego's border area asked for police protection against night marauders from Mexico, citing near 50 percent unemployment and inflation in the Mexican border areas as contributing to the desperation behavior.

And finally, although by no means exhausting the range of conflict issues in the border area, there is the attraction of medical attention on the U.S. side. It is sadly inadequate in Mexico and pregnant mothers know that if they can give birth to a child inside the U.S. they will have a vague future chance at U.S. immigration when the child reaches age 21. At Cochise County Hospital in Arizona officials say their problem epitomizes a generalized situation on the border. That hospital had 234 delinquent accounts during 1976 for a total of nearly $74,000 in unpaid bills owed by Mexican citizens. An Arizona court decision prohibits a hospital from refusing to grant emergency care regardless of a person's nationality or legal status. The local taxpayers ultimately pay the bills for these services. Not all medical costs, of course, are for maternity services, but where there is a new U.S. citizen involved he or she cannot be deported even though the illegal alien mother can. In most cases the mothers opt to take their children back to Mexico and use the birth certificate as a basis for getting on the eligibility list for eventual immigration. Not surprisingly, this has left resentment among taxpayers on the U.S. side.[39]

The health-care problem becomes more costly in larger jurisdictions like San Diego. There it was estimated that the cost to San Diego County of reimbursing the University of California Hospital for services rendered to Mexican nationals that could not be recovered was slightly in excess of $0.5 million for fiscal year 1974/75.[40] Only that one hospital in the San Diego area kept records which could be useful here. The other hospitals justified their lack of information on three grounds: that it is an administrative burden to keep nationality and alien legality statistics, that false addresses provided the hospital make detection impossible until bills are returned unpaid, and that persons who are known to be illegals are not admitted to the hospitals except in emergency status in which case the hospitals absorb the cost. However, the San Diego Board of Supervisors has provided a section in its Administrative Code which generally requires any hospital under its Department of Medical Institutions to provide emergency care to anyone in serious need.[41]

A study published during late 1976 in the Mexican journal *Foro Internacional* contained a profile of the illegal Mexican alien as one who "remains tied to agricultural labor, is illiterate, without skilled training, socioeconomically marginal, and is exploited on both sides of the Mexico-U.S. border."[42] The study also points to one development paradox of Mexico as a cause of the exodus, that is, with the adoption of mechanized agricultural and industrial techniques the unskilled rural peasant and many urban proletarians become increasingly unnecessary. But this vast lumpenproletariat has been exposed to the comforts and advantages of modernity (at least they know there is a better life) without having acquired the ability to achieve them. Cast in terms of the theory of "relative deprivation," the mojados and alambristas have a level of goal expectations that exceeds considerably their perceived ability to achieve the same.

It can be argued, according to the Mexican study, that a new dependency relationship has been created that requires the continued flow of migrants, legally or clandestinely, to satisfy industrial, agricultural, and service needs in the receiving country and as an escape valve for the population pressures and balance-of-payment needs of the sending country. The flow of migrants is encouraged to some degree by the firmly entrenched hispanic subculture in many parts of the United States which helps facilitate the population movement and makes possible, often without intending to, much of the human exploitation.

A final and important human dimension would be the number of wetbacks there are during a recent normal year in the United States. That is impossible to answer definitively since a census of illegals is impossible to take. The answer is further complicated by multiple apprehensions of the same individuals, often within a matter of a 48-hour period. As stated previously, for every alien apprehended it is believed that quite a few more go undetected. The San Diego County study cited earlier states that in fiscal year 1974/75 slightly in excess of 200,000 illegals were apprehended in that county alone and that 97.5 percent of these were Mexican nationals, the majority of whom were between 18 and 35 years of age. My St. Louis study found a similar age majority, despite the greater distance from the border.

Interestingly, the San Diego County study also contends that the proportion of Mexican males apprehended was 87 percent, but this figure excluded the San Ysidro border crossing, the principal port of entry for all of California. Looking at San Ysidro (an extension of the City of San Diego) alone, 75 percent of the illegals apprehended there turned out to be Mexican females, a reversal of the overall county and national trend. This may be explained in part by the relatively short distance between the San Ysidro border crossing and the shopping or other social attractions of urban San Diego. In contrast, my St. Louis study found almost no apprehensions of Mexican females, suggesting that the distance from the border may be a controlling factor. Thus, the quantity of aliens may vary among the numerous entry points according to sex, distance from large U.S. urban areas, and other variables including time of year. For instance, the coming of winter to the central plains of the United States may mean that more illegals will either congest in the border states of the United States awaiting spring or that they will wait longer on the Mexican side to find the best opportunity for crossing. Changes in U.S. immigration law (for example, the Western Hemisphere Bill of 1976) or enforcement policy may also affect the numbers of illegals who are apprehended.

Public discussion of President Carter's proposals for granting amnesty to illegal aliens during 1977 and 1978 led to increased pressure on the border as many Mexicans misunderstood the issue (or were misled), believing that amnesty meant that crossing the line would mean automatic legal status or citizenship. The human impact of simply opening the issue to public discussion was felt almost immediately along the border. One example: at Douglas, Arizona, in May 1977 a group of aliens was apprehended after having abandoned a homemade railway hand car which they had manufactured in distant Michoacán. The vehicle, which I photographed, reflected great ingenuity on the part of the Mexicans. They admitted they hoped to coast all the way "down hill to Los Angeles" on it, having heard that it was then certain that if apprehended they would be granted amnesty. This, of course, reflects the desperation with which Mexicans seek to abandon their country.

Enforcement weakness and growing desperation in Mexico have kept the flow of aliens coming. Corruption in Mexico is also seriously to blame. Most poignant has been the use of children for crime and vice activities as the search for a socioeconomic escape valve continues. Witness:

> Some Mexican child criminals are reported by juvenile officials to have been kidnapped from the Mexican interior *or sold by their impoverished parents* for as little as $50 to $75, then taken to border city slums, where they are trained in crime. When they fall ill or become too well-known to either the American or Mexican police, they may be taken to some Mexican city away from the border and abandoned to shift for themselves. . . . [In 1976] . . . 2,280 Mexican children aged 8 to 17 were picked up for crimes in border cities of California, Arizona, New Mexico and Texas, but only one in seven was charged and held. The others were turned over to the Border Patrol and sent back to Mexico.[43]

COMMUNITY IMPACT: SELECTED INTRA-U.S. EXPERIENCES

Presumably, the issue of slavery in the United States was settled once and for all by the Civil War and subsequent legislative action. But near the wealthy retirement community of Sun City, Arizona, in April 1977 it was doubtful whether such was the case. Less than two miles from Sun City we saw, and photographed, modern slavery. The slaves were illegal Mexican aliens employed by a prominent member of Arizona Citrus Growers, Inc., an agrobusiness consortium whose groves we inspected in the Phoenix area. Several of the fence jumpers spoke with us in detail about how they had arrived, how they had done it before, and of the misery to the south that drove them north. They confirmed this writer's suspicion that coming to the Arizona-Sonora border in search of work in one of the border industries was futile for most.[44]

One man in particular, having come all the way from Querétaro in central Mexico, said he had nothing to lose by continuing north. He had a wife and nine children in Querétaro and no way to feed them there. Besides, he had been apprehended in the United States before, given good treatment and good food by the Border Patrol, and then sent back. But through the grapevine of smugglers he knew that on the outskirts of wealthy Sun City there would be a job awaiting him.

There were an estimated 60 to 70 illegals in the area I visited on April 21, 1977. Entrance into that particular citrus grove was difficult and a resident familiar with the area had to lead us. The illegals had been told to stay under cover of the trees when they were not working so as to avoid INS surveillance. Without entering all the adjacent groves we could not count the total number of illegals in the entire citrus area but it must have been well into the hundreds, this within a space of probably no more than five square miles.

Coincidentally, on the very day of our excursion into the orange and lemon groves a suit was brought on behalf of six Mexican laborers identified only as "Juan Doe I through VI." The class-action suit was filed in federal court in Phoenix by the Maricopa County Legal Aid Society Legal Services for Farm Workers in the community of El Mirage. The suit charged, among other things, that some 90 growers who comprise Arizona Citrus Growers, Inc., pay illegally low wages.[45] The suit further alleged that some 400 workers were affected but could not be named for fear of reprisals from their employers. It was charged that the growers recruited laborers illegally in various parts of Mexico in violation of the Farm Labor Contractor Registration Act of 1963 in that Arizona Citrus Growers, Inc. was not registered with the secretary of agriculture as a farm labor contractor.[46] Although the employing of the illegals itself was not in violation of the law at the time, their recruitment and transportation from Mexico or the arranging thereof would be a felony under U.S. immigration statutes. It was further alleged that the growers assigned false Social Security numbers to the illegals for pay purposes.[47]

What we learned from the Juan Doe illegals themselves, however, was even more revealing. Our man from Querétaro earned about $9 per day with no guarantee as to his hours, just whatever the foreman decided (United Farm Workers unionized pickers earned on the average three times that much with overtime for extra work). The illegal alien workers were expected to sleep among the orange trees. They stretched plastic sheets, cardboard, old cloth, and other makeshift devices to give them partial cover from sun and rain. They had arrived during the spring months when the nights were cold by anyone's standards, but the Mexicans slept in light clothing and blankets and on the ground. Not even a real tent or anything that could be called a shack was in sight. Debris and human excrement were strewn about (no sanitary facilities existed) and there was no electricity, hence any raw foods had to be consumed at once.

The men were forced to purchase their provisions at the company-owned store where they paid over $1.00 for a dozen eggs, $4.00 for one chicken (raw) and some beans, over $2.00 for a six pack of beer, and similarly exaggerated prices for other basic items. The men were not sure on pay day whether they were having the correct amount of their debt subtracted from their pay (for which they signed in cash terms). Money sent to loved ones in Mexico had to be handled through the foremen who charged a fee for purchasing a postal money order. It was bad, said our man from Querétaro, but still better than trying to work in Mexico. He was helping his family and had money order receipts to prove it. Even though his life was that of a slave, his large family back home ate because of his sacrifice.

More significantly, however, the grower in question (and his foremen) were profiteering. The consensus seemed to be that they could make a fair profit and still pay decent wages even if they insisted on employing illegal aliens. Other growers in Arizona and California were showing a respectable profit by employing union labor. Slavery seemed an anachronism with no legal, social, or economic justification (apart from blatant greed and gross neglect of human rights). Any of the aliens who protested, or sought to make food purchases at independent markets charging competitive prices, were threatened with being fired or turned over to the INS. That threat, plus the needs of families in Mexico, was sufficient to keep the illegals in line, all that is except for the six Juan Does who filed suit. We were told that there is a statutory provision whereby illegal aliens may not be expelled from the United States while they are party to a litigation in process. The use of the Juan Doe identification was intended to keep the plaintiffs from being singled out for firing. It would not, of course, save the illegal workers in the citrus groves from INS raids, once their presence had been made public by the suit.

Herbert E. Walsh, chief patrol officer for the Tucson Sector of the Border Patrol, expressed concern for the human rights of the illegals. He stated in a private interview that little would be gained by raiding the citrus groves under then-existing conditions given low INS manpower in the Phoenix area and in light of current immigration laws, except as to improve physical conditions for the illegals by putting them into clean living circumstances and guaranteeing their physical well-being. Walsh and his colleague Gene Wood stated that the principal concern of the Border Patrol is effective law enforcement and to prevent exploitation of the Mexican workers. They also stated that employers like the citrus producers are magnets and that until the law is changed to penalize them for attracting and hiring illegals, and for exploiting them, the current immigration laws would be nearly uninforceable.

An even more notorious case than the one we inspected personally is that of the Arrowhead Ranch, owned by the powerful Goldmar Corporation of Arizona, and which is contained in the IRE report.[48] On the same day of our interviews we succeeded in penetrating Arrowhead Ranch and found similar living conditions to those described above. We did not, however, find any aliens. Previously unfavorable publicity given to the Arrowhead operation by the IRE report may have forced operating changes upon the management, that is, they may have learned to hide their wets better. And we, like the IRE reporters, were menaced by a circling aircraft and patrol cars which began searching for us shortly after our entry into the area. The high sensitivity of the Arizona growers to exposure vis-a-vis their profiteering from the use of illegal alien labor suggests that a great deal of money must be at stake in these operations. Of course, not all Arizona growers profiteer from illegal labor.

From the standpoint of community impact, such cases of worker abuse are of importance to labor organizations like the United Farm Workers (UFW) who are already at a disadvantage in their organizing efforts due to the Arizona right-to-work (no union shop) law. Moreover, UFW officials in Arizona like Daniel Morales insist that there exists a more-than-adequate labor supply of native Americans including Chicanos plus a number of legal resident aliens who need the seasonal agricultural work. At the time of our interviews, nevertheless, the UFW had only one contract with an agrobusiness farm in the Phoenix area. It was believed that most fruit and vegetable growers in the area bolstered their profits by using nonunion and, wherever possible, illegal alien labor. The given community impact issue in Arizona, bluntly stated, is whether agricultural profits, labor wage demands, and consumer price interests can be reconciled equitably and legally while at the same time safeguarding human rights.

In many respects it is more interesting to study the illegal Mexican alien phenomenon in an interior community like St. Louis than along the international border in that the migrant workers who are apprehended inland have already penetrated the Border Patrol (which operates only in the immediate border area contiguous to Mexico) and have avoided the various state and local police agencies. They have, for the most part, either been smuggled by a syndicate or have come via the informal underground railway, as it is known. These interior aliens are more likely to have a measurable community impact out of proportion to their numbers than are the thousands who rush the border areas nightly and are routinely sent back to Mexico. As far as St. Louis is generally concerned, the underground railway begins somewhere in Texas (usually Laredo or El Paso) and terminates in Chicago or Detroit.

St. Louis is a convenient stopover place for those who may have sufficient cultural skills to live in an area which does not have a major Latin barrio as does Chicago, where one can get along virtually without knowing English. St. Louis is also attractive for migrant agricultural laborers who are seasonally employed on vegetable farms and orchards both in Missouri and Illinois. Foundries and other heavy industries in the St. Louis area, plus the railroads, have been an important source of employment for illegal Mexican aliens. Many who do not find work in Chicago return (or are sent) to St. Louis.

The region has known its tragedies involving Mexican aliens but the scale of such happenings has never been great enough to attract such major public attention as is the case in Arizona. An example of problems involving the underground railway as it passed through the St. Louis area can be seen in August 1973. In that month a truck carrying a group of mojados crashed near Sikeston, Missouri, killing several of the aliens and seriously injuring a number of others. Witnesses reported that the men were being transported like cattle in the doomed vehicle. Newspaper accounts stated that on arrival either in St. Louis or Chicago these aliens were destined to pay exorbitant rates to landlords specializing in running safe houses and that the men could expect to receive poor wages by U.S. standards. The driver of the truck in the Sikeston crash was a Chicano from Orange Grove, Texas, who collected $50 a head in exchange for driving the wets to St. Louis and Chicago. The underground railway often requires drivers to make straight-through runs without sleep, and in the Sikeston crash the driver apparently lost control of his vehicle due to fatigue. He was charged with criminal violations of both U.S. and Missouri statutes.[49]

We asked the Mexican Consul in St. Louis, the Honorable Manuel Esparza, what his government was able to do for its nationals who fell into difficulties of the type described above. He stated in a personal interview that in the Sikeston case the Mexican Consulate sent lawyers to try to collect damages for the aliens who had been exploited.[50] He said his government is very concerned for the rights of aliens in the United States. My general impression from reviewing a number of hardship cases is that the Mexican Consulate in St. Louis makes a commendable effort to assist its citizens who enter the United States illegally and who fall victim to misfortune. This is not necessarily true of all Mexican consulates throughout the United States.

Of the 4,000 illegal aliens estimated to be residing in the greater St. Louis area, some 95 percent are probably Mexicans. In 1975 it was calculated that illegal aliens earned an average wage of $3.45 per hour in the area, but some wages went as low as $1.00 per hour and others as high as $11,000 per year.[51] Also it is not known how many illegal aliens receive welfare payments in St. Louis proper. Missouri state law does not require the checking of one's resident status as a condition for receiving welfare. In recent years INS-St. Louis has apprehended from 300 to 600 illegal aliens annually of all nationalities, but 95 percent of the total were Mexicans.

The officer in charge of INS-St. Louis since 1972 has been Michael J. Nolan. He told a reporter of the changes he had seen in the character traits of the Mexican aliens over his more than ten years of professional service: "Twenty years ago they were much more passive. Today there is open contempt and open defiance. The younger ones will test you. They say, 'I'll see you in two weeks!' and you do see them, walking down the street."[52] Nolan also commented that the illegals often got back to St. Louis before the detention officer who had accompanied them to the Mexican border. He estimated in 1976 that some 25 percent of those apprehended in St. Louis had been there before.[53]

In 1977 Nolan offered me this additional comment on the changing character of the illegal Mexican alien. He said:

> There is also another phenomenon that we have tracked over the years, and that is the type of alien, the Mexican male, we are apprehending is not making the mistake (I use that term loosely) of his father. In other words, he is remaining unmarried. He comes to St. Louis with relatively few family responsibilities and is spending a larger proportion of his earnings on consumer goods, so-called luxuries, than he actually sends back to his family in Mexico. Five to ten years ago the average Mexican we picked up normally had one small suitcase or a shopping bag filled with a few rudimentary articles of clothing. Among the young today we are increasingly finding stereo sets, television sets, digital watches, etc. . . . It appears that many Mexicans today are more sophisticated and recognize the pitfalls of a large family or of marrying at an early age.[54]

On the basis of data gathered over roughly two years we can say that the typical illegal Mexican alien in St. Louis is between 20 and 25 years of age and comes from the border state of Chihuahua or from the more distant state of Michoacán. In the latter case it is believed on the basis of existing literature,[55] and my interviews with old hands in the INS-Border Patrol, that since World War II patterns have been established whereby the people of certain regions, even villages, would form their own informal syndicates for placing people with given U.S. employers. The sending of people annually to these same employers became a family tradition in many cases. Thus we note from a statistical profile based on the I-213 forms that in the case of Michoacán a great number of illegals found working in St. Louis steel and foundry enterprises came from the village of El Llano in the *municipio* (roughly a county) of Samora and also from the municipio of Cherán.[56] Informants in the St. Louis area having personal knowledge of Michoacán stated that the family operations out of El Llano in particular were interrupted by the 1976–77 area control operations of INS-St. Louis and that many of the El Llano people began going to Waukeegan, Illinois, where they also enjoyed firm job placement contacts. Documentary evidence supports this deliberate change in established behavior patterns by the illegal Mexican aliens.[57]

With the exception of the border states, there seems to be a tendency for sizable numbers of illegals to come from some of the poorer states like Durango, Michoacán, and Zacatecas. A study by Weaver and Downing contends that between 1930 and 1971 some 73 percent of Mexican migration (legal and illegal) to the United States came from the states of Michoacán, Guanajuato, Jalisco, Nuevo León, San Luis Potosí, Chihuahua, Durango, and Zacatecas.[58] I am not entirely sure that St. Louis is the best arena for sampling the typical Mexican migrant according to state-by-state origin. I am more confident that St. Louis is likely to be typical of inland cities generally in terms of the overall spectrum of illegal Mexican alien input.

My inquiry in St. Louis found that illegal aliens may be employed to fill hazardous or unpleasant jobs which American citizens find unacceptable, and they may also be used to impede unionization of a given shop. Illegals are often considered a more stable work force vis-a-vis unpleasant working environments. At times they may serve to camouflage illegal activities on the part of a given employer. A potential combination of all these elements emerged from a specific operation that was carried out by INS-St. Louis during several months in 1976. It was the biggest such undertaking on record for that field office. The climax of the operation occurred during October when a search warrant was executed against an automobile shredding and metal recycling plant in the East St. Louis, Illinois, area.

Investigators Gerald Jacobson and David Gross of INS-St. Louis were able to locate several former employees of the metal shredding firm who testified that numerous foreign workers who spoke only Spanish were employed at the establishment in question. They also found another informant who testified that on several nights after the gates were locked (during 1976) new automobiles without license plates drove up to the front gate of the same auto shredding and metal recycling company. The informant said the drivers of the cars were instructed by the foreman to drive them inside the gate. The gas tanks and tires were immediately removed from the vehicles and put off to one side. Then a crane was used to pick up these new cars and put them into the shredder, and of course the cars were completely destroyed beyond any recognition. The informant believed that this was not the only occasion on which such a practice was carried out, but he said this was the only time he had personally seen it.

The testimony of this informant led the INS investigators to suspect that the recycling operation might be involved in the disposition of stolen cars, cars that had been used for criminal purposes, or perhaps for committing insurance fraud. For that reason it was decided to bring other law-enforcement agencies, including the FBI, the Internal Revenue Service, and the Illinois State Police, into the investigation. It was suspected that using fearful illegal Mexican aliens to work in a crime-related plant might be a silence-buying device to reduce the chances of employees reporting illegal or otherwise suspicious activity (like the deliberate destruction of new cars).

Ultimately a number of Mexican aliens were apprehended at this East St. Louis plant and all confessed their illegal status in the United States. This evidence is contained on separate pages that are in the INS-St. Louis file which I cite here as STL 50/37.

One of these confessions is highly revealing. It is included here because it illustrates clearly how the given company used illegal Mexican aliens to its advantage. The questions, in Spanish, are being asked by investigator Gerald Jacobson with the name of the respondent omitted here:

Q. Of what country are you a native and citizen?
A. Mexico.
Q. When and through where did you last enter into the United States?
A. I first went to Los Angeles by car, and then to Chicago by airplane, and then to Fairmont City, Illinois, by bus.
Q. When and where were you born?
A. I was born March 15, 1951, at Rancho Medianega which is near Jalostotitlán, Jalisco, Mexico.
Q. Have you or any members of your family ever been admitted to the United States for lawful permanent residence?
A. No.
Q. Have you ever entered the United States before this time?
A. I entered the Unites States illegally in July 1975 by jumping the line.
Q. Did you pay anyone to smuggle you into the United States?
A. Yes, I paid a person in Tijuana $200 to take me across the border to Los Angeles.
Q. How did you obtain employment after arrival in the United States?
A. In Mexico, Antonio Romo told me that he had worked at this company before. He told me that I could go with him there to get a job.
Q. Did you prepare any type of an application at the company to obtain a job?
A. Yes.
Q. Who did you talk with at this auto shredding company about obtaining a job?
A. Nicolás.
Q. Did you show Nicolás a Social Security card when he employed you?
A. No, Nicolás wrote a number down and told me that I would be working under the name Leon Ramirez.
Q. Do you have or did you ever have a Social Security card?
A. No.
Q. Do you think that Nicolás knows that you are illegally in the United States?
A. I think so.
Q. Did you run to hide yesterday when the "Immigration" arrived?
A. Yes.
Q. Who told you to run?
A. No one in particular, but everyone started yelling that Immigration was coming.

He then signed a statement to the effect that his was true testimony, that he was not forced to sign the statement but that he did it voluntarily, and that the statement was translated to him in Spanish accurately before he signed it. Other apprehended Mexicans gave similar confessions. All were apprehended in the one section of the whole plant which had never been unionized—the wets had served their purpose.

A "FORTRESS AMERICA" AGAINST MEXICAN ALIENS?

There may not be much point in trying to divide the blame between the United States and Mexico on the illegal aliens question, although some of it can be divided. On this side the Congress is to blame for not providing a set of immigration laws with teeth that will enable rapid and just punishment of immigration violators. This means both the aliens who are flagrant repeat violators and unscrupulous U.S. employers who deliberately exploit aliens. On the Mexican side the governmental corruption is so horrendous, respect for human rights so low, and poverty so severe that the exodus will not be stopped without radical, perhaps revolutionary, action.

Mexican governments are guilty of using the United States as an escape valve for a population problem they are unwilling to solve. North American employers are guilty of taking advantage, indeed of capitalizing whole industries, on the presumed availability of cheap, desperate, illegal Mexican labor. Much U.S. prosperity is founded upon the continued misery of Mexican citizens. This point was dramatized by an encounter which is reliably said to have happened to Leonel Castillo, President Carter's new choice as commissioner of INS. Castillo, a Mexican-American with impressive political credentials, was approached at a Houston cocktail party by a drunken Texas construction firm executive. The conversation went as follows: " 'You get me some Mescans, you hear?' the construction man said in a slur of words and thoughts. 'Real Mescans! I don't want no Chicanos or blacks or white trash. I want Mescans!' "[59]

Such Anglos as the speaker above are surely to blame. There are also some Chicanos who should be blamed, for assuming that any criticism of Mexico or effort to halt the illegal migration is a slur against their perceived ethnicity.[60] The Mexican-American community in the United States probably stands to lose more than any other group by the continued influx of illegals. Stopping it is just good social and economic sense, not racism.

Ultimately, we may have to shut off the border to Mexican aliens. That would be morally repugnant to almost everyone and would be an unfortunate last resort. In contrast, and at the far opposite of the spectrum, is the proposal that we open the border completely and abolish all immigration laws. That might work if we could also abolish or absorb the Mexican political system.

We can't. We had the chance to do that in the war of conquest against Mexico which ended with the Treaty of 1848. That was our opportunity to absorb Mexico. It is utopian to speak of it today, unless of course Mexico just becomes totally bankrupt and asks to be absorbed (and some speculators have entertained that possibility as well). Most of the various intermediate proposals for a Mexican "Marshall Plan" overlook the sorry record of failure compiled by the Alliance for Progress.[61] Feeding money into a corrupt political system does not bring about development or social justice.

The United States clearly has a vested interest in not dislocating the economy of Mexico and in avoiding social upheaval there (although Mexico's internal political corruption is likely to produce that anyway). It is an economic fact that Mexico buys billions of dollars more from us than we buy from them. Also, every job that is created in Mexico is potentially one less Mexican jumping the line in the Arizona desert (potentially, providing the employment conditions in Mexico are humane and the wages not those of starvation).

A trade agreement signed in December 1977 with Mexico was intended to reduce U.S. tariff barriers against some Mexican goods and stimulate the Mexican economy. Considerable discussion has been devoted to helping Mexico create labor-intensive industries. President López Portillo has, in fact, criticized the United States for its quota embargo against Mexican-made shoes, a product that is of good quality and can be exported successfully into the United States.[62] The Mexican shoe industry could be expanded and made labor-intensive. But when the debate gets seriously to the point of suggesting that a genuinely independent Mexican economy be created, there is relative silence from both North American business and labor. A truly strong Mexican economy is seen in those sectors as just as much of a threat as the illegal migration is viewed elsewhere.

American business is in an especially anomalous, almost bizarre, position in fearing economic growth, yet pretending to contribute to it via the twin-plants border industries and through direct investments in Mexico, and at the same time capitalizing itself partially on the continued availability of people who will work cheap because they are desperate. And U.S. labor groups adopt an untenable position by arguing that U.S. citizens are being displaced by aliens when the labor unions have been unable, or unwilling, to force employers to make those jobs in question attractive enough so that Americans will take them. There is, of course, the likelihood that many jobs simply cannot be made acceptable to Americans, as long as the welfare and unemployment compensation alternative exists.

Turning to the Mexican side of the coin, a perceptive American journalist elicited the comment from a Mexican executive for Volkswagen that political and economic collapse were inevitable. He commented wryly that perhaps former president Luis Echeverría had the right idea: "We mortgage the country to American banks and then default. Then you take us over. That will be the only solution for Mexico."[63] The same reporter was given testimony that is believed typical concerning Mexican attitudes toward remaining in their country versus illegal migration to the United States. A young man in La Manzanilla said that all of the men on his street went to work illegally in California where the average laborer could hope to earn $750 dollars a month, just about what it would take him a whole year to earn by staying in Mexico. These respondents said that they and everyone else would go to California if given the chance: "We would all go . . . all of us. There is nothing for us in Mexico."[64] The reporter also found a certain skepticism on the part of Mexicans about the alleged sufferings of the American Chicanos, "whose difficulties millions of Mexicans would give anything to have."[65] It is clear that the Mexicans would also give anything to take those Chicanos' jobs as well.

The absence of a clearly defined policy on Mexican illegal immigration is demoralizing to the INS and the Border Patrol as evidenced by a letter to President Carter that was published in a national news magazine, written by a concerned Border Patrol officer.[66] But there are also those who offer such utopian counsel as "let the aliens in," the title of a contemporary article in another magazine.[67] That particular writer went so far as to claim that "instead of aliens being a burden to the rest of us, it's the rest of us who are a burden to the aliens."[68] Citing various studies where jobs in California were vacated by illegal aliens and could not be filled by American citizens, this article charges unrealistically to INS the responsibility for job placement of citizens and ignores the responsibility or refusal of employers to make jobs sufficiently attractive so that Americans will take them. Keeping jobs miserable is a ready justification for exploiting the already poor Mexicans who, in relative terms, see themselves better off taking a miserable job on the U.S. side.

Adding to the overall complexity of the issue is the inevitable tendency in some sectors to relate illegal Mexicans in the United States to the problem of Americans who behave illegally (or enter illegally) in Mexico. Manuel Esparza, the Mexican consul in St. Louis, told us that most Americans go to his country as law-abiding tourists or to retire and they are most welcome. He also said that there are other Americans who enter Mexico illegally to escape justice on this side of the border or who go to seek drugs. Esparza showed a picture from Mexico of some badly dressed American hippies, calling them marijuanos and compared them unfavorably to the Mexican illegals who come north looking for work. He argued that American movies have tended to make Mexico look like a "paradise for criminals," and he added that U.S. citizens who go to Mexico illegally are almost always moral criminals, whereas the Mexican aliens were not—they are not law-breakers in his view, they are simply workers without papers.[69]

The Mexican consul's view is not completely at odds with that of the man responsible for enforcing immigration laws in St. Louis. In response to an opinion we put forth, Officer-in-Charge Michael J. Nolan told us, "You're right when you say that a solid answer is a modified Bracero Program. We too are finding that many, many of the illegals that we apprehend and process in this office would be very happy to work part time in the U.S. and then return to their own homes . . . regardless of the squalor, and maybe a more sophisticated and younger Mexican national today would prefer a long-term residence in the U.S."[70] Such a Bracero Program, administered via U.S. consulates and beyond the bite of Mexican corruption, is a partial solution, but it can be the basis on which diplomatic efforts can be mounted to force internal change in Mexico without disrupting its economy and political life radically. The alternative may be "Fortress America," followed by internal upheaval in Mexico, and probably a Castro-type solution fashioned behind a "cactus curtain" (and in all candor, this could be materially desirable from the point of view of most Mexicans if the Cuban experiment were to be replicated in Mexico).

Finally, those who would "let all the aliens in" should consider that in certain parts of the United States (specifically in southern Texas) this country has not done a very good job of integrating, with dignity, the Hispanic population we now have and to encourage more is likely to aggravate existing resentments. Witness this comment by a Chicano boy in Texas who had to deliver milk to an all-Anglo school:

> While I was putting the cases away, and carrying out the empty bottles, and waiting for the principal to sign his name, I'd hear the teachers talking. They said they'd hate to teach us Mexicans, because we are inferior and it is a waste of time. I wanted to go punch them all in the face . . . I dream of revenge, but that will never happen.[71]

But this boy may have revenge from an unexpected source, and it could be a Pyrrhic victory for all concerned. A Mexican commentator writing on the front page of one of Mexico's controlled press organs, or official newspapers, described the population situation on his side of the border as a time bomb which could go off at any moment.[72] This, he argued, was because the attraction of workers to the border in search of the myth (or reality) of opportunity on the other side had created an intolerable situation of pressure on Mexico's urban border areas which those municipal governments are not equipped to contend with. He noted the seriousness of Mexico's prostitution and drug problem and quoted Feliciano Calzada Padrón, a PRI official, as to the gravity of the cultural incompatibility (he called it cultural rejection) the illegals experience on the U.S. side. This supports the lesson of the above quotation about teaching children of Mexican descent.

But it is significant that this journalist, using the front page of the Mexican establishment press, also admitted that there were crooks *(enganchadores)* on both sides and that the ultimate losers were the illegal migrants. Via this article, PRI spokesmen called openly for a new treaty with the United States to provide a legal and regularized coming and going of Mexican laborers as they are needed and with safeguards for human rights. Clearly, to effect such a solution will require radical changes in value-behavior patterns on both sides of the border—before the time bomb explodes.

NOTES

1. I am aware of the semantic controversy surrounding use of the expression "illegal aliens." Some Hispanic groups object to the term as a slur on their ethnicity and national origin. No such offense is intended here. But any Mexican citizen who jumps the fence in the Arizona desert without proper inspection and documents is an illegal alien. Using the expression "undocumented workers" is merely a word game. Many of the illegals are, in point of fact, not undocumented but carry documents proving them to be illegal Mexican aliens.

2. Letter from Eric Sevareid to Kenneth F. Johnson, July 24, 1974, giving permission to reprint this commentary.

3. Such a profile is included in Kenneth F. Johnson and Nina M. Ogle, *Mexico's Silent Invasion,* a report to the INS and the U.S. Congress on border problems and illegal migration. See especially Chapter 5 of that report for the statistical profile done in the St. Louis area.

4. As quoted in Arizona *Daily Star,* January 17, 1977.

5. Julian Samora, *Los Mojados: The Wetback Story* (Notre Dame, Ind.: University of Notre Dame Press, 1971), p. 4.

6. The tendency for Mexico to become an increasingly poor nation in both relative and absolute senses is set forth by Roger Hansen in *The Politics of Mexican Development* (Baltimore: Johns Hopkins University Press, 1971), pp. 71 and 87–88.

7. For the first time in 22 years the Mexican government began a series of devaluations of the peso approaching 60 percent starting in August 1976. The peso was allowed to float and seek out its free market value.

8. For a view of socioeconomic problems elsewhere on the border, see John A. Price, *Tijuana: Urbanization in a Border Culture* (Notre Dame, Ind.: University of Notre Dame Press, 1973).

9. *Newsweek,* March 11, 1946.

10. *Newsweek,* October 25, 1948.

11. *Nation,* May 5, 1951.

12. Ibid.

13. Samora, op. cit., p. 46.

14. Ibid.

15. *Newsweek,* September 1, 1952.

16. *Newsweek,* May 25, 1953.

17. Ibid.

18. *Business Week,* February 1, 1972.

19. Ibid.

20. Ibid.

21. The visitor's pass (I-186 card) is given to Mexicans who reside in their part of the immediate border area (subject to approval) and allows them to cross the border into the adjoining part of the United States for shopping and social purposes, but not for working. The resident alien card (I-151 green card) is given to those who have regularized their status for work or immigrant purposes and to those aliens who are married to U.S. citizens. Mexicans with visitor's passes often violate the terms of this document and work on the American side of the border, thereafter returning to their Mexican homes at night, but others simply melt into the interior of the United States looking for work. They, in turn, often mail back their I-186 cards to a friend with similar

looks who will try to use it in a crossing. Holders of I-151 cards may lawfully work in the United States, but many of them also lend these cards to help others enter illegally. Counterfeiting rings in Mexico fabricate a range of documents to help illegals migrate north.

22. *U.S. News and World Report,* July 23, 1973.

23. Ibid.

24. *U.S. News and World Report,* December 13, 1976.

25. Another collateral law (P.S. 94-484, October 12, 1976) applied severe restrictions to the entry of aliens in the medical profession, excepting those who are entering programs of study with the intent of returning to their native countries. This law has been referred to sardonically as the American Medical Association's Protective Bill. It was passed under AMA pressures to halt the rapid increase in medical doctors immigrating legally to the United States under Department of Labor certification that a scarcity of doctors existed.

26. See the Domestic Council Committee on Illegal Aliens *Report* issued by the Department of Justice, December 1976. See also John Kendall's series of articles beginning January 9 in the Los Angeles *Times.*

27. Kendall, op. cit.

28. Ibid.

29. Ibid.

30. Ibid. There are those who argue that the illegals pay more than their share of taxes; but that judgment must be weighed against the total additional costs of any kind they cause for society. That total is still an enigma, but the figure is certain to be high.

31. City of Los Angeles Police Department, *The Illegal Alien Problem and Its Impact on Los Angeles Police Department Resources* (Staff Briefing Paper), January 1977.

32. The Border Patrol has sometimes been victimized with complaints of brutality when these acts were, in fact, committed by U.S. civilians. On September 1, 1976, Congressman Augustus Hawkins of California wrote to Commissioner Chapman alleging that such human rights viclations had occurred. It was learned that the Mexican aliens who had been tortured were victims of U.S. civilians and of Mexican authorities, not the Border Patrol.

33. Late in 1977 two anglos accused of torturing Mexican aliens were acquitted by a Bisbee, Arizona, jury. None of the jury members were of Mexican descent, despite the large Chicano population of Cochise County where the trial occurred.

34. In September 1976, President Echeverría made a public issue of the treatment of Mexican wetbacks in the United States by including an oblique reference to this in his State of the Nation speech.

35. San Diego County, *Report on Mexican Migration* (Report of the San Diego County Immigration Council), December 1975, pp. 114–24.

36. Edmund Villaseñor, *Macho* (New York: Bantam Books, 1973), p. 81.

37. Arizona *Daily Star,* January 8, 1977.

38. Arizona *Daily Star,* February 14, 1977.

39. Ibid.

40. San Diego County, op. cit., p. 69.

41. My general impression from talking with public administrators, be they in the health field or some other, is that there is a widespread reluctance to disclose (or even ask for) information as to an individual's alien status. This is probably a reflection of the ingrained American "melting pot" social ethic which has been the underlying factor in our past immigration policy (with occasional xenophobic exceptions, for example, orientals in California during World War II).

42. As cited in *Proceso,* February 12, 1977, p. 10.

43. See Everett R. Holles's article in Denver *Post,* March 30, 1977.

44. The issue over the twin plants border industries (maquiladoras) is that U.S. materials are often assembled on the Mexican side using cheap labor and under special tariff strictures. This was developed during the late 1960s following the suspension of the Bracero Treaty in an effort

to provide some new sources of employment for Mexicans. Evidence is that the maquiladoras have attracted more people than they can absorb and many of the displaced engage in vice activities including international smuggling and illegal migration. It is also known that some American firms have displaced U.S. citizen workers and moved plants to the Mexican border to take advantage of the cheap labor, thereby leaving resentment on the U.S. side. See Lawrence E. Koslow and Rodney R. Jones, "The Mexican-American Border Industrialization Program," *Public Affairs Bulletin* (Arizona State University, Institute of Public Administration) 9, no. 2 (1970). Mexican doctors reported during 1977 a high incidence of mental disease and emotional problems associated with working in the maquiladoras, many of which have a bad reputation for abusing workers (*El Imparcial,* February 18, 1977).

45. Arizona *Republic,* April 22, 1977.
46. Ibid.
47. Ibid.
48. The following is taken from the Investigative Reporters and Editors, Inc. Report, which ran in series for 23 consecutive days ending April 4, 1977, in the Arizona *Daily Star* and was carried by numerous newspapers in other parts of the country. Its general focus was vice and corruption in Arizona and on the Mexican border. The following is reprinted with permission from Arizona *Daily Star,* March 20, 1977.

A mammoth Arizona citrus farm partly owned by the brother of Senator Barry Goldwater has profited for more than a decade from the sweat of illegal Mexican aliens who have been paid meager wages and forced to live in unhealthy conditions.

Members of an Investigative Reporters and Editors (IRE) team who ignored the menace of a gun-toting guard at Arrowhead Ranch, northwest of Phoenix, discovered that aliens there

Paid $100 or more a head to "coyotes" (alien smugglers), one of whom callously left a boy with an injured leg in the desert to face 120-degree heat with only a gallon of water and a bit of marijuana.

Lived amid their own excrement and garbage in orange-crate shelters and fly-infested camps shielded from curious eyes by black plastic sheets hung on trees.

Worked from dawn to dusk for as little as $5 a day, a pittance bled down by Social Security deductions and food prices they say were inflated by their overseers.

Robert Goldwater is president of Goldmar (Arrowhead Ranch) and serves on its board of directors. There is no question that the Senator (Barry Goldwater) is aware that his brother hires aliens. It is legal to hire such aliens, though it is illegal to knowingly harbor them (illegals).

49. Taken from the Saint Louis *Post-Dispatch,* August 5, 1973.
50. Interview by Nina M. Ogle, July 15, 1977. Officials of the Mexican Consulate were provided with a transcript of this interview and asked if they wished to make corrections. At the time of this writing no response had been received. We have thanked Mr. Esparza for his courteous attention and cooperation.
51. Based upon a series of articles done by Marsha Venuti for the Northwest County *Journal,* especially May 26, 1976.
52. Ibid., June 2, 1976.
53. Ibid. This is a notable figure when compared with similar estimates for Arizona. The numbers of ill-fated and desperate (often very young) Mexicans who rush the border at night repeatedly (and with multiple arrests) made Arizona officials reluctant to venture estimates—this is understandable and is, once again, part of the problem one encounters in trying to research an illegal population.

54. From a statement taped specifically for this writer by Michael J. Nolan on June 29, 1977 (transcript on file).

55. See Thomas Weaver and Theodore Downing, eds., *Mexican Migration* (Tucson, University of Arizona Press, 1976).

56. A discussion of this migratory phenomenon is found in Chapter 5 of Johnson and Ogle, op. cit.

57. The bulk of the evidence in this case consists of letters from home, or about to be sent home, in the possession of apprehended Mexican aliens.

58. Weaver and Downing, op. cit.

59. From James Flanigan, "North of the Border–Who Needs whom?" *Forbes,* April 15, 1977, p. 37.

60. In reply to an article published in the Arizona *Daily Star* on May 15, 1977 (which focused on Mexican corruption as a part of the explanation for so many Mexicans wanting to leave their country), a dean at the University of Arizona wrote an article which ignored most of the argument in question but seemed to be expressing wounded pride under the presumption that Mexicans in general had been criticized (when, in fact, only the Mexican government had been attacked). The article by Adolfo Quezada appeared in the Arizona *Daily Star,* May 31, 1977.

61. See, for instance, Jerome Levinson and Juan de Onís, *The Alliance That Lost Its Way* (Chicago, Quadrangle Books, 1970).

62. Flanigan, op. cit., p. 41.

63. Gene Lyons, "Inside the Volcano," *Harpers,* June 1977, p. 54.

64. Ibid., p. 52.

65. Ibid., p. 45.

66. Frank C. Dupuy, "No Support From Washington," *U.S. News & World Report,* April 25, 1977, pp. 36–37.

67. Stephen Chapman, "Let the Aliens In," *Washington Monthly,* July/August 1977. Other lenient views on handling the alien problem have been given to Congress by Wayne Cornelius of the Massachusetts Institute of Technology. His study and evidence, based on interviews in Mexico with so-called illegals or ex-illegals raises questions as to the reliability of the results given the atmosphere in which the research was conducted. Cornelius stated: "There is ... no direct evidence of displacement of native Americans by illegal Mexican workers, at least in those sectors of the job market where the Mexicans typically seek employment." From the *Congressional Record —House,* H 7061-68 (July 13, 1977) and H 7064. My study in St. Louis tends to contradict Cornelius's view. In fact, only a matter of weeks after the raid on the auto shredding company, U.S. citizens (who had been hired to replace the illegals who were apprehended and sent back to Mexico) were complaining that they had been dismissed without cause and that the "shop was once again being filled with Spanish-speaking wetbacks." The latter is based upon confidential interviews with affected persons who plan to take legal action in the matter.

68. Ibid., p. 43.

69. Interview by Nina M. Ogle, July 15, 1977.

70. Taped comments by Michael J. Nolan, June 29, 1977.

71. Robert Coles, "Our Hands Belong to the Valley," *Atlantic Monthly,* March 1975, p. 78.

72. Jesus Saldaña H., writing in *El Heraldo de México,* July 30, 1977. Fortunately, I received for the revised edition of this book several valuable suggestions from General Leonard Chapman, Jr., former commissioner of INS. He points out that in addition to the projected growth of the overall Mexican population by the year 2000 it will be critical to consider the ratio of growth in Mexico's available labor force vis a vis the total population. He also cautions as to the potential impact of the growth within the United States of an alienated and extralegal subculture, not just of Mexican nationals, but of illegal aliens of many nationalities. This phenomenon poses a real policy issue for the near future having ramifications ranging from public health to law enforcement to economic security.

Nine

On Mexico's Political Future: Alternative Views of a Psychological Impasse

Optimistic prognoses of Mexico's political future still emanate from the pens of some North American academics and journalists.[1] What is significant in much of this literature is that, try as the authors might to the contrary, the impolite term "corruption" inescapably creeps in. Corruption is at the heart of Mexico's political dilemma, its psychological impasse. Perhaps, then, the best way to conclude this work is to consider some of the alternative views of the Mexican dilemma which have emerged in recent years.

One study of the government staple-goods-distributing agency CONASUPO (touched on in Chapter 5) treats the efficacy of this program which is intended to alleviate both rural and urban material penury. Despite a heavy research dependency upon officialdom, the author recognizes that a series of corrupt intermediaries have acted to rob the small Mexican farmers of the benefits which CONASUPO was intended to give them.[2] The study describes the politicking within the bureaucracy which eats up valuable time and dilutes the impact of new policy formulations, if and when they materialize. The study reveals how bureaucrats running a grain subsidy program tried to hide their own corruption and failure by pretending to the farmers that all would be remedied with the coming of a new sexenio. Just how the victimized farmers were supposed to feed their families in the interim is not clear (perhaps they were expected to become wetbacks), but the author tries to soften the blow of what has been said by assuring the reader that the personalized corruption of Mexico is not like the widespread spoils systems that existed during the nineteenth century in the United States. It is argued that such a comparison is spurious because Mexico is not a two-party system and thus there is no "large, organized, and committed movement for reform of its operations."[3]

Of course there is no such movement for reform when, in the words of another writer, the regime treats bona fide opposition groups as if they were enemy nations.[4] And merely citing the absence of an effectively organized opposition (without mentioning the baneful role of electoral fraud and official terrorism) is not ipso facto to demonstrate that there is no opposition nor that the bulk of the people like the regime. My observations and testimony over the years lead to the inescapable conclusion that Mexicans are enormously unhappy with their political system, while still maintaining some residual loyalty toward Mexico as a social system. The phenomenon of illegal migration, and the testimony of many migrants as to perceptions of their government versus their social choice of residence, supports this conclusion.

Often the tie-in between a corrupt political system and popular alienation is lost through verbiage. Simply applying esoteric jargon—"the Mexican political system . . . is . . . a corporate and authoritarian regime, dominated by a party-bureaucratic apparatus and pervaded by extensive clientelist relationships among the population and the political elite"—[5] will not change the fact that around 40 percent of Mexico's available work force is unemployed and that rather than rely upon CONASUPO bureaucrats, some 10 percent of Mexico's population prefer to migrate illegally to the United States (and probably 50 percent would try to do so if they had the chance). It is hard, therefore, for me to agree with optimistic prognoses of Mexico's future based upon the belief, no matter how sincerely held, that the Mexican political system, partly because of its authoritarianism, has the inherent flexibility to meet and solve a wide variety of crises and demands. This I would relegate to the province of doubt.

Constructive, loyal political opposition simply has not been institutionalized in contemporary Mexico. Thus the nation is denied the potential benefits of change which might result from the existence of a truly opposition political sector, one which could distinguish itself within the body politic by forcing the system to generate and accept concrete reforms. This point emerges from another study done of the decision by the Mexican government during 1963 to implement the profit-sharing provisions of the constitution. The author of that study concludes essentially that the profit-sharing decision was designed to perpetuate the existing political system, not to threaten seriously the balance of collaboration between PRI's labor sector and major sectors of Mexican business and industry, but still give the impression that a major step forward had been taken toward bringing the revolutionary principles of 1917 to fruition.[6] The author lists as factors which account for the decision the fact that President López Mateos was a former labor minister, the pressure of the example of the Cuban revolution, and the president's desire to carve a revolutionary image for himself. Of course it is also true that the same president had put down labor protests in 1958 and 1959 using methods which smacked more of the Porfirian dictatorship, hence he had the need to improve a tarnished image.

As the foregoing pages have demonstrated, especially those dealing with poverty, it is no surprise to note that the profit-sharing decision of 1963 has benefited few if any poor Mexicans. Nonetheless, it may have helped to keep the system from falling apart. What is most striking about this case, however, is the relationship the decision had to forces from the principal opposition party PAN. It was PAN that seems to have made an issue out of profit sharing during its 1960 national convention by pledging to implement the existing provisions of Article 123 of the Constitution of 1917. The PAN, of course, was not allowed to take the initiative in congress and the study cited above acknowledges that any such congressional move by the PAN would have been defeated.[7] The PRI was not then mature enough to allow its principal opposition to be the originator of legislation implementing the existing constitution.

The author cites a PAN campaign poster used in 1964, the year after the profit-sharing decision was taken, to the effect that the regime had moved thanks to pressure from the PAN. But the author then adds that the PAN's demand for profit sharing cannot be *the* cause of López Mateos's action, yet admits at the same time that López Mateos could not postpone the decision indefinitely since the PAN had drawn public attention to the fact that a key provision of the constitution having broad popular implications had not yet been implemented.[8] This is precisely what the novelist Carlos Chavira Becerra, the former PAN deputy cited earlier, had said in stressing that if a good idea came out of the opposition it would be tabled for a decent amount of time and then embraced as the PRI's own.[9] The problem lies in that when the "good idea" finally does get embraced by the PRI it may have been distorted or watered down to the point that its social impact will be nil. Thus the author of the decision-making study concludes: "The government was the primary beneficiary of the profit-sharing decision."[10] Corruption, the deliberate confusing of public and private goods and goals, entered in here; the government benefited, not the needy public. Thus it is that the psychological impasse of political alienation in Mexico intensifies.

Here a special caveat is in order as a matter of fairness. It is not that I wish to disparage other analysts of Mexican politics. Surely those cited herein have made contributions in their own chosen way and have done it sincerely. Yet I am unable to forget that much jargon of the social sciences seems to become a verbal mold into which empirical reflections about political life must be fitted. So rather than say bluntly that we are confronted with massive bureaucratic corruption in which thousands of peasants are robbed of their income, we talk instead about the diseconomies of clientelist politics. Instead of admitting straight away that the government itself is the principal beneficiary of most decisions that are publicly lauded as great revolutionary policy advances, the whole thing must be cast in the more respectable and rigorous vocabulary of systems analysis. This often carries with it the implicit bias that what "is" is therefore the natural and hence the correct state of things to be and to come. One who has worked personally and directly in Mexico's phenomenal world may become skeptical of social science qua science as a general epistemological position from which to work. It has even been speculated that the concept of ideology might be more useful in some analytic situations than the concept of science.[11] This may ultimately prove to be the case in the study of Mexican political alienation.

Without casting an oar further into those troubled semantic waters it is possible to talk of the evidence which Mexican thinkers themselves have put down on paper and which reflects on Mexico's political psychology and alternative futures. In this book, as in some previous works, I have leaned heavily on the humanistic side of the evidence-writing process for political insight. The distinguished novelist Luis Spota wrote two recent novels about the Mexican political process. His works *Palabras mayores* (1975) and *Sobre la marcha* (1976) depict the ethical basis of political life within an authoritarian single-party system which is suffering internal decay. He mixes in sex, and sexual perversion, in ways that have political relevance. One of these mixtures occurs when the tapado ritual is about to be performed in the process for selecting a new president. Among the contenders is the brilliant and popular tourist minister Marat Zabala. He is deliberately smeared by a competing camarilla which circulates a spurious document alleging that Zabala committed a homosexual act when he was 16 years old and had communicated venereal disease to his victim in the process.[12] The fabrication of a reckless novelist you are tempted to say! But is this not almost identical to what happened in real life to the rector of the University of Sonora as a device for breaking student resistance to the PRI's electoral fraud during 1967 (see Chapter 7)? In that case the PRI actually committed the political-sexual atrocity so as to film the act and use this to destroy one of its critics. Yet the infighting depicted by novelist Luis Spota becomes even more vile. Another presidential candidate, Avila Puig, receives a cassette tape containing excerpts from private conversations he had held during the previous three years, thereby demonstrating that his lines were tapped by his competitors during all that time. More fabrication you say! But on the front page of the June 20, 1977, edition of the critical review *Proceso* appears a story of officially sponsored espionage by wiretap. Inside is a list of wiretap victims ranging from opposition political figures to wealthy executives and people within the government itself. No novelist invented this one. Watergate conditions are the order of the day in Mexico. Thus, as Luis Spota put it, one can destroy or at least damage a political actor by depicting him "as a sodomist in a country where the male cult of machismo is a permanent rule."[13]

Herein lies a curious anomaly, and a potentially significant one. If manliness or machismo is a permanent cult in Mexico as so many authors have suggested, then why would trickery, deceit, and treason be standard political skills? Surely the more macho thing to do would be to confront one's competitors and defeat them on the battleground of skill, wit, and merit. This would not include surreptitious combat, Watergate skills, passing out spurious handbills or faking damaging photographs and films. True machismo would also mean the PRI defeating the PAN via an honest electoral process, rather than by resorting to ballot fraud. If one looks at it carefully, the central Mexican political ethic may not be machismo but rather the vengeful enanismo which Oscar Monroy Rivera said it was. Enanismo, dwarfishness, is synonymous with cowardly weakness. The ethic says repress at Tlatelolco, don't negotiate. Negotiation is feminine behavior. Here we are again at a psychological impasse. And many deaths plus bitter alienation result.

Evidence of disorder in the Mexican political character may be seen in the treatment many North Americans have received at the hands of Mexican officialdom. It will be remembered that at the close of 1977 an agreement was reached between the United States and Mexico for exchange of prisoners. This was the culmination of efforts by a few American journalists, fewer U.S. congressmen, and quite a few distressed American families. One of the most vigorous efforts to expose the abuse of human rights of American prisoners in Mexico was made by the Arizona journalist Bill Waters. A special report which he published in 1975 cited State Department ineptness and lack of concern for the plight of U.S. citizens in Mexican prisons who had been tortured, forced to sign bogus confessions, extorted, and denied the basic rights granted to them under the United Nations Universal Declaration of Human Rights to which Mexico is a signatory.[14]

Quoting congressional sources, Waters's revelations included the probability that the U.S. Drug Enforcement Agency had given Mexican police the notion that confessions should be beaten out of suspected smugglers as a partial way of stopping the northward flow of drugs. The State Department, it seemed as of 1975, was not concerned with prevailing international law precluding such atrocities. With the release of the first Americans and their press conferences in San Diego during December 1977, it was clear that the human rights which should have been guaranteed under existing international law were grossly violated in Mexico.[15] Is this, then, not more evidence of inherent weakness in the Mexican political character? Mexican wetbacks in the United States, even those who are accused of crimes, have the right to legal counsel and the right *not* to be tortured. Americans accused of nearly anything in Mexico are given electric shock treatments, or otherwise threatened, and denied interpreters when such are needed, until confessions are signed.[16]

The Mexican political character is reflected in presidential acts. Since the Mexican president is supposed to be the tlatoani, the modern counterpart of the ancient Aztec sacrificial priest, it is fitting to ask how macho he really is in dealing with the cross pressures which come to bear upon him. Does he take strong, decisive, manly action and face the consequences squarely? As of this writing it is probably unfair to make a judgment in this respect on President López Portillo, who is in the early years of his sexenio. But we can judge his predecessor, especially in terms of one of his last acts while in office. This involves land for food production. Land tenancy is one of the most critical of

Mexico's problems and it will continue to be during the decade of the 1980s. The way President Echeverría chose to handle a land distribution case as his term came to an end reflects both on his political psychology and on the land problem itself.

On November 19, 1977 (days before Luis Echeverría's sexenio was to end), the president expropriated by decree some 250,000 acres of fertile land in Sonora and granted it to a throng of approximately 8,000 peasants. In so doing Echeverría sidestepped an order by his nation's Supreme Court interpreting the constitutional provisions on land tenancy in favor of some 600 large landowners. The dilemma to be resolved centered on the legal stricture that any one person was limited to owning 250 acres of irrigated land in Mexico. The property owners had traditionally interpreted "persons" to mean individual members of large families, thus laying a basis for vast landholdings by a single family. Echeverría, bowing to pressures from within his party's own agrarian sector (and no doubt seeking to carve for himself a final niche in Mexican revolutionary history along with Cárdenas), decided that families were single persons and therefore anything in excess of 250 acres per family could be expropriated.

The Sonora conflict became bloody at times. Celestino Salcedo, leader of the PRI's agrarian sector, came under attack by landowners about the country. Land invasions occurred in other states. Especially sensitive was the situation in Sinaloa, Sonora's southern neighbor (these two states constitute something of a Mexican breadbasket in and of themselves).[17] Evidence was published to the effect that thousands of peasants from the poorer states of Durango, Zacatecas, and Michoacán, easily identifiable by their use of huaraches in place of shoes, were being trucked into Sonora and Sinaloa.[18] It is these same poorer states which, not coincidentally, contribute most of the illegal Mexican aliens who come to the United States looking for work. Moving them en masse into the northern states without guaranteed employment probably added more pressure to an already difficult border situation.

It was clear that López Portillo was to inherit a hot potato as it were. He could not repudiate his predecessor by annulling the land expropriation decrees. Ultimately López Portillo arranged to pay off most of the disgruntled Sonora farmers who then proceeded to try to buy back (or extort back) their lost properties. But there was an even greater national issue here. How could the small farms turned over haphazardly to peasants be made economical so as to feed Mexico and still gain foreign exchange? That issue will yet have to be resolved by the López Portillo administration. And it is not this writer's intention to ignore the existence of great injustice in the land tenure patterns that were prevalent, and still are, in Sonora and Sinaloa. These are other facets of a desperate crisis facing a country whose burgeoning population cries for work and food. Echeverría, still trying to mold his desired international image as a Third World leader and champion of the masses, acted cynically and deliberately in his final presidential days, knowing full well that his successor would have to bear the brunt of the uproar caused by the land expropriations. Echeverría escaped facing it. That was hardly macho behavior. It was more like the cowardly dwarfishness which Oscar Monroy Rivera applied to Echeverría in the works on enanismo that were cited earlier (see Chapter 7).

Thus the enano syndrome is central to understanding the psychological impasse of contemporary Mexican politics. There is little reason to expect this condition to change in the foreseeable future, although some apocalyptic event might give rise to a more optimistic prognosis. When no high officials can be held accountable for breakdowns in the political system, be it at Tlatelolco, San Cosme, or in Sonora, then it is unreal to expect the average Mexican to lead an exemplary life either.

What kind of life can Mexicans be expected to lead when nearly half the population is under 16 years of age, the average life span has increased from approximately 45 in the 1950s to around 65 in 1978, and there is no way in the visible future way for the nation to create over 1 million new jobs per year that would be needed to absorb all these people? Crime and illegal migration are solutions for many, anarchy and suicide for some. Communism is a solution for others. But communism, says Octavio Paz, has an internal contradiction which links it anomalously with capitalism. It cannot really thrive without capitalism as its target. Says Paz, "The differences between the Mexican Communist Party and the Monterrey capitalist barons may be large but both groups believe that industrial development is the salvation of Mexico."[19] Moreover, fascist capitalists and communist anticapitalists have traditionally had to compete for the allegiance of the same proletarian people. This inherent conflict lends itself to further ideological clashes, thereby deepening the psychological impasse. Rural proletarian uprisings during the Echeverría sexenio led by Ramón Danzós Palomino and others demonstrated this conflict situation. These were accompanied by urban protests (like bus drivers in Puebla who were forced to work 16 to 20 hours per day for meager wages) of workers and students. The government's fear of the universities as centers of resistance was manifest in its repressions in Puebla and elsewhere. And all the while alienation on the political right was building.[20]

When Chilean President Salvador Allende was killed in September 1973, President Echeverría declared a period of mourning. This did not sit well with the captains of industry in Monterrey, much less so when one of their number, Eugenio Garza Sada, was assassinated by extremists of the left. President Echeverría heard himself denounced at graveside for encouraging an atmosphere in which left-wing terrorism would flourish. An effort to further discredit the president was made by those who told the press that Mrs. Echeverría's family (the Zunos of Guadalajara) had themselves made a fortune based on armed violence and threats.[21] To the conservative capitalists, Echeverría was a Mexican version of Allende bent on turning the nation over to communism. To the Marxist left, Echeverría was a conspirator of Yankee imperialism and its Mexican lackeys. The basis for an ideological clash was there; it is likely to remain there, and the psychological impasse will be broken only with great upheaval and pain.

Octavio Paz calls Mexico a patrimonial regime, in the style of the seventeenth century, but with somewhat more liberty than existed under the viceroys. Nevertheless, he adds, Mexican governments continue to treat public goods as if they were private. There is no effective political opposition to curb this, no real political parties. That is why PRI President Reyes Heroles finds it necessary to proclaim a new era of political reform in the late 1970s. If real political parties existed, he would have no reason to pretend such an undertaking.[22] Less-critical voices like José Luis Reyna disagree. Political reform is continuing, he says, but this does not mean democratization of all Mexico. It means the expanding of the PRI so as to incorporate "new tendencies into the established political system."[23]

When we speak of system reform in Mexico, of making politics more open to competing groups and more sensitive to demands from within the PRI itself, we seem inescapably to return to the central behavioral norm of corruption. Corruption in Mexico is associated inextricably with coyotaje and mordidas. It has been explained to me that the practice of paying off officials to make the administration work can be traced back to Cortés. One writer attributes to Cortés the saying, "Our illness of heart is cured only with gold," and he adds that the Indians, when originally confronted by the Spaniards, found that the way to escape the cruelty of their conquerors was with gifts of gold, a magic touch—the system of coyotaje and mordidas in Mexico may have begun with that discovery.[24] And with it went the ultimate and inevitable descent of Mexico into the throes of socioeconomic inequality and misery. This was the legacy which José López Portillo would inherit, the presidency of a country whose per capita wealth distribution was only one-eighth that of its northern neighbor, in which 5 percent of the population with the highest income received close to 40 percent of the total income of the nation while 20 percent of the poorest families shared only slightly above 4 percent of the same national yield.[25]

In a certain sense Mexican society, its economy, and political life are reflected in its penal institutions, themselves a microsocioeconomic and political system. It has been observed that Mexican prisons, unlike those of Canada or the United States, are allowed to operate as free-enterprise market economies with a kind of competitive barter-oriented political system functioning at the same time. It is possible to use prisons to extract a micromodel of Mexican society and to see clearly the role of corruption, that is coyotaje and the mordida, within it. In the study of Tijuana done by John Price, this penetrating summation emerges:

> The payment of mordidas sanctions and perpetuates in the prison society a practice of circumventing the law. Instead of promoting a legal conscience

and a genuine respect for the law among the prisoners the system promotes a set of brutal situational ethics. The extreme inequalities that the system promotes are also inhumane. New inmates who are poor or too sick to work may barely survive. Instead of treating drug addiction the administration has allowed the prison to become an easy place to buy drugs.[26]

This excellent, yet tragic, statement can be applied to the whole of Mexico and reflects upon a number of important system capabilities whose functioning is stultified by the ethic of corruption. Corruption and its tolerance generate extralegality as the rule, not the exception. Moreover, the extralegality is commonly accompanied by human brutality and torture, like the circumstances inside Sonora prisons described in the eyewitness account by Alejandro de Galicia that was cited in Chapter 7.

A kind of social Darwinism operates in the prisons and throughout Mexican society with the sick and weak dying out and the moderately strong relegated to the perpetual role of exploited pariahs. And instead of seriously moving to cure its ills, the custodians of the political system profit from a continuation of those very ills and mask their complicity behind rituals of symbol manipulation. The counsel offered by Price for Mexican penologists could be applied to the entire political system: "Mexican penologists need to insist that some regimentation is humane and that disregard for the law within the prison promotes a general disregard for the law in the wider society."[27] The trouble is that for most of its people Mexico is a gigantic prison, but without enlightened penologists.

Mexico might salvage itself from total atrophy and collapse by taking advantage of that lingering sense of identity which many of the illegal migrants to the north reflect, the innate pride, spiritual satisfaction, and dignity of being Mexican socially but perhaps not politically. If the social attachment of Mexicans could be transferred to the political system it might save Mexico from some kind of jacquerie, or millenarianism, or any number of forms which civil strife and war can take. Inevitably, as in the counsel of Daniel Cosío Villegas, this would mean giving competing interest and ideological groups a *real* share in the exercise of national political power. It would mean *real* accountability imposed upon an avaricious bureaucracy, jealous of privilege, and parsimonious in the sharing of the public wealth. In short, it would require that a *real* distinction be made and enforced between public goods and private ones. That would end coyotaje and bribes as the rule, rather than the exception. Presumably it is the above ills which President López Portillo's promised political reforms will be aimed at curing.

But if the reform promises of the current sexenio should turn out to be mere rituals, symbolic manipulations with slogans and empty paper victories, then the year 1982 could see a Mexico substantially different from what it is today. Regardless of Mexico's internal policy changes, of the reality of reform, external forces will affect it. The intermingling of Mexico's economy with that of its northern neighbor is always a major consideration. Another recession or worse in the United States would be disastrous for Mexico. Thus Mexico has a built-in motive to send its petroleum products north at realistic prices, just as it has a built-in advantage in keeping the flow of American tourists coming southward. Improved treatment of those tourists will be imperative. Mexico also has an inescapable interest in continuing to solve its unemployment and overpopulation problems by sending wetbacks northward. The United States could seriously disrupt Mexico socially, economically, and politically by effectively stopping the illegal migration. And the United States has, as observed in earlier chapters, reason to avoid such disruptions in Mexico. There is also another imponderable about which precise information is lacking, the degree to which key regions of Mexico depend economically upon the production and export of narcotics for sale in the United States. Although this is difficult to prove, educated guesses strongly suggest that parts of Sinaloa, Jalisco, and Michoacán could be adversely affected in a grave manner should the narcotics traffic to the north be really ended.

Throughout this book the hint has been dropped that one solution to the problems of Mexico, both domestic and international, would be for the United States to absorb Mexico in one way or another. Even such antigringo ideologues as former president Luis Echeverría are quoted as smiling privately upon this strategy. Probably the most profound barrier to absorption (putting aside legal and practical considerations) is the nature of the Mexican national consciousness whose formation I discussed in Chapter 1. Studies such as that of Price cited above note the reluctance of Mexicans and Anglos to mix personally even though they may coexist peaceably, what he called a "mutual conspiracy of silence on significant personal levels . . . neither society knows much about the other."[28] This can best be observed in the border areas and in those retirement communities for Americans which have been established deep into Mexico. Yet it is clear that American Anglos and Mexicans can coexist, probably with less friction than is found between the same Anglos and the American native blacks—and this despite the language barrier.

Perhaps, then, the gradual absorption of Mexico via migration (be it legal or illegal) is the only viable solution, *provided* that the ethic of coyotaje is smothered and eliminated in the process. Perhaps the great gift that the United States can give to Mexico is legal guarantees for human rights and an enforced distinction between public and private goods, this to be accompanied by governmental effectiveness and accountability, be it within the context of a single-party system or via some other arrangement. And perhaps the Mexican gift to Americans can be a renewed commitment to human sensitivity, indeed to sensuousness in the most positive sense of that term, as applied to the relations among humans. This latter capability has been threatened by the decline of the traditional family in North America. But also in Mexico it has been menaced by the disruption of forced migration, both domestic and international, and by the predatory ethic of corruption in which Mexicans are taught to prey upon each other. Perhaps a symbiosis of the two societies will eventually bring to fruition the dream of Mexico's great philosopher José Vasconcelos, the coming of a "cosmic race."

There is no fixed reason why Mexico cannot accomplish some of the vital reforms it so desperately needs within the context of the single-party political system. Other cultures within the Third World (or Fourth World if you prefer) do offer examples of the successful functioning of a single-party system, but the key seems to be that corruption was eliminated. This may have been due to the enlightened leadership of a key person, or to religion or some other influence or tradition. It is the contention of Tanzania's Julius Nyerere that much of Africa since 1960 has been afflicted with political traumata because of corruption, poor leadership, and tribalism. In fact, Tanzania is somewhat unique in Africa in that it still has a functioning and popularly elected parliament. The Tanzanian experience may be relevant comparatively to that of Mexico; the latter, of course, being a much older state in total years since independence. It is contended by one analyst that

> before independence, Tanzanians were advised that they needed to have
> several parties in the country. This theory was tested and found wanting. Not
> a single one of the two opposing parties won seats in the first two elections.
> As a result the Tanzanians moved to a single-party system with opposing
> candidates within that political entity. The leaders realized that they had to
> follow the verdict of the electorate. . . .[29]

Thus the role of a loyal opposition, and its accompanying ability to hold governments accountable to the electorate, was instilled within a single-party framework. But the ideology of Tanzania, known as familyhood *(ujamaa)*, was distinctly humanistic and distributive, not vengeful and exploitive. We cannot pour over the historical circumstances which might account for the obvious differences when the comparison is made with Mexico, nor can we predict the future of Tanzania. In Mexico it seems that at least one key element which is missing is institutionalized respect for the dignity and basic rights of the individual human, something which cannot exist along with institutionalized coyotaje.

The Mexican playwright Rodolfo Usigli, writing at the upsweep of the Cárdenas-era reforms, contended that "Mexico needs its heroes in order to live."[30] My own suspicion is that both Mexico and Mexicans need their heroes, in the first instance to bolster a sagging image of legitimacy and in the second to provide an emotive, albeit deceiving, sense of security in the midst of a world that is arbitrary and cruel. As Martin Needler has correctly observed, Mexicans are raised in an insecure and capricious environment, one which may lead them to seek out the security of authoritarianism. But it is not the studied authoritarianism of the German-Prussian tradition; rather, since the Mexican authority is visited upon children by a father who is frequently absent from the home and is capricious, "one either commands or obeys in an anarchy of personal power, not in an ordered world of duty and regulations. Thus the Mexican is a rebel and a would-be dictator, not a fanatical cog in a state machine."[31] By claiming a monopoly of legitimacy for itself the PRI can demand unquestioning obedience. But it is no longer able to command affection. That must be earned, and brutal repression of critics, especially those within the PRI, is not the way to do it.

Zapata, Rubén Jaramillo, and Lucio Cabañas could be physically liquidated. Respectable political ideologues who seek to reform the PRI from within may be broken socially via bizarre filmings and spurious news releases. Excess humanity can be bulldozed out of their slums and encouraged to migrate north illegally or simply left to starve. Mexico is in no way a welfare state that is prepared, at least not yet, to care for the misery of its citizenry. Yet, the PRI has served one of the purposes for which it was created: the avoidance of armed civil war which rent Mexico for much of its history. Yet violence in anomic uprisings and in organized guerrilla insurgency seems to have increased throughout the decade of the 1970s. It is impossible to know for sure since reliable figures on the Mexican violence are, at best, informed estimates.

Throughout this work I have been reluctant to involve myself with the more global issues of economic development and its relationship to political development.[32] The approach taken herein can best be described as a human-rights approach, one that has been heavily influenced by the political theorist-psychologist Christian Bay. Contrary to the Benthamite formula of adding pleasures and subtracting pains, ostensibly to achieve the greatest happiness for the greatest number, the Bay approach requires that governments remove freedom constraints affecting all citizens who do not themselves seek to deny the freedom of their fellow men. This approach further posits that no one's particular freedom should be achieved at the expense of another's. Minorities should be the ones who decide when their interests have been victimized; therefrom comes the basic contention that "a society is as free as its underdogs are."[33] A top-priority goal for democratic and humanitarian politics must be that of safeguarding a measure of freedom for each individual.[34] Probably the most cryptic expression of Bay's human-rights approach involves the following generalized value judgment:

> The protection of each individual's more basic human rights has priority over the less basic human rights even of large numbers of individuals. And the most basic human right is physical inviolability, which can be forfeited only by individuals who present a manifest and immediate threat to the physical inviolability of others.[35]

Thus, the right to stay alive and not suffer physical violence or emotional distress at the hands of others is the most basic of human rights. I would carry this to the point of natural law by arguing that a general and discoverable behavioral norm among all human beings is the desire to be free from physical or emotional distress, no matter how they may be caused. Just as no one welcomes the fear of political repression, neither do they welcome the fear of famine or flood (resulting from a governmental policy of benign neglect, or corruption in the use of public funds so that famine and flood may occur as the consequence of malfeasance). It is therefore incumbent upon any state in which the good life is to be a priority goal to remove those barriers to human self-fulfillment and to eliminate physical and emotional repression.

Scholars are far from agreement as to whether political democracy is the best form of government to achieve this; indeed, there is much disagreement as to the most appropriate criteria for democracy itself.[36] It is therefore suggested that a distinction be made between political democracy and social democracy, the latter allowing for the possibility of a social welfare state administered by a benevolent authoritarian regime which might come to power by ostensibly nondemocratic means.[37] Social democracy (providing for people's welfare needs and equitable wealth-sharing), it is argued, can materialize under a benevolent dictatorship, a political style not easily identified and documented anywhere in Latin America including Mexico. As noted in Chapters 1 and 3, there is an ample basis in power and tradition for a Mexican president to become a truly benevolent authoritarian. The reforms President López Portillo has promised could make him into just that. The uncertainty lies in the degree to which he dares to erode the "apostolic succession" process which brought him into power, whether radical political changes can be made in Mexico without precipitating the alienation of any of the principal power blocs including the military and its elite corps, los penecilinos, who are potentially available to intervene in the political system as is the case in so many Latin American countries.

The nub of the political dilemma of psychological impasse lies in the urgent need to bring about radical and lasting value change, perhaps via some apocalyptic occurrence. President López Portillo did pledge to attack Mexico's political corruption. That, to be sure, would be radical change. The staying power of such change is another matter. Prosecuting those responsible for the shameful Bay of Flags scandal (see Chapter 5) would only be scraping off the tip of the iceberg and would have real meaning only if *all* parties responsible, no matter how high in the PRI they might be found, are castigated. Reforming CONASUPO or the Mexican social security system would have meaning only if the benefits of those programs ultimately reached out to all unfortunate Mexicans. Promising to do it in the next sexenio is deceitful, inhumane, and will do little to forestall the human volcano which may erupt.[38] Brutalizing tourists from the United States, jailing them to extort their families, does little to improve international relations nor does it persuade Americans to be more generous in their treatment of illegal Mexican aliens. Spraying a few opium and marijuana fields with poison serves only the interests of the corrupt if the same helicopters used, and given by the United States, are later employed to transport the contaminated narcotics northward. Creating exaggerated peasant hopes for land tenancy does not solve Mexico's basic problem of not enough food for too many people. Repressing critics into silence augurs poorly for the cause of any reform.[39]

The PRI, with its monopoly on political legitimacy and coercive force, can avoid atrophy, violent revolution, and class warfare in Mexico if it is willing to eliminate the norm of corruption and instill a broad set of impartial and firmly enforced legal guarantees for the human rights of all those living in and visiting in Mexico. Perhaps it is not, as suggested above, that Mexico needs its martyrs, but rather that the PRI needs menacing phantoms as justification for its continued dictatorship. The essential dogma of the PRI is that only the PRI, and those not yet purged from it, are true inheritors of Mexico's revolutionary tradition. But embracing dogma means ipso facto that freedom of opinion must be severely restricted. How, then, can reform occur? Perhaps in Mexico it cannot without another civil war or some form of unification with its northern neighbor. The words of the wise Third World theoretician Nyerere come to mind: "No party which limits its membership to a clique can ever free itself from fear of overthrow by those it has excluded."[40]

And, finally, why has Mexico created its own set of demons from which it must eternally escape? Following the classic statement by Samuel Ramos, in his discussion of the Mexican *pelado* (a poor devil whose outward naughtiness cloaks his inferiority complex) the Mexican has a dual personality. The pelado's schizophrenia enables his fictitious personality to obscure his real one (like Octavio Paz's treatment of the Mexican masks which are periodically discarded when the real self emerges, often violently). But the fictitious personality engenders self-distrust. This impairs the Mexican's perceptions of reality, that is, corruption may not be perceived as damaging to the total society. The macho cult of virility is intimately related to the ambivalent Mexican's drive toward self-fulfillment, even though he knows that he harms himself. An exaggerated professing of nationalism can be a drive for self-fulfillment in the political arena. It is macho, hence self-fulfilling, for the PRI to win all the electoral posts, even by fraud, and then enhance its self-image through bequeathal of a handful of deputies to the opposition parties. The Mexican in his social, economic, and political life works for immediate gratification, much as in Banfield's "amoral familism" and, as Ramos puts it, he has "suppressed from his life one of its most important dimensions—the future."[41] The psychic insecurities detailed by Ramos result in distrust, susceptibility, aggression, and impulsiveness. This, then, translates into political graft, corruption, repression, and human atrocities. The potential for upheaval is ever present.

This argument becomes even more credible when a contemporary PRI supporter cites evidence much to the same effect, that the Mexican is by nature sad; but sadness can be cloaked until the final threshold of tolerance is reached and then there may be an explosion. This gives the Mexican an aggressive individualism, leading him away from any spirit of civic collaboration and toward self-indulgence in mysticism, sexual exploits, and a psychic refuge into religion and cultism.[42] It comes down to an innate psychological impediment to society working as a collectivity and with a singularity of purpose. Each Mexican is bent upon his own self-enrichment at the expense of everyone else. This is a war of all against all and ultimately there can be only losers. Perhaps this explains the apparent pessimistic abandon of Carlos Fuentes at the end of his magnum opus, *Terra Nostra.*[43] Although Fuentes does not so predict, we can hypothesize that for Mexico's political norms to be changed significantly, some apocalyptic event must purge Mexico and Mexicans of their psychic distress, much of which may be traced back to the confabulations involving Quetzalcóatl and Guadalupe, Cortés and Moctezuma, that were taken up in Chapter 1. Perhaps such an event will be civil war, a jacquerie, or a form of ethnocide—the absorption of Mexico and its culture into that of its northern neighbor.

If not, the end could be as in *Terra Nostra,* a complex work which I cannot pretend to have understood thoroughly, but which seems to foresee Mexico continuing its schizophrenic life toward a tragic end, one with the Catholic cathedral erected over the trembling ruins of serpentine Aztec murals, the seat of government still cemented above the fallen palace of the Aztec empire and boasting a leadership chamber of pale men who are also "hunchbacked and dwarfish" *(jorobados y enanos)*.[44] Fuentes's reference to dwarfishness has an obvious relation to the theme of Oscar Monroy already established in the foregoing pages. It is part of the outcome of a life dedicated to rapine, greed, oppression, and of centuries of defeat for noble human aspirations. In *Terra Nostra,* by the year 1999, Mexicans may well have become resolved to their condition as a "protectorate of Anglo-Saxon democracy."[45] And Fuentes queries whether in the end it will be necessary for them all to die just in order to punish the worst evil-doers.[46] Inevitably, says Fuentes, Mexico will not be able to feed over 100 million people by the year 2000 and mass extermination may be the only realistic policy. Then it will be appropriate to brainwash the public, as in Aztec times, so that they will accept human sacrifice as a religious necessity, the Aztec tradition of eating human hearts united with the Christian tradition of God's surrogate being sacrificed on the cross.[47]

The above synthesis and observations were drawn from uniquely Mexican sources. They were not arrived at via anything remotely approximating the scientific method. The concept of ideology as explained in note 11 is perhaps a more realistic approach here. For it is on the basis of ideology (deeply felt and widely shared beliefs) plus subconscious character traits that the business of Mexican government and politics is conducted. On that point Mexico's humanistic political writers seem to have reached a consensus; their nation's political edifice has rotten spiritual timbers, its future is not hopeful. For some time to come Mexico's PRI will continue to ask the Mexican people to endure hardship, but at the same time to be proud and patriotic; the people will continue to appeal to the cult of Guadalupe, asking her to play the schizophrenic dual role of violated woman (so that the defensive male cult of machismo may thrive in its self-defeating way) and at once to be the patroness saint who will protect Mexico from misfortune—and as always, Mexico will continue to fear the demons which it itself has created.

NOTES

1. Although most writers (who are not outright apologists for the PRI) admit that there is much room for change, it is nonetheless common to find essentially positive conclusions which are at variance with my own vis-a-vis the status and thrust of Mexican politics. In the interest of fairness I wish to draw the reader's attention here to other views. Among the optimists is L. V. Padgett, *The Mexican Political System* (Boston: Houghton Mifflin, 1966 and 1976). An example of an optimistic journalist would be Richard Salvatierra of the Tucson *Citizen* who wrote on December 1, 1977, a hopeful resume of the López Portillo political reform effort that promised to give a greater and more real voice to opposition forces. This journalist also admits that the social pressures in Mexico are "explosive" and credits López Portillo with having held some inflationary forces (like wages) in check. As of this writing one can only hope that Salvatierra's cautious optimism is justified.

There are other recent analyses of Mexican socioeconomic-political life which lean toward the optimistic side. Note David Ronfeldt's book, *Atencingo: The Politics of Agrarian Struggle in a Mexican Ejido* (Stanford, Calif.: Stanford University Press, 1973). See especially his discussion on pp. 224–25 of the ejidatarios' willingness to wait for another sexenio in order to have their complaints attended to when there would be change of personnel in the agrarian reform bureaucracy. Considerable economic optimism is expressed by John B. Ross in *The Economic System of Mexico* (Stanford, Calif.: California Institute of International Studies, 1971), pp. 106–07. Other scholars have attempted to maintain a more value-neutral position by applying statistical methods to data which they believed to be valid. One of the central figures in the development of quantitative history is James Wilkie of UCLA whose writings have stimulated a great deal of controversy. Two critics of Wilkie wrote, "We agree with his implicit premise that one should not judge ideology merely by the proclamation of goals; one should also examine what is done . . . [as well as] what one believes should be done. . . ." From Kenneth M. Coleman and John Wanant, "On Measuring Mexican Presidential Ideology Through Budgets: A Reappraisal of the Wilkie Approach," *Latin American Research Review,* Spring 1975, pp. 84–87. They assert, insofar as Mexican presidential decisions in budget allocation are concerned, that Ruíz Cortines and Díaz Ordaz were relatively conservative, giving greater subsidies to rich states than to poorer ones, whereas López Mateos was more ideologically oriented, taking populist cues from the political arena, and that he overwhelmingly gave subsidies to states where the PRI made a poor showing in the previous presidential election. Such value-neutral research has its place as a counterpoise to more normative and value-laden approaches such as my own. The critical dilemma for the quantitative history researchers is, of course, being sure that the budgetary data they manipulate are the genuine article. Finally, but by no means exhausting the range of sources, an optimistic historical view of the allegedly ongoing Mexican revolutionary process is found in Frederick C.

Turner, *The Dynamic of Mexican Nationalism* (Chapel Hill: University of North Carolina Press, 1968). The inquiring reader should consult some of the above sources as a way of evaluating my admittedly more negative views.

2. Merilee S. Grindle, *Bureaucrats, Politicians, and Peasants in Mexico* (Berkeley: University of California Press, 1977), see specifically pp. 88–89. This study reveals a high degree of personalism in the CONASUPO bureaucracy, the placement of confidence workers who owe their jobs to personal ties, a significant amount of infighting among competing camarillas, and time wasted while bureaucrats try to protect their jobs into the next sexenio. The usual result is a high degree of turnover and many losers, hence, roots of more political alienation. A careful reading of this study indicates the increasing difficulty which the PRI is having in containing its own members in the face of scarce budgetary resources. Another valuable aspect of this study is its insight into the secrecy which surrounds policy formation (see p. 110) and this in itself tells something of the dilemma facing quantitative analyses based upon officially provided data.

3. Ibid., p. 177.

4. Evelyn P. Stevens, *Protest and Response in Mexico* (Cambridge, Mass.: MIT Press, 1974), p. 259.

5. Grindle, op. cit., p. 177.

6. Susan Kaufman Purcell, *The Mexican Profit-Sharing Decision: Politics in an Authoritarian Regime* (Berkeley: University of California Press, 1975), pp. 133–47.

7. Ibid., p. 61.

8. Ibid., p. 62.

9. See *La otra cara de México* (Mexico: La Nación, 1966).

10. Ibid., p. 146. A valuable study of another Mexican bureaucracy, the IMSS (Instituto Mexicano de Seguro Social), or social security system, shows the regime, once again, to have been the principal beneficiary of public policy administration. The author shows that in the short run the IMSS Programs have contributed to political stability in Mexico by guaranteeing the well-being of bureaucratic elites, but it is the already powerful who benefited, not the weak and needy. In serving principally the urban unionized workers (part of the PRI's CTM and labor sector), the IMSS benefits those workers who least need social security and, after some years of existence, IMSS has been able to cover only about 18 percent of Mexico's population. The impression left by this study is that revolutionary rhetoric is clearly a mask for a greedy system dedicated to satisfying the elites who formulate social security policy. See Guy F. Poitras, "Welfare Bureaucracy and Clientele Politics in Mexico," *Administrative Science Quarterly,* March 1973, pp. 24–25.

11. In this connection see Willard A. Mullins, "On the Concept of Ideology in Political Science," *American Political Science Review,* June 1972, especially p. 508, which contains the following:

There are, of course, significant differences between science and ideology. In science one aspires to a self-critical, analytical, "objective" understanding of phenomena without reference to normative categories which assign value to alternative courses of action. Seeking to maximize intellectual clarity, science is not concerned with dilemmas of policy, choice, or commitment. In politics, however, it is necessary to understand situations in terms of their moral significance for human beings, and the normative language of ideology provides reasons for supporting one social arrangement rather than another, reasons why this or that political program should be instituted, defended or abandoned. Science may be the final arbiter of an ideology's "factuality." Ideology, however, comprehends situations in a way which science cannot for ideology, unlike science, is able to portray the "facts" in terms of their relevance for human wants and aspirations.

It is in the spirit of the above-quoted position that I raise the question about the usefulness of a strict adherence to the scientific method as an approach to the study of alienation or ideology in Mexican politics, given the prominence of deeply felt beliefs whose factuality may be less important than the fact itself that they are shared and acted upon.

12. As portrayed in Luis Spota, *Palabras mayores* (Mexico: Editorial Grijalbo, 1975), p. 149.

13. Ibid., p. 314. The use of sexual perversion as a politically destructive tactic appears in one of its most gross forms when used by the poet-journalist Horacio Espinosa Altamirano, in *Apocalipsis apócrifo* (Mexico: Ediciones Universo, 1975). This work would be considered pornographic by some, but given the context of the author's having been a victim of official repression his choice of this means of expression is perhaps understandable. Altamirano sets forth the story of governmental repression against him, and against the journal *Por Que?* for which he often wrote, in his book *Campo militar numero uno* (Mexico: Ediciones Ballesta, 1976). Altamirano and the Menéndez brothers Roger and Hernán were imprisoned and tortured by the Mexican police and military in September 1974. The presses and offices of *Por Que?* were destroyed to prevent publication of material damaging to the PRI and favorable to the guerrilla leader Lucio Cabañas whose episode was discussed in Chapter 6. It is appropriate to underscore such tactics as pornography used by the PRI's opposition not only because the PRI itself used and continues to use the same weapons (as in the case of Sonora, 1967) but because admitted PRI ideologists even defend openly the use by the regime of what is called "fiction" as a way of holding on to power. Fiction in this sense is meant to include libelous statements, defamations, and other inventions to give the appearance that power is unquestionably in the PRI's control, this as admitted by PRI theorist Rodolfo Siller Rodríguez, in his *La crisis del Partido Revolucionario Institucional* (Mexico: Costa-Amic, 1976), especially pp. 111–13. The theme of sexual perversion in the literature of socioeconomic-political protest may be a signal of the desertion of intellectuals from Mexico as a geographic entity, a phenomenon singled out by Crane Brinton and others as foreshadowing atrophy and revolution.

14. Among the human-rights violations committed against Americans in Mexico were "incommunicado jailings, confiscation of property and torture—cattle-prodding, finger-breaking, injuries to the sex organs, and severe beatings" not to mention outright murder. See Bill Waters's special copyrighted publication, "Mexico Owes Justice to Foreign Prisoners," by Arizona *Daily Star*, 1975.

15. Ibid.

16. Ibid. The totality of this evidence, coupled with the testimony of the Mexican writers cited herein, reveals an acute sadism as one psychological constant in the Mexican politicoadministrative character. The above-cited writings of Horacio Altamirano are especially relevant here as well.

It is worthwhile dwelling momentarily on the matter of sadism as a character trait, even in view of the quite probable risk that I will be accused of ethnic bias or racism. The PRI has chosen, in some cases, to castigate its own people (that is, PRI members found guilty of some transgression) in a much more severe fashion than opposition party members or North American aliens. In my own case I was treated relatively well, subjected to about one week's captivity and mental torture to secure my signing a confession that I was not permitted to read. However, we should examine the case of Jorge Issachtts Corrales for comparative purposes. Issachtts, a Mexican Jew immigrated from Transjordan (before it became part of the state of Israel), was a member of the PRI's political machine in Baja California and had even worked close to several governors. He was also a bank accountant in the Ejido Development Bank (Banco Nacional de Crédito Ejidal) in Baja California, a government-owned enterprise. Issachtts discovered a 50 million peso embezzlement ($4 million at that time) which ultimately implicated high PRI officials in both Baja California and Sonora. To defend itself the regime accused Issachtts of the embezzlement (the investigation had gone too far to be covered up and a scapegoat had to be found). Issachtts was imprisoned but not brought to trial. His revelations had implicated former governor Luis Encinas who had been the target of Monroy Rivera's wrath. At various times he was offered a "sentence" if he would pay for it. After more than four years in prison his wife, fearing that he would die, agreed to mortgage their only remaining property near Mexicali in exchange for her husband's freedom. He told me via intermediaries in the spring of 1977 that in all likelihood he would be forced to lose everything. Even his physical security was in doubt since his captors chose to release him from prison without documents. This made it possible for any Mexican law officer to arrest Issachtts at any time for mere nonpossession of identification, it kept him from negotiating a tourist exile in the United States, and it made difficult his option of taking advantage of Israel's law of return inasmuch as without credentials he was virtually a man without a country. As of this writing his future is clearly in doubt, but this is an example of the vengeance that thrives within the bosom of Mexican officialdom. Issachtts wrote several books while in prison which were smuggled out and circulated clandestinely, including *La sentencia: el derecho de los fuertes* (Mexico: Costa-Amic, 1973) which was prohibited from public distribution but reissued under the same title in Argentina during 1976. He also wrote *Yo acuso* (Mexico: Costa-Amic, 1976) which treats the Biebrich scandal in Sonora and accuses the ex-governor of complicity in a range of evil doings. Also by Issachtts is *Volveré a vivir* (Mexico: Costa-Amic, 1974). Throughout these works he presents rich but tragic testimony as to the tortures and human atrocities that are committed in Mexican prisons.

17. A thorough analysis of Mexican agriculture in a contemporary historical perspective (of which I have been privileged to read several parts) is J. W. Barchfield's *Agrarian Policy and National Development in Mexico* (New Brunswick, N.J: Rutgers University, Transaction Books, 1978).

18. See Bill Waters's article in Arizona *Daily Star,* November 21, 1976.

19. As quoted in *Proceso,* December 5, 1977, p. 8.

20. See Bill Waters's prize-winning series, "Uneasy Neighbor," copyright by Arizona *Daily Star,* 1974.

21. Ibid., and also a report in *Time,* September 16, 1974.

22. *Proceso,* op. cit., pp. 8–9.

23. Ibid., p. 17.

24. Samuel Máyenz Puente, "Matices de la mordida," *Proceso,* November 21, 1977, p. 38.

25. *Proceso,* November 14, 1977, p. 8.

26. John A. Price, *Tijuana: Urbanization in a Border Culture* (Notre Dame, Ind.: Notre Dame University Press, 1973), p. 128.

27. Ibid. The judgment of Price is confirmed in the testimony of Issachtts cited above and also in the previously cited testimony of Alejandro de Galicia as to conditions in Sonora prisons.

28. Price, op. cit., p. 15.

29. From William R. Duggan and John R. Civille, *Tanzania and Nyerere* (Maryknoll, N.Y.: Orbis Books, 1976), p. 163.

30. Rodolfo Usigli, *El gesticulador* (Mexico: 1937; Appleton-Century-Crofts version, 1963), p. 101.

31. Martin C. Needler, *Politics and Society in Mexico* (Albuquerque: University of New Mexico Press, 1971), p. 80.

32. I am aware, for example, of Samuel Huntington's work that was cited earlier plus a range of works on developmentalism including Helio Jaguaribe's *Political Development: A General Theory and a Latin American Case Study* (New York: Harper & Row, 1973). In that mammoth undertaking the author builds on the intellectual foundations constructed by Huntington and others. It seems that Jaguaribe's theory of political development has three basic aspects: development of the capabilities of the political system, development of the contribution of the political system to the overall development of the society, and development of the responsiveness of the political system, with the qualitative and quantitative increase of its representativeness, legitimacy, and serviceability (quoted from p. 196). Here, and in the long discussion that follows, it seems that development is defined as development. Nevertheless, if one focuses upon key concepts like capabilities and representativeness and legitimacy, and if these are used as a gauge for the

performance of the Mexican political system vis-a-vis the well-being of its citizenry, it is quite clear that the status quo leaves much to be desired, especially so in terms of the human rights approach which I wish to embrace herein.

33. From Christian Bay, *The Structure of Freedom* (New York: Atheneum, 1968), p. 7.

34. Ibid., p. 59.

35. Ibid., p. 115.

36. See Kenneth Johnson, "Research Perspectives on the Revised Fitzgibbon-Johnson Index of the Image of Political Democracy in Latin America, 1945–75," in *Quantitative Latin American Studies Methods and Findings,* ed. James Wilkie and Kenneth Ruddle (Los Angeles: UCLA Latin American Center, 1977).

37. Rodolfo Siller Rodríguez, the PRI supporter and theorist cited above, says that the legislative power in Mexico has gravitated to the president because the individual legislators are too cowardly or too lazy to exercise what is rightfully theirs and as a consequence the executive power has usurped the powers of the judiciary, the states, and the municipalities. With this testimony from within the PRI itself, it seems clearly possible for some president, perhaps López Portillo or his successor, to assume the reformist role of a benevolent authoritarian. See Siller Rodríguez, op. cit., pp. 187–88.

38. It is noteworthy that PRI supporter Siller Rodríguez cites the social potential in Mexico for a "violent explosion" asserting that the Mexican adopts superficial happiness to hide his innate sadness (the same theme developed in Octavio Paz's classic *El laberinto de la soledad*) and that the Mexican takes politics seriously only when he sees his rights trampled upon and he has lost his last ounce of patience (Siller Rodríguez, op. cit., p. 190). Siller Rodríguez also presents public opinion survey evidence showing that scarcely 3 percent of a national cross section expressed an interest in politics whereas over 50 percent expressed interest in a combination of sexuality, eroticism, mysticism, and religion (ibid., pp. 189–90). The Mexican, so it seems on all the evidence, has an incredible capacity to endure abuse, even self-inflicted abuse, as part of the many rituals to steel himself against a hostile environment. But when the threshold of endurance is crossed the explosive potential, once latent, may erupt uncontrollably as in the anarchy associated with the revolutionary years between 1910 and 1917 or more recently at the Tlatelolco massacre. Curiously, writing just before the tragedy of Tlatelolco, Victor Alba stressed that Mexico was indeed a democratic country whose people had confidence in the regime and in the social mobility it could provide. *The Mexicans* (New York: Praeger, 1967), pp. 237 and 240.

39. As cited above, the PRI's repression of Issachtts Corrales and its lack of internal reform capability reveal a great unwillingness to hear unpleasant facts or to admit them. Despite Siller Rodríguez's above-cited exercise in self-criticism, his negative evaluations are directed against offices and institutions, not powerful contemporary individuals as is the writing of Issachtts and Monroy. A psychological syndrome associated with some forms of dictatorship is developed by William T. Daly and may be applicable to the PRI as an institution (or to the president himself as an enshrinement of power). Daly writes: "The raising of . . . ideology above discussion . . . the insistence on mass adulation of the leader's person, as an extension of populism; omnipotence fantasies and the refusal to hear unpleasant facts . . . [all] lead to megalomania and terror." See *The Revolutionary: A Review and Synthesis,* (Beverly Hills, Calif.: Sage Publications, 1972), p. 33.

40. Duggan and Civille, op. cit., p. 176.

41. Samuel Ramos, *Profile of Man and Culture in Mexico* (New York, McGraw-Hill, 1962), pp. 60–65.

42. Siller Rodríguez, op. cit., pp. 190–91.

43. Carlos Fuentes, *Terra Nostra* (Mexico: Joaquín Mortiz, 1975).

44. Ibid, p. 735.

45. Ibid., p. 737.

46. Ibid., p. 779.

47. Ibid., p. 734.

Selected Bibliography
on Mexican Politics

BOOKS

Agee, Philip. *Inside the Company: CIA Diary.* Harmondsworth, England: Penguin, 1975.

Aguilar, Manuel G. *La derrota de un régimen.* Hermosillo, Mexico: Imprenta Regional, 1971.

Alba, Victor. *Las ideas sociales contemporáneas en México.* Mexico: Fondo de Cultura Económica, 1960.

———. *Mexicans: The Making of a Nation.* New York: Praeger, 1967.

Alisky, Marvin. *Sicartsa: The Mexican Government's New Complex to Make the Steel Industry Self-Sufficient.* El Paso, Tex.: University of Texas Press, Center for Latin American Studies, 1975.

Altamirano Espinosa, Horacio. *Apocalipsis apócrifo.* Mexico: Ediciones Universo, 1975.

———. *Campo militar numero uno.* Mexico: Ediciones Ballesta, 1976.

Amaya, Juan Gualberto. *Los gobiernos de Obregón, Calles, y regímenes "peleles" derivados del callismo.* Mexico: Editorial del Autor, 1947. (*Note:* this self-edited book, regarded by some as a collector's item, is available in the University of Arizona library under the reference number 972-082-A489).

Arrecillas, Antonio D., ed. *México: realidad política de sus partidos.* Mexico: Instituto Mexicano de Estudios Políticos, 1970.

Ayala Anguiano, Armando. *El día que perdió el PRI.* Mexico: Editorial Contenido, 1976.

Balam, Gilberto. *Tlatelolco: reflexiones de un testigo.* Mexico: 1969.

Barchfield, J. W. *Agrarian Policy and National Development in Mexico.* New Brunswick, N.J.: Rutgers University Press, Transaction Books, 1978.

Barresen, Donald. *Mexico's Border Industrialization Program.* Lexington, Mass.: Lexington Books, 1971.

Beals, Carleton. *Porfirio Díaz: Dictator of Mexico.* Philadelphia, Penn.: Lippincott, 1932.

Benveniste, Guy. *Bureaucracy and National Planning: A Sociological Case Study in Mexico.* New York: Praeger, 1970.

Bezdek, Robert R. *Electoral Oppositions in Mexico: Emergence, Suppression, and Impact on Political Processes.* Unpublished Ph.D. dissertation, Ohio State University, 1973.

Braddy, Haldeen. *Mexico and the Old Southwest: People, Palaver, and Places.* Port Washington, N.Y.: Kennikat, 1971.

Brandenberg, Frank. *The Making of Modern Mexico.* Englewood Cliffs, N.J.: Prentice-Hall, 1964.

Brodman, Barbara L. *Mexican Cult of Death in Myth Literature.* Gainesville, Fla.: University Presses of Florida, 1976.

Bustamante, Jorge. *Espaldas Mojadas: Materia Prima para la Expansion del Capital Norteamericano.* Mexico: El Colegio de Mexico, 1975.

Cameron, Charlotte. *Mexico in Revolution.* New York: Gordon, 1976.

Camp, Roderic A. *The Education of Mexico's Political Elite.* Milwaukee: University of Wisconsin Center for Latin America, Center Discussion Paper No. 62, 1978.

———. *Mexican Political Biographies: 1935–1975.* Tucson: University of Arizona Press, 1976.

Carlos, Manuel L. *Politics and Development in Rural Mexico: A Study of Socioeconomic Modernization.* New York: Praeger, 1974.

Castillo, Heberto, and Francisco Paoli Bolio. *¿Porque un nuevo partido?* Mexico: Editorial Posada, 1975.

Chavira B., Carlos. *La otra cara de México.* Mexico: La Nación, 1966.

———. *Macario Vázquez.* Mexico: Editorial Jus, 1968.

Clendenen, Clarence C. *The United States and Pancho Villa.* Ithaca, N.Y.: Cornell University Press, 1961.

Cline, Howard. *Mexico: Revolution to Evolution: 1940–1960.* New York: Oxford University Press, 1963.

Cockcroft, James. *Intellectual Precursors of the Mexican Revolution, 1900–1913.* Austin, Tex.: University of Texas Press, 1968.

Coleman, Kenneth M. *Public Opinion in Mexico City About the Electoral System.* James Sprunt Studies in History and Political Science, No. 53, University of North Carolina, Chapel Hill, N.C., 1972.

Consejo Nacional de Huelga. *El móndrigo.* Mexico: Editorial Alba Roja, 1968. (*Note:* this unauthored book is believed to have been commissioned by President Díaz Ordaz himself to help cast the blame for the Tlatelolco massacre on other members of his own regime).

Cornelius, Wayne A. *Politics and the Migrant Poor in Mexico City.* Stanford, Calif.: Stanford University Press, 1975.

Cosío Villegas, Daniel. *El estilo personal de gobernar.* Mexico: Joaquín Mortiz, 1974.

————. *El sistema político mexicano.* Mexico: Joaquín Mortiz, 1972.

————. *Historia moderna de México.* 8 volumes. Mexico: Editorial Hermes, 1948–65.

————. *La sucesión: desenlace y perspectivas.* Mexico: Joaquín Mortiz, 1975.

————. *La sucesión presidencial.* Mexico: Joaquín Mortiz, 1974.

Creel, G. *Mexico: The People Next Door.* New York: Gordon, 1976.

Cumberland, Charles C. *Mexico: The Struggle for Modernity.* London: Oxford University Press, 1968.

Daly, William T. *The Revolutionary: A Review and Synthesis.* Beverly Hills, Calif.: Sage, 1972.

de Galicia, Alejandro. *De visita en la prisión.* 3d ed. Mexico: Costa-Amic, 1975.

De Lara, L. Gutiérrez, and Edgcum Pinchón. *Mexican People: Their Struggle for Freedom.* New York: Gordon, 1976.

de Mora, Juan Miguel. *Las Guerrillas en México y Jenaro Vázquez Rojas.* Mexico: Editora Latino Americano, 1972.

————. *Por la gracia del señor presidente (México: la gran mentira).* Mexico: Editores Asociados, 1975.

————. *T-68 (Tlatelolco 1968).* Mexico: Editores Asociados, 1973.

Demaris, Ovid. *Poso del Mundo: The Mexican-American Border.* Boston, Mass.: Little, 1970.

Edmundo, Jardón A. *De la Ciudadela a Tlatelolco.* Mexico: Fondo de Cultura Popular, 1969.

Estrada, Antonio M. *La grieta en el yugo.* San Luis Potosí, Mexico: Editorial del Autor, 1963.

Fagen, Richard R., and William S. Tuohy. *Politics and Privilege in a Mexican City.* Stanford, Calif.: Stanford University Press, 1972.

Fernández, Julio A. *Political Administration in Mexico.* Boulder, Colo.: Bureau of Governmental Research, University of Colorado, 1969.

Fuentes, Carlos. *Terra Nostra.* Mexico: Joaquín Mortiz, 1975.

Fuentes Díaz, Vicente. *Los Partidos Políticos en México.* Mexico: Editorial Altiplano, 1972.

García Cantú, Gastón. *El Socialismo en México, Siglo XIX.* Mexico: Era, 1969.

————. *La Hora de los Halcones.* Puebla: Universidad Autónoma de Puebla, 1976.

————. *Política Mexicana.* Mexico: UNAM, 1974.

García Rivas, Heriberto. *Breve historia de la revolución mexicana.* Mexico: Editorial Diana, 1964.

Glade, William P., Jr., and Charles W. Anderson. *The Political Economy of Mexico.* Madison, Wisc.: University of Wisconsin Press, 1963.

Godines, Prudencio, Jr. *Que poca mad . . . era!* Mexico: Editorial del Autor, 1968.

González Casanova, Pablo. *La democracia en México.* Mexico: Ediciones Era, 1965.

González Morfín, Efraín. *El cambio social y el PAN.* Mexico: Ediciones de Accion Nacional, 1975.

Greenberg, Martin. *Bureaucracy and Development: A Mexican Case Study.* Lexington, Mass.: Heath Lexington, 1970.

Griffiths, B. *Mexican Monetary Policy and Economic Development.* New York: Praeger, 1972.

Grindle, Merilee S. *Bureaucrats, Politicians, and Peasants in Mexico: A Case Study in Public Policy.* Berkeley and Los Angeles, Calif.: University of California Press, 1977.

Guerra Utrilla, José. *Los partidos políticos nacionales.* Mexico: Editorial America, 1970.

Hansen, Roger D. *The Politics of Mexican Development.* Baltimore: Johns Hopkins Press, 1971.

Hellman, Judith Adler. *Mexico in Crisis.* New York: Holmes & Meier, 1978.

Issachtts Corrales, Jorge. *La sentencia: el derecho de los fuertes.* Mexico: Costa-Amic, 1973. See also a special edition of this work published by the author in Buenos Aires, Argentina, in 1976.

———. *Volveré a vivir.* Mexico: Costa-Amic, 1974.

———. *Yo acuso.* Mexico: Costa-Amic, 1976.

Jaguaribe, Helio. *Political Development: A General Theory and a Latin American Case Study.* New York: Harper & Row, 1973.

Jaramillo, Rubén M., and Froylán C. Manjarrez. *Rubén Jaramillo, autobiografía y asesinato.* Mexico: Editorial Nuestro Tiempo, 1967.

Johnson, Kenneth F. *Mexican Democracy: A Critical View.* Boston, Mass.: Allyn & Bacon, 1972.

Johnson, William Weber. *Heroic Mexico.* New York: Doubleday, 1968.

Kamstra, Jerry. *Weed: Adventures of a Dope Smuggler.* New York: Bantam, 1975.

King, Timothy. *Mexico: Industrialization and Trade Policies Since 1940.* New York: Oxford University Press, 1970.

Lafaye, Jacques. *Quetzalcóatl and Guadalupe: The Formation of Mexican National Consciousness 1531–1813.* Chicago: University of Chicago Press, 1976.

Levinson, Jerome, and Juan de Onís. *The Alliance that Lost its Way.* Chicago: Quadrangle Books, 1970.

Lewis, Oscar. *The Children of Sánchez.* New York: Random House, 1961.

———. *Pedro Martínez.* New York: Vintage, 1964.

López, Jaime. *10 años de guerrillas en Mexico.* Mexico: Editorial Posada, 1974.

Mabry, Donald J. *Mexico's Accion Nacional: A Catholic Alternative to Revolution.* Syracuse, N.Y.: Syracuse University Press, 1973.

Magaña, Manuel C. *Poder láico.* Mexico: Ediciones Foro Político, 1970.

Maldonado, Braulio. *Baja California: Comentarios Políticos.* Mexico: Costa-Amic, 1960.

Malloy, James M., ed. *Authoritarianism and Corporatism in Latin America.* Pittsburgh, Penn.: University of Pittsburgh Press, 1975.

Mancisidor, José. *La Revolución Mexicana.* Mexico: Ediciones El Gusano de Luz, 1958.

Medina Valdés, Gerardo. *Operación 10 de junio.* Mexico, Ediciones Universo, 1972.

Menéndez Rodríguez, Mario. *Yucatán o el genocidio.* Mexico: Fondo de Cultura Popular, 1964.

Monroy Rivera, Oscar. *A la espera del día (frontera sin agua).* Mexico: Costa-Amic, 1975.

―――. *Ayer: recuerdos de infancia.* Mexico: Costa-Amic, 1973.

―――. *El cazador de estrellas.* Mexico: Editorial Libros de Mexico, 1968.

―――. *El mexicano enano.* Mexico: Editorial Diana, 1967.

―――. *El profeta del silencio.* Mexico: Costa-Amic, 1974; Editorial Diana, 1975.

―――. *El señor presidente de Enanonia.* Mexico: Costa-Amic, 1973.

―――. *La burgesía y la opresión en la noticia.* Mexico: Costa-Amic, 1976.

―――. *León de Galán.* Mexico: Editorial Libros de Mexico, 1977.

―――. *México y su vivencia dramática en el pensamiento vasconcelista.* Mexico: Editorial Diana, 1975.

―――. *Poemas de juventud.* Mexico: Editorial Stylo, 1958.

―――. *Sonora: en torno al valor de mi pueblo.* Mexico: Editorial Libros de Mexico: 1967.

―――. *Un extraño en el puerto.* Mexico: Editorial Libros de Mexico, 1969.

Montes, Eduardo. *¿Cómo Combatir al Charrismo?* Mexico: Ediciones de Cultura Popular, 1972.

Morena Sánchez, Manuel. *Mexico: 1968–1972: Crisis y perspectiva.* Austin: Institute of Latin American Studies, University of Texas Press, 1973.

Natividad Rosales, José. *La Muerte de Lucio Cabañas.* Mexico: Editorial Posada, 1975.

―――. *¿Quién es Lucio Cabañas?* Mexico: Editorial Posada, 1974.

Needler, Martin C. *Politics and Society in Mexico.* Albuquerque, N.M.: University of New Mexico Press, 1971.

Padgett, L. V. *The Mexican Political System.* 2d. ed. Boston: Houghton Mifflin, 1976.

Padilla, Juan Ignacio. *El sinarquismo.* 2d. ed. Mexico: Ediciones UNS, 1953.

Paz, Octavio. *El laberinto de la soledad.* Mexico: Fondo de Cultura Economica, 1959.

————. *Posdata.* Mexico: Siglo Veintiuno Editores, 1970.

————. *El arco y la lira,* Mexico: Fondo de Cultura Económica, 1972.

Pérez Chowell, José. *Requiem para un ideal: la liga 23 de septiembre.* Mexico: Editorial V Siglos, 1977.

Porfirio Miranda, José. *El cristianismo de Marx.* Mexico: Editorial del Autor, 1978.

Price, John A. *Tijuana: Urbanization in a Border Culture.* Notre Dame, Ind.: University of Notre Dame Press, 1973.

Purcell, Susan Kaufman. *The Mexican Profit-Sharing Decision: Politics in an Authoritarian Regime.* Berkeley and Los Angeles, Calif.: University of California Press, 1975.

Quirk, Robert E. *Mexico.* Englewood Cliffs, N.J.: Prentice-Hall, 1971.

Ramos, Samuel. *Profile of Man and Culture in Mexico.* Austin, Tex.: Pan American Paperbacks Series, University of Texas Press, 1962.

Reyna, José Luis, and Richard S. Weinert, eds. *Authoritarianism in Mexico.* Philadelphia, Penn.: Institute for the Study of Human Issues, 1977.

Reynolds, Clark W. *Mexican Economy: Twentieth-Century Structure and Growth.* New Haven, Conn.: Yale University Press, 1970.

Rivanuva, Gastón. *El PRI: El Gran Mito Mexicano.* Mexico: Editorial Tradición, 1974.

Romanucci-Ross, Lola. *Conflict, Violence, and Morality in a Mexican Village.* Palo Alto, Calif.: National Press Books, 1973.

Romero, J. Rubén. *La vida inútil de Pito Pérez.* Mexico: Editorial Porrúa, 1969.

Ronfeldt, David. *Atencingo: The Politics of Agrarian Struggle in a Mexican Ejido.* Stanford, Calif.: Stanford University Press, 1973.

Ross, John B. *The Economic System of Mexico.* Stanford, Calif.: California Institute of International Studies, 1971.

Ross, Stanley, ed. *Is the Mexican Revolution Dead?* New York: Knopf, 1966.

————, ed. *Views Across the Border: the United States and Mexico.* Albuquerque, N.M.: University of New Mexico Press, 1977.

Russell, Philip. *Mexico in Transition.* Austin, Tex.: Colorado River, 1977.

Samora, Julian. *Los Mojados: The Wetback Story.* Notre Dame, Ind.: University of Notre Dame Press, 1971.

Schmitt, Karl M. *Communism in Mexico: A Study in Political Frustration.* Austin, Tex.: University of Texas Press, 1965.

Scott, Robert E. *Mexican Government in Transition.* Urbana, Ill.: University of Illinois Press, 1964.

Semo, Enrique. *Historia del Capitalismo en México.* Mexico: Era, 1973.

Sepúlveda, Bernardo, and Antonio Chumacero. *La Inversión Extranjera en México.* Mexico: Fondo de Cultura Económico, 1973.

Siller Rodríguez, Rodolfo. *La crisis del Partido Revolucionario Institucional.* Mexico: Costa-Amic, 1976.

Silva Herzog, Jesús. *Breve Historia de la Revolución Mexicana.* 2d. ed. de Cultura Económico, 2 vols. Mexico: Fondo 1972.

Simpson, Lesley Byrd. *Many Mexicos.* Berkeley: University of California Press, 1960.

Spota, Luis. *La plaza.* Mexico: Joaquín Mortiz, 1972.

————. *Palabras mayores.* Mexico: Editorial Grijalbo, 1975.

Stavenhagen, Rodolfo. *Sociología y Subdesarrollo.* Mexico: Nuestro Tiempo, 1972.

Stevens, Evelyn P. *Protest and Response in Mexico.* Cambridge, Mass.: MIT Press, 1974.

Tannenbaum, Frank. *Peace by Revolution—An Interpretation of Mexico.* New York: Columbia University Press, 1933.

Taylor, William B. *Landlord and Peasant in Colonial Oaxaca.* Stanford, Calif.: Stanford University Press, 1972.

Thompson, Wallace. *The Mexican Mind: A Study of National Psychology.* Boston, Mass.: Little, Brown, 1922.

Turner, Frederick C. *The Dynamic of Mexican Nationalism.* Chapel Hill, N.C.: University of North Carolina Press, 1968.

Ugalde, Antonio. *Power and Conflict in a Mexican Community.* Albuquerque, N.M.: University of New Mexico Press, 1970.

———, and others. *The Urbanization Process of a Poor Neighborhood.* Austin, Tex.: University of Texas Press, Institute of Latin American Studies, 1974.

Usigli, Rodolfo. *El gesticulador.* 2d. ed. New York: Appleton-Century-Crofts, 1963 (first edition 1937).

Valadés, José C. *El presidente de México en 1970.* Mexico: Editores Mexicanos Unidos, 1969.

Vasconcelos, José. *La raza cósmica.* Mexico: Austral, 1948.

Velázquez, Manuel. *Revolución en la constitución.* Mexico: Costa-Amic, 1969.

Vera Estañol, Jorge. *La revolución mexicana.* Mexico: Editorial Porrúa, 1957.

Vernon: Raymond, *The Dilemma of Mexico's Development.* Cambridge, Mass.: Harvard University Press, 1963.

Villaseñor, Edmund. *Macho!* New York: Bantam, 1973.

Von Sauer, Franz A. *The Alienated "Loyal" Opposition.* Albuquerque, N.M.: University of New Mexico Press, 1974.

Warman, Arturo. *Los Campesinos: hijos predilectos del régimen*. 4th ed. Mexico: Editorial Nuestro Tiempo, 1975.

Weaver, Thomas, and Theodore Downing. *Mexican Migration*. Tucson, Ariz.: University of Arizona Press, 1976.

Wilkie, James W. *The Mexican Revolution: Federal Expenditure and Social Change Since 1910*. Berkeley: University of California Press, 1967.

Womack, John, Jr. *Zapata and the Mexican Revolution*. New York: Vintage, 1969.

Zubirán, Salvador, et al. *La Desnutrición del Mexicano*. Mexico: Fondo de Cultura Economica, 1974.

SELECTED ARTICLES

Adie, Robert F. "Cooperation, Cooptation, and Conflict in a Mexican Peasant Organization." *Inter-American Economic Affairs* 24, no. 3 (Winter 1970): 3–25.

Alisky, Marvin. "CONASUPO: A Mexican Agency Which Makes Low Income Workers Feel Their Government Cares." *Inter-American Economic Affairs* 27, no. 3 (Winter 1973): 47–59.

———. "Mexico versus Malthus: National Trends." *Current History*, Vol. 66 (May 1974): 200–03.

———. "Mexico's Population Pressures." *Current History* 72 (March 1977): 106–10.

Anderson, Bo, and James D. Cockcroft. "Control and Cooptation in Mexican Politics." In *Dependence and Underdevelopment: Latin America's Political Economy*, edited by James D. Cockcroft, André Gunder Frank, and Dale L. Johnson. New York: Anchor, 1972.

———. "Control and Cooptation in Mexican Politics." In *Latin American Radicalism*, edited by Irving L. Horowitz. New York: Vintage, 1969.

Arriola, Carlos. "La crisis del Partido Accion Nacional." *Foro Internacional* (April–June 1977).

Astiz, Carlos A. "Mexico's Foreign Policy: Disguised Dependency." *Current History* 66 (May 1974): 220–23.

Ayres, Robert L. "Development Policy and the Possibility of a 'Livable' Future for Latin America." *American Political Science Review* 69, no. 2 (June 1975): 507–25.

Barkin, David. "Mexico's Albatross: the U.S. Economy." *Latin American Perspectives* 2 (Summer 1975): 64–80.

Becker, Jacklyn, and others. "The Dope Trail." *Contemporary Drug Problems* 1 (Summer 1972): 413–52.

Berry, T. "Mexico Workers' Housing Fund Attacks A Giant Problem." *Architectural Record* 159 (June 1976): 37–49.

Bizarro, S. "Mexico's Government in Crisis." *Current History* 72 (March 1977): 102–05.

Camp, Roderic A. "A Reexamination of Political Leadership and Allocation of Federal Revenues in Mexico, 1934–73." *The Journal of Developing Areas* 10, no. 2 (January 1976): 193–211.

―――. "El sistema mexicano y las decisiones sobre el personal político." *Foro Internacional* 17, no. 1 (1976): 51–83.

―――. "Losers in Mexican Politics: A Comparative Study of Official Party Precandidates for Gubernatorial Elections, 1970–75." In *Quantitative Latin American Studies,* edited by James W. Wilkie and Kenneth Ruddle. Los Angeles: UCLA Latin American Center, 1977.

―――. "Mexican Governors Since Cárdenas: Education and Career Contacts." *Journal of Inter-American Studies and World Affairs* 16, no. 4 (November 1974): 454–81.

―――. "The Cabinet and the Técnico in Mexico and the United States." *Journal of Comparative Administration* 3 (August 1971): 188–214.

―――. "The Middle-Level Technocrat in Mexico." *The Journal of Developing Areas* 6, no. 4 (July 1972): 571–81.

―――. "The National School of Economics and Public Life in Mexico." *Latin American Research Review* 10, no. 3 (Fall 1975): 137–51.

Cochrane, James D. "Mexico's New Científicos: The Díaz Ordaz Cabinet." *Inter-American Economic Affairs* 21, no. 1 (Summer 1967).

Cockcroft, James D. "Coercion and Ideology in Mexican Politics." In *Dependence and Underdevelopment: Latin America's Political Economy*, edited by James D. Cockcroft, André Gunder Frank, and Dale L. Johnson. New York: Anchor, 1972.

Coleman, Kenneth M., and John Wanant. "On Measuring Mexican Presidential Ideology Through Budgets: A Reappraisal of the Wilkie Approach." *Latin American Research Review* 10, no. 1 (Spring 1975): 77–88.

Cornelius, Wayne A. "Urbanization and Political Demand Making: Political Participation Among the Migrant Poor in Latin American Cities." *American Political Science Review* 68, no. 3 (September 1974): 1125–46.

de Navarrete, Ifigenia M. "La distribucion del ingreso en Mexico." In *El perfil de Mexico en 1980.* Mexico: Siglo XXI, 1970.

Elliott, J. H. "The Triumph of the Virgin of Guadalupe." *The New York Review of Books* (May 26, 1977), pp. 28–30.

Flanigan, James. "North of the Border—Who Needs Whom?" *Forbes* (April 15, 1977), pp. 37–41.

Fuentes, Carlos. "Mexico and its Demons." *The New York Review of Books* (September 20, 1973), pp. 16–21.

Furlong, William L. "Peruvian and Northern Mexican Municipalities: A Comparative Analysis of Two Political Subsystems." *Comparative Political Studies* 5 (April 1972): 59–83.

Garibay, Ricardo. "El hambre: un horizonte negro nos espera." *Proceso* 2, no. 40 (August 1977). A three part series.

Garza, David T. "Factionalism in the Mexican Left: The Frustration of the MLN." *The Western Political Quarterly* (September 1964): 447–60.

González Casanova, Pablo. "Mexico: The Dynamics of an Agrarian and 'Semi-Capitalist' Revolution." In *Latin America: Reform or Revolution?*, edited by James Petras and Maurice Zeitlin. Greenwich: Fawcett, 1968.

González Gollaz, Ignacio. "La posibilidad de JLP." *Visión* (June 1, 1976).

González Navarro, Moisés. "Mexico: The Lop-Sided Revolution." In *Obstacles to Change in Latin America,* edited by Claudio Veliz. London and New York: Oxford University Press, 1969.

Grayson, G. W. "Making of a Mexican President, 1976." *Current History* 70 (February 1976): 49–52.

Grimes, C. E., and Simmons, Charles E. P. "Bureaucracy and Political Control in Mexico: Towards an Assessment." *Public Administration Review* 29, no. 1 (January–February 1969): 72–79.

Gruber, Wilfried. "Career Patterns of Mexico's Political Elite." *The Western Political Quarterly* 24, no. 3 (September 1971): 467–82.

Johnson, Kenneth F. "Ideological Correlates of Right Wing Political Alienation in Mexico." *The American Political Science Review* 59, no. 3 (September 1965): 656–64.

―――. "Research Perspectives on the Revised Fitzgibbon-Johnson Index of the Image of Political Democracy in Latin America, 1945–75." In *Quantitative Latin American Studies Methods and Findings,* edited by James W. Wilkie and Kenneth Ruddle. Los Angeles: UCLA Latin American Center, 1977.

―――, and María Mercedes Johnson. "Human Sacrifice in Mexico: The Modern Aztec Style of Development versus Despair." *Intellect* 103, no. 2364 (March 1975): 362–66.

Koslow, Lawrence E. and Rodney R. Jones. "The Mexican-American Border Industrialization Program." *Public Affairs Bulletin* 9, no. 2 (1970): 1–5. Published by Arizona State University, Institute of Public Administration.

Lottman, H. R. "Mexican Publishing: A Struggle Against Illiteracy, Poverty and Piracy—But With Powerful Government Support." *Publisher's Weekly* 211 (January 10, 1977), pp. 42–44.

Lyons, Gene. "Inside the Volcano." *Harpers* 254, no. 1525 (June, 1977), pp. 41–46.

Martínez Ríos, Jorge. "Los campesinos mexicanos: perspectivas en el proceso de marginalización." In *El perfil de México en 1980,* vol. 3. Mexico: Siglo XXI, 1972.

Mayenz Puente, Samuel. "Matices de la mordida." *Proceso* 2, no. 55 (November 21, 1977): 38–39.

Maza, Enrique. "Estrangulamiento de la conciencia política." *Proceso* 2, no. 11 (15 de enero de 1977): 40–41.

McCoy, Terry L. "A Paradigmatic Analysis of Mexican Population Policy." In *The Dynamics of Population Policy in Latin America,* edited by Terry L. McCoy. Cambridge, Mass.: Ballinger, 1974.

Meyer, V. J. "Women in Mexican Society." *Current History* 72 (March 1977): 120–23.

Monson, Robert A. "Political Stability in Mexico: the Changing Role of Traditional Rightists." *Journal of Politics* 35 (August 1973): 594–614.

Mullins, Willard A. "On the Concept of Ideology in Political Science." *The American Political Science Review* 66, no. 2 (June 1972): 498–510.

Needleman, Carolyn, and Martin Needleman. "Who Rules Mexico? A Critique of Some Current Views on the Mexican Political Process." *Journal of Politics* 31, no. 4 (November 1969): 1011–34.

Niblo, Stephen R. "Progress and the Standard of Living in Contemporary Mexico." *Latin American Perspectives* 2 (Summer 1975): 109–24.

O'Donnell, Guillermo. "Reflections on the Patterns of Change in the Bureaucratic-Authoritarian State." *Latin American Research Review* 13, no. 1 (1978): 3–38.

Perissinotto, G. "Mexican Education: Echeverría's Mixed Legacy." *Current History* 72 (March 1977): 115–19.

Poitras, Guy E. "Welfare Bureaucracy and Clientele Politics in Mexico." *Administrative Science Quarterly* 18 (March 1973): 18–26.

Prieto, Raul. "Elefantes negros." *Proceso* 1, no. 6 (December 11, 1976): 46–47.

Reyna, José Luis. "Redefining the Authoritarian Regime." In *Authoritarianism in Mexico,* edited by José Luis Reyna and Richard S. Weinert. Philadelphia: Institute for the Study of Human Issues, 1977.

Roberts, Robert E. "Modernization and Infant Mortality in Mexico." *Economic Development and Cultural Change* 21 (July 1973): 655–69.

Scott, Robert E. "Politics in Mexico." In *Comparative Politics Today: A World View,* edited by Gabriel Almond. Boston: Little, Brown, 1974.

Sheridan, T. L. "Mexican City Tourists Never See: Netzahualcoyotl." *America* 133 (November 22, 1975): 351–54.

Stevens, Evelyn P. "Legality and Extra-Legality in Mexico." *Journal of Inter-American Studies and World Affairs* 12, no. 1 (January 1970): 62–75.

————. "Mexican Machismo: Politics and Value Orientations." *The Western Political Quarterly* (December 1965): 848–57.

————. "Protest Movements in an Authoritarian Regime: The Mexican Case." *Comparative Politics* 7, no. 3 (April 1975): 361–82.

Taylor, Philip B. "The Mexican Elections of 1958: Affirmation of Authoritarianism?" *The Western Political Quarterly* 13 (September 1960): 722–44.

Tuohy, William S. "Centralism and Political Elite Behavior in Mexico." In *Development Administration in Latin America,* edited by Clarence E. Thurber and Lawrence S. Graham. Durham, N.C.: Duke University Press, 1973.

————. "Psychology in Political Analysis: the Case of Mexico." *The Western Political Quarterly* 27 (June 1974): 289–307.

Unzueta, Gerardo. "Requiem para un sarcófago (nota sobre la ideología burguesa de la Revolución Mexicana." *Nueva Epoca* (February 1969).

Villarreal, René. "The Policy of Import-Substituting Industrialization, 1929–75." In *Authoritarianism in Mexico,* edited by José Luis Reyna and Richard S. Weinert. Philadelphia: Institute for the Study of Human Issues, 1977.

Wilkie, James W. "On Quantitative History: the Poverty Index for Mexico." *Latin American Research Review* 10 (Spring 1975): 63–75.

Womack, John. "Unfreedom in Mexico." *The New Republic* (October 12, 1968), pp. 27–31.

Index

About the Author

KENNETH F. JOHNSON is Professor of Political Science, University of Missouri, St. Louis. Previously he was Associate Professor in the Political Science Department at the University of Southern California, where he was also Chairman of the Latin American Studies Program.

Dr. Johnson is co-author with Ben G. Burnett of *Political Forces in Latin America* (2nd ed. 1970). His articles have appeared in such journals as *American Political Science Review,* and *Latin American Research Review.* Professor Johnson holds a Ph.D. from the University of California, Los Angeles.